S0-AFU-434

THE
WORLD SYSTEM
AND THE **EARTH SYSTEM**

THE
WORLD SYSTEM
AND EARTH SYSTEM
THE

GLOBAL SOCIOENVIRONMENTAL

CHANGE AND SUSTAINABILITY

SINCE THE NEOLITHIC

ALF HORNBORG &
CAROLE L. CRUMLEY, Eds.

Left
Coast
Press
Inc.

Walnut Creek, CA

LEFT COAST PRESS, INC.

1630 North Main Street, #400

Walnut Creek, CA 94596

http://www.LCoastPress.com

Copyright © 2006 by Left Coast Press, Inc.

All rights reserved. No part of this publication may be reproduced, stored in a retrieval system, or transmitted in any form or by any means, electronic, mechanical, photocopying, recording, or otherwise, without the prior permission of the publisher.

Library of Congress Cataloging-in-Publication Data

The world system and the Earth system : global socioenvironmental change and sustainability since the Neolithic / edited by Alf Hornborg and Carole L. Crumley.

   p. cm.

  ISBN 1-59874-100-4 (alk. paper)— ISBN-13 978-1-59874-100-1

  ISBN 1-59874-101-2 (pbk. : alk. paper)—ISBN-13 978-1-59874-101-8

  1. Ecology. 2. Climatic changes. 3. Environmental sciences. 4. Human ecology.

5. Social ecology. I. Hornborg, Alf. II. Crumley, Carole L.

  QH541.W57 2006

  304.2—dc22   2006020200

Printed in the United States of America

This paper is acid free and meets the minimum requirements of ANSI/NISCO Z39.48-1992 (R 1997) (Permanence of Paper).

Text design by Detta Penna

Copyedited by Stacey Sawyer

Cover design by Andrew Brozyna

09 10 5 4 3 2

This book is dedicated to the memory of
Andre Gunder Frank
(1929–2005)

Contents

Preface

This book is one of two volumes emerging from the conference on *World-System History and Global Environmental Change*, arranged by the Human Ecology Division of Lund University, Lund, Sweden, on September 19–22, 2003. I gratefully acknowledge generous funding from the Bank of Sweden Tercentenary Foundation, which covered the bulk of our expenses, as well as additional funding from the Swedish International Development Cooperation Agency, the Swedish Research Council, the Swedish Environmental Protection Agency, and the Swedish Research Council for Environment, Agriculture and Spatial Planning. I also want to thank Christian Isendahl for efficiently handling the practical details of conference organization, my co-editor Carole Crumley, for competently commenting on several chapters that particularly required her expertise in historical ecology, and Bob Denemark for invaluable assistance in editing Gunder Frank's posthumous chapter. Finally, I thank Jennifer Collier, Stacey Sawyer, and Detta Penna for helping me turn a pile of papers into a book.

Alf Hornborg

Contributors

Thomas Abel is Assistant Professor of Anthropology at Tzu Chi University in Taiwan. • **Björn E. Berglund** is a paleoecologist and Professor Emeritus of Quaternary Geology at Lund University, Sweden. • **Christopher Chase-Dunn** is Distinguished Professor of Sociology and Director of the Institute for Research on World-Systems at the University of California, Riverside. • **Alfred W. Crosby** is Professor Emeritus of American Studies, History, and Geography at the University of Texas, Austin. • **Carole L. Crumley** is Professor of Anthropology at the University of North Carolina, Chapel Hill. • **John A. Dearing** is an environmental scientist and Professor of Physical Geography at the University of Liverpool, England. • **Bert J. M. de Vries** has a background in theoretical chemistry and is senior scientist at the Netherlands Environmental Assessment Agency and part-time Professor of Global Change and Energy at the Copernicus Institute for Sustainable Development and Innovation, Utrecht University, The Netherlands. • **Nina Eisenmenger** is a researcher and lecturer at the Institute of Social Ecology, Klagenfurt University, Austria. • **Andre Gunder Frank** (1929–2005) was an associate of the Luxembourg Institute for European and International Studies, and Senior Fellow at the World History Center, Northeastern University, Boston. • **Jonathan Friedman** is Directeur d'études at the École des Hautes Études en Sciences Sociales in Paris and Professor of Social Anthropology at Lund University, Sweden. • **Stefan Giljum** is an ecological economist and researcher at the Sustainable Europe Research Institute, Vienna, Austria. • **Thomas D. Hall** holds the Lester M. Jones Chair in Sociology at DePauw University in Greencastle, Indiana. • **Karin Holmgren** is Professor of Physical Geography at Stockholm University, Sweden. • **Alf Hornborg** is an anthropologist and Professor of Human Ecology at Lund University, Sweden. • **Kristian Kristiansen** is Professor of Archeology at the University of Gothenburg, Sweden. • **Thomas Malm** is a biologist and anthropologist and Associate Professor at the Human Ecology Division, Lund University, Sweden. • **Daniel S. Mandell** did graduate work in anthropology and environmental studies at the University of California, Santa Barbara and Berkeley. • **Betty J. Meggers** is director of the Latin American Archeology Program, National Museum of Natural History, Smithsonian Institution, Washington DC. • **George Modelski** is Professor Emeritus of Political Science at the University of Washington, Seattle. • **Emilio F. Moran** is the James H. Rudy Professor of Anthropology, Professor of Environmental Sciences, and Adjunct Professor of Geography at Indiana University, Bloomington. • **Helena Öberg** is a PhD candidate in Physical Geography at Stockholm University, Sweden. • **Frank Oldfield** is a physical geographer and Professor Emeritus at the University of Liverpool, England. • **Susan C. Stonich** is Professor of Anthropology, Environmental Studies, Geography, and Marine Science at the University of California, Santa Barbara. • **William R. Thompson** is Rogers Professor of Political Science at Indiana University, Bloomington. • **Peter Turchin** is Professor of Ecology and Evolutionary Biology at the University of Connecticut, Storrs.

Conceptualizing Socioecological Systems

ALF HORNBORG

The relation between society and nature has no doubt always been a central concern of human beings. Whether we turn to the earliest written records from Mesopotamia or China, or to the myths and metaphors of contemporary indigenous peoples, the interface between human and nonhuman spheres of life is a pervasive theme for reflection and cosmological elaboration.

In modern research, too, there is hardly a science that does not provide some perspective on the complex, multifaceted, and often problematic relation between the human and the natural. A major problem for this research, however, is the very distinction between a "societal" and a "natural" domain. This conceptual split is at the foundation of the division of social and natural sciences, and it continues to make communication between researchers in these two categories difficult and often antagonistic.

This book tries to capture some of the trends in recent thinking about this topic as we enter the twenty-first century. It brings together researchers from a wide spectrum of sciences to explore the possibilities of merging some concepts, methods, and perspectives from different fields that might help us gain a better understanding of the profound changes that our social and natural systems have undergone during the past few millennia. What unites the contributors to this volume is not only the ambition to transcend the distinction between social and natural science but generally also the reasons and even the recipe for doing so. The reasons derive from the current concern with global problems of sustainability and the growing conviction that such problems can be addressed only through transdisciplinary collaboration between social and natural science. The recipe for such collaboration, to most of the contributors, is the concept of "system."

Working in parallel, and generally without much knowledge of one another,

1

social and natural scientists have for several decades struggled to understand how the different parts of their respective domains fit together. One camp has discovered how human societies are globally interconnected in a shifting "world system" of trade, politics, and information flows. The other camp has developed an understanding of how ecosystems are connected in a common "Earth system" with planetary dynamics that affect all its constituent parts. From their various vantage points, the authors of this book's chapters suggest ways in which these two global systems in turn are linked to each other. As we have become accustomed to thinking of our world as a single and coherent globe suspended in space, we more easily acknowledge that changes in the world system and changes in the Earth system may be recursively connected. The most concrete example of this change in thinking is probably our current concern over global warming. However, although an important one, climate change is only one of the ways in which the connections between global social and ecological processes are revealing themselves to us.

At the Lund conference that spawned this book, participants were invited to discuss the sociopolitical dimensions of environmental change as well as the ecological dimensions of long-term social change. Some contributors inevitably leaned more toward the kinds of approaches that are dominant in the human sciences, whether providing richly empirical case studies in environmental history or quantitative analyses of the environmental effects of international trade (Hornborg, McNeill, & Martinez-Alier 2007). Others, that is, the contributors to the present volume, seemed animated by the prospects of modeling or even simulating the dynamics of socioecological systems over time. At one point, Emilio Moran demonstrated a brief computer reconstruction of global changes in land cover, illustrating in a few seconds several millennia of deforestation and other environmental transformations. At another point in the program, the archeologist Andrew Sherratt showed us a similar simulation, of the same brief duration, but now of the global expansion of trade routes during a comparable time period. It struck us how essential it is that these two dynamic snapshots of the Earth system and the world system be brought together, at least conceptually.

In Chapter 1, anthropologist Carole Crumley outlines the approach of "historical ecology" (cf. Crumley 1994), demonstrating how versatile researchers must learn to be if they have the ambition to reckon with both sociocultural and biophysical factors in understanding how landscapes change over time. Her rare capacity to communicate with social as well as natural scientists is reflected not only in the ease with which she connects landscape ecology, climatology, complex systems theory, and epistemology but also in her profound familiarity with the traditional obstacles to communication between representatives of what C. P. Snow long ago called the "Two Cultures." Whereas humanists can be overly on their guard against attempts to reduce society and social change to reflections of biophysical processes, natural scientists are often naive about how "nature" is imbued with culture and politics. Crumley suggests that recent research on complex systems offers a way to accommodate, without reductionism, the study of human history and culture within a biophysical framework. I would add that such an integrative project would have to be careful about using words such as "accommodate," "within," and "framework," because they could easily be perceived as the vehicles of an imperial project. It would, in fact, be equally plausible to propose that the study of ecosystems can be accommodated within a semiotic framework (cf. Hornborg 2001b). Flows of signs and flows of matter and energy are ubiquitous in all complex systems, and the different conceptual frameworks and the methodologies for studying them need to be granted equal standing, rather than one accommodated "within" the other.

The importance of mutual respect between the two research traditions is well argued by geographer Frank Oldfield in Chapter 2. Although clearly embedded in the Earth-system discourse, he observes that it is only part of the framework needed to unite biophysical and human perspectives. Intriguingly, he speculates that the contrasting records of environmental impacts in Italy and northern England during the Roman period might in part reflect the political economy of imperial Rome, with different attitudes to land management in the core and the periphery. Oldfield also demonstrates the wisdom of hindsight drawn from environmental history when he expresses doubts about the assumption of global control that often seems to underlie normative and prescriptive discussions of "sustainable development."

In Chapter 3, geographer John A. Dearing discusses some prospects and technicalities of modeling past socioenvironmental change so as to make it possible to anticipate the future. He acknowledges some of the problems in trying to simulate something as unpredictable as human behavior, but he suggests that successful modeling of emergent, macro-scale phenomena may be possible without having recourse to the lowest-level "rules"—for example, those that generate individual action. This is a significant observation from a natural scientist, considering the traditional view that natural scientists tend toward "micro-determinacy" and social scientists toward "macro-determinacy" (for example, Rose, Kamin, & Lewontin 1984; Steiner 1993; Weiss 1969). It seems that at least some parts of the natural and social sciences may now be converging toward recognition of "macro-determinacy," whether the macro-system is the Earth system or the world system. (Simultaneously, however, an increasing number of social scientists seem to resort to micro-determinacy in accepting genetic explanations of human behavior; cf. Duster 1996.) Although the technical details of modeling complex systems are beyond the horizons of most anthropologists, including me, I assume that a major challenge must be to accommodate the very recursivity between micro- and macro-levels. At a very general level, I sympathize with the early warnings of Gregory Bateson (1972a) against delegating to computers our responsibility for pursuing knowledge.

In Chapter 4, anthropologist and systems ecologist Tom Abel applies the modeling framework of Howard T. Odum to "world systems" as conceived by Immanuel Wallerstein, Gunder Frank, Chris Chase-Dunn, Tom Hall, and others (Frank 1995; Chase-Dunn & Hall 1991, 1997, 1998; Wallerstein 1974–1980). Odum's main concern was the flow of energy through social and natural systems; this thermodynamic perspective on the metabolism of world systems raises several relevant questions about the biophysical requisites and constraints of human societies. One such question concerns the issue of social system boundaries. Although the world-system concept emerged precisely to show that total units of social reproduction are more inclusive than are individual nations, nation-state boundaries continue to shape our image of the spatial extent of separate "societies" within the core and the periphery. Political boundaries are not identical to social system boundaries in the sense of reproductive totalities but can be both less and more inclusive (Hornborg 2007). Colonialism and political imperialism can be viewed as attempts to make the political and the economic coincide, but the metabolic flows sustaining modern nations are generally very far from congruent with their political reach. Another question raised by Abel concerns the possible connection between metabolic pulsations, such as Odum identified in ecosystems, and the pulsations that world-system analysts are tracing in human history.

World-system pulsations are precisely the topic of Chapter 5, in which sociologist Tom D. Hall and ecologist Peter Turchin argue that pulsations or cycles are in themselves indications of the existence of a system of some kind. Drawing on models from population ecology, they review various possible approaches to the apparently synchronized oscillations between demographic and socioeconomic expansion and decline in areas as far apart as eastern and western Asia over the past two millennia (cf. Chapter 9). Among the factors considered are climate change and the simultaneous "resetting" of several local cycles by other exogenous events such as political conquest and empire formation. The chapter is not primarily concerned with the empirical identification of such synchronicities but rather with the theoretical system models that can be used to account for them. It thus also includes a section on how to analyze the dynamics of demographic oscillations in preindustrial England, proposing that a significant and potentially driving factor was the degree of sociopolitical (in)stability. The underlying assumption in this chapter, as in the two preceding ones, seems to be that the dynamics of different kinds of complex systems, whether ecosystems or societies, share some regularities that can be approached with the aid of abstract models originally designed to represent the organization of biological systems, for example, evolutionary learning processes (cf. Chapter 12).

In Chapter 6, the anthropologist Jonathan Friedman challenges such assumptions by reviewing his own pioneering work, in the 1970s, in modeling the dynamic interface of social and ecological systems in Southeast Asia over the long term (Friedman 1979). He recalls how, as a student, he revolted against the functionalism and "adaptationism" of cultural materialism and cultural ecology and instead turned to Marxist models emphasizing structural contradictions, crises, and transformations (Friedman 1974). This critique of the view of socioecological systems as cybernetic "adaptive machines" is still valid today. The risk with applying biological models to social systems continues to be that subsystems are assumed to promote the survival of the larger system, an assumption that lacks support either in theory or in historical evidence. Whether attributed to mystical cultural wisdom or conscious decision making, the notion of a societal rationality geared to collective survival must be recognized as wishful thinking, not as a sociological or historical fact (cf. Hornborg 2005). Where Edmund Leach (1954) had seen a social-structural oscillation understandable in its own terms, Friedman saw recurrent contradictions between expansive socioeconomic structures and a fragile natural environment.

Friedman's early observations on the pulsating socioecological systems of Highland Burma were later expanded into a general concern with how global systems of states and international trade define the conditions of reproduction of local populations and polities. In this chapter, he shows how this perspective was applied to other historical cases such as Oceania and the ancient Mediterranean area. The pulsations or cycles that he identifies are generated by the structural properties of social systems, rather than by some general dynamics common to all complex systems. These structural properties can be described in terms of culturally specific institutions and contradictions, as he does in all the above-mentioned cases, but Friedman simultaneously recognizes the recurrent patterns of hegemony and decline that riddle human history and that seem to tell us something more general about the dynamic of global social systems. Although socioecological systems are not regulated by metaphysical autopilots, this is not to say that they do not exhibit regularities over time.

In Chapter 7, the geologist Björn E. Berglund uses data from paleoecological studies as well as archeology and history to discuss landscape changes in northwestern Europe from 4000 B.C.E. to 1400 C.E. He reviews eight time periods of particularly dynamic change, five of which were characterized by deforestation and agricultural expansion, and three suggesting regression, reduced human impact, and regeneration of forests. There is significant synchronicity between events in different parts of the region, which Berglund tentatively attributes to shared climatic fluctuations. However, cumulative changes in technology, society, and the landscape permitted a successively greater expansion of agriculture with each new opportunity. He thus offers a dynamic model emphasizing the recursive interaction between climate, ecology, technology, and society.

A similar recursivity between climate and society is recognized by geographers Karin Holmgren and Helena Öberg, who in Chapter 8 trace the impact of climate change on social systems in southern and eastern Africa during the past millennium. As in the previous chapter, paleoclimatic data are correlated with archeological and historical evidence. Records of food availability, intensity of agropastoral production, settlement history, and politics tend to match the climate data. Moreover, the authors suggest that the often inverse variation in rainfall between equatorial eastern Africa and subtropical southern Africa may have been a factor prompting migrations from the former to the latter area at the end of the first millennium C.E.

In Chapter 9, sociologists Chris Chase-Dunn and Tom D. Hall and ecologist Peter Turchin examine the causes of the above-mentioned demographic synchrony between East Asia, on the one hand, and the West Asian/Mediterranean region, on the other. In their search for possible causes of this synchrony, they discuss climate change, epidemics, trade cycles, and incursions of nomads from the steppes of Central Asia (cf. Chapter 10). Although they do not arrive at any definitive conclusion, their consideration of alternative hypotheses and methodologies for validating them is illuminating. The authors also present several more general observations on world-system analysis, partly building on previous work (for example, Chase-Dunn & Hall 1997, 1998). One such observation is that cultural homogeneity is not a good measure of cohesion within bounded social systems, since interaction instead tends to produce heterogeneity (cf. Chapter 14). Another important point is that the assumptions of cultural ecology about the local environmental determination of sociocultural institutions, discussed in Chapter 6, are quite inadequate for the study of world systems. However, the authors do not wish to argue that social institutions have become progressively less ecologically determined but rather that ecological constraints have become progressively more global.

The archeologist Kristian Kristiansen provides in Chapter 10 the link between eastern and western Asia by focusing on the emergence of a dynamic interaction zone in central Eurasia in the third and second millennia B.C.E., later known as the Silk Road. He proposes that the expansion of mobile pastoral societies was recursively linked with deforestation and the expansion of open grasslands, facilitating long-distance trade and interaction. By the end of the second millennium B.C.E., Kristiansen suggests, this vast steppe linked the extremes of the Eurasian continent "to a common historical pulse."

In Chapter 11, the political scientist William R. Thompson examines the common "political-economic rhythm" of ancient Mesopotamia and Egypt from 4000 to 1000 B.C.E. The parallels in the timing of regime changes and general turmoil in the two areas suggest yet another case of synchronic pulsations. Thompson tests several hypotheses and concludes that a strong case can be made for finding recurrent water scarcity problems, and thus ultimately climate change, underlying conflicts, regime changes, and the collapse of trade networks. He emphasizes, however, that to invoke a climatic factor is not equivalent to environmental determinism. Although similar environmental changes may have affected the civilizations of Mesopotamia and Egypt at roughly the same times, their responses were as different as their social structures and belief systems. Moreover, climate-induced problems with water scarcity and other problems such as hinterland incursions should not be seen as alternative explanations of decline but as factors that could cumulatively reduce the capacity of core areas to deal with these and other challenges.

Political scientist George Modelski discusses in Chapter 12 the concept of "dark ages" as reflecting periods of adjustment of imbalances in the world system, generally characterized by zero growth, economic redistribution, and ecological regeneration. Using data on world population and urbanization, he identifies such phases approximately every second millennium, for example, the second millennium B.C.E. and first millennium C.E. Modelski observes that such periods are significant ingredients in long-term social transformations, providing new opportunities for subsequent periods of expansion. Although he suggests that we have entered yet another period of adjustment, he believes that information technology, democracy, and improved global governance will alleviate its effects, compared to those experienced in the past. This chapter raises some questions regarding why world-system pulsations happen to fit so conveniently into 1,000-year slots, whether dark ages are to be viewed as systemwide—even when Islam was flourishing in the first millennium C.E.—or only as "localized 'dark spots,'" and whether we really entered a new period of "readjustment" already in 1850, considering that growth and accumulation since then have been unprecedented. These questions aside, the chapter provides important data on long-term trends in world population growth and urbanization, drawing on many years of research on world cities and global demography.

In Chapter 13, archeologist Betty J. Meggers argues against the recent suggestions of several other archeologists and some historians and geographers that some areas of pre-Columbian Amazonia may have had considerably higher population densities than suggested by the indigenous social systems encountered by Europeans since the seventeenth century. She argues that the poverty of Amazonian soils would have precluded dense sedentary settlement and dismisses the recent finds of anthropogenic Dark Soils (*terra preta*) as insufficient evidence of such settlements. Meggers concludes that archeological, historical, and ethnographic data do not support the occurrence of dense settlement and intensified land use in the region. She also observes that the Amazon area is highly vulnerable to climate change, exemplified by the four mega-Niño events that have been documented around 500, 1000, 1200, and 1500 C.E. All in all, Meggers thus maintains her position, grounded in cultural ecology, that the natural environment strictly constrains sociocultural development in the Amazon Basin (Meggers 1971).

In Chapter 14, I present a somewhat different perspective on the relation between social and ecological systems in prehistoric Amazonia. My point of departure is that, for millennia, the region has been integrated by relations of long-distance exchange connecting different parts of Amazonia with one another and with adjacent regions such as the Andes and the Caribbean. Drawing on historical accounts, ethnographic analogies, and linguistics, I argue that this world-system-like trade network, rather than migration, was the main factor in explaining ethnolinguistic differentiation, social stratification, economic specialization, and environmental change. Contrary to Meggers, I believe that we should take seriously the possibility that deposits of *terra preta*, as well as the systems of raised fields discovered on the moist lowland savannas of Bolivia and Venezuela, are the remains of dense sedentary settlements that emerged in response to socioeconomic processes stimulated by the opportunities for trade and stratification. Although it is obvious that ecology and climate affect sociocultural processes, it is equally obvious that sociocultural processes—always embedded in specific systems of meanings—have an impact on landscapes and ecosystems.

Anthropologist Emilio F. Moran begins Chapter 15 by reviewing some of the major threats to sustainability presently faced by humanity. He observes that the core of our problems may be the incongruity between our (global) economic reach, manifest in our consumption of resources from all over the world, and our (local) cognitive reach, which does not encompass the distant environmental impacts of our consumption patterns. He strongly urges us to improve our capacity to obtain information on the environmental consequences of our behavior. In the final part of his chapter, Moran shifts from an activist to an academic tone of voice, reviewing some recent research on the dynamics of human–environmental systems approached through studies of land use and land-cover change. Of particular significance in relation to several other chapters in this book is his reference to studies showing that land-cover change can drive "regional-to-local" climate change. Although most of the chapters that mention climate focus exclusively on the impact of climate change on societies (but cf. Chapters 5 and 16 for other exceptions), it seems that recent global warming is not the only example of causality working in the opposite direction. The impact of the world system on the Earth system is today global and conspicuous enough to be scientifically monitored, but anthropogenic climate change at the regional-to-local level may have been with us for millennia. This recursivity between society and nature is inherently difficult to deal with, whichever analytical or methodological frameworks we apply.

In Chapter 16, Bert J. M. de Vries asks what modern people concerned with sustainability can learn from the past. He summarizes some recent research by archeologists and paleoscientists on the socioecological processes involved in the transition from hunting and gathering to sedentary agricultural societies in the Near East after around 10,000 B.C.E., and seems optimistic about the possibilities of simulation. The models he presents emphasize the feedback loops, or recursivity, between societal and ecological factors. Such cybernetic approaches, going back to the work of, for example, Kent Flannery (1972), continue to risk adopting a functionalist outlook (cf. Chapter 6), as illustrated by de Vries's reference to systemic "pathologies" and to the underlying systemic rationality of social stratification, specialization, trade, priests, and warriors. Building on Joe Tainter's (1988) proposition that socioecological decline or collapse tends to be the result of diminishing returns to complexity, de Vries concludes his chapter by suggesting that explicit and intentional "simplification" may be the best recipe for sustainability. Although the attempts to connect theories of ecological succession with Mary Douglas's culture theory seem superfluous, de Vries's recipe for sustainability appears valid enough without these theoretical embellishments.

In Chapter 17, anthropologists Susan C. Stonich and Daniel S. Mandell discuss the emergence of new, transdisciplinary discourses on human–environmental interaction. Judging from their search of the *Web of Science* for peer-reviewed articles using these labels as keywords, the frameworks of "political ecology" and "sustainability science" have in recent decades eclipsed those of "cultural ecology" and "human ecology." Moreover, the authors note that adherents of political ecology and sustainability science tend to diverge in terms of publication patterns and general outlook on human–environmental relations. Political ecology emerged in the 1970s as a reaction to the preoccupation of cultural ecology with local homeostatic processes and adaptation, and to its neglect of global political economy (cf. Chapter 6). Recently, however, political ecology appears to have become so diverse in terms of theoretical perspectives and methodologies—for example, the tensions between scientific and constructivist approaches—that it no longer represents a coherent field of study. Meanwhile, proponents of sustainability science appear to perceive political ecology as "politics without ecology." The authors argue that sustainability science needs to build on the accomplishments of political ecology. Not to do so, they warn, would be to once again reinvent the wheel. The chapter illustrates how the pervasive divide between scientists and humanists (cf. Chapter 1) continues to reassert itself, constantly jeopardizing every new attempt to create integrated frameworks for understanding socioecological systems.

Anthropologist Thomas Malm in Chapter 18 challenges the common metaphor that uses isolated oceanic islands to represent the fragility of Earth in space. Reviewing the fate of Easter Island and other Pacific Islands after the arrival of Europeans, Malm instead argues that the most serious fragility of such islands has had less to do with isolation than with inclusion in the world system. It is precisely as a consequence of their being incorporated into global economic and political structures that the Pacific Islands have suffered most in terms of epidemics, slave raids, unhealthy diets, garbage disposal, resource extraction, nuclear tests, and a host of other threats to their sustainability.

In Chapter 19, the historian Alfred W. Crosby reflects on epidemic diseases as phenomena at the interface of social and ecological systems. The chapter, as did the previous one, begins by arguing that civilization—or the world system, if you will—has created problems that generally did not afflict our precivilized ancestors. The emergence of sedentary farming settlements and cities, perfect breeding grounds for rats and bacteria, brought unprecedented health problems. Until a mere two centuries ago, cities were "demographic sumps." Long-distance trade among urban elites conveyed exotic diseases as well as exotic goods. Problems accelerated with improvements in transportation technology and the expansion of global commerce. Crosby recounts the history of influenza pandemics from the first unambiguous cases in the eighteenth century to the one that occurred in 1918–1919, whose impact on San Francisco he traces in greater detail. Although not nearly as feared as, for example, cholera, because of its low mortality rate, influenza killed more people in the nineteenth century than did any other pandemic. Crosby concludes that pandemics inevitably will continue to surprise us far into the future. Although perhaps not conventionally recognized as socioecological phenomena, epidemics exemplify the very intersection of nature and society. Crosby's classic *Ecological Imperialism* (1986), which deals with how the expansion of a world order dominated by Europeans was aided by the competitiveness of their biological luggage, is thus an exemplary study of the interaction of the world system and the Earth system.

The notion of "ecological imperialism" could equally well have been used to denote the kind of phenomenon discussed in the final two chapters—that is, unequal ecological exchange between different parts of the world system (cf. also Hornborg, McNeill, & Martinez-Alier 2007). In Chapter 20, the ecological economists Nina Eisenmenger and Stefan Giljum apply the concept of societal metabolism and the methodology of material flow analysis to investigate the claims of world-system theorists regarding unequal trade and the division of labor between cores and peripheries. They find that, in terms of biophysical resource flows, the developing countries in their sample tend to be net exporters, whereas the European Union (EU) and Japan are net importers. Moreover, when juxtaposed with average prices of each traded ton of materials, the statistics show that developing countries tend to export great quantities of resources at low prices in order to be able to import small quantities of materials with high economic value. In other words, the market prices set by the world system orchestrate an unequal exchange of material resources between different regions of the Earth system. Although the notion of "exchange" between society and nature that recurs in studies of societal metabolism is unfortunate, suggesting that there are system boundaries between social and ecological systems (cf. Chapter 4), this assumption does not detract from the value of being able to show that there is an unequal exchange of biophysical resources between distant segments of the global socioecological (that is, world *and* Earth) system, facilitating development and infrastructural accumulation in some regions at the expense of other, economically and ecologically impoverished ones. Such distributional and political dimensions of global sustainability are inextricably interwoven with the more naively conceptualized issue of not damaging the viability of our Earth system beyond repair.

In the final chapter, Andre Gunder Frank discusses unequal trade within the nineteenth-century world system. In his final years, he obviously glimpsed the potential of a biophysical perspective on the world system, experimenting with the thermodynamic concept of entropy to account for its polarities between increasing complexity and order (in the core) and increasing socioecological disorder (in the periphery). Although many would prefer to view the notion of sociopolitical entropy as no more than a metaphor, an integrated socioecological perspective should perhaps take seriously the observation that sociopolitical complexity, too, requires inputs of negative entropy (order) in the form of energy and materials (cf. Chapters 4 and 20), and produces entropy (disorder) through its own metabolism (Hornborg 2001a). Frank argues that the societal displacement of entropy from cores to peripheries, although more obvious today (for example, the consequences of global warming), can be discerned already in the nineteenth century. Although the validity and details of each such proposed example of entropy displacement still remains to be worked out, the general outlook holds promise for yet closer integration of our studies of the world system and the Earth system.

Part I

Modeling Socioecological Systems:
General Perspectives

CHAPTER 1

Historical Ecology: Integrated Thinking at Multiple Temporal and Spatial Scales

CAROLE L. CRUMLEY

That man is, in fact, only a member of a biotic team is shown by an ecological interpretation of history. Many historical events, hitherto explained solely in terms of human enterprise, were actually biotic interactions between people and land. The characteristics of the land determined the facts quite as potently as the characteristics of the men who lived on it. A land ethic, then, reflects the existence of an ecological conscience, and this in turn reflects a conviction of individual responsibility for the health of the land. Health is the capacity of the land for self-renewal. Conservation is our effort to understand and preserve this capacity.

Aldo Leopold, *A Sand County Almanac* (1949)

The alarming condition of our planet necessitates that we respond both to global changes that make local differences and to local practices that influence global change. We are thoughtful primates, proud of our intellectual and technical accomplishments. But the truth is that we are only part of a complex network of elements and relations that make up planet Earth. Within this enormous ecosystem we live our lives influenced by events and conditions that began long ago and far away.

My aim in this chapter is to bridge the gulf dividing the *Two Cultures*, C. P. Snow's (1959) term for the division between physical and biological sciences on the one side and the social sciences and humanities on the other. To

15

explain this focus I should offer some personal background. I read Snow's essay in high school and was horrified to realize that I would soon have to choose "between camps." I avoided having to make that choice owing to an early and abiding interest in *archeology*, a discipline whose practice unequivocally requires both the sciences and the humanities. This meant, however, that my professional life would be spent trying to master very different areas of study and engaging in shuttle diplomacy among them. So I am trained in paleoclimatology, geomorphology, archeology, anthropology, ethnohistory, and classics; I have some familiarity with complex systems theory, ecology, history, and geography. For thirty years I have been studying the historical ecology of Burgundy, France. We have been able to trace environmental worldviews—what Aldo Leopold terms a *land ethic*—over 2,800 years' time and to connect local Burgundian practices with environmental, economic, and social changes at the global scale (Crumley 2000; Crumley & Marquardt 1987; Gunn et al. 2004). It is with these tools that I pursue the practice and implications of historical ecology, hoping to help construct a theoretical and practical framework that will bridge the Two Cultures gulf. Other historical ecologists have different tools in their toolbox and diverse interests.

Historical ecology traces the complex relationships between our species and the planet we live on, charted over the long term (Crumley 1987a, 1994, 1998, 2001; Balée 1998; Egan & Howell 2001). It is a term new to both ecology and to history[1]; practitioners take the term *ecology* to include humans as a component of all ecosystems, and the term *history* to include the Earth system as well as the social and physical past of our species. Historical ecologists take a holistic, practical, and dialectical perspective on environmental change and on the practice of interdisciplinary research. They draw on a broad spectrum of evidence from the biological and physical sciences, ecology, and the social sciences and humanities. As a whole, this information forms a picture of human–environment relations over time in a particular geographic location. The goal of historical ecologists is to use scientific knowledge in conjunction with local knowledge to make effective and equitable management decisions.

Development of an interdisciplinary grammar and the identification of shared concepts and understandings are fundamental to the practice of historical ecology (Newell et al. 2005). A good example of such development is the term *landscape*, a unit of analysis in many academic disciplines (archeology, geography, geomorphology, ecology, architecture, art, regional planning) and also a concept recognized by the general public. Such concepts, along with widely held understandings about the way the world works—what anthropologists call *cultural models*—provide the basis for decisions about which practices are maintained or modified and which ideas are given substance. Landscapes retain the physical evidence of these understandings. They record both intentional and unintentional acts and reveal *both* the role of humans in the modification of the global ecosystem *and* the importance of past natural events in shaping human choice and action. In short, landscapes are read and interpreted by everyone, as likely to promote lively discussion in a gathering of citizens as in a group of scholars from various disciplines.

A working definition of landscape is the spatial manifestation of the human–environment relation (Marquardt & Crumley 1987:1). Landscape is thus a convenient idea that serves as an initial (but never the only) *spatial scale* of analysis. This is for two reasons. First, landscapes do not have an intrinsic temporal or spatial or cognitive scale (for example, one can speak of the medieval landscape of Europe or New York's Central Park landscape), but what all landscapes have in common is that they allow us to follow changes in the interaction of humans with their environment over some specified amount of time. Thus "the medieval landscape of Europe" assumes that different elements and relations pertained in Roman or Renaissance or contemporary times and that "Europe" itself was a different size and shape and meant something else. Second, all landscapes are in both real and cognitive "flux" as they are physically modified and imagined in myriad ways.

The landscape "scale" is thus powerfully integrative, enabling the simultaneous study of both the physical environment and human activity, and leading the investigation of factors that helped form a landscape—such as its geology, or an historical event, or an invasive species—to data aggregated at other scales. As with spatial scales, multiple *temporal scales* are necessarily part of the analysis as data sets with different temporal ranges are collated. Together, spatial and temporal scales are limited only by available data and the research question, and they can include a spatial range from microscopic to global and a temporal range from very recent events to deep geological time.

By integrating evidence from many different disciplines, the history of human–environment interactions may be sketched for a particular locale. The unique characteristics of every place challenge researchers to integrate a congeries of empirical environmental and cultural information. This necessarily requires the abandonment of notions of "nested" variables—often collectively termed *hierarchies*—common in biology and appropriated by other disciplines. In the real world, both environments and societies present themselves as mosaics, the temporal and spatial boundaries of which are fluid and crisscross one another (de Vries 2002, 2005; Marquardt & Crumley 1987; Nicholas 2001; Pickett & White 1985; Wiens 1976; Winterhalder 1984). Complex systems theory offers a means by which this nonhierarchical, nonlinear organization may be conceived in the term *heterarchy* (Crumley 1987b, 1995,

2001, 2003; Ehrenreich et al. 1995; Hofstadter 1979; Marquardt & Crumley 1987; McCulloch 1945; Minsky & Papert 1972). The fundamental utility of this term for rethinking human–environment relations will be explored below.

The social and environmental history of each region of the world may be investigated using archeology, archival materials, oral tradition and history, and proxy measures drawn from the Earth sciences for studying the area's previous and current environmental characteristics. Of obvious importance are rules for analyzing and combining diverse categories of evidence. For each category, the customary disciplinary techniques and protocols are respected (for example, in the analysis of pollen or soil or the excavation of an archeological site), but the structure of the inquiry as a whole is synergetic: collectively researchers exchange information and construct the overall design of the research, then continue to communicate as the work advances, together modifying the research design and working out problems as necessity arises.

Inasmuch as historical ecology begins with the presumption that contemporary landscapes are the result of multiple factors that have interacted in complex ways throughout history, independent data sets provide an important cross-check in building consensus among collaborators. For example, oxygen-isotope dating of Kenyan geomorphological samples places a flood event sometime during a ten-year period in the mid-nineteenth century; oral tradition associates the flood with the initiation of an age-grade in 1856 or 1857. If the evidence from the two sources is contradictory (oral tradition places the flooding in 1888), specialists then return to their data with new queries. (How accurate is the chronological control? Could there have been more than one flood event?) Thus the advantages of both multidisciplinary research (specialists work alone using appropriate techniques) and of interdisciplinary research (specialists cooperate and discover new aspects of their data) are combined.

While this working arrangement between the Two Cultures may sound ideal, everyone knows that very real battles are being fought. Rather than following Snow into a dualistic world where warring camps send emissaries who more often than not meet a bad end, I suggest a means by which the perception of great dissimilarity between the two may be erased and a third great river of knowledge—older than either—be joined with them. This latter is the empirical approach that carried our most distant human ancestors into the present (Mithen 1996). How was its value lost to us? Three influential and interrelated movements in Western intellectual history—the Enlightenment, the formation of the first nation-states, and positivism—have led the majority of intellectual elites and a considerable portion of the general public to abjure traditional knowledge, an empirical tool with which humans have always made their way in the world. In its place is an almost religious belief in our ultimate redemption by a sophisticated technology; somehow we will be saved from the outcome of our reckless use of chemicals, bioengineering, nuclear physics, and fossil fuels.

Do not mistake the arguments among the Two Cultures combatants as simply academic; they are profoundly political. Everywhere their discourse advocates the dismissal of empirically derived qualitative information in favor of quantifiable data; the ridicule of indigenous knowledge in favor of technological superiority; the adoption of a definition of complexity that favors hierarchical power over democratic principles. These premises, argued in scholarly articles innocently housed in dusty libraries, nonetheless underwrite global agendas that threaten the planet and impoverish humanity.

Historical ecologists regard history and politics as inseparable. For example, changes in a landscape can be viewed as a history of shifting social power (Crumley 1987a; Mann 1986).

Viewed from the present day, landscape history is invariably tied to contemporary politics of compliance, often contrasting scientific and institutional goals with traditional societies' practices and public awareness and participation (Brosius 2001; Johnston 1994, 1997, 1998, 2001). One need only think of contested cities such as Jerusalem or contested monuments such as Devil's Tower in Wyoming, where Native American religious traditions are pitted against the very different interests of ranchers, sport climbers, and the Park Service. The study of collaborative schemes for solving such community and institutional differences of opinion on environmental issues has made surprising headway in recent years. Some of these schema—collective bargaining, stakeholder participation, role playing, and the European Union's term *concertation* (meaning cooperative dialogue)—produce solutions that are widely acceptable. The study of such schemes underscores the fundamental role of values and perceptions in forming worldviews. Stakeholders challenge, debate, and come to understand others' positions, and underlying values are examined in a new way (Newell et al. 2005; Poncelet 2001). This does not mean that organic gardeners are converted to the use of pesticides but that the focus of the discussion becomes the stewardship of the Earth and not confrontation. The collective value, then, is environmental well-being and not the iron-clad correctness of one's own position. These democratic schemes for consensus move away from the inviolate authority of Science while still valuing its insights, and concede the necessity of democracy in assuring compliance. Historical ecology can shepherd these new ways of encouraging agreement: rather than policy makers assuming that their management strategies are superior to indigenous ones, historical ecologists can demonstrate that indigenous and popular strategies are also empirically derived and potentially useful.

In many nonwestern societies, ecological knowledge, resource management systems, and worldviews are inseparable; a large literature in anthropology documents creative indigenous solutions to environmental problems (Balée 1998; Bates & Lees 1996; Berkes 1999; Berkes, Colding, & Folke 2003; Berkes & Folke 2002; Brosius 2001; Crumley 1994, 2000, 2001, 2003; Lansing 1987, 1991, 1994; Kempton, Boster & Hartley 1995; Netting 1981, 1993; Rappaport 1968; Swesey & Heizer 1977; Trawick 2002). In cognitive anthropology, the analysis of worldviews has come to be known as the study of cultural models (Holland & Quinn 1987). These models make connections among different types of information and enable prediction and explanation. They are cultural because they are shared and reproduced within a society, and in time become traditional. Diverse cultural models of nature underpin every society's thinking about the environment (Kempton, Boster, & Hartley 1995), and the politics of these differences fuels environmental justice movements (Johnston 1994, 1997, 1998, 2001).

Science-based modeling is quite different. Modelers rarely begin with actual data but theorize about relations among elements. A good example is that of climate modeling, which begins with a set of assumptions about how "drivers" of climate (for example, insolation, greenhouse gases) interact. Modelers then change the parameters of the model to see how they affect the system. This approach necessarily means that the models need to be kept simple; even then it takes a phalanx of parallel processors a considerable amount of time to run the models. There is little room to include empirical behavior of the system in the form of historic climate and other proxy data.

I recall the open derision of any scientific link between climate and human history from National Oceanic and Atmospheric Administration (NOAA) atmospheric scientists (mostly modelers) as late as a 1992 conference organized by archeologist Ervan Garrison and applied anthropologist Shirley Fiske. Circumstances have changed in the interim, and atmospheric scientists are now more interested in climate history, thanks to the work of some modelers, but much of the burden has rested on historians, geographers, archeologists, and palynologists to demonstrate the utility of historical analogues (for example, Crumley 1994; Gunn 2000; Hughes 1975, 1994, 2001; PAGES Newsletter 2000; Pfister 1999; Pfister, Frenzel, & Glaser 1992; Redman 1999).

Even there, of course, there have been enormous difficulties. The first crude attempts to link human activity and the environment placed humans in an unequal relation with their surroundings (Huntington 1907, 1924). Led by social scientists and humanists, the rightful critique of this determinist effort remains a vivid part of their disciplinary socialization, spilling over into tensions between sociocultural anthropologists on the one hand and archeologists and physical anthropologists on the other. One example: I once shared with a cultural anthropologist a taxicab from the airport to the annual American Anthropological Association meetings. I responded to her question about my interests by saying that I study relationships between long-term climate change and human societies. She looked horrified, physically moved away from me on the taxicab's back seat, and said, "but that's Environmental Determinism, isn't it?" She said not another word to me for the rest of the ride.

How might these two very different notions of models be combined? Although one approach is primarily inductive (cultural models) and the other deductive (computer models), both are empirical, require creativity and learning, and their utility can be judged. Why not invite interested modelers of both kinds to a conference where the keynote speech addresses points of similarity in the two approaches rather than differences?

In the current climate of hostility, perhaps the most important characteristic of historical ecology is that it celebrates the open-minded quest of scientific inquiry, the phenomenological intensity of the human experience of *place*, and the empirical basis for both. Moreover, the study of changes in the temporal and spatial configurations of landscapes, in conjunction with work in cognition, offers practical means of integrating the natural and social sciences and the humanities. The historical ecology of any part of the world is always an unfinished manuscript, passed from hand to hand, critiqued, debated, amended, and revised. The approach values insights from the past as well as the present, employs the knowledge of science and society, stimulates creative thinking about the mitigation of contemporary problems, and encourages locally and regionally developed answers to global situations in which sensitive cultural issues play an important part.

Intellectual Architecture for the Global Scale

Three concepts that draw on intellectual traditions already familiar to many of us could leverage the next stage of integration. They are a revival and expansion of *multi-scale ecology*, the exploration of *complex systems theory*, and incorporation of the alternative form of social order termed *heterarchy*.

Revitalizing Multi-Scale Ecology

First used by natural scientists in the late nineteenth century, the term *ecology* (from the Greek *oikos*, dwelling) emphasizes the reciprocal relationships among living and nonliving elements of our world. Growing in concert with systems theory, ecology emerged as a discipline in its own right by the 1960s. The generation that came of age at about the same time our species first set foot off-planet (1969) could hardly help but note the contrast between American postwar materialism and the growing human, economic, and environmental toll in Viet Nam. They were the first eager students of the new academic discipline of ecology, which became for them shorthand for the relation of our species to all facets of its *oikos*. For many, the first view of our blue planet and the compelling spirituality of the Gaia hypothesis inspired a definition of ecology that included all scales (local to global) of relations among living and nonliving elements and that explicitly included humans.

The discipline of ecology has since bifurcated, and its emphasis has undergone a scalar shift. Today microecology, with ties through cell and molecular biology and genomics to schools of medicine and public health, dominates the field; macro-ecology (for example, wildlife ecology, landscape ecology, Earth-systems ecology) trains fewer practitioners and garners fewer research dollars than does its larger and better-connected twin. Although Russian scientists pioneered the concept (Budyko 1980), only recently has the West perceived the need for a global-scale ecology. Broader scale ecologies (for example, landscape ecology) are increasingly important, but even there lessons from the social sciences and humanities have been incorporated slowly. For example, many ecologists still think of ecosystems as "natural" and human presence there as invariably negative, even including the scholarly presence of the research scientists themselves (for example, Forman & Godron 1986; Naveh & Lieberman 1990). This quest for "pristine" ecosystems to study (that is, ones ostensibly "without human impact"), and the tendency to leave time out of their considerations of systemic function and structure, has caused North American ecologists in particular to stumble over definitions of "wilderness" and its management. Criticisms from within and outside ecology have resulted in the search for a framework that draws on the strengths of systems theory, relates myriad anthropogenic and exogenous factors, and integrates all temporal scales and every spatial scale from microscopic to global.

The editor of a journal that publishes papers in both ecology and history analyzed manuscript reviewers' comments and found that scientists consider historians' (mostly qualitative) approaches imprecise and their styles of argumentation histrionic; historians perceive scientific (mostly quantitative) methods to be mechanistic and their findings trivial (Ingerson 1994). Historians concentrate on both intended and unintended consequences of human action and offer convincing examples of the plastic role of history and culture, but they usually have less command of the biophysical systems that also condition human activity. For their part, many scientists remain naive about how "natural" systems are shaped by politics, belief, and history. Journals such as *Landscape Ecology, Ecological Restoration*, and *Ecological Applications* offer a forum for integrated approaches.

The Two Cultures divide between science and the humanities costs twentieth-century ecology not only the insight of multiple spatial scales but also that of time. But it was not just ecology that forgot history and structure in the rush to model process; so too did geography, much of anthropology (including even archeology for a time), physics, and climatology (with the exception of H. H. Lamb 1972–1977, 1995). Ecology could learn much from geology by working at multiple temporal as well as spatial scales and embracing geology's interpretive dialectic between structure and process.

Adapting Complex Systems Theory to Human Societies

Systems theory was a major influence on ecology from the outset, and complex systems have been a focus of research since the 1930s (Bateson 1972b; Ellen 1982). The benefits of systems thinking are considerable, but there have also been significant criticisms. Chief among several issues is the charge that the approach is inherently reductionist and leads to the modeling of simpler and simpler systems. Just the reverse is required if we are to study our planet, where conjoined human and physical systems make it the most complex dissipative system known.

The most recent iteration of complex systems research offers new ways to study the dynamics of coupled human–environment systems (for an overview see Johnson 2001). Key universal features are: *integration* (holism), *communication* (emergence or self-organization), and *history/initial conditions* (chaos). These correspond to key features of *social* systems: integration (culture), communication (language, society), and history/initial conditions (traditions, structures and materials, strategies, and habits of mind). Thus communication has emergent properties: two (or more) communicating entities have different attributes than each does alone and together can generate new forms (Jantsch 1982; Kauffman 1993, 1995; Langton 1992; Mithen 1996).

The development of communication is important for both the emergence of cognition in human history and the formation of community. The reproductive aspect of emergence (termed *allopoiesis*) satisfactorily characterizes the reproductive and dynamic aspects of human communication, language, and social organization, which persist in collective memory and material culture, are passed on from generation to generation, and are transformed (Climo & Cattell 2002; Connerton 1989; Crumley 2000; Gunn 1994; Maffi 2001; McIntosh, Tainter, & McIntosh 2000; Nora 1984). This is, of course, an essential definition of culture and a valuable entry point for social scientists.

This new systems thinking has opened an important door between the social and biophysical sciences, in that it can accommodate the results of human cognition (religion, politics, and systems of formal knowledge such as science).

Many of us, already familiar with "old" systems thinking and criticisms of it, can find refreshing potential in contemporary complex systems research, which offers a means by which human history and culture can be accommodated in a biophysical framework without reductionism.

Re-Visioning Social Organization

From the earliest human societies to the present day, coupled individual creativity and collective flexibility have met with success. Thus biological diversity has a correlate in human societies: the toleration of difference in individuals and groups and of variety in circumstances increases societal choice and offers a reserve of alternative solutions to problems. Similarly, organizational flexibility—economic, social and political—enables societies to adjust to changed circumstances.

Although there exist several useful vocabularies for discussing the organizational characteristics of society, twentieth-century American archeology was dominated by one: the framework of band, tribe, chiefdom, and state (Service 1971). Using this framework, considerable flexibility was attributed to bands and tribes, but much less to stratified societies (chiefdoms and states). The difference was seen primarily in terms of increasing "complexity," defined not as the more richly networked systems of complex systems theory but as increasingly nested, hierarchically organized systems manifest in hierarchies of power and their attendant systems of communication. Yet while hierarchical organization characterizes many aspects of state power, hierarchy alone does not capture the full range of organizational relations. Alternative forms of social order and state power—coalitions, federations, leagues, unions, and communities—are just as important to state operation as they are in more egalitarian groups like bands and tribes.

Terming such groupings *associations*, Service noted their importance. Unfortunately, subsequent archeological theory disregarded this avenue and concentrated instead on how elites constructed power pyramids. Yet as the September 11, 2001 events demonstrate, power flows in many channels (Samford 2000) and can be manifested entirely outside the framework of state hierarchies and beyond their control. In complex systems terminology, this is termed *chaos* or surprise, and it is related to systemic negligence in engaging other dimensions of power (Crumley 2003).

Hierarchy (the classic, pyramidal organizational form) is a structure composed of elements that on the basis of certain factors are subordinate to others and may be ranked (Crumley 1979:44, 1987b:158; see note 2).

Another way of viewing the meshwork of dimensions and levels in large societies is as a *heterarchy*, the relation of elements to one another when they are unranked, or when they possess the potential for being ranked in a number of different ways depending on conditions. Understood from a heterarchical perspective, sources of power are counterpoised and linked to values, which are fluid and respond to changing situations. This definition of heterarchy and its application to social systems is congruent with Warren McCulloch's research into how the brain works (McCulloch 1988). A strong influence on the complex systems theorist Kauffman (1993, 1995:xx), McCulloch first employed heterarchy (1945) to examine independent cognitive structures in the brain, the collective organization of which he terms *heterarchy*. He demonstrates that the human brain adjusts by re-ranking values as circumstances change. McCulloch's heterarchical "nervous nets" are the source of the brain's flexibility. Thus an individual can simultaneously be against abortion rights and for the death penalty (or vice versa). The context of the inquiry and changing (and frequently conflicting) values (Bailey 1971; Cancian 1965, 1976; Crumley 1987b) mitigates this logical inconsistency and is related to what Bateson (1972b), following Russell, terms *logical types*. Priorities are re-ranked relative to conditions and can result in major structural adjustment.

McCulloch's insights about the autonomous nature of information stored in the brain and how parts of the brain communicate revolutionized the neural study of the brain. They also solved major organizational problems in the fields of artificial intelligence and computer design (Minsky & Papert 1972). What McCulloch realized was that information stored in bundles as values in one part of the brain may or may not be correlated with information stored elsewhere; in computer terminology, subroutine A can subsume ("call") subroutine B and vice versa, depending on the requirements of the program. Rather than the "tree" hierarchy of the first computers, those today use an addressing (information-locating) RAM (Random Access Memory) system that is heterarchical, more like a network or a matrix (De Landa 1997).

Another example of the utility of complex systems theory is in the critique of ecologists' theories of ecosystem structure and process (Winterhalder 1984). While a shared goal is to define change over time, the difference is in how it is seen as occurring, whether in an "orderly" (linear, hierarchical) fashion or in a more dynamic manner. Frederic Clements's influential paradigm of succession involved the idea of orderly, linear, and predictable stages—early succession, mid-succession, and climax—in which there was no room for human activity except as "disturbance" of "natural" processes. Informed by complex systems theory, historical ecology traces geographically specific, dynamic human–environmental relationships that are not bound by the old laws of equilibrium and stasis.

In summary, heterarchies are self-organizing systems in which the elements stand counterpoised to one another. In social systems, the power of various elements may fluctuate relative to conditions, one of the most important of which is the degree of systemic communication. Hierarchies and heterarchies of power coexist in all human societies. Societal dilemmas in which values are in conflict are resolved by achieving a novel, transcendent state that either ranks competing values relative to one another (hierarchy) or does not allow them to be definitively ranked (heterarchy). At each successive level of integration and over time, new ordering principles come into play. Thus, conflict or inutility leads to suspension of old forms but ensures the preservation of useful elements through communication to provide creative new solutions to challenges, that is, transcendence of older forms. In these novel forms societies retain near-term flexibility, although there is of course no guarantee that the new form is more stable than the old or that tensions will not reappear in another guise. For example, revitalization movements such as the Native American Ghost Dance or the "born again" phenomenon seek transcendence through individual and collective rededication based on both new information and the retention of selected old values; this is also termed *maze-way reformulation* (Wallace 1970).

The addition of the term *heterarchy* as a descriptor of power relations in so-called complex societies (Crumley 1979, 1987b, 1995b) is a reminder that there exist in every society forms of order that are not hierarchical, and that interactive elements in complex systems need not be permanently ranked relative to one another. Although a heterarchical ("egalitarian") form of order has long been recognized in smaller ("simpler") societies, it has been rejected as an appropriate organizational form for states. It is both impractical and inaccurate to exclude such a fundamental adjustment mechanism from the characterization of more populous political forms. The more successfully a society consolidates power and melds distinct hierarchies (for example, religious, political, economic) into hyperhierarchy or hypercoherence, the less flexibility there is in dealing with surprise (Crumley 2001, 2003). The current theoretical paradigm in archeology and elsewhere, which falsely assumes that the only form of complex order is hierarchy, no longer explains data collected in many parts of the world (Ehrenreich, Crumley, & Levy 1995). Complex systems theory and the concept of heterarchy can reinvigorate the interpretation of social systems and shed new light on the relationship between environmental change and societal collapse.

An Interdisciplinary Effort

Clearly, humans must respond both to global changes that make local differences and to local practices that drive global change, employing every means at our disposal. We must search for common ground, in relatively new terrain and on relatively neutral terms. The term *environment* must encompass the built environment, the cultural landscape, and nature wild and tame. The definition of *ecology* must include humans as a component of all ecosystems. The term *history* must include that of the Earth system as well as the social and physical past of our species.

Construction of an integrated framework has proven difficult, in large part because of the scalar incompatibility of human activity with planetary-scale atmospheric phenomena. Patterns of settlement and land use, emissions, and extractive procedures must be investigated at regional and local scales. However, aggregated human behavior in regard to global-scale changes (for example, climate) must be verified at the macro-scale through methods involving parallel change events in widely dispersed regions. Growing scientific understanding of the interconnectivity of the atmosphere, hydrosphere, biosphere, and geosphere in the global system provides reasonable background cause-and-effect linkages and cyclicity, but wide-ranging social science theory and methods must be articulated to meet global science and attribute broader systemic causation. Without environmental and cultural information at local and regional scales, there exists no opportunity to test and refine global models; without planetary-scale confirmation of the long-term effects of human activity, arguments over values (embedded in property rights, social justice, environmental policy, and other issues) will not abate.

Policy makers everywhere are *ad hoc* students of causation. They address myriad issues in which human and environmental conditions are inextricable. Situations they must anticipate and to which they must respond require enormous knowledge at multiple scales of time and space. After all, there is no reform without compliance; history and society, messy as they are to integrate into scientific research, are of fundamental importance (Johnston 1994, 1997, 1998, 2001).

All dissipative systems—including human societies—are subject to profound change. In that there is no guarantee of progress, we are a species like any other. For humankind, this means that we are not inevitably on a rising stair of accomplishment but may find ourselves in the blink of an eye in a condition much more dire and hopeless than at any time in that part of human history red in tooth and claw. We must review a description of the world that is solely mechanistic and denies spirituality as an essential characteristic of the human species. We have allowed pragmatic arguments to triumph in almost every quarter and to relegate emotions to a small, closely moderated compartment of our psyche. While they were not the earnest ecologists some have imagined, our human forebears did at least see that the sun, the heavens, the earth, the waters, their fellow creatures, and they formed a single system, and held all sacred. While they too made management mistakes, they did not lose sight, as have we, of the integrated nature of the Universe.

Historical ecology marshals a powerful array of conceptual and practical tools, permitting the integrated investigation of change driven by conditions at global, regional, and local scales. It honors the values, knowledge, and sensibilities of people at all times and places. It is also a practical guide for research, encouraging interdisciplinary discoveries, aiding conservation, and amplifying creative and integrative explanation. In it we have a means by which we can study ourselves as a conscious species in conjunction with the history of our planet. Historical ecology can show us how our world works, how we are not bystanders but instigators of change in the world, and how we must now act on its behalf.

Notes

1. For an overview of historical ecology see Crumley 1994 and Balée 1998. Don S. Rice attributes the first use of the term to the archeological palynologist Edward S. Deevey, who directed the Historical Ecology Project at the University of Florida in the early 1970s. Historian J. Donald Hughes uses the term *environmental history* in his 1975 book, but with a human ecologist, an economist, anthropologists, and other historians contributed to *Historical Ecology: Essays on Environment and Social Change* (1981) edited by historian Lester J. Bilsky. Anthropologist Alice Ingerson organized a session on historical ecology at the 1984 American Anthropological Association annual meeting. She sought to address the chasm between cultural and environmental studies in anthropology, and to explore political economy and social history approaches. I first used the term as the title of a chapter in *Regional Dynamics: Burgundian Landscapes in Historical Perspective* (1987a) edited with William H. Marquardt, and subsequently edited a School of American Research volume entitled *Historical Ecology: Cultural Knowledge and Changing Landscapes* (1994a). Since the early 1990s ethnographer and cultural ecologist William Balée has been fostering historical ecology; together we have edited the *Historical Ecology Series* for Columbia University Press (Balée 1998; McIntosh, Tainter, & McIntosh 2000). Restoration ecologists Dave Egan and Evelyn A. Howell have edited *The Historical Ecology Handbook: A Restorationist's Guide to Reference Ecosystems* (2001). A recent search of Web sites employing the term found dozens of references representing a variety of projects. Most, but not all, of these sites explicitly address the relation between the environment and human activity.
2. For further reading about heterarchy and its connection to brain research, computer design, artificial intelligence, and social organization, see, for example, Bateson 1972b; Crumley 1979, 1987b, 2001, 2003a, 2003b; Crumley & Marquardt 1987; Ehrenreich, Crumley, & Levy 1995; Kontopoulos 1993; McCulloch 1945, 1988; Minsky & Papert 1972; Mithen 1996.

CHAPTER 2

Toward Developing Synergistic Linkages between the Biophysical and the Cultural: A Paleoenvironmental Perspective

FRANK OLDFIELD

Increasingly, global change research communities are highlighting the need to develop closer links between biophysical and cultural perspectives and approaches. For someone trained as a geographer in the United Kingdom some 45 years ago, this kind of goal seems both less innovative and perhaps less achievable than it may seem to many working on either side of the divide, but coming from other disciplines. The goal seems less innovative because it closely parallels one of the recurrent themes in geography, that of reconciling, perhaps even finding common ground between and to some extent uniting, the "physical" and "human" branches of the subject; less achievable, because most attempts within geography have foundered on the sheer difficulty of sharing a common conceptual framework. Just as the conceptual frameworks differ, so inevitably do views on the reasons for the difficulties. This perspective is a personal one, colored by a long career almost entirely on the biophysical side of the divide.

One of the research areas within which there is clearly a growing and increasingly successful merging of biophysical and cultural/socioeconomic perspectives, to the point of synergistic, functional interaction rather than interwoven narrative, is in the development of Integrated Assessment Models and the scenarios they can generate. As far as I can judge, and despite exciting conceptual developments in historical ecology (for example, Crumley 1994a), very little comparable is happening in paleo-research. This leads me to the rather paradoxical view that the desired merging is currently more readily achievable in "cyberspace" than in past reality. No doubt the need for—hence the funding available for—groups developing future scenarios that unite a wide range of biophysical and socioeconomic perspectives provides a powerful incentive. At

29

the same time, questions about the future create an unusual inferential context. Not only is there shared uncertainty when story lines stretch beyond the limits of secure empirical underpinning; most of the future scenarios developed are, by definition, unverifiable in the short term. Could it be that these qualities that distinguish the shared context of "futures" research reduce the mutual vulnerability that might otherwise arise in the participating groups? There is also more comparability in methodologies between future-oriented social and biophysical scientists than between their more traditional counterparts, as well as a relaxation in the degree to which each is likely to be trammeled by his or her respective disciplinary traditions, with their tendency to entrench academic imperialism (and xenophobia). From these considerations, we may conclude that just as there is a divide between the biophysical and the sociocultural, there is an equally significant one between scientists focusing on present and future patterns and processes and scientists dealing with the past. Both divides need to be addressed.

If, for the moment, we turn to the past, we may perhaps come closer to addressing the problem of the gap between biophysical and cultural perspectives by considering the modes of research currently adopted in the paleo-research community. Although these modes defy rigid classification, we can propose a rather loose taxonomy for them based on the dominant purpose underlying various modes:

1. narrative reconstruction of the past sequence of events;
2. establishment of time-slice "realities";
3. provision of the recent antecedents to present-day environmental systems;
4. post-hoc hypothesis testing; and
5. elucidation of processes and process interactions.

These categories overlap and are not necessarily mutually exclusive, but they lead me toward my next main point—namely, that the merging of biophysical and cultural perspectives is easiest to achieve in the case of the first research mode, that of narrative, or sequential reconstruction. There are many parallels in research mode between the paleoecologist and the historian (see Figure 1). Moreover, narrative can be achieved safely without contravening embargos from the cultural side of the fence on deterministic or oversimplified, mechanistic thinking. In conceptual terms, narrative also falls comfortably within what Head (2000) explores and illustrates extensively under the term *contingency*, by which she means "the historical particularity of sets of circumstances." This concept closely parallels that of "emergence" in chaos

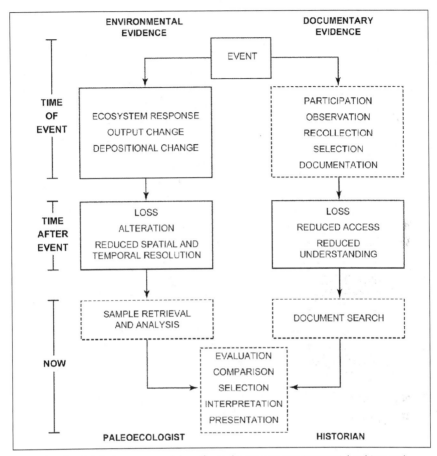

Figure 1 • Parallels between research by paleoecologists using environmental archives and historians using documentary archives (from Oldfield & Clark 1990).

theory. Interwoven narrative is not sufficient if we are aiming to develop more generalizable perspectives from combining the cultural and the biophysical. I would claim that the fifth mode is the most important.

In present-day paleoenvironmental research, many of the best elucidations of past processes and process interactions are the result of close collaboration between the data and the modeling communities. There are many examples of this ranging across themes as diverse as the mid-Holocene desiccation of the Sahara and the ascription of recent climate change to particular combinations of forcings and feedbacks. Might this type of interaction suggest a way forward for merging biophysical and cultural perspectives on past changes in societies and ecosystems at a level that embraces functional interactions and leads to real synergy? The study by Dean and colleagues (1999) could be a pointer in the right direction.

All this brings us to the not very original suggestion that whether we are dealing with interactions between humans and their environment in the past or the future, the conceptual framework within which diverse perspectives may best be linked is one that places strong emphasis on models and modeling. To what extent are there emerging paradigms that recognize this and provide some kind of framework within which future dialogue can take place fruitfully?

We may begin by trying to articulate some criteria that the framework and the methodologies that it includes should meet. I believe that Cronon (1992) set us on the right path in his brief critique of postmodernist approaches to environmental history, though still very much within the framework of narrative reconstruction. He proposed three criteria that narratives of environmental history must meet: They should not contradict known facts about the past; they should not contravene our present understanding of environmental and ecological processes; and we should be prepared to recognize that, as individual scholars, we act within a pattern of affiliations—both academic and nonacademic—and that from this arise preconceptions as well as a collective critique and a context of evaluative constraints. These criteria seem to me to serve the empiricists well, irrespective of which side of the human/biophysical divide their interests and expertise may lie.

Is it possible to develop a similar set of criteria for model development? An ideal set of criteria for the biophysical realm might require that all models satisfy the following:

1. internal consistency;
2. compliance with all applicable biophysical laws;
3. compatibility with the constraints imposed by secure and relevant data; and
4. robust performance under a range of credible boundary conditions.

The second criterion may need to be relaxed to some degree, because we recognize that the dynamics of the Earth system at no time generate ideal steady states and will therefore always fail to conform to any requirement for perfect conservation of energy. Consideration of the third criterion leads us toward a duality in the relationship between models and data. For some purposes, the criterion may serve quite well, but it is often the case that models are developed from a fusion of fundamental theory and statistical relationships in such a way that independently derived empirical data can serve as a test of their credibility. Data may therefore serve at the stage of model development and at the later stage of model evaluation, though the same data cannot be used at both stages. Increasingly, this circumstance has led to a relationship between models and data analogous to Popper's scheme of deductive science. Looked at from a Popperian perspective, the model, as initial hypothesis, can be falsified by independently derived data. Improving the model to bring it closer to compatibility with the data and enhancing the quality of the data in order to provide increasingly secure and well-defined constraints thus go hand in hand in the search for explanatory models that do not contravene the best available data. Such models may then serve as refined and unfalsified hypotheses.

If, as seems likely, our windows into the future continue to take the form of model-based scenarios or "story lines" and if, as is manifestly the case, future data are unavailable, model building and testing must rely, for its empirical inputs, both on what we can observe and measure now and what we can reconstruct from the past—which brings us to the final criterion. In the largely mechanistic biophysical world and despite all the hurdles imposed by stochastic processes, nonlinear behavior, and emergence, it is reasonable to take the view that the performance of a model developed to simulate present and future processes and interactions can be tested by applying it to periods in the past when forcings and boundary conditions were markedly different. When paleosimulations are inconsistent with data for the target period, this inconsistency seriously undermines confidence in the robustness and future applicability of the model. Consistency between model simulations and data from the past may be regarded as an essential, if not necessarily sufficient, indicator of the likely reliability of future simulations. In this rather simplified formulation, our study of the past serves not simply to improve our knowledge of past states, rates, and processes as antecedents to the present and future; it also serves as a basis for testing our ability to understand the processes and their interactions, and for evaluating the extent to which we have been able to develop, from these insights, models and simulations consistent with our empirical knowledge.

Broadening the scope of the model-data interactions to include human systems in all their interconnected complexity takes me well beyond the limits of my personal competence. All I can do is ask colleagues on the other side of the "divide" to what extent the preceding scheme of model-data/present-past-future interactions is applicable within their realm. Note that it depends strongly on a degree of fundamental conformity of relationships through time that allows past, present, and future to be treated in a similar way, no matter how dramatically different the boundary conditions and process interactions may be at different times. Even a partial and qualified affirmative may open up a methodological framework for future synergy. One area within which this already appears to have been given is in reconstructing past land cover (Petit

& Lambin 2002) and predicting future land use (Lambin, Rounsevell, & Geist 2000; Veldkamp & Lambin 2001).

We now return to the broader question of paradigms that may provide a wider, overarching context within which any emerging methodology may be set. Recent writings have pointed toward several possibilities.

Starting from the biophysical side of the bridge, the emerging concept of Earth System Science (ESS) provides one kind of framework. The Earth system, of which the climate system is only a part, may be seen as a dynamic entity, consisting of coupled, strongly interacting processes and biogeochemical cycles. Hutjes and colleagues (1998) observe that "it becomes more and more widely recognized that the fundamental properties of the climate system . . . do not depend on the capacity of separate subsystems, or on the unidirectional driving of one component on the other. Rather, the Earth system behaves as a dynamic entity, consisting of coupled, strongly interacting processes and biogeochemical cycles." In the forthcoming International Geosphere-Biosphere Program (IGBP) synthesis (Steffen et al. 2004), the Earth system is defined as "broadly the suite of interacting physical, chemical, and biological global-scale cycles (often called biogeochemical cycles) and energy fluxes which provide the conditions necessary for life on the planet." It is clear from a huge array of literature that over the last century, the human population of the planet has become a major force in virtually every aspect of the Earth system. The concept of Earth System Science thus embraces human activities as they affect the functioning of the planet and its capacity to serve as a context for life, especially that of our own species. Overall, I would guess that the perspective of ESS is less anthropocentric than humanists would wish. Humans enter in as participants, even major drivers of change in the system. Less attention is given to the nature of social organization or to human perceptions and priorities as these affect societal responses. My impression is that ESS is only part of the framework needed to unite biophysical and human perspectives.

Developing from and going beyond ESS toward a grand view of its significance, both fundamental and normative, is Schellnhuber's (1999) proposal that we are witnessing a second Copernican revolution, one in which, for the first time, we can strive to understand the complex workings of the Earth system as a whole in sufficiently complete and quantitative terms to both model and manage it. Whether or not one can fully accept the normative (and potentially highly prescriptive) aspects of Schellnhuber's formulation, the focus on sustainable development is one shared by many across the biophysical/human divide. But I see it more clearly as a shared goal than as a concept easily translatable into a framework for integrated, collaborative research embracing the past as well as the future. For me, the key question is, can sustainable development, as a goal, be translated into a research agenda that avoids the taint of global control that emerges from Schellnhuber's analysis? Different analysts have responded to this in different ways.

Taking the rather different view favored by writers such as Funtowicz and Ravetz (1992, 1993), Haug and Kaupenjohann (2001), and Saloranta (2001), we may ask if the only type of research that is sufficiently responsive to the combination of urgency and uncertainty, provoked by fears of the consequence of global change, is that in the "postnormal" mode set out by these authors. They highlight what they see as a discontinuity between traditional science and the role in which scientists responsive to the demands of future policy makers are cast (see below). This seems quite unsatisfactory to anyone who has worked to integrate research on past, present, and future changes by stressing the time continuum between them, that is, the extent to which any present "baseline" is conditioned by past processes and the need to understand and quantify long term changes.

By integrating the past with the present and the future, will it be possible to strengthen the human dimensions of future scenarios, thereby helping to bridge more effectively the gap not only between the biophysical and the human but between "normal" and "postnormal" science? Reference to the latest Intergovernmental Panel on Climate Change report (IPCC 2001) shows how the evaluation of current trends and of the scientific basis for modeling the climate input to future scenarios has been crucially informed by reconstructions of past climate variability. To what extent can similar progress be achieved with regard to human societies and decision-making processes? This issue brings us back to one of the questions already posed above. It is worth noting at this stage that the main difference between biophysical and human scenario-building is not simply that of uncertainty. For example, it is doubtful whether the uncertainties attached to estimates of the level of future greenhouse gas emissions are either wider or less readily quantifiable than those attached to the role of water vapor and clouds as feedback agents in the atmosphere of the future. As already noted, it is rather an issue of whether it is possible to find patterns that adequately capture quantifiable conformity in human behavior through time, despite the spatial and temporal discontinuities in cultures. As Haug and Kaupenjohann (2001) note: "Although calibration may adapt models to data sets of the past, it does not assure predictive capacity, nor validity." Further, they envisage that science may split into an "academic branch" and a "managerial, public policy branch," and that modeling for science per se and modeling for decision making may diverge. Their analysis thus disconnects future-oriented, hence policy-oriented, science from traditional science by stressing several aspects that lie outside the traditional scientific realm—the relevance of values, self-organization, and indeterminacy in the complex, transdisciplinary systems requiring evaluation.

My personal view is that this alleged dichotomy is constructed, in part, through caricature; moreover, that the interchange and the synergy between the two modes of science are both achievable and essential. If I am correct, then our studies of the past should have a key role to play, but, in some of the most important areas of research, those who ignore the past have hijacked the agenda. One of the reasons for this is that knowledge of past processes and interactions is more likely to constrain scenario development and impair its fluency than to facilitate it. Where the only criteria are apparent credibility and acceptance by users, testing against independently derived empirical data runs the risk of becoming redundant. Somehow, there must be a fully *shared* and open-minded appraisal of the past involving those whose primary task is to develop future scenarios and those who strive for empirically based reconstructions of the past, whether from a biophysical or a cultural standpoint. Kenneth Boulding (1973) once noted that, "whereas all experiences are of the past, all decisions are about the future . . . [I]t is the great task of human knowledge to bridge this gap and find those patterns in the past which can be projected into the future as realistic images. . . ."

One possible way forward is for researchers from both sides of the biophysical/cultural divide to pose questions arising from their own studies and experience that seem to require both kinds of perspective. Out of these questions may develop hypotheses linking both kinds of processes interactively. These in turn should generate models that can be tested against the full range of empirical evidence. At the stage where testable models are developed, there might be a much better chance of using the insights gained from the past to inform the business of providing future impact scenarios. Perhaps this strategy is a long shot, and it certainly is not a simple research agenda, but I can see no other way of bridging the several gaps outlined in this paper—between biophysical and cultural perspectives, empirical and model-based modes of research, and past reconstruction and future scenario development.

The best I can offer as partial starting points are some of the questions that have arisen in my own mind from those times when my research has been concerned with past human impacts on the environment. Two sets of questions will suffice as illustrations. First, throughout the long span of environmental history reconstructed from Holocene pollen diagrams from many sites from western Europe, the sequences of deforestation and associated soil erosion take several forms. In some cases, the first discernable impact suddenly transforms the surrounding environment dramatically, and there is no full recovery (see, for example, the records from Lago Albano in Guilizzoni & Oldfield 1996). Elsewhere, the first impact triggers gradual changes that are never reversed (see, for instance, Godwin 1944): they seem to be essentially incremental. In other regions, there is a lengthy sequence of alternation between forest and open land before one or other becomes established to the point of persisting until the present day (see, for example, Oldfield 1963). What factors underlie these differences? Are they a simple function of the initial resilience or otherwise of the preimpact ecosystem? Do ecosystem characteristics combine with regional climate to create spatial and temporal gradients of ecosystem vulnerability? Are the differences the result rather of contrasts in the type of land use or the persistence and intensity of human exploitation? How may these several influences interact to generate the different kinds of sequence observed?

Second, recent studies both from the region around Rome, where the records are rather localized (Guilizzoni & Oldfield 1996; Ramrath, Sadori, & Negendank 2000), and from the Adriatic, where the sediment and pollen source areas are very extensive (Oldfield et al. 2003a), the history of deforestation and of soil erosion giving rise to changed and accelerated sedimentation shows two periods of intense impact, the first from the Bronze Age, the second from Medieval times. Relatively little environmental impact appears to have occurred during the Roman period. By contrast, in northern England, there are sites where the impact of deforestation during late Iron Age and Romano-British times was more severe than anything before or since (Oldfield 1963); Oldfield et al. 2003b; Oldfield & Statham 1966). What is the basis for this contrast? Is it a question of historical contingency, reflecting the earlier history of the two regions, with the "damage" already done in the Mediterranean environments? Is it linked to the different opportunities for agricultural production offered by the contrasted climates in the two regions? Does it reflect, in part at least, the nature of the political economy of imperial Rome, with strongly contrasted attitudes to land management in core and peripheral regions? Surely more than one of these potential explanations is involved. Might it be possible to develop models linking these factors together in an explanatory framework to generate testable post hoc simulations?

Finally, what are the conceptual barriers that have to be overcome to make for better interactions? I suggest that they fall into two categories: "intrinsic" and "affective." Among the intrinsic barriers are questions of repeatability, predictability, and falsifiability, as considered briefly above. Each of these interlinked concepts may be thought of as generating a spectrum along which biophysical and cultural processes will often occupy very different zones. As for affective barriers, one of the strongest (as perceived from the biophysical side of the divide) is the need for cultural/social scientists to place their work in a theoretical framework, the adoption of which would radically alter its interpretation. Somehow, we need to learn how to overcome both kinds of barrier through mutual curiosity and respect.

CHAPTER 3

Integration of World and Earth Systems: Heritage and Foresight

JOHN A. DEARING

This chapter addresses one of the pressing problems of our time: how do we anticipate future human–environmental conditions in the face of interacting economic, social, and biophysical changes? The chapter summarizes how past complex interactions between nature and society may be identified, described, and analyzed using a methodology that combines documentary, archeological, instrumental, and sedimentary archives within spatially defined landscape units. The scope of this approach is illustrated with "parallel histories" compiled from a historical rural case study in China covering the last millennium. Here I argue that an optimum methodology for anticipating future changes uses parallel histories as the means for validating rule-based simulation models, such as cellular automata. The problems and limitations of the methodology are discussed, with the main conclusion that regional aspects of world history and Earth systems have a shared heritage that can, in many locations, be identified and analyzed sufficiently well to provide an understanding of past socioenvironmental interactions. A new phase of model development and experimentation can be expected to improve our theoretical understanding of socioenvironmental change and environmental foresight.

The Past Becoming the Future

We all have a qualitatively different view on the way human society interacts with the natural environment. But a consensus would probably not fall too short of the view that the long-term security of all societies will depend in part on our ability to combine more effectively our knowledge of the natural environment and society: the functioning of each and their two-way interaction. Attempts to visualize the complexity of these interactions are rarely made, but the Swedish artist, Öyvind Fahlström, produced a number of maps and models in the 1970s that portrayed the world system at that time. In purely qualitative and subjective terms, he defined the links between different sociopolitical systems, economics, population, natural resources, and pollution. In 1973 he created the "Garden—A World Model" comprising a physical "interlocking 3-D puzzle" created from abstract colored shapes suspended at different levels within the confines of a "garden." His preliminary work, "Study for World Model (Garden)," captures the train of thoughts and observations that underlie the model. These are categorized according to his views on the capitalist drivers of the global environmental crisis (*The Tie*), the unbalanced relationships between resources, population pressure, and economics (*The Conflict*), and the alternative futures of planning, fascism, or revolution (*The Choice*). It is a chaotic cartoon that includes sketches of political leaders and regional environmental crises set within a time dimension, centered on the 1970s, which stretches from the recent past into the near future. In short, it provides a pictorial representation of the multidimensional web of interactions that link Earth and world systems. Fahlström's futures included "low profile military imperialism," "holography," "biology/genetics," "extrasensory perception," "energy crises," and accelerated growth to feed profit-based economies.

Thirty years on, we recognize the veracity of many of these elements and links, and even predictions, while rejecting the importance of others. But it is also clear that neither Fahlström nor anybody else was able to foresee other major developments. In the early 1970s, environmental scientists were yet to compile compelling evidence for global warming driven by human actions, the medical sciences could only guess at the cumulative effects of HIV/AIDS, and political scientists had not anticipated the break-up of centrally planned economies. In creating new institutions such as the Kyoto Protocol, modifying regional demographic profiles, and redefining geopolitical goals—just three developments of many—have dramatically altered the functioning of the world system and the way that we now perceive its future path. The past becoming the future follows diverse parallel and linked lineages. Multidimensionality, interactions, and complexity may be the implicit watchwords of Fahlström's images, but they are also a reminder, if we need it, that the difficulties of describing and explaining the past and the current world system are nothing compared to the problems of foreseeing its future.

The link between complex systems, science, and Fahlström's art is conveniently summed up in Edward Wilson's statement: "The love of complexity without reductionism makes art; the love of complexity with reductionism makes science" (Wilson 1998:58). Whether Fahlström loved the complexity he observed or was simply driven to grappling with it (and one strongly senses the latter), it is obvious that descriptive models can provide only the starting point on the road toward the creation of workable and dynamic complex models that may help us anticipate our future. Some writers cast a more pessimistic view than Wilson's on the ability of science to solve humanity's complex problems, making open declarations of uncertainty. They argue that we may be close to a point where scientific advance slows down in the face of the challenges to find appropriate scientific methodologies that can realistically handle complexity (Horgan 1996; Pollack 2003).

This chapter embraces these challenges: how should we develop and apply scientific method to the creation of predictive models that embrace the complexity of Earth and world systems? It considers our current understanding of past socioenvironmental systems in the light of complexity theory in order to identify appropriate model requirements. It argues for existing modeling approaches to be explicitly embedded within histories of socioenvironmental interaction. It proposes a methodology that combines natural and social sciences in a framework whereby complexity theory, reductionism, and synthesis each plays a role.

Complex Socioenvironmental Systems

With the impetus of recent climate projections and population growth models for the present century, the ability of nations and regions either to mitigate the worst trends or to adapt to future scenarios is now prioritized in international scientific agenda. Journal editorials (Lawton 2001), global science declarations (Amsterdam Declaration 2001), and global research agendas (for example, International Geosphere-Biosphere Program; United Nations) argue forcefully for a new focus on the Earth as a complex set of interacting subsystems (see Figure 1), where nonlinear change is likely to be the rule rather than the exception. In recent years, systems thinking has been dominated by the rapid developments in the field of nonlinear system dynamics and complexity theory. Complex adaptive and interactive systems are characterized by feedbacks, thresholds, and self-organization. In the twentieth century, these theories were originally driven by findings from physics and biology, with a strong emphasis on abstract mathematical models. Partly as a result, the implications of complexity theory have yet to disperse fully among the environmental and social sciences, where there has been a reluctance to embrace its concepts and methodological tools. Exceptions include Manuel De Landa's (1997) rewriting of European environmental history over the last millennium in terms of "geological" and "biological," nonlinear progressions, and Peter Allen's (1997) attempts to model urban landscapes through the application of complex systems theory. In

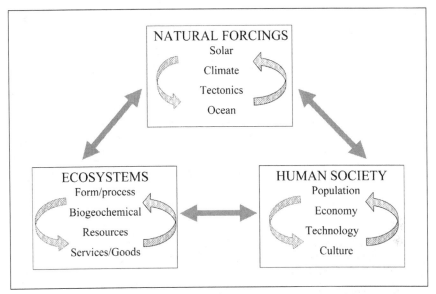

Figure 1 • Schematic illustration of the potential interconnections among society, natural forcings, and ecosystems. Bidirectional arrows represent potential flows of energy, matter, and information *among* the three state systems that may define externally driven causality and feedback. Circular arrows *within* each box represent internal dynamical processes.

some fields, the developments have simply fueled long-standing debates about methodology: the merits of "reductionism," the avoidance of "physics envy," the grappling with "space-time," or the meaning of "physical determinism" (see review by Massey 1999). A longer overview of the development of nonlinear dynamic theory would perhaps offer two broad lessons. First, many of our traditional descriptions and labels for the function and form of real world systems, often based on linear precepts, are too narrowly defined or inappropriate. Second, there has been a general failure to translate nonlinear concepts and abstract mathematical models into accessible and workable models that are appropriate for addressing real world problems.

We can apply these lessons to the study of complex socioenvironmental landscape systems. These systems are defined here as zones at the atmosphere-Earth interface where humans live, procure food, fiber, and water and where as individuals and societies they formulate and carry out environmental management decisions. All landscape systems are webs of interconnections among the natural world, socioeconomic conditions, and culture; some of these systems are tightly bound within fairly definable boundaries, whereas others are more open with links that may extend worldwide. Within each system an improved understanding of how it operates is needed in order to identify natural environments and communities at risk to projected future change, and to improve the basis for formulating appropriate environmental management policies, particularly for long-term sustainable development. These are truly complex and nonlinear systems characterized by a myriad of components and processes interacting between the physical environment and society, many contingent on the history of change that each has experienced. Inevitably, for any specific system there are wide ranges of potential social and environmental impacts and choices of management strategies. One element of our general understanding of how such systems change is to consider their heritage: the historical background to the modern natural, cultural, and social environments.

Heritage

The phrase "learning from the past" is often applied to several methodological approaches in which the study of past environments provides information about current states. The paleoenvironmental research community has a long track record in reconstructing past biophysical environments from geochemical, magnetic, and microscopic analyses of natural environmental archives, such as peat and other sediment sequences (Dearing et al. 2006a). There are now reconstructed trajectories of change over past decades to millennia for biophysical processes that include climate, vegetation, soil erosion, flooding, surface water acidification and eutrophication, and atmospheric pollutants. In some cases, these time series have provided a key perspective for the current environmental condition (for example, Dearing et al. 2006a; Oldfield & Dearing 2003), allowing definition of baseline levels or prehuman impact conditions against which restoration targets or appropriate ecosystem management strategies can be defined. A key element of the global warming debate has been the ability of paleoclimate reconstructions to demonstrate that modern temperatures are the highest during at least the past 10,000 years. Some trajectories allow the testing of alternative hypotheses of the cause of current environmental stress, as in the case of lake acidification. In all these cases, the role of human activities and social systems are normally inferred or remain nonspecific. Paleoenvironmental studies have been combined with archeological findings to provide an insight into the relative impacts of human activities and natural climate change on past environments, but not until recently have research programs explicitly combined paleoenvironmental reconstructions with documentary evidence for social change provided by environmental historians (for example, IGBP-PAGES Focus 5 program "Past Ecosystem Processes and Human-Environment Interactions" 2001). Such studies aim to provide an improved understanding of socioenvironmental systems through a combination of narrative and empirical

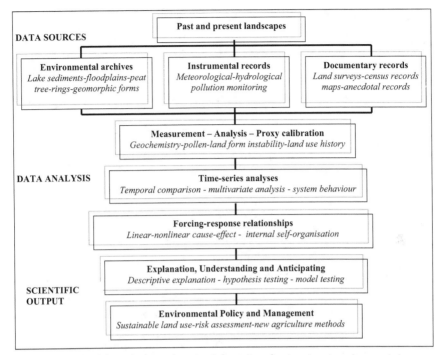

Figure 2 • Methodological scheme for using information about past socioenvironments to enhance our understanding of present and future conditions in local/regional contexts (for example, river/lake catchments). Boxes show the methodological path that links data sources (environmental archives, instrument records, and documentary records) to data analysis and output in terms of improved explanation and environmental policymaking (author's figure displayed at www.liv.ac.geography/PAGESFocus5).

analysis, within a framework that overcomes the temporal constraints imposed by methods based on observation and instrumentation (see Figure 2).

A summary of an ongoing case study in China illustrates the method. In southwestern subtropical China generally, high population densities and high population growth on cultivated plains and terraced valleys are placing great strain on already limited natural resources. Lake Erhai, in Yunnan Province and its catchment (~2,500 km^2) are situated in the Himalayan foothills, with a history of socioenvironmental interactions stretching back at least 6,000 years. The catchment is home to the Bai minority peoples, their distribution closely mapping onto the extent of the mountainous catchment boundary that rises to over 4,000 meters above sea level. Modern communities suffer from the effects of tectonic activity, extreme climate events, soil erosion, flooding, and nutrient enrichment of surface waters but are gaining materially through ongoing actions to promote the city of Dali as a regional industrial and tourist center. The tension between development and the need for sustainable management provides a pressing need to understand natural resource use, particularly linked to water control, the governance of common property, and the adaptive capacity of local communities, many of which belong to poorly represented ethnic minorities.

These modern concerns are superimposed on a long history of crises driven by environmental and political change. Over the past 1,800 years, the area has witnessed dynastic, colonial, communist, and postcommunist regimes, each apparently influencing the nature of local peoples' interaction with their physical environment. As a result, there are legacies of past actions that we can deduce from documented history and observation (Elvin et al. 2002). For example, ninth century hydraulic engineering on the western plain still forms the basis of modern irrigation. Also, it is fairly certain that the population pressures and social tensions of the late Ming period led to minority ethnic groups deforesting fragile slopes, which in turn led to substantial construction of flood-protection dikes that still require maintenance today.

These narratives can be examined further in conjunction with time-series of environmental processes derived from paleoenvironmental study (Shen et al. 2006). The compilation of documentary evidence for social change and reconstructions of natural environmental processes produces a set of "parallel histories" that forms the basis for hypothesizing interactions between climate, human activities, and the natural environment (see Figure 3). For example, the erosion record drawn from the lake sediments suggests that the geomorphic system may have now reached a state of relative stability compared with earlier periods: a state that has emerged from the multitude of local interactions between changing rainfall, slope angle, vegetation and land use, and engineering works over the previous decades and centuries, rather than having been caused by a change in any particular factor or any single event. The complexity of the whole lake-catchment system exists across a wide range of spatial and temporal scales. Land-use decisions made at one spatial scale and at one instant in time reverberate into other spaces and other times. There may be significant differences between the timescales of human activity and environmental responses, with some responses taking place over far longer timescales than are available for instrument data. Thus, the contrasting trends for erosion and nutrient losses (Figure 3) suggest that, at Erhai at least, these processes are not related to the same practices or locations of activities. Also note that these two processes differ in the way each responds to the phases of human activity identified: erosion responds fairly rapidly to changes in forest

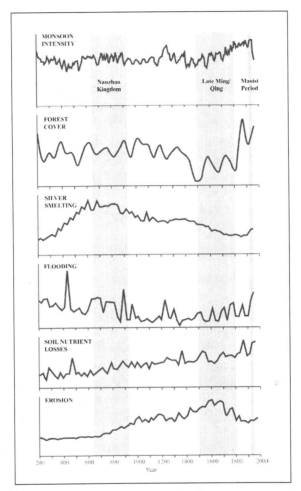

Figure 3 • Parallel histories of climate, human activities, and ecosystem responses for the landscape around Lake Erhai, Yunnan Province, China, 200–2000 c.e. based on lake sediment analyses and compilations of local environmental history. Selected trajectories are shown for climate (monsoon intensity: Wang et al. 2005), human activities (forest cover: % pine pollen; silver smelting: lead concentrations), and environmental process responses (flooding: > 45µm particle size; nutrient losses: phosphorus concentrations; erosion: magnetic susceptibility). Vertical bars show periods of known historical stresses on the natural environment of the Erhai catchment: Nanzhao kingdom: silver smelting and hydraulic engineering; late Ming-early Qing: deforestation, upland cultivation, and river diking; and the Maoist period: deforestation (after Elvin et al. 2002; Dearing et al. In prep.; Shen et al. 2006).

cover and periods of environmental stress, whereas the nutrient losses remain relatively unconnected while rising continuously over nearly two millennia.

Combining paleoenvironmental and documented data in these ways therefore maximizes our capability both to improve our understanding of process drivers and responses and to identify key aspects of system behavior, such as emergent forms and thresholds. Ultimately it may be possible to improve the conceptualization and measuring of phenomena such as current landscape sensitivity, adaptive capacity, and social vulnerability. Where the concern about environmental change extends into future decades, rather than years, the argument made here is that these parallel records are the best resources available for making judgments about how the future socioenvironmental system will evolve. But how do we make these judgments? However detailed and penetrating, a full narrative derived from analysis of all available past records will not be able to generate alternative strategies for sustainable management *that can be tested* for their accuracy in informing the future. The power of socioenvironmental reconstruction and narrative can be utilized fully to inform alternative views of the future only when they can be married to simulation modeling.

Let us review the needs of such models from the perspective of what we already know about long-term socioenvironmental change and complexity theory. The changing Chinese landscape presented in the case study is portrayed as a series of parallel histories. But these are in fact representations of independent data sources rather than independent histories, and importantly the interactions between the lineages are inferred rather than known. In reality, the changing system is less a set of parallel lineages and more an evolving web of interactions between the social and the biophysical systems (Capra 1996). The multifarious nature of interactions between those processes and environmental states that we can measure or envisage (let alone the ones we cannot) leads to a blurring of spatial and temporal scales. As already noted, the case study portrays the process of emergence, a concept that describes the formation of highly complex systems at a macro-scale from the relatively simple interactions of system components at the micro-scale, without explicitly identifying the functional relationships between variables. Historical case studies therefore reinforce the nonlinear and contingent nature of the modern socioenvironmental system but also underline the challenge for simulation models whose goal is to extend socioenvironmental dynamics into the future: that is to be functionally and dynamically realistic. As Wilson (1998:93) says, in referring to the construction of mathematical models that can capture the key properties of systems, "success in this enterprise will be measured by the power researchers acquire to predict emergent phenomena when passing from general to more specific levels of organization. That in simplest terms is the

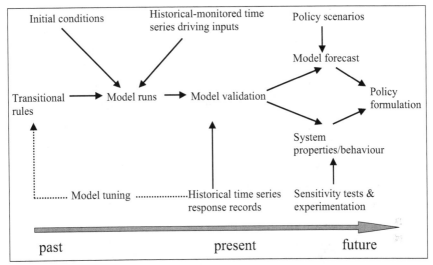

Figure 4 • Possible methodological scheme for linking parallel histories to cellular simulation models. A simulation model for environmental responses (for example, flooding, soil erosion) is run up from the past (from left to right) using historical data to define initial starting conditions, driven by appropriate time-series (for instance, climate, population) and validated against further historical data (for example, lake sediment-based erosion rates). Once the model is developed and validated sufficiently well to capture the nonlinear properties of the system it is driven forward from the present by socioenvironmental scenarios (for instance, climate projections, land-use projections) to simulate likely system responses and hence appropriate management policies.

greatest challenge of scientific holism." At the heart of Wilson's statement is the dichotomy in scientific methodologies between those that follow a reductionist path and those that tackle systems holistically.

Any method that promises to understand the holistic behavior of systems needs to include fundamental rules, the means to synthesize these into emergent phenomena, and, crucially, the means to test the accuracy of simulations. A proposed methodology (see Figure 4) tests the models by comparing their outputs in time and space with observed historical phenomena in the direction of emergence: from the past to the present. Testing simulation models by comparison with paleoenvironmental records is already an important aspect of climate modeling and has been central to unraveling the individual and the combined roles of alternative climate drivers in producing twentieth-century global warming. But the relative tractability of the fluid dynamics of climate systems contrasts sharply with the intrinsically more complex nature of socioenvironmental systems, particularly in terms of cross-scale process interaction and the nature and timelines of emergent phenomena. Socioenvironmental systems are characterized by the growth of far longer-lived emergent phenomena at all scales: social institutions, social structures, ecosystems, and geomorphic forms. Thus the main requirements for socioenvironmental simulation models at local and regional scales are to capture the simultaneous growth of emergent phenomena that can be observed historically—as in the Erhai case study—over a variety of timescales and within spatially defined zones. These tested models can then be run forward (Figure 4) to simulate future systems under different scenarios of environmental and societal change, allowing the opportunity to test alternative hypotheses and to run "what if" experiments.

Foresight through Simulation

Cellular automata (CA) models appear to satisfy many of these requirements because they simulate interactions between processes represented by fundamental rules. Cellular automata were originally created as toy models to simulate the complexity of hypothetical systems but have now graduated to applications in the natural and social sciences. At their heart lies a spatially explicit landscape defined as a series of contiguous cells. Each cell has a number of rules that determine how neighboring cells will change. At each time step, the state and the conditions of each cell are updated to provide new states and conditions for the rules to operate on. Through continuous interaction, the rules generate emergent patterns and features, capturing along the way the feedbacks, time lags, and leads that prove so intractable to alternative methods. Complex and unpredictable behavior is typical of even simple toy models whose cells have rules for whether they should turn black or white according to the state of neighboring cells (Wolfram 2002).

CA models can be classified according to the level of functional rules used, the means by which and the timescales over which the model is validated, and the extent to which the activities of human agents and decision making are made explicit. Tucker and Slingerland (1997) and Coulthard, Macklin, and Kirkby (2002) have pioneered the use of mathematical biophysical cellular models in catchment hydrology with low-level rules (relating to fundamental processes of energy and matter expressed as mathematical equations), long timescales ranging from decades to millennia, but with limited inclusion of agents. The basic cell in Tom Coulthard's CAESAR model is a cube with edge ranging from 1 m to 50 m, subdivided to represent the land surface and the subsurface horizons. Each divided section of cube has embedded mathematical algorithms to characterize hydrology, hydraulics, and sediment transport processes. The interactions between cubes for any defined catchment are driven by regional rainfall, temperature, and land-use records (or their reconstructed equivalents) acting as inputs to the equations at each time-step. Environmental changes are expressed as sequential maps or as time-series of outputs from the whole catchment. For example, the sediment generation curves simulated over the last 10,000 years for upland catchments in the United Kingdom (see Figure 5) capture the same trend and frequency-magnitude behavior that is seen in aggregated time-series of alluvial activity produced from dated stratigraphic sections (Coulthard, Lewin, & Macklin 2005; Coulthard, Macklin, & Kirkby 2002).

Similar models have been developed for coastal zones. For example, Costanza and Ruth (1998) describe the use of the generic STELLA computing language to develop a simulation model of the Louisiana coastal wetlands. Set up with a spatial scale of 1 km², the model simulates the changing nature of the Louisiana coast over 50–100 year timescales as a function of management alternatives and climate variations. A similar approach has been adopted by Dearing and colleagues (2006b) in the CEMCOS model of estuarine sediment dynamics, operating at a spatial scale of 2,500 m² and driven by wave gauge and tide data. The model will be used to simulate coastline and bathymetric changes over the next decades in the face of a rapidly rising sea level, projected changes in wave regime, and alternative coastal management options. The model outputs will be tested against historical sequences of British Admiralty Charts that show the emergence of sandbanks, mudflats, and channel changes over the past 200 years. In these three examples, human agents are brought into play mainly to set future scenarios for hard engineering options or land-use change: the models are essentially low-level, rule-based biophysical models.

In contrast, the inclusion of human agents involves the use of high-level rules (essentially equations or statistical relationships describing group behavior) and often a restricted history. For example, many models simulate regional dynamics (for example, White & Engelen 1997) and urban development (for instance, Benenson & Torrens 2004) over annual to decadal timescales. Li and Gar-On Yeh (2000) use land-use suitability indices as rules to drive a CA model of urban sprawl of Dongguan, on the Pearl River, China, using maps from 1988 and 1993 to validate the model outputs. Wu and Martin (2002) model the potential growth of London as a function of land-use probability scores defined by proximity to, for example, transport networks. They validate the model for 1991 and 1997. In a review of the limitations of CA modeling, Torrens and O'Sullivan (2001) point to the constraints imposed by the simplicity of CA models and how this simplicity has to be compromised to accommodate action-at-a-distance processes. They argue that there should be

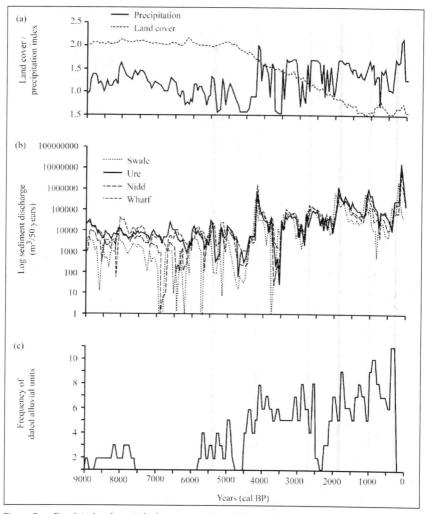

Figure 5 • Simulated sediment discharge using the cellular CAESAR model for northern England rivers compared to alluviation records for the past 9,000 years: (a) paleoenvironmental proxy time series for precipitation and vegetation cover that drive the model; (b) CAESAR-modeled output of sediment discharge for four river catchments; and (c) frequency of observed dated alluviation records. The timings of modeled peak sediment discharge correlate well with observed frequency record of alluviation (vertical grey bars). The *periods* of high sediment discharge tend to be linked to precipitation maxima, whereas the increasing *trend* in magnitude of sediment discharge toward the present seems to be driven by the declining land (vegetation) cover (Coulthard, Lewin, & Macklin 2005; Coulthard, Macklin, & Kirkby 2002).

more direct links between rules and theory, and an emphasis on *why* models should be developed rather than *how*. But these problems apart, there are ongoing developments that are likely to see improved CA-based modeling: through integration with GIS, new macro-level models, and, in ecology, the development of individual-based approaches (for example, Gimblett 2002). With the increased availability of computer grid systems, processing power is unlikely to impose a major constraint. Perhaps most headway toward the development of integrated socioenvironmental models has been gained through the agent-based models (ABMs), particularly among the researchers attempting to model changes in land cover and land use (for instance, Lambin, Geist, & Lepers 2003). Validation has largely come through sequential maps of land cover derived from satellite imagery since the 1960s. ABMs combine a cellular model of a landscape with an agent-based model that introduces decision making (Parker & Berger 2002). The way in which decision makers (agents) and the environment are represented in a model can fall into one of four combinations (Couclelis 2002) depending on whether agents and environment are each analyzed (empirical rules) or designed (theoretical rules). The ideal model for simulating the future, and one that comes closest to the requirements of long-term socioenvironmental models, is a validated model in which both agents and environment are analyzed: that is where both have relatively low-level rules, as in the case of the biophysical models.

It is at this point, however, that the lack of process theory for decision making, particularly the inclusion of political and institutional decision making, is seen to represent a fundamental challenge to successful modeling (Couclelis 2002; Parker & Berger 2002). This lack raises the whole question of how to deal with systems in which the available level of rules is not uniform across the biophysical and the social spheres. In the Chinese example, it is feasible to model the flooding and erosion processes using standard hydrodynamic and sediment equations as low-level rules, but at which level is it feasible to derive rules for socioeconomic processes: the individual farmer, the village, or the county? Figure 6 illustrates the problem more generally with respect to the levels of rules that exist in geophysical, biological, and social systems. Wilson's (1998) description of the potential reductionist-holistic lineage of the social sciences (Figure 6, column 3) shows the *potential* to explain macro-scale phenomena through reductionism, from societies to gene-culture evolution and ultimately human genetics. In contrast, the explanatory lineage for geophysical systems (Figure 6, column 1) shows that there are already sufficient low-level rules to make rule-based modeling feasible in many cascading landscape systems. For biological systems (Figure 6, column 2), the level of rules for which we have confidence is intermediate between those for society and geophysical systems.

GEOPHYSICAL	BIOLOGICAL	SOCIETY	
global environments earth system science – geology, ecology, climatology, hydrology, oceanography	**global environments** earth system science – biology, ecology, climatology, hydrology, oceanography	**global human societies** world system science – social sciences, human geography, sociology, economics, politics	HOLISM 'HIGH LEVEL' RULES
forms and associations (soil-vegetation, regional climate patterns) ecology, climatology, environmental science	**biological communities** (ecosystems) ecology, sociobiology	**gene-culture evolution** (diverse cultures) anthropology, archaeology, sociobiology	
abiological evolution (weathering, tornadoes) geomorphology, meteorology, ecology, pedology	**biological evolution** (diversity of individuals) behavioural genetics, evolutionary biology	**biological evolution** (diversity of individuals) human behavioural genetics	
chemical interactions (molecules) physics, chemistry	**biochemical interactions** (DNA, RNA) cognitive neuroscience	**biochemical interactions** (DNA, RNA) cognitive neuroscience, cognitive psychology	REDUCTIONISM 'LOW LEVEL' RULES

Figure 6 • Suggested hierarchies of explanatory rules in geophysical, biological, and social systems arranged in three columns from high-level to low-level rules (top to bottom). Here, "low level" refers to one end of a scientific spectrum, where the goal is to understand phenomena through rules, equations, and so on for micro-scale processes based on scientific laws of energy and matter, representing the ultimate goal of reductionism. "High level" refers to the other end of the spectrum, where the goal is to understand phenomena through rules that relate to relatively macro-scale system behavior, representing the goal of holism. The boxes give examples of phenomena studied at each level and the associated academic disciplines. The vertical arrows show the generally accepted span of currently available explanatory rules with dotted lines suggesting possible extensions in the foreseeable future (developed from Wilson 1998 and extended by the author).

Despite recent advances in developing rules for social processes (Ball 2004), it is common for writers to argue that low-level rules for social phenomena are simply unrealistic. As Massey (1999:272) notes, "although humanly meaningful phenomena may not be reducible to the phenomena studied by the natural sciences, they may be emergent from them. There may be real similarities in the abstract pattern of functioning of the inorganic, the biological, and the sociocultural, but in each sphere it is necessary that we specify the actual, particular "mechanisms" through which this functioning occurs." Others take the contrasting view and accuse the social sciences of not having progressed toward the development of rigorously defined theory, where explanation of phenomena is provided by webs of causation across adjacent levels of organization. Wilson (1998) argues that social scientists by and large spurn the idea of hierarchical ordering of knowledge that unites and drives the natural sciences: never do they embed their narratives in the physical realities of human biology and psychology, which he argues is the driving force of cultural evolution. Rather they seek to explain social phenomena not through individuals, but through ordering and classifying social phenomena without making the scientific progress toward a web of causal explanation. As such they remain at the stage of natural history where hermeneutics, the close analysis and interpretation of data, plays a large part of the method (Wilson 1998). In some ways, these criticisms apply to many paleoenvironmental studies that, while providing a rich source of material that describes environmental change, only infrequently generate theory. We therefore have social sciences that are often ahistorical and seemingly uncoupled from cognitive processes. However, the environmental sciences have strong roots in reductionist science and, as demonstrated above, excellent records of evolution and past changes, but with the exception of climatology they have still failed to find a unifying framework from which theory and predictions can be developed. In developing simulation models that integrate aspects of Earth and world systems, the task is to find overlapping and complementary units and tools that can be applied to the interface and that can accommodate the relevant spatiotemporal scales of interacting autogenic and endogenous changes. A comparison of the three columns in Figure 6 suggests that the commonality in the level of rules is placed at a fairly high level, perhaps signaling a fundamental barrier to simulating emergent phenomena from interactions of low-level rules. But if our goal is not the complete unity of knowledge but rather the more modest desire to develop workable and useful models, there may be shortcuts. There are two points to consider.

First, the behavior of systems is likely to be even more complex than the relatively simple emergence of phenomena driven by multiple iterations of interacting rules. Stewart (1997) argues for punctuations in this process, with emergent features at one level providing the basis for a different set of simple rules to operate and to produce emergent features at a higher scale still. In other words, intermediate emergent forms or "resting points" (Stewart 1997) are likely to exist as essential antecedents of the emergent phenomena in question. Cohen and Stewart (1994:417) distinguish between complex systems that arise from the interaction of simple rules alone ("simplexity") and those that arise from the interactions of simple systems that change and erase their dependence on initial conditions ("complicity"). In the latter, simple rules produce features that then become the important elements of rules that produce the next level of complexity. Intuitively, socioenvironmental systems fall into this category, where different subsystems interact through feedback to produce new dynamics that cannot be understood from the underlying rules of any of the subsystems. Thus the presence of rules that while different in detail give rise to the same emergent phenomena suggests that *there is little to be gained in necessarily reaching for the lowest-level rules*. Cohen and Stewart (1994) use the term *fungibility* to describe these rules, which is analogous to Wolfram's (2002) use of the term *universality* when dealing with simple CAs, and the concept of "equifinality" commonly used in geomorphology to describe convergent pathways. Cohen and Stewart (1994) argue that the existence of nonunique rules for the same phenomena makes a truly reductionist approach to complexity, and by analogy to CA models, unwarranted: that there may be numerous pathways to the production of larger-scale phenomena dependent on context. From this we might even speculate that the precision of rules and the dependence on initial conditions may not be so crucial to the successful simulation of future phenomena *as context and external influences*. In this respect, it is noteworthy that the cellular phenomenological model SimDelta produces realistic complex behavior *without any low-level rules* for processes (Guy Engelen, pers. comm.). Thus, the implication is that in future projections it is the accuracy of the projected drivers that may be more important than the precision of the rules and features that describe the landscape.

As a consequence, a second point to consider is how we should judge the success of a simulation model. Simulation models that can capture nonlinear behavior in observed historical sequences should be able to inform us about how future external forcings may give rise to threshold-dependent change, the likely timescales over which change may evolve and, indeed, which of the alternative actions under our control should be avoided or selected (Dearing et al. 2006c). Thus, integrated, CA-based socioenvironmental models may have less predictive value in terms of the precision and accuracy of specific phenomena over short timescales, but they potentially have great value to strategic decision making and scoping alternative scenarios in the longer term: we essentially trade quantitative accuracy and precision for realism. Since we currently have so little insight into future socioenvironmental change, any models that demonstrate an ability to capture realistic nonlinear behavior should be highly valued.

Our current knowledge and theory do not allow us to define with any certainty the optimum structure of the proposed socioenvironmental models. We probably have to recognize the importance of trial-and-error approaches, particularly in selecting the appropriate rule level or, as illuminated in the Chinese case study, the appropriate spatial and timescales required to evolve the emergent features that we observe today. When modeling soil erosion on a hill slope, we may intuitively choose rules pertaining to particles rather than molecules, but the truth is that we do not really know where the "resting points" are until we experiment with simulation models. Similarly we can only debate the relevant time line (Ming or Mao?) out of which has emerged the highly sensitive modern landscape around Lake Erhai. Model development through experimentation at different process levels and spatiotemporal scales can be expected to significantly advance theory about socioenvironmental systems. We are entering a phase of simulation-model development, where our highest level of certainty lies in the parallel histories that we can construct. The design of new simulation-modeling research programs should acknowledge this wealth of information, for it is our heritage that holds the key to developing new theory about socioenvironmental change.

Conclusions

Understanding local and regional changes in integrated Earth and world systems demands consideration of nonlinear dynamics and complexity theory. Sets of parallel histories derived from reconstructed biophysical records, instrument data, and documents provide a sound basis for studying the long-term dynamics of past socioenvironmental systems.

Making the shift from studies of our environmental heritage to gaining foresight into future socioenvironmental states requires a methodological framework in which mathematical models simulate emergent phenomena, which are in turn tested by comparisons with parallel histories.

Spatially explicit, cellular automata-type models show much promise in this respect, allowing the emergence of macro-scale phenomena through the continuous interaction of rules at lower levels. Limitations to current CA/agent-based models include poorly understood rules for social systems, and short timescales for validation. However, the nature of emergence may mean that low-level rules are not always required.

Model success should be seen in terms of the correct simulation of observable nonlinear behavior. In generating alternative futures, such modeled system behavior will often be more important for policy formulation than the accuracy and precision of spatiotemporal details. Experimentation with simulation models is essential for understanding modeling needs.

In general, there is a paucity of theory about how socioenvironmental systems are affected by different combinations of management decisions, internal organization, and external forcings. Integrated socioenvironmental simulation models may not only provide decision-support tools for strategic management policies but also contribute to developing theory about the functioning of these systems.

CHAPTER 4

World-Systems as Complex Human Ecosystems

THOMAS ABEL

Reflecting on the impressive breadth of perspective that has been applied to the study of world-systems, Straussfogel (2000:169) recently observed, "Perhaps a little ironically, the only way world-systems have not been much considered is as a *system*." She proceeds to advocate "dissipative structures" theory (Prigogine & Stengers 1984) and the revolutionary systems thinking that it engenders for "open" natural systems including world-systems. From this perspective, the relationship between world-systems and the environment is forced to center stage: "Seen as a multileveled complex system exhibiting the properties of a dissipative structure, the [world-] system-environment relationship looms as crucial" (Straussfogel 2000:175). This chapter takes up the important challenge of furthering the integration of world-systems theory with environmental and complex systems science.

World-systems can be productively conceived as complex systems: complex human ecosystems. Complex systems are a general class of phenomena found ubiquitously in nature. While definitions vary, complex systems can be described as open, dissipative structures that self-organize into forms that are multi-scaled and hierarchical, that exhibit emergent properties, that make use of information at many scales from genes to culture, and that exhibit complex dynamics of pulse and collapse, discontinuous change or "surprise," and nonlinearity, leading to multiple stable states.

World-systems, comprising core, semiperiphery, and periphery, are by definition multi-scaled and hierarchical structures. Conceptualized as "complex human ecosystems" (Abel & Stepp 2003), world-systems are material and energetic self-organizing systems that are multiple-scaled in *space* and bounded in *time*, exhibiting complex dynamics that includes pulse, collapse, cycle, and chaos. As ecosystems, they are spatial entities that capture and use energy and materials, structured by information from many scales. As complex systems they are self-organizing phenomena with emergent properties. As "human ecosystems," they are dominated by the material assets, social organization, and cultural models at their disposal.

Since its conception (Wallerstein 1974), the world-system concept has inspired research and generated debate. Wallerstein's original model was of a multi-state system of capitalist countries bounded in space and time, with a division of labor and trade relations that favored a core of one or several nations over a surrounding periphery of other nations. Since that time there have been efforts to extend the model back in time to precapitalist social formations (Abu-Lughod 1989; Chase-Dunn & Hall 1995, 1997; Frank & Gills 1992). There has been interest in redefining its boundaries politically (Modelski 1987), symbolically (trade in luxury goods) (Schneider 1977), and otherwise. Some have sought to compare and possibly combine it with the concept of "civilization" (Wilkinson 1995). This chapter covers such definitional debates and proposes a complex human ecosystems definition of world-systems. This definition of world-systems has implications for understanding sociocultural cycles as well as the larger process of cultural evolution, and this chapter explores these implications.

Ecosystems as Complex Systems

Pickett and Cadenasso (2002:2), following Odum (1959), following Tansley (1935), define an ecosystem very flexibly as "any size so long as organisms, physical environment, and interactions can exist within it. Given this . . . ecosystems can be as small as a patch of soil supporting plants and microbes; or as large as the entire biosphere of the Earth. However, all instances of ecosystems have an explicit spatial extent. The extent must be specified and bounded." They proceed to fully explore the ecosystem as a concept, model, and metaphor. Of special interest for my discussion at this point is the "spatial" feature of this definition. An ecosystem boundary, at whatever size determined by the analyst, is not placed around an animal, plant, or human institution such as government or economy. An ecosystem, in "all instances," is an explicitly spatial entity, a physical space on Earth that encompasses interacting biotic and abiotic complexes, a location "as small as a patch of soil . . . or as large as the entire biosphere."

There is a simple reason why the ecosystem is a spatial concept. Ecosystems are open energetic systems that exist on Earth because energy flows through them, energy from lunar gravity, from Earth deep heat, and especially from the sun. When these energies reach the Earth's surface they interact with living organisms and nonliving substrates, self-organizing into the structures and processes of an ecosystem. Ecosystems are thus spatial entities, constructed by the convergence of energies at or near the Earth's surface.

Simon Levin (1998:431) characterizes ecosystems as "prototypical examples of complex adaptive systems." Self-organization divides natural systems into multiple temporal and spatial scales. A product of maximizing energy dissipation, nature is conceived to be discontinuous across scales, forming lumps or wholes in nested hierarchies (Holling, Gunderson, & Peterson 2002:77–88). Ecosystems are nested within the biosphere, while simultaneously composed of nested scales selected by biological, chemical, and physical processes.

Natural, open, self-organizing ecosystems are not static in time but exhibit fluctuations, both regular and unpredictable. Ecosystems are thought to be sometimes more and sometimes less resilient to perturbations, and for reasons that are difficult to predict. Fluctuations from small or large scales, both internal and external to the ecosystem, can lead to transformations. The pulsing or fluctuations of ecosystems is now felt to be a common property of complex systems, most thoroughly explored as an "adaptive cycle" by Holling (1987; cf. Figure 8). Ecosystems, like other complex systems, are thus multi-scaled, hierarchical, self-organizing systems that exhibit fluctuations in both time and space.

Complex Human Ecosystems

A "human ecosystem" is depicted with a systems diagram in Figure 1 (Abel 2003; Abel & Stepp 2003).[1] The sun is the most important energy source for ecosystems, delivering gravitational and solar energy and creating weather, wind, rain, and seasonal fluctuations, although lunar gravity (tide) and Earth deep heat (uplift) are other essential sources (see the circle on the left) (Odum 1996). Gradients of sunlight and fluctuating patterns of wind and rain have had defining impacts, it now appears, on the pulsing growth and collapse of human ecosystems, including world-systems (de Menocal 2001; Gill 2000; Weiss & Bradley 2001). These impacts will be discussed below along with other temporal dynamics of world-systems.

Concentrations (of energy, materials, structure, and information) within a human ecosystem include natural resources and sociocultural storages ("storage" tanks, Figure 1). Natural resources in Earth systems are commonly partitioned into categories of "renewable" (sun, tide, uplift), "slow-renewable" (timber, topsoil, groundwater), and "nonrenewable" (coal, oil, natural gas, metals) resources. This categorization scheme is based on the turnover time

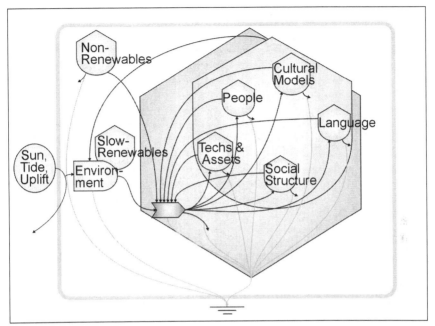

Figure 1 • Human ecosystem. A human ecosystem is spatially defined to include energy inputs, a physical substrate ("a patch of soil"), natural resource storages ("storage" tanks), and a human sociocultural system. A sociocultural system is a general term that applies to aggregates of humans at any scale, from foragers to chiefdoms, archaic states, modern states, and world-systems. The ecosystem context of the sociocultural system is represented in highly aggregated form to the left in the diagram. Important sociocultural storages are shown and discussed in the text.

relative to human life spans. For example, coal or oil, while renewable on the timescale of geological processes, are *non*renewable at the scale of people or even civilizations. A convincing model of a sociocultural system should include "storages" of material assets, social structure, cultural models, and language, as well as the interactions between these components, the natural environment, and the people that continuously produce and renegotiate their forms (Abel 2003). These components always co-occur, with none occurring before another.

A point to emphasize is that no storages are static—that is, not population, technologies, assets, topsoil, groundwater, social structure, or any other such factors. Even when a system appears to be changing very little, its storages are depreciating and must be replenished. This fundamental principle of nature is called the Second Law of Thermodynamics, or "Time's Arrow" (Prigogine &

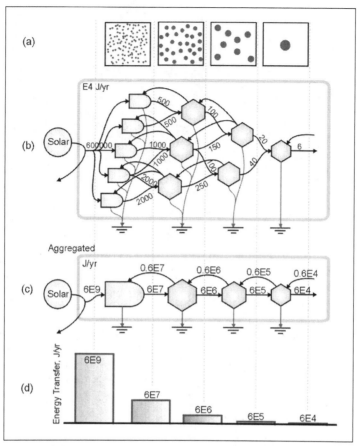

Figure 2 • Energy transformation hierarchy (adapted from Odum 1996:23). (a) Spatial view of units and territories; (b) energy network including transformation and feedback; (c) aggregation of energy networks into an energy chain; (d) bar graph of energy flows for the levels in an energy hierarchy. It is a principle of systems science (Odum 1996) that open systems, such as ecosystems, are non-equilibrium thermodynamic systems that self-organize into energy transformation hierarchies. Figure 2 depicts a hierarchy from four different perspectives. Figure 2b shows a typical hierarchy that could be an ecosystem with plant producers on the left and animal consumers on the right, concentrating food in a food web that is capped by one or several top carnivores. The energy that moves through that web is highlighted in the Figure 2d bar graph, with energy amounts shrinking as they move through the web.

Stengers 1984). In Figure 1, both the sociocultural system configuration and the environmental inputs are dynamic, constantly forming and reforming in the energy flux of an open natural system. Both culture and nature are highly dynamic, neither being merely the static backdrop for the other.

Complex human ecosystems can be redrawn in a form that displays the structural hierarchy within. Figure 2 depicts Odum's hierarchy of energy transformations, ubiquitous in self-organizing complex systems, illustrating Odum's (1996:16) proposed Fifth Law of Thermodynamics. An ecosystem is an obvious example, in which solar energy is converted to plant and animal biomass in hierarchical food webs, depicted in Figure 2b. At each step in a hierarchy, energy is lost as concentrations are made into species with "emergent" properties (complex proteins, mobility, landscape builders). Figure 2c is an aggregated diagram of Figure 2b, which emphasizes the energy transformations and reduces and consolidates the complexity into a visually simpler form.

Figure 1 can be redrawn, as in Figure 2b-c, by replacing the single "social structure" storage with an energy transformation hierarchy (Abel 2003). This diagramming convention can be applied to any human ecosystem and will be used in the world-systems diagram below (Figure 5).

World-Systems in Space

With this conceptual background, world-systems will now be discussed as complex human ecosystems, bounded in space and time. As far as we know, our universe is one single universe. Energy impinges on the Earth from far reaches and near. One biosphere, not more, envelops our globe. There are no boundaries in nature. Yet there are discontinuities. It is argued that self-organization leads to gradients (Wicken 1987), that nature forms lumps or wholes in nested hierarchies, as was just described (see also Holling, Gunderson, & Peterson 2002:77–88). In theory, a scientist can draw a boundary around anything he or she wants to study. In practice, however, it is more convenient to take advantage of the discontinuities in nature. Physiologists do not normally divide a person in half but rather make use of the (permeable) natural boundary of our skin.

Ecosystem scientists also seek discontinuities in defining a unit of study. One such common unit is a watershed. Within a watershed there are countless pathways of energy and material flows. Certainly animals and seeds cross watershed boundaries, but because so much physical, chemical, and biological work in ecosystems is done by rainfall there exists a gradient or discontinuity along the edge of natural drainage, that is, along the watershed "boundary." Another example is an island ecosystem, which might be bounded by its

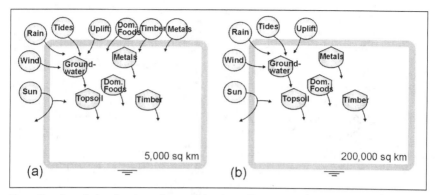

Figure 3 • Boundaries of early modern world-systems. Two options for boundaries around an early modern world-system. Note that these two drawings show only sources and storages and omit any flows or interactions, as were depicted in the previous diagrams. The focus here is boundaries, and not internal structure.

shoreline but is more logically defined to include the near-shore production of reefs or estuaries, down to the effective limits of sunlight. The biosphere as a whole is the largest scale for life on Earth. But nested within it is a hierarchy of self-organizing systems, from ecosystems to chemical cycles.

A number of researchers have attempted to define the boundaries of world-systems. Christopher Chase-Dunn and Thomas Hall have summarized and grouped the different conceptualizations of world-system boundaries into four categories (Chase-Dunn & Hall 1995, 1998). Some argue that trade in prestige goods is the largest important interaction network for world-systems and should therefore constitute its spatial limit (Schneider 1977). Chase-Dunn and Hall label this model "prestige goods exchange network (PGN)." Others believe that military alliances among a group of states in regions defines the world system (Wilkinson 1987), what Chase-Dunn and Hall call "political/military interaction networks (PMNs)." The most inclusive world-system boundary they define is a social network, called the "information exchange network (IN)." The most restricted world-systems boundary, which they call the "bulk goods exchange network (BGN)," coincides with Wallerstein's original formulation for world-systems, which focuses on trade in primary commodities.

A complex human ecosystem model of world-systems would focus on gradients in the flows of essential energies, natural resources, domesticated foods, or minerals, roughly equivalent to the BGN model. These are the necessary material foundations of any human ecosystem and sociocultural system within it. Once included, this ecosystem scale contains the necessary and sufficient

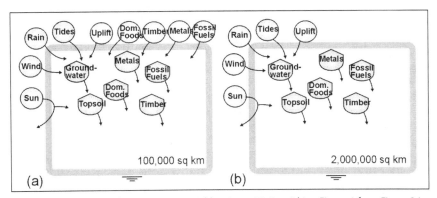

Figure 4 • Boundaries of contemporary world-systems. Distinguishing Figure 4 from Figure 3 is the addition of "Fossil Fuel" sources and storages. Fossil fuels are such an important addition to the provisioning of contemporary world-systems that they deserve special distinction.

ingredients for self-organization of the multi-scaled world-system structure.

These considerations support Wallerstein's formulation of the BGN model because of its spatial and material orientation, which can productively articulate with ecosystems and complex systems theory. Furthermore, this design compensates for an omission in the typologies of cultural evolution in anthropology, viz. a category for extra-state social formations, a level more inclusive and qualitatively different than archaic states or empires.

Figure 3 depicts two models of an early modern world-system. The "Golden Age" Dutch world-system of the seventeenth century is an example (Wallerstein 1974). In Figure 3a, a boundary is drawn around Holland. Within that boundary, important storages supporting the human sociocultural system include surface and ground water, topsoil, peat, domesticated food production, some timber, and mining. However, the Golden Age Dutch world-system depended on timber from Scandinavia, grain from the European heartland, and other key inputs such as salt from the southern Caribbean. From a human ecosystems perspective, the boundary of the Dutch world-system is thus better drawn around those bulk-goods-producing regions as peripheries, feeding natural resources to the Holland core. Figure 3b therefore draws the boundary just wide enough to reduce the flows of essential goods across its border by expanding it to include the resource-producing regions.

Figure 4 is a model of contemporary world-systems that is similar to Figure 3. Figure 4a includes a "too small" world-system boundary with inputs of primary commodities of domesticated foods, timber, metals, and fossil fuels.

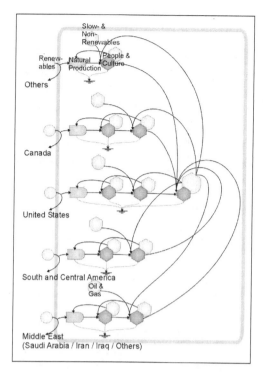

Figure 5 • A "Cold War" world-system with a U.S. core. A modern capitalist world-system of nations defined by bulk-goods trade unequally forming the core, which can be measured in ecological-economic terms (see Abel 2003).

Figure 4b represents a more inclusive boundary. This design has implications for defining twentieth-century world-systems. By this account, the last century would have begun with perhaps three world-systems, a dominant European-centered system, a U.S.-centered system, and a Japan-centered system. The Cold War world witnessed the expansion of a Soviet-centered system and decline of the Japan-centered system (Figure 5 depicts the U.S.-centered system). Note also that countries or regions may at times fall outside any world-system, as did China and Indonesia after the collapse of the Japan system and the contraction of the European system after World War II.

Figure 5 is a world-system conceived spatially and located in time. It is a multinational division of labor organized by trade flows. Note especially that each nation is represented in human ecosystem terms, as a spatial entity constructed "from the ground up," with energy sources and local storages of natural resources, all supporting a sociocultural hierarchy (compare to Figure 2c). The nations are then joined together by trade flows into a world-system. The innovation of the world-system is that it creates a larger spatial scale and thus a greater area for energy convergence.

By this conceptualization, today there is a single hegemonic U.S.-E.U.-Japan world-system, though China may be in the center of an emergent new

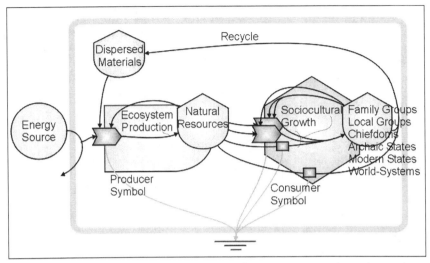

Figure 6 • Pulsing sociocultural systems. Coupled producers-consumers with recycling can be a pulsing organization. The storages have different spatial and temporal scales (Odum & Pinkerton 1955).

system. Yet considering the slow growth of global energies, the world future more likely holds for us decomposition of the existing world-system, the end of a "secular cycle," rather than composition of new systems (Abel 2000:414–428). This is explained in the next section.

World-Systems in Time: Storages and Pulsing

In dissipative structures theory, when an energy gradient exists between a storage and a sink, or between a source and a sink, self-organization occurs that has the effect of hastening the dissipation of energy (Prigogine & Stengers 1984). The process of self-organization is inherent in the thermodynamics of inorganic and organic matter and energy. Energy dissipation is revealed to be a highly creative process.

Self-organization often leads to pulsing patterns, the building of energetic storages followed by their autocatalytic consumption and dissipation, depicted in Figures 6–8 (Odum & Pinkerton 1955; Holling 1987). In Figure 6, the system of multi-scaled self-organization is a pulsing system that produces the cycle in Figure 7. Examples include fire-controlled ecosystems, locust outbreaks, or cross-catalytic chemical reactions. It is expected that this pulsing pattern would also be observed with storages used by humans. It is well known that small farmers who use slash-and-burn techniques occupy an area only

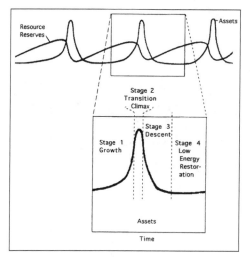

Figure 7 • Pulsing. Typical cycle in which pulsing of consumer assets alternates with productive restoration of resources. Four stages are defined to aid discussion (from Odum and Odum 2001:78, reprinted with permission).

long enough to consume the storages of nutrients; then they move on. In more complex human systems such as chiefdoms or archaic states, pulse and collapse have been observed, as in ancient Greece (Runnels 1995), the Maya of Yucatán (Culbert 1988), and the Roman Empire (Perlin 1991). In the world-systems literature, there is growing interest in this pulsing and collapsing of sociocultural systems and their human ecosystems at different scales (Bosworth 1995; Chase-Dunn & Hall 1998; Frank 1995). So-called civilizations such as the Andean or the Chinese are better conceived as systems repeatedly pulsing and collapsing in space and time (Marcus 1998; Wallerstein 1995).

Perhaps the best known pulsing and cycling model today is the "Adaptive Cycle" proposed by Holling (1987), a general pattern with four phases: exploitation, conservation, crisis/release, and reorganization. Odum's pulsing model fits this pattern (Odum & Odum 2001), as do other cycling models (Figure 8).

In complex human ecosystems, cycles are nested, as in Figure 9. Figure 9 gives only an indication of the complex pattern of nested scales of pulse and collapse that exist in open systems in nature. Not surprisingly, the history and prehistory of humans and human ecosystems has been complex, filled with pulse and collapse of whole systems or parts of them. For world-systems, collapse does not mean the disappearance of peoples or nations but rather the decomposition of core-periphery bulk trade networks and the return to single state-scale organization or, in the peripheries especially, decomposition into even smaller-scaled social formations resembling chiefdoms, located within the political shells of nation states (as today in Somalia, the Ivory Coast, Burundi, and so on).

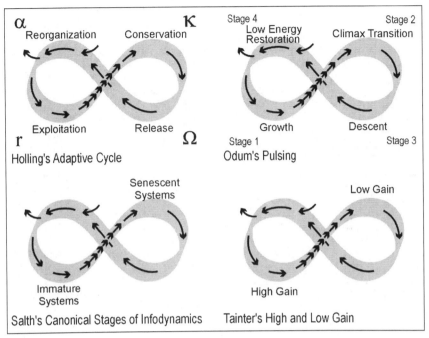

Figure 8 • Cycles in complex systems. The "Adaptive Cycle" has been extensively discussed and elaborated (Gunderson & Holling 2002; Gunderson, Holling, & Light 1995). Odum has emphasized a similar model of growth, transition, descent, and low energy restoration, a design which he contends maximizes self-reinforcing energy flows in many systems (Odum & Odum 2001; Odum & Pinkerton 1995). His model does not have the resolution of detail into important mechanisms of release and reorganization that Holling's does. Salthe's (2003) model of canonical stages of infodynamics is another cycling model, as is the High Gain/Low Gain model of Tainter and colleagues (2003).

Implications for World-Systems Theory

World-systems theory thus reconceived has implications for some unsettled issues. Two of particular interest to other world-systems theorists are explored below, suggesting both the promise and the novelty of viewing world-systems as complex human ecosystems.

Cycles in Sociocultural Systems

Cycles have captured the attention of world-systems research in recent years. Here I consider three often-studied cycle types. "Kondratieff cycles" (K-waves) have been much discussed (Frank 1995; Straussfogel 2000; Thompson 2000).

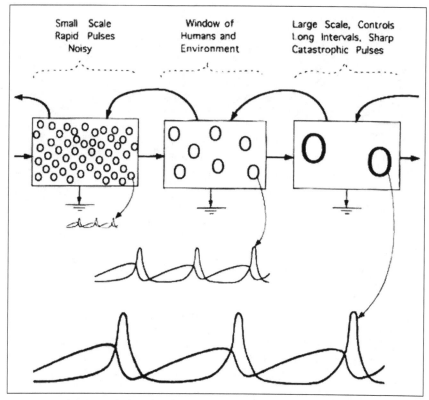

Figure 9 • Pulsing at multiple scales of space and time. Sketch showing the pulsing for three scales of time and space. Larger scales have sharper pulses and longer interpulse periods. Many nested cycles are conceivable for the biosphere (from Odum and Odum 2001:82, reprinted with permission).

As Turchin and Hall (2003:39) explain: "The basic dynamic is that a new technology allows economic expansion. Eventually the market saturates, and competition increases, and the expansion slows until another cycle, based on yet another new or renewed technology, develops."

In terms of Figure 1, a new technology is equivalent to expanding the storage of "Assets and Technologies," which would recursively amplify the capture of more natural resources, resulting in "economic expansion." In addition, because all sociocultural storages are linked, the other storages will grow, including population, social structure (division of labor), cultural models, and even language (that is, adding new vocabulary, or— if the growth is sustained enough for the sociocultural system to expand its reach spatially—expanding the language hegemony, as English has expanded its reach and varieties today[2]).

It does not suffice to explain the contraction of a K-wave, however, in terms of "the market saturates, and competition increases." In a complex human ecosystem there are real physical limits that always restrain growth, here represented by limits to nonrenewable resources (oil, coal, metals), but also to slow-renewables such as timber or groundwater, or full renewables such as agricultural produce. Furthermore, within the interconnected sociocultural system, real economic growth eventually leads to growth of *all* storages (as just explained)—population growth, division of labor, cultural models—which also draw on resources and which hasten the restricting effect of physical resource limits. Resource limits from any of many scales, plus the burden of maintenance of all interrelated cultural storages, including the new division of labor, new cultural models, and so on, together contribute to the decline phase of the K-wave.

A special consideration for recent cycles is that economic growth during the last 150 years has been riding the fossil fuel wave, which has clouded our collective view of natural limits (and fueled a global population explosion) by providing energy for real growth in all sectors. This has given us the false impression that economic expansion can occur whenever technological innovations appear. From the longer history of technological innovations, we know this to be untrue. The "new technology" that starts a cycle must appear at a time when necessary storages are available from many spatial and temporal scales of humanity and the environment, including all the necessary natural resources plus an appropriate division of labor, possessing the necessary cultural models and language skills.

"Hegemonic cycles" are the century-long cycles "in which one state in a core dominates a world-system through economic and political power, typically without overt coercion" (Turchin & Hall 2003:39). A hegemonic cycle, therefore, refers to the expansion and contraction of an explicitly bounded spatial entity (a world-system). This cycle, however, can again be explained with reference to resource limits. First, the logic of spatial expansion is understandable as the means to capture untapped resource storages in virgin forests, topsoil, and mineral deposits. This leads to sociocultural system expansion as a whole, with its many requirements for maintenance. As resource storages are consumed unsustainably, especially the slow-renewables timber and topsoil with turnover times of 50–200 years, and the maintenance of world-system organization remains high, the system reaches a point of instability and contracts.

"Secular cycles," that is, "periodic waves of state breakdown accompanied by oscillations in population numbers" (Turchin & Hall 2003:39), by this account are the same phenomenon. In other words, by explaining hegemonic cycles human-ecologically instead of as the result of "power" fluctuations, I am proposing a model of macro-scale dynamics for sociocultural systems.

Where this explanation differs from many others is in its account of a highly dynamic and pulsing environment, a complex interconnected human presence often stressed by its own weight of numbers, and fluctuating boundaries of the human ecosystem and its associated resources. Because sociocultural systems always occur within human ecosystems, *space* is a fundamental factor in understanding all components and their dynamics in time. Archeological and ethnographic evidence tells us that spatial fluctuation is the rule, not the exception for sociocultural systems. Only with the relatively recent advent of fixed nation-state boundaries have human ecosystem boundaries ever been stable for long. And that stability was perhaps a short interlude, for world-systems theory would contend that actual human ecosystem boundaries have become both larger-than-states and fluctuating.

Evolution in Sociocultural Systems

This complex human ecosystems model has many implications for the long tradition of cultural evolutionary theory in anthropology (Carneiro 1970; Flannery 1972; Harris 1977; Johnson & Earle 1987; Morgan 1877; Service 1975; Spencer 1860; Steward 1955; White 1959), which has recently generated much interest among world-systems researchers (Chase-Dunn & Hall 1998; Sanderson 1990). I will raise only two issues regarding the subject that can illuminate my definition of complex human ecosystems (see Abel 1998 and Abel 2000:341–428 for further discussion).

First, in Figure 1, we can see that the source of culture change is not restricted to single "prime movers" such as "population pressure" or its predecessor "technological progress." In fact, characterizing any but the earliest cultural evolution theory as linear or driven by "prime movers" is an over-simplification of what was already recognized in its day as a highly systemic process (Carneiro 1970; Flannery 1972; Harris 1977). More recent accounts from anthropology (for instance, Johnson & Earle 1987) and world-systems (Chase-Dunn & Hall 1998; Sanderson 1990) have become more overtly systematic. For example, Chase-Dunn and Hall's dynamic "iteration model" accounts for many interrelated variables in the process of cultural evolution: technological change, population growth, intensification, environmental degradation, population pressure, emigration, circumscription, conflict, and hierarchy formation.

Cultural evolution conceived in terms of the complex human ecosystems model is an emphatically systematic account. Change in open self-organizing systems is expected, incessant, and directional, owing to the teleomatics of energy dissipation (Prigogine & Stengers 1984). A sociocultural system is conceived as a self-organizing system of amplification, constraint, and pulsing dynamics with many shifting limiting factors within ecosystems and within itself (population density being only one). For instance, sociocultural complexification may be simultaneously pushed (for example, by population pressure), pulled (for instance, by agricultural innovation), squeezed (for example, by approaching water limits, topsoil depletion, spatial contraction due to warfare, and so on), collapsed (for instance, by geologic pulses such as volcanoes, weather pulses such as large-scale hurricanes, climate change, loss of resilience, and so forth), in more ways than I can list.

Chase-Dunn and Hall's "iterative" model is a better approximation of this, although it emphasizes the "push" of population pressure and offers only an unelaborated environment with incomplete dynamics and theorizing of its own. Within the material constraints of a dynamic environment and model of production should be situated the human symbolic systems of cultural models, which have structures and dynamics of their own. Intentionality and agency can be understood to self-organize with a highly dynamic human and extra-human environment. This complex nexus of human ecosystem causality is what is represented by a simplifying systems diagram such as the one in Figure 1.

Second, there has been much discussion in the world-systems literature about extending the concept back in time to include precapitalist social formations that anthropologists have called bands, tribes, chiefdoms, and archaic states (Harris 1977; Johnson & Earle 1987). The point has been made, for example, that capital accumulation, a determinant characteristic of the modern world-system, has precapitalist roots in early states (Ekholm & Friedman 1982), and has perhaps "*always* been a driving force of world development" (Gills 1995:137).

I would prefer to see this initiative turned on its head. Considered in terms of the human ecosystems model (Figure 1), the autocatalytic structure of capitalist accumulation is unsurprisingly pervasive in human social formations, as it is in nature generally. Rather than applying Wallerstein's world-systems model, which is a useful referent to specific capitalist multistate entities, back in time to all social formations, I would argue for reserving that term as it is, and adopting a more general term, that is, complex human ecosystems, which encodes a general model of structure, function, and complex dynamics.

Conclusions

World-systems theory can be enriched by a close relationship with ecosystems and complex systems theory more generally. The history and prehistory of humans and human ecosystems take on a radically different appearance when conceived in terms of systems of energy and their complex transformations.

Permanence is replaced by flow, fluctuation, and cycling. Space becomes a dynamic and critical dependent variable.

Rather than extend the concept of world-systems to encompass "kin-based" foragers, local groups, chiefdoms, or archaic states (including empires), I argue instead that it is more useful to maintain these distinct terms. The "world-system" concept has a place in this typology of social formations. It has served well to uncloak nationalist ideologies and reveal the system connections *between* nations that have real and often oppressive effects.

To call everything a world-system is to dilute the concept of its analytical strength. I do not believe that my world-systems model is more "correct" than that of the prehistorians or civilizationists. Intriguing properties of "cycling," inequality, hierarchy, and spatial scales should be expected and can be found in social formations generally. However, general processes deserve a general name, such as human ecosystems. Calling them all world-systems subtracts from the usefulness of the concept, which is its final measure of success.

How does this complex human ecosystems model differ from other models of cultural evolution or world-system formation? It emphasizes that the "environment" is a "moving target," not a permanent stage for the human play. It defines world-systems in space and time. It expects to find pulse and collapse, and at multiple temporal and spatial scales. And it locates world-systems in a natural world, a dynamic open system with material and energetic limits that must be considered in any account of our history or future.

Notes

1. This paper applies many of the conventions developed by H. T. Odum to understand and depict ecosystems and complex systems. The work of H. T. Odum spanned systems of all types. In forty years of active research, he and his brother E. P. Odum helped define the modern field of ecology. In the last fifteen years, his work was rediscovered by complex systems scientists (for example, Depew & Weber 1995; Van de Vijver, Salthe, & Delpos 1998). What makes it complex systems science? In brief, much of his research focused on the self-organization of natural, open, thermodynamic systems that creatively build themselves and dissipate energy (Odum 1983; Odum 1988; Odum 1995; Odum & Pinkerton 1955), systems sometimes called "dissipative structures" (Prigogine & Stengers 1984). Other complex systems domains of his work are (1) autocatalytic, nonlinear dynamics, (2) pulsing or chaotic systems (Odum & Pinkerton 1955), (3) hierarchy (Odum & Odum 2001), and (4) scale (Hall 1995). In recent years this work directly led him and colleagues to the creation of a form of ecological economics called "emergy" accounting (Odum 1996;

Odum, Odum, & Brown 1998). Emergy accounting has been used to evaluate sustainability (Odum 1994), international trade equity (Odum & Arding 1991), and global forecasting (Odum & Odum 2001).

2. With the most dynamic economy and often the largest military, the hegemon also disseminates its language, culture, and economy as "global" standards (Grimes 2000:47).

CHAPTER 5

Lessons from Population Ecology for World-Systems Analyses of Long-Distance Synchrony

THOMAS D. HALL AND PETER TURCHIN

In this chapter we have several objectives. First, we observe that processes within world-systems are often characterized by cycles or waves: chiefdoms cycle, empires rise and fall, and the modern state system undergoes a "power cycle" or "hegemonic sequence." Furthermore, all world-systems "pulsate," that is, expand rapidly, then more slowly, or even contract (Chase-Dunn & Hall 1997). Because spatial waves of expansion/contraction occur across all types of world-systems, such pulsations cannot be rooted in a specific mode of production or mode of accumulation. Rather, these cycles are themselves evidence that polities and world-systems are dynamical systems with various feedback loops. Second, we want to explore the issue of spatial influences and how they interact with various social factors in world-systemic processes, especially the synchronization of cycles across great distances. Third, we suggest some potential empirical tests of these models, and propose that, whether or not these models work, the exploration of them will deepen our understanding of social evolutionary processes. Fourth, we argue that this is not an exercise in reductionism, nor is it an attempt to remove actors from the system model. Rather, it helps clarify how structures change, how they constrain behaviors, and conversely, how behaviors can act on those evolutionary processes.

Following Butzer (1997), if there is any systemness to a system, changes should permeate it. Rephrased somewhat, cycles *are* evidence of some sort of *system*. Previous research has shown that there is a broad degree of synchrony between the sizes of empires and city populations in Europe, west Asia, and east Asia (reviewed in Chapter 9). By contrast, Indic empires are far less correlated with the other Eurasian regions. A similar pattern is observed in population dynamics. Figures 5a and 5b in Chapter 9 show the populations of the four Eurasian macro-regions (taken from McEvedy & Jones 1978). There is an increasing trend affecting all population trajectories, which is presumably a result of sociocultural evolution. We are interested in the fluctuations around the trend, and therefore we have de-trended all series by the technique known as "differencing" (Box & Jenkins 1976). When log-transformed population data are differenced, we obtain relative population growth rates. Focusing on the growth rates during the better-studied period of 800–1800 C.E., we observe that all regions except south Asia appear to fluctuate in synchrony (Chapter 9, Figure 5b). In fact, the degree of synchrony apparently increases toward 1800.

These data are very "noisy," so the findings *may* be an artifact of the data. However, the patterns hold with various refinements, which strongly suggests that the following theoretical and empirical issues are worthy of further investigations: (1) that there are cycles in populations, city sizes, empire sizes, and so on and (2) that there is some correlation, or synchrony, between east and west Asia, and less with south Asia, which echoes the claim made by Teggart (1939).

The other world-systems puzzle is that Afroeurasia has been linked, at least at the information and luxury goods exchange levels, for two and half millennia or more (Chase-Dunn & Hall 1997). Thus, events and processes in Europe cannot be explained solely by examining European processes, a conclusion strongly supported by Pomeranz (2000) and Hobson (2004). However, the degree of Afroeurasia-wide linkage fluctuated, so that world-systems at opposite ends of Afroeurasia were nearly isolated for long periods of time. One question raised by this puzzle is why these rise/fall processes at the western and eastern ends of Afroeurasia have been linked during the last two millennia (see Chapter 9). For example, increases and decreases in the territorial sizes of empires and the population size of cities correlate between east Asia and west Asia-Mediterranean, yet, there appears to be little linkage to cyclical processes in south Asia. Interestingly, archeologists have noted apparent parallels in the rise and fall of ancient cultures in what is now southeastern and southwestern United States (Neitzel 1999).

There are at least three subissues here: (1) why these instances link east-west and not north-south; (2) why there are cycles; and (3) how those cycles become linked, especially over great distances. As a working hypothesis we suggest that Diamond's (1997) thesis may be applicable. Given similar environments, or biomes, similar kinds of social systems may be in evidence along an east-west axis. If those systems are characterized by, or include, cyclical processes, what are the phase relations among their various cycles? Do some cyclical systems become linked, for example, phase-locked or phase-shifted? Or do they oscillate independently? The questions are how and why? Our third point is that once analyzed and described, these linkages can be subjected to more rigorous testing.

One very interesting finding from animal ecology is that certain types of synchronization of predator-prey cycles actually produce rapid evolution of prey populations as a direct response to the synchronous linking (Turchin 2003a). In other words, the linking, or synchronization, of cycles can itself be a mechanism of evolution that pushes social change in one direction rather than another.

We want to insert two caveats here, however. First, we are not being teleological. Rather, we are claiming that, under certain circumstances, some types of change are more likely than others. This should lead to questions about the roles of agency and praxis in social change. It may also help us better understand how and why the result of intended change can lead to unexpected results, such as in the French revolution, the revolution of 1848, and the Russian revolution. The second caveat is that we cannot simply apply biological models directly to social processes. Social evolution tends toward convergence, whereas biological evolution tends toward divergence (Sanderson 1990). These caveats and data problems notwithstanding, we argue that we can learn much about social evolution by exploring and applying models derived from the natural sciences. We begin with a review of population ecology.

What Ecological Theory Says about Synchrony

Ecologists have long asked themselves why many oscillatory population systems exhibit large-scale spatial synchrony. Charles Elton (1924) speculated why lemming peak years should be synchronized across much of Norway. He also observed that the ten-year lynx cycle is synchronized over the whole taiga region of Canada in the Hudson Bay Company data on lynx pelts. P.A.P. Moran developed statistical approaches for analyzing such synchrony and proposed a formal mechanism to explain it, known in the ecological literature as "the Moran effect" (Bjornstad, Ims, & Lambin 1999; Moran 1953). The idea is that synchronized exogenous shocks to local oscillating systems will cause them to come into synchrony even when the exogenous shocks do not themselves display much periodicity (Ranta et al. 1997; Ranta, Kaitala, & Lindstrom 1999). A key issue in these investigations was determining which mechanisms may cause synchrony.

Synchronizing Mechanisms

Ecologists have classified mechanisms that induce spatial synchrony along two continua: exogenous versus endogenous, and local versus "global." A factor X is called an exogenous mechanism if it is not part of the feedback loop: X affects the variable of interest, while the variable of interest does not affect X. By contrast, an endogenous factor is one that is part of a feedback loop: the

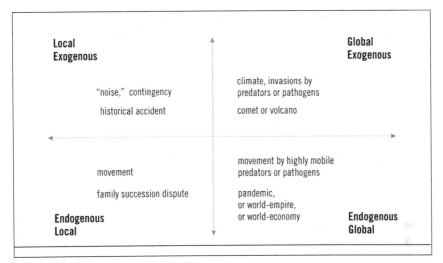

Figure 1 • Dimensional continua of mechanisms of spatial synchronicity.

variable of interest affects X, and then the change in X affects the variable of interest. Of course, we do not always (or even often) know all the feedback loops that affect the dynamics of the variable of interest. Thus, in practice, we call endogenous only those mechanisms whose feedback influences are explicitly taken into account. For example, in human-dominated ecosystems, the usual assumption that climate affects population, but population does not affect climate, does not necessarily hold. Chew (2001) shows that early human civilizations so denuded forests and salinized agricultural land that they may indeed have changed local, if not regional, climates. Some of these changes may be systemwide (see also Butzer 2005). Thus, some climatic changes may need to be modeled as endogenous, rather than exogenous processes.

Ecological theorizing uses the terms *local* and *global* somewhat differently from their usage in world-systems analysis. A local mechanism is one whose effects fall off with distance. By contrast, a global mechanism affects all points in the relevant space similarly, without any regard to how far these points are from one another. Thus, "global" in the ecological sense might be glossed as "systemwide" in world-system analysis. For clarity, we use "planetary" when we mean the entire world and "global" when we mean "systemwide."

Given these two dimensions (endogeneity and locality) we can define four regions of a universe of potentially synchronizing processes (see Figure 1 and, for more detailed explication, Turchin & Hall 2003). Ecologists have tended to concentrate on two: the global exogenous mechanism and local endogenous mechanism. The most discussed global exogenous factor in ecology is climatic variation. It is a quintessentially exogenous process because variation in temperature and rainfall can have a very strong effect on survival and reproduction of organisms, while fluctuations in population numbers almost never have an effect on weather (although for humans this is not necessarily true).

In any case, close examination of specific mechanisms shows that the global-local distinction defines a continuum, and not a dichotomy. For world-systems analysis, given the potential effects of human activity on climate (see Chew 2001), clearly global or systemwide mechanisms would be a massive volcanic eruption or collision with a sizable comet. Alternatively, if there is a truly exogenous climatic shift (due, say, to sun spot cycles or some such mechanism that humans could not affect) and if it were planetary, then we should see global synchrony, across Afroeurasia, Meso- and South America, southeast Asia, and sub-Saharan Africa. This would still require some subsidiary explanation for the already documented lack of synchrony in south Asia.

The quintessential local endogenous mechanism is movement. It is endogenous because the number of organisms spreading from a source depends very much on the population density at the source. It is local, because organisms do not "teleport." Rather, the density of dispersers declines with the distance from source. We note that movement may also refer to other components in the dynamical system, such as predators or pathogens. Socially, disputes in family succession among elites, as among the Mongols, who had competing lines of succession (laterally and lineally), would be examples (Barfield 1989; Chase-Dunn & Hall 1997:Ch. 8). Rules of succession or descent vary between cultural groups and are thus typically localized. Such rules do change but usually only very slowly, often pushed by changes in the ecology of production and adaptation. Under certain circumstances, movement may be exogenous or global or both. Movement would be exogenous when the area is subjected to recurrent invasions of predators or pathogens. Finally, imperial policies might be an endogenous global factor, for example, the widespread effects of the Roman Empire on its various frontiers.

Types of Oscillatory Dynamics

The efficacy of different mechanisms described above to synchronize oscillations depends on the nature of the dynamics characterizing the synchronized systems. The key distinction is between stable and chaotic oscillations. Chaos is defined as bounded oscillations with sensitive dependence on initial conditions (Eckmann & Ruelle 1985). The faster trajectories diverge, the more sensitive to initial conditions (and therefore the more chaotic) the system is.

The same argument applies to the behavior of two identical or very similar systems. If their dynamics are stable, then the two systems starting from similar initial conditions tend to oscillate in synchrony. Small random perturbations will keep them out of perfect synchrony but the stable nature of the two systems will act to bring the two trajectories back in synchrony. By contrast, two identical chaotic systems starting even from very similar initial conditions will rapidly diverge and oscillate asynchronously (the "butterfly effect"). Small random perturbations make this process of divergence even faster.

In general, exogenous drivers are not powerful synchronizing mechanisms. A substantial degree of spatial synchrony requires, first, that local dynamics are stable (nonchaotic) and, second, that the exogenous factor acts globally (that is, is systemwide). The Moran effect is the mechanism of entrainment.

Endogenous factors such as movement have a greater potential for inducing spatial synchronization, especially where cycles are stable. Ranta and colleagues (1999) showed that even relatively low rates of movement can induce a near-perfect synchrony of locally cycling populations. This property of nonlinear systems is called *phase-locking* (Bjornstad, Ims, & Lambin 1999). However, systems with locally chaotic dynamics will remain uncorrelated by movements.

Summary

A few themes emerge from this review. First, spatial synchrony is promoted when two local systems are driven by similar dynamical mechanisms. Second, processes that act globally (that is, on a systemwide basis) promote large-scale spatial synchrony. Third, the type of local dynamics affects very much whether any particular mechanism will induce synchrony. Systems with stable oscillations can be synchronized over vast geographic distances by global exogenous influences. Fourth, endogenous factors such as movement may result in a very high degree of synchrony and phase-locking, but the spatial extent may not be great, because the effect of movement attenuates rapidly through space. Additionally, endogenous processes may cause out-of-phase cycles. Fifth, chaotic systems are very difficult to synchronize either by exogenous or endogenous mechanisms. Only global catastrophes that reset all locations to approximately the same initial conditions can impose some (fleeting) degree of synchrony on chaotic systems. Examples include events such as collision with a large comet or a massive volcanic eruption.

Implications for World-System Research

East-West Synchronicity and Global Climate

Ecological theory suggests several hypotheses to account for synchronous changes of empire sizes in west and east Afroeurasia, the simplest one being the effect of an exogenous global factor—climate. World-system theorists have already suggested this explanation (see Chapter 9). In a study of historical demography, Galloway (1986) shows that populations of western Europe and China increased and decreased roughly in parallel with solar activity.

Another explanation might be the long-term effects of the Mongol conquest and empire, which briefly connected east and west Asia but also started a series of remarkably coherent oscillations in Central Asia and adjoining regions. The huge territory conquered by the Mongols during the early thirteenth century was ruled by four separate Chingissid dynasties. According to Turchin (2003b: Ch. 7), these four polities appear to reflect so-called Ibn Khaldun cycles of around a century. The Ibn Khaldun cycle, named after the fourteenth-century Arab sociologist who first described it, is a kind of secular wave that tends to affect societies with elites drawn from adjacent nomadic groups. The dynamics of an Ibn Khaldunian world-system are determined by the interaction between a sedentary, agrarian state and surrounding steppe or desert pastoral "tribes." The sedentary state region is the site of recurrent episodes of state building and collapse. It is inhabited by an indigenous commoner population that provides the productive basis of the society. The steppe or desert is inhabited by stateless tribes that periodically conquer the agrarian region and establish a ruling dynasty there. Steppe or desert tribes thus supply the elites (nobility) for the sedentary state. Ibn Khaldun cycles tend to last about four generations, or a century.

This is an alternative way of approaching the analyses of Barfield (1989) and Chase-Dunn and Hall (1997:Chapter 8). As Barfield notes, however, the Mongol conquest was exceptional with respect to the usual strategy employed by the Central Asian nomads. First, the Mongols succeeded in capturing much vaster regions, owing to innovations in organization introduced by Chinggis. Second, instead of merely exploiting sedentary states, the Mongols actually conquered large empires, and then governed them. Finally, the Mongol empire broke apart owing to their rules of dynastic succession, which emphasized both lateral and linear descent. These extensive Mongol conquests also disrupted the Ibn Khaldun cycles, in effect resetting them in several different areas simultaneously.

Thus, the Chinggisid dynasties went through typical Ibn Khaldun cycles of about a century, and all experienced collapse at approximately the same time. In China, a native dynasty expelled the Mongols after one cycle, whereas in Russia and Iran the steppe dynasties went through two cycles before giving way to native rulers. Incidentally, the central Eurasian steppes continued to undergo Ibn Khaldun cycles, until their conquest and division between the Russian and the Chinese empires (Barfield 1989). What is remarkable is the degree of synchrony in the sociopolitical dynamics of the settled regions initially conquered by the Mongols in the thirteenth century. One possible explanation of this pattern is that an initial catastrophic event—the Mongol conquest—reset all regions to approximately the same initial conditions. Thereafter, each region oscillated as a result of its endogenous dynamics, but because oscillations were driven by similar mechanisms, political collapses occurred at about the same time.

Asynchronous South Asia

If we accept Jared Diamond's (1997) observation that, in the absence of formidable barriers, east-west movement along similar latitudes and climates is easier than north-south movement that traverses different ecological zones, we can construct an explanation for east-west Asian synchronicity, and the absence of synchronicity with south Asia. An additional factor is the Himalayan Range, which present a formidable barrier to contact and exchange. While there has been extensive traffic across the Himalayas, it may not have been sufficient to synchronize the various systems. Steppe nomads seldom made incursions into south Asia. Central Asian influence on India was transmitted indirectly via the Iranian plateau.

Two additional factors give tangential support to this supposition. First, although bulk goods, large populations, and armies rarely moved between south and central Asia, travelers and ideas did so extensively. The spread of Buddhism and of silk and other luxury goods are familiar examples. Both illustrate the critical difference between the various world-system boundaries of bulk goods and military-political exchanges, on the one hand, versus information and luxury goods, on the other (see Chapter 9). Second, south Asia had tremendous effects on southeast Asia. Again there is the spread of Buddhism, but also other cultural features, as well as trade in luxury goods. Yet, if the east-west versus north-south differential is at work, there should be some synchrony between south Asia and southeast Asia, and less synchrony between southeast Asia and east Asia. But this remains an issue in need of careful empirical study. Philippe Beaujard (2005) examines relations between south Asia and Europe and to a lesser extent between south Asia and southeast Asia. His finds strongly suggest that this second factor is very important in accounting for south Asian asynchrony.

A second explanation for asynchronous dynamics in south Asia is the effect of climate. A cold, wet climate leading to problems in most of Eurasia might have been a boon for south Asian agriculturalists. The two hypotheses, that is, movement (of people, goods, and ideas) and global climate, are not mutually exclusive.

A possible third explanation for asynchronous dynamics in south Asia is that local, that is, endogenous, processes may have differed significantly between south Asia and the rest of Asia. This would seem less likely, but it is a possibility that warrants consideration. Currently we do not have sufficient data to discriminate among these explanations. Still, the arguments and analyses presented here suggest ways in which these issues might be addressed empirically.

Summary Thus Far

We cannot simply map biological models directly onto social processes. Rather, our approach needs several additional ingredients for success. On the empirical side we need a more detailed database on the territorial dynamics of all polities within Afroeurasia. We also need data on the spatiotemporal dynamics of other variables that may affect synchrony, such as epidemics and climate. Some databases already exist, for example, Biraben's (1975) compilation of places affected by the Black Death in Europe and the Mediterranean. Other kinds of databases, such as on climate change, are in the process of being developed (for instance, Mann 2000).

On the theoretical side, we need a better understanding of processes that may cause oscillations and synchrony. What would be particularly useful in the study of synchrony would be estimates of the rates of movement for different kinds of phenomena, for example, goods, pathogens, ideas, and people.

Such a research program would be expensive in time and money. We argue, however, that such an investment is warranted. Recent results that suggest sociopolitical cycles and wide-scale synchronicity within Afroeurasia have been described as "intoxicating" (Denemark 2000). Unraveling the complex interactions causing these empirical regularities will require sophisticated quantitative tools. In the following section, we present a brief example to illustrate the type of analysis and types of data needed for such research.

Synchrony and Phase-Shifts in Socioeconomic Variables: An Example of Analysis Using Data from Preindustrial England

In the previous section we outlined our general vision of the research questions and methods of approaching them. However, we realize that some readers may not be familiar with quantitative techniques of data analyses, which have been recently developed for investigating dynamical systems, and therefore this section provides an illustration. More specifically, we have two goals: (1) to illustrate how time-series techniques can reveal synchrony and phase-shifts, and how such results can be useful in testing various mechanism-based explanations of the observed patterns; and (2) to provide an illustration of some mechanisms underlying secular waves, using data for preindustrial England (before 1800). The results we report come from Turchin (2005) and Turchin and Nefedov (2007); here we simply summarize this work without going into technical details.

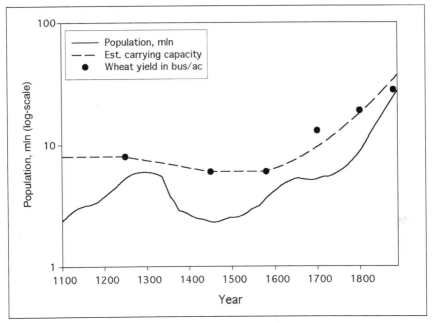

Figure 2 • England: Population and carrying capacity.

We begin the analysis with data on population dynamics in England and Wales (Wrigley et al. 1997). There are two features of the data that are immediately apparent. First, there is a very long increasing trend, which appears to accelerate around 1800 (see Figure 2). The forces explaining this trend are not controversial and have to do with the English Industrial Revolution. The second feature of the empirical curve is the oscillations around the trend, with an average duration of about 300 years. Our main interest is in the oscillations, so somehow we need to remove the trend. De-trending is best done when we have some mechanistic basis for it. In this case, we can estimate the carrying capacity of England by multiplying the acres of arable land with the average wheat yield per acre, and dividing by the amount of wheat needed to support one person per year. It turns out that carrying capacity is primarily driven by the evolution of wheat yields (the circles in Figure 2). Now that we have the curve for carrying capacity (shown with a broken line in Figure 2), it is a simple matter to express the observed population numbers in terms of proportion of carrying capacity exploited (see Figure 3, dotted line). The de-trended— or relative—population exhibits two oscillations with peaks around 1300 and 1640. According to the standard methods of time-series analysis, the periodicity in this data is statistically significant.

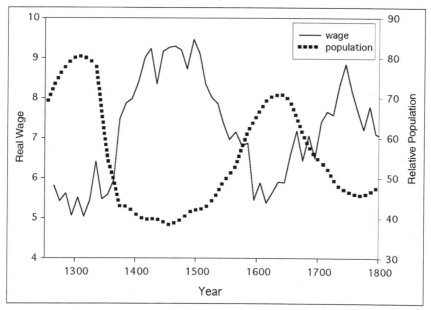

Figure 3 • England 1250–1800: Real wages by year.

The next step is to examine the potential interactions between the population oscillations and some other socioeconomic variables. The obvious place to start is the data on wages, since one of the venerable theories for demographic cycles, advanced by T. R. Malthus (1798), proposes that increased population leads to lower wages, and lower wages, in turn, cause population to decrease. Data on real wages (that is, nominal wages deflated by the cost of a standard bundle of consumables) in England was published by Allen (2001). Plotting these data together with population (Figure 3), we see that both variables oscillate with the same period, but completely out of phase—that is, when population reaches a peak, real wage hits a trough, and vice versa. Plotting the data in a phase-plot (a graph in which each variable is plotted along its own axes), we see that the trajectory moves back and forth along the same, essentially one-dimensional path (see Figure 4). But as explained in (Turchin 2003b), such a pattern in the phase-plot is inconsistent with the hypothesis that the dynamical interaction between the two variables is what drives the cycle. In a cycle, the two interacting variables are always phase-shifted with respect to each other by approximately one-quarter of the period. In a phase plot, this phase shift generates a circular trajectory. Thus, we conclude that there must be another variable, which we have not yet identified, that drives the population cycle. It is clear that changes in population and in real wage are related (in fact, it is

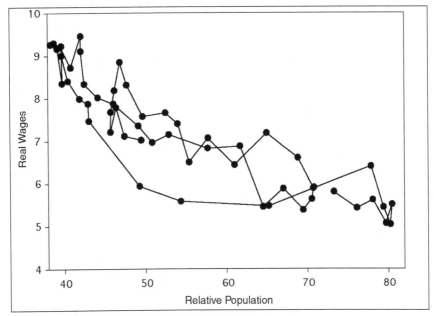

Figure 4 • England 1250–1800: Real wages by relative population.

uncanny how closely real wage dynamics mirror the population curve), but the nature of the relationship would not produce the long-term cycle that we observe.

What other variables can we examine? We know that the mid-fourteenth-century population collapse in England was associated with an epidemic of bubonic plague—the Black Death. The population decline in the late seventeenth century was also associated with plague (for example, the great plague of London). Biraben's (1975) data on plague prevalence provide us with an index of plague intensity, that is, the number of locations reporting plague outbreaks. We plot Biraben's data (solid curve) together with population data (dotted curve) in Figure 5a (the curves stop at the end of the seventeenth century, because the bubonic plague became extinct in England at that time). We observe a striking parallelism between the movements of the two curves. When plotted in the phase space, the trajectory again traces a one-dimensional path (Figure 5b). Using the same logic as in the case of the real wage, we must again reject the hypothesis that population cycles are driven by interaction with epidemics, since the phase relations are wrong.

A third variable that we can examine is the frequency of internal warfare. This index was constructed by Tilly (1993) and Sorokin (1937) by merging the lists of revolutions, civil wars, and major rebellions but excluding such

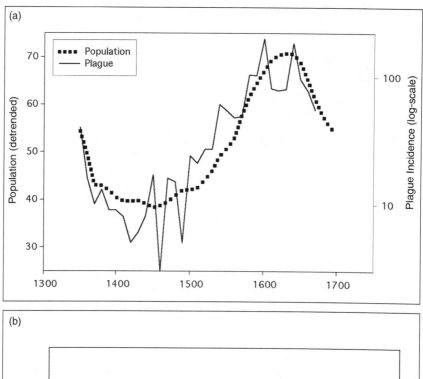

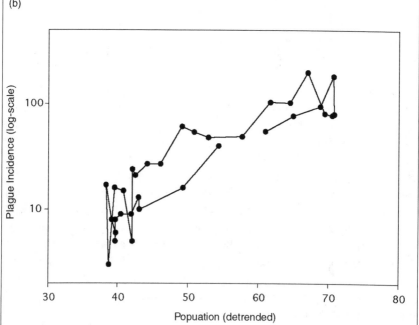

Figure 5 • (a) England 1350–1700: De-trended population by year; (b) England 1350–1700: Log of plague incidence by de-trended population.

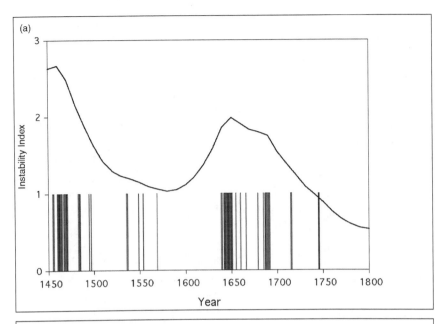

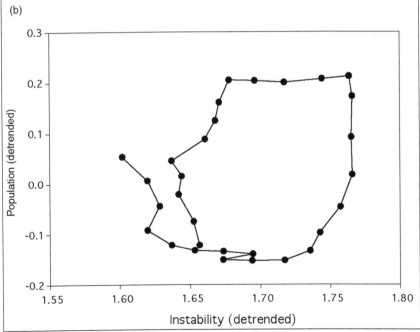

Figure 6 • (a) England 1450–1800: Instability index by year; (b) England 1450–1800: Population by instability (both de-trended).

events in Ireland, where they reflect colonial activity of the English empire, rather than sociopolitical dynamics internal to England proper. The resulting index assigns "1" to years with civil war and "0" to years without civil wars (the vertical spikes in Figure 6a). In order to use this variable in the time-series analysis we must smooth it; the smoothed curve is shown as a solid curve.

Plotting population and sociopolitical instability in the phase plot, we observe a pattern that is qualitatively different from those obtaining in the case of real wages and epidemics. Now we see that the trajectory traces a circle in the phase space (Figure 6b). This pattern is consistent with the hypothesis that it is the dynamical interaction between population and instability that drives the observed secular cycle. However, this analytical result cannot be taken as conclusive proof of the hypothesis, because we have not exhaustively examined all possible social variables that in principle could provide an explanation for the oscillations.

In summary, this example illustrates how we can capitalize on the phase relationships between various dynamical variables in order to test hypotheses about mechanisms that underlie the observed cycles. Thus, we found that population and disease prevalence oscillated completely in synchrony, which leads us to reject disease as the factor responsible for oscillations. In fact, disease apparently plays the role of reducing the amplitude of oscillations: it is highest when population is at the peak (and therefore helps to prevent further population growth) and lowest when population is in the trough (facilitating population increase). By contrast, sociopolitical instability is highest when population is already declining, and therefore it acts to accelerate the decline and increase the amplitude of the cycle. Real wages, however, are completely out-of-phase with respect to population dynamics. It may seem strange that wages act in the same way as epidemics, but this point can be better understood by looking at an inverse real wage, or an index of "misery" (see Figure 7). Here we see that the index of misery acts precisely as the plague. Thus, misery (and, by implication, real wage) is a factor that, like the epidemic, tends to reduce the amplitude of oscillations: when population is high, misery is also high and prevents further population increase owing to its effect on increased mortality and reduced birth rate. Malthus was correct in that there definitely is a connection between population change and economic misery, but he was wrong in suggesting that the interaction between population and misery causes cycles.

Conclusions

From this analysis we conclude that real wages and disease act as first-order factors in driving cycles that respond without a lag. However, these factors

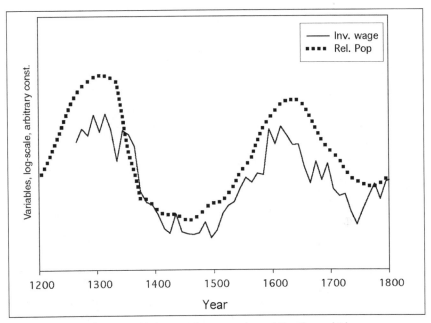

Figure 7 • England 1250–1800: Inverse of wages and population (log scale) by year.

are incapable of driving the observed oscillations. Rather, we observe that sociopolitical instability acts as a second-order factor that is phase-shifted with respect to population density and that can potentially drive the cycle.

Our theory, following Goldstone (1991:25), is that population growth in excess of the productivity gains of the land leads to state fiscal crisis because of persistent price inflation. This in turn leads to expansion of armies and rising real costs. Population growth also leads to an increased number of aspirants for elite positions, which puts further fiscal strains on the state, leading to increased intra-elite competition, rivalry, and factionalism. These strains on the state lead to popular discontent because of falling real wages, rural misery, and urban migration. Intensification of these trends eventually causes state bankruptcy and consequent loss of military control, giving way to elite movements of regional and national rebellion. A combination of elite-mobilized and popular uprisings reflects the breakdown of central authority. This sociopolitical instability affects population growth (Turchin 2003b) through higher mortality owing to increases in banditry, internal war, and starvation but also through migration, emigration, spread of disease, lower birth rates, and infanticide. These trends combine to lower productive capacity through destruction of infrastructure (for example, irrigation, flood control) and abandonment of exposed lands.

Final Comments

We return, finally, to the issue of synchrony. We argue, but have not demonstrated, that secular cycles—long-term oscillations in socioeconomic variables—are common to all tributary world-systems and component states of world-systems. To explain why some areas experience related, synchronous cycles in population size, population growth or change, city size, and state or empire size, we need to discover mechanisms that link them. What we learn from theories developed in natural sciences (and specifically, models of population ecology) is that the linking mechanisms need not be of the same duration, or even cyclical, nor do they need to be exceptionally strong. Relatively weak links, such as trade in preciosities or prestige and luxury goods, low levels of migration, and spread of disease, are sufficient to bring about synchrony. Climate shifts, especially those that are "global" in the population ecology sense (that is, "systemwide"), could certainly also bring about synchrony.

Future research needs to focus on these mechanisms. The linkage between east and west Asia, but not with south Asia, suggests either that the mechanism is *not* global climate change or that somehow the relevant climatic shifts occurred only north of the Himalayan chain. An alternative explanation might be a parallel linkage between south and southeast Asia that was sufficiently strong to bring those areas into synchrony and block synchrony with the regions of northern Eurasia. Whatever the results of future research on these issues, we will understand more profoundly how various structural dynamics shape and limit processes of social and ecological change. The linkage of cultures in precontact southwest and southeast North America (Neitzel 1999) appears to suggest that synchronous linkage has long been a significant factor in social evolution and has played an important role in shaping human–environmental interactive dynamics.

CHAPTER 6

Sustainable Unsustainability: Toward a Comparative Study of Hegemonic Decline in Global Systems

JONATHAN FRIEDMAN

Social and cultural anthropology has for a hundred years been occupied with issues of human variation, cultural creativity, technological innovation, and what is often referred to as social and cultural evolution. In interaction, often quite intense, with archeologists and ancient historians, there has been a diverse production of models of the social history of our species. I have myself been very much involved in this broad attempt to discover the nature of long-term processes, a perspective that has become much diminished in the field of anthropology since the 1980s, not least under the aegis of social and cultural anthropologists themselves. During this period there has been a focus on ethnographic research and a rise of a strongly present-oriented ethnography that eschewed both historical and comparative research. In this chapter I review some of the arguments that propelled the development of what I call a global systemic anthropology.

In the late 1960s and 1970s Columbia University[1] was the major center of cultural materialism and neoevolutionism. Cultural materialism and cultural ecology were highly functionalist and what might be called adaptationist in their approach. The latter emerged in the late 50s as an attempt to demonstrate the rationality of exotic institutions and practices often assumed to be irrational or at least arational manifestations of primitive and even not so primitive cultural schemes or mentalities. The rationale of this new approach was one in which apparently strange phenomena such as pig feasts, the potlatch, and sacred cows were accounted for in terms of their practical functions. Rather than functionally integrating the social order, the rationality of such institutions concerned the relation between society and the natural environment. There was little place for crises, for systems that did not work, and explanation was mostly a question of ecological adaptation itself. A reaction developed to this approach that had become dominant during the 60s in the United States and even, albeit to a lesser extent, in the Marxist anthropology that was emerging in Europe at the time, the time being the mid to late 60s. The approach that was proposed was one in which social systems are not conceived as adaptive machines but as systems of social reproductive processes whose properties are incompatible with one another and that in their dynamics often lead to crisis, even collapse, and historical transformation (Friedman 1974; Murphy 1970; Sahlins 1969).

This approach was applied quite early to a study of the Kachin and neighboring societies of Highland Burma, Assam, and Yunnan (Friedman 1998, 1979), making substantial use of historical ethnography, ancient history, and archeology to try to understand the way in which different social forms could be said to be historically related to one another. The model contained a number of hypothetical frameworks. The first was that the dominant social strategies of social reproduction are not self-monitoring for major trendlike results, especially those that might generate systemic crisis. They are not organized around negative feedback functions. They are not, then, preorganized for adaptation but, on the contrary, for accumulation of power and control. This entails that they can outstrip their limit conditions of reproduction. In the analysis of tribal social reproduction among the Kachin of Highland Burma it was found that logics of reproduction tended toward the hierarchization of lineages and the development of increasingly larger chiefly polities. The reproductive process is structured through two kinds of circulation, the alliance structure and the ritual feasting structure.

Prestige is gained via competitive feasting at particular ritual occasions in which a great deal of food and beer is distributed and cattle are sacrificed. The ability to give large-scale feasts implies that one is closer to the ancestor-gods who provide fertility, which means that one is closer in kinship terms to these gods or that their immediate ancestors are closer or even identical to such gods. This is a process of transformation of prestige into descent from high-ranked ancestor-deities. Prestige is then transformed into rank via a system of "generalized exchange" in which women descend from higher to lower ranked groups. The global effects of this logic are the accumulation of sacred rank at the top of the social order and the production of indebted slaves at the bottom. This leads to demographic expansion of the chiefly domain as increasing numbers of lineages are connected, via the extension of exchange links, at the same time as those of lower rank become indebted as the cost of alliances increase. This is sometimes referred to in terms of the inflation of bridewealth, one led by chiefly competition. The chiefly lineages are able to maintain the competition because of their increasing access to the labor input of a larger portion of the population, as well as the import of labor as the result of warfare. This entire process occurs on the basis of swidden agriculture in sensitive conditions whereby a fallow rate of 1/14 is the limit for the maintenance of soil fertility. But this ratio deteriorates with intensification, and productivity declines as a result, which in turn entails that increasing amounts of land become necessary to maintain the demand for total production. Chiefs can carry this out, but commoners lose out, having access neither to more land nor to slaves, and so they drop out, becoming slaves themselves or at least living in conditions of increasingly difficult indebtedness. Ultimately there develops a situation of revolt. The chief may be deposed or even killed and people re-disperse into the forest areas and live in small egalitarian communities. But the social logic remains unchanged, and the process is repeated. This is what I have referred to as the short cycle of expansion and contraction.

There is a longer cycle as well. Historically, the cycles of expansion lead to long-term degradation of larger areas and then in turn to the transformation of the social order. Declining levels of productivity and higher population densities prevent the rapid emergence of hierarchy for a complex of reasons that are detailed in other publications (Friedman 1998, 1979). There is an emergence of more egalitarian but still competitive social forms, a major increase in warfare, and the transformation of the nature of power. The generous chief is historically transformed into a warring big-man, an "antichief," and finally a headhunter. The emergence of antichiefs along this historical trajectory reveals a great deal about the transformation of power. These chiefs, often chosen from among youth, against their will, are not allowed any role in fertility rites, to give feasts or other gifts, nor to engage in sex with their wives for a specified number of years. Fertility rites themselves deal increasingly with maintaining standards rather than with increasing wealth. While the expansionist chiefdoms call their acquired slaves "grandchildren," the imploded end-version of this cycle is one in which ancestral power is a scarcity, so that potential slaves are killed and transformed into ancestral fertility and the heads of victims are placed in sacred groves where they too are sources of ancestral force. This model attempted to account for a particular logic of accumulation, one that transformed production into prestige, then into rank, and finally into sacred position within an already extant cosmology in which rank is inscribed in a cosmological hierarchy of ancestral efficacy, whereby the most senior (that is, highest ranked) ancestors are the source of increasing fertility. The short cycle is related to the expansion and collapse of chiefly hierarchies, whereas the long cycle is linked to a more permanent transformation of the social order itself. The long cycle of intensification is also part of a dialectical relation between the

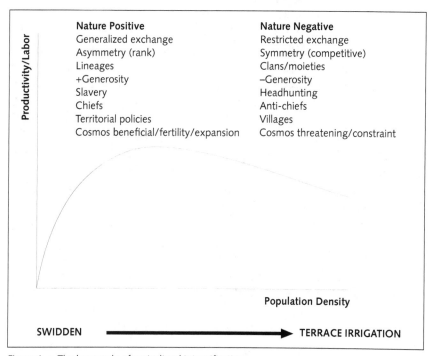

Figure 1 • The long cycle of agricultural intensification.

particular logic of social accumulation and the conditions in which it occurs, producing long-term ecological degradation.

Figure 1 shows a condensed summary of a series of other graphs that detail the transformation of "tribal" systems and that include the development of states in some conditions and the devolution of the social order in others. This particular graph refers only to the long-term devolutionary process. It might seem paradoxical that swidden agriculture is associated with expansion and irrigation with decline. This is because terracing here occurs in a rainfall zone in which swiddening has become far too improductive to support the social order. Terracing allows the maintenance of total production quotas but is very difficult to expand without major inputs of labor. It is also far less productive in terms of labor inputs, thus not really adequate to an expansionist economy. The conditions of hydraulic irrigation in riverine plains are quite different with respect to both productivity and growth capacity. Some authors have tended to reduce the relation between the social order and nature to a quasi-Darwinian relation in which societies "chose to fail or survive," primarily by destroying or improving their ecological base (Diamond 2005). Diamond is aware of the complexity of such phenomena, but his analysis is one of different factors, such as population growth, climate change, cultural rigidity, self-serving power elites, and so on, that do interact in the process of decline but in which ecological factors are primary, since the proper function of social actors is to adapt to their ecological conditions. The approach adopted here, while focused on issues of "crisis" and even "collapse," suggests that such phenomena, while related to ecological conditions, are better accounted for in terms of the internal incompatibilities of social systems themselves.

Whereas Diamond's assumptions imply a rather direct relation between whole societies and environmental limits, our own model conceives of environmental limits as the outermost but not necessarily the determinant cause of decline. This might be expected from a natural science perspective, one that does not depart from the dynamic and quite specific nature of the social systems involved. This accounts for the need to seek culprits, the particular factor, or even a combination of factors that accounts for decline. However, if such factors have no independent existence but are linked systematically within larger processes of social reproduction, then the different weights accorded to one or another "factor," for example, population growth versus cultural rigidity, can be understood as part of the same overall process. It is not a question of either/or, or even of both/and. It is a question of systemic relations between variables or aspects of a larger process. It is worth remarking that Diamond's work is very similar to the discussions in the 1960s of social evolution and ecological adaptation (for example, Harris 1977, 1979; Boserup 1965, 1966; Harner 1970) that I referred to above.

Global Systems

What was missing in earlier analyses of particular societies was the contextualization of this pulsating process within the larger regional field of imperial states and major trade systems. In subsequent work, following several initial essays by Kajsa Ekholm (Friedman) (1976, 1980; see also Ekholm & Friedman 1979, 1980; Friedman 1976), we developed what we called global systemic anthropology. Crucial here is the point of departure for the analysis, the processes of social reproduction of populations, processes that can transgress the borders of any particular polity and that define the larger arena within which units reproduce themselves.

The global systemic approach was applied to the macro-history of the Pacific. Here the logic of accumulation was not based on feasting even if feasting continued to have a role in the social order of these societies. Instead control over valuable trade items, or prestige goods, which, for any particular population, either came from the outside or were monopolized by a central node that was difficult to maintain, implied control over an entire population's social conditions of reproduction. The specific character of such goods is that they are necessary for marriage and other life-cycle exchanges as well as being a sign of social status. Such systems are widespread in the ethnographic and even the archeological literature (see Hedeager 1978; Kristiansen 1998a). Evolutionists had envisioned the Pacific in terms of a movement from egalitarian and big-man-based Melanesia to chiefly Polynesia; however, it was striking that it was Melanesia that had the most densely populated territories and clearly the most ancient settlements. The results of our research led to a model in which a prototypical social order based on monopoly over trade goods/prestige goods associated with the Lapita period of Oceanian history was transformed in different ways in the eastern and western parts of the Pacific. Here the classical interpretation was reversed. The Lapita societies were conceived as stratified societies based on the monopoly over long-distance trade in prestige goods, which in Melanesia became increasingly fragmented owing to loss of monopolies and which in eastern Polynesia was transformed into a system based on warfare and theocratic feudal power owing to the collapse of long-distance trade. In Western Polynesia and Southern Melanesia (Tonga-Fiji-New Caledonia) the original prestige goods model was more or less maintained for a longer period owing to the stability of monopoly trade systems in the area.

Comparing Hegemonies in World-System History

In the two examples cited above, the focus is on social orders organized on the basis of kinship. More recent work has moved us in the direction of so-called civilizations, including our own. Here the issue of hegemony in world-systemic terms is fundamental. One project has concentrated on ancient world-systems including the Middle and Late Bronze Age and the Hellenistic era (Ekholm 2005; Friedman & Chase-Dunn 2005). These periods display developed and complex economies with relatively clearly defined center/periphery structures. The competition among a number of centers, shifts in hegemony, and long-term intensification are characteristics of such systems. The issue of the existence of capitalism in such systems is also of interest. It might be suggested that competition and accumulation in such systems can be understood in terms of a Weberian model of capital as abstract wealth or perhaps "real-abstract," whereby a highly liquid valuable symbolizes an increasingly generalized form of wealth and thus capital. The Hellenistic imperial project grew out of the decline of the Athenian hegemony in Greece, the export of capital to both the Middle East and to Macedonia, and the military expansion of Alexander,

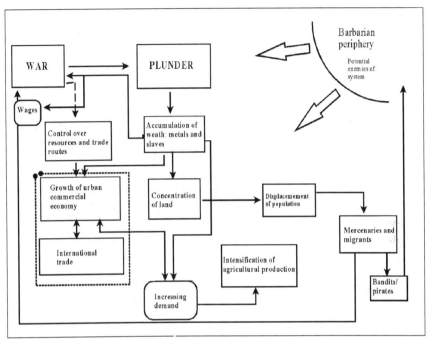

Figure 2 • Hellenistic state economies: A military-industrial complex.

following the plans of his father Philip. The goal of this expansion was the conquest of the known world, including the Mediterranean and Egypt as well as the Middle East as far as India, the playing field previously established in the Bronze Age. One might suggest that the shifting hegemonies in the Hellenistic period, in which Ptolemaic Egypt became the major historical center, ended, in fact, with the expansion of Rome, which can be seen, in systemic terms, as the last Hellenistic state. The entire period, only a few centuries in length, was organized in terms of a military-based economy that, extending the Roman model (Hopkins 1978), can be represented as in Figure 2. Here the capitalist economy develops within the envelope of the military machine, which is also the principal wage labor employer.

Endpoint

The Roman consolidation of the Hellenistic field of conquest represents the final stage of this dynamic period. There are excellent descriptions of economic and political processes throughout this era, and a wealth of literature and archival material including letters provides important insights into the social life of the entire period. Here we can speak of a truly complex economy in which the accumulation of abstract wealth or money plays an important role, a capitalist system, I would maintain, that dates back to earlier epochs in the Middle East. The typical trajectories of such systems include the geographical shift of centers of accumulation over time. The reason for this shift is related to the increasing costs of maintenance in centers of accumulation that become relatively expensive in relation to surrounding hinterlands and potential competitors. This leads to a period of decentralization of accumulation as "capital" is exported to other areas, and the center eventually becomes dependent on the import of products from its own exported capital.

It is important to situate the specific historical context of the Hellenistic states in order to properly articulate what might seem specific to the more general aspects of the dynamics of the period. This was a period of increased and increasing competition, one that might be understood as an intensification in relation to the earlier Classical Greece/Persian Empire era. The important aspects of the Hellenistic decline can be summarized as follows:

1. States confront increasing financial difficulties.
2. Polities begin to fragment into smaller entities that become independent and even attempt to conquer state power.
3. Cultural politics increases within the larger state and imperial orders. This is exemplified by the combined rise of Jewish nationalism in Israel and the diasporization of Jewish identity in Egypt.
4. There are invasions by "barbarians" from Central Europe and Asia. It appears that unstable relations exist throughout the period, but there is evidence that the northerners, whether Celts/Gauls or Scythians, are engaged as mercenaries or specialist producers, as peripheral functions of the larger states in periods of hegemonic expansion. It is in the decline of such states, in situations where they cannot afford to pay mercenaries or purchase peripheral goods to the same degree, that invasions become more aggressive and often successful.
5. Increasing internal conflicts take the following forms:
   a. class conflict including slave revolts;
   b. ethnic conflict in the eastern states;
   c. intradynastic conflicts over succession;
   d. increasing warfare between states and within former states now fragmented into smaller entities.
6. Increase of oriental cults that fill the gap following the decline of the Olympian gods and the disintegration of this early version of "modernism" (Walbank 1993:220).

7. It is interesting that, of the philosophies of the period, Stoicism was adopted by expanding Rome, representing as it does a kind of universalist modernism, whereas Cynicism and Epicurianism are closer to a postmodernist relativism (cf. Cheney 1989). Diogenes, for example, while a cosmopolitan, was closer to the cultural version of that position in his relativistic openness to all differences. Similarly neo-Confucianism in east Asia has embraced figures such as Habermas (Tran van Doan 1985) in its search for a common modernist denominator, while the West has imploded into postmodern factionalism. This is not to say that China is today's Rome, but simply that there is an interesting distribution of tendencies that needs to be understood in systemic terms.

Hegemonic Decline

The issue of decline depicted above is one that can be applied to many so-called civilizations. It is the common endgame of a series of waves of expansion/ contraction of centers that replace one another as hegemonic in particular periods. This is also the case with the history of Western development since the end of the Middle Ages, a period that, in terms of the global field, coincided with the simultaneous decline of the Arab empires within which Europe had previously been a supply zone periphery. The general model, much oversimplified here, is depicted in Figure 3. The envelope curve might be said to represent the limits of expansion of the system as a whole based on technological capabilities and limits of extraction of "natural resources" defined as a function of a particular socially organized technology. This is a complex issue, of course, and cannot be dealt with here in any depth. It might be understood in terms of the limits of a particular energy resource, such as wood, or oil in today's world, which has set off a scramble for alternative forms of energy, but it might also be something related to the maintenance of exchange such as tin in the Bronze Age.[2] It is the demands of the social order that specify which resources are strategic, rather than the converse. There are also more general limits of functioning of a social system or world-system that are directly linked to degradation of the environment. But such degradation must be understood as the degradation of the conditions of functioning of the social order. The fact that Highland New Guinea as well as much of northern China display high levels of ecological degradation does not necessarily correspond to social decline. It all depends on the specific needs or demands of the social system itself. In our own research, the envelope is rarely the direct cause of decline. The ecological basis of an expansive system might well be put under a great deal of strain, but there are intervening mechanisms that tend to play a more immediate role in decline

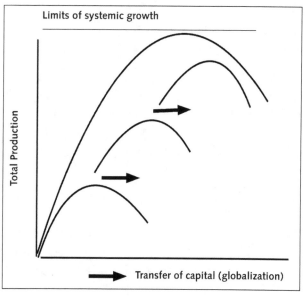

Figure 3 • Hegemonic shifts and system cycles.

even if there is clearly an interaction between levels of exploitation of nature and dominant strategies and relations within the social order. Regarding the particular historical period stretching from the decline of Athenian hegemony to the Roman Empire, we can make the following suggestions (see Figure 4).

The limits of systemic growth can be understood as the threshold of exhaustion of the system. This limit, as suggested above, is related to both technoeconomic factors and to contradictory tendencies within the system as a whole. It is rarely, as suggested, reducible to ecological limits as such even if rates of depletion can be extreme. The structure of human social orders in general can be understood as systems of reproduction containing numerous strategic logics that are autonomous from one another in terms of their internal properties yet joined in the larger reproductive process. The autonomy of internal properties implies the possibility of incompatibility among the various logics of the reproductive process. Almost all human social systems are accumulative and competitive.[3] The dynamics of such systems can easily be described in terms of positive feedback processes, and this implies a high probability that limits of systemic compatibility can be exceeded. The transgression of such thresholds usually results in crises, and the latter can be more or less catastrophic for the societies and populations involved. The examples referred to here contain such contradictions. In the first example, chiefs are deposed as the result of revolts, and chiefly polities collapse, not as a direct result of environmental degradation

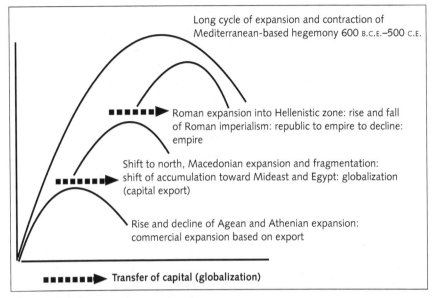

Figure 4 • Mediterranean hegemonic cycles.

but as a result of the way such degradation is filtered through the social order. Chiefs continue their expansionist activities because they gain increasing control over the total population and access to labor that offsets declining productivity. At the same time, increasing numbers of households enter a condition of debt slavery because the expansion of chiefly activities inflates the total debt, that is, demand for repayment in the system. The Kachin word for debt (*hka*) is also the word for revolt. The collapse of the polity leads to population dispersal and a return to an initial state of equality among lineages, but the process begins all over again. The natural limits of the system are reached only when the general population density of the area increases beyond a given threshold.

Similarly, in commercial civilization, declines occur within the absolute limits of the system because the primary contradictory tendencies of accumulation of abstract wealth lead to periodic breakdowns and hegemonic shifts, as a result of what some might call overaccumulation of capital, in which further productive investment declines and fictitious accumulation of "paper" wealth becomes dominant, eventually leading to financial crises. Italy, Holland, and England did not decline as hegemons for environmental reasons. However, as the system as a whole continues to expand, such pulsations can eventually strain the system to its resource limits. This accounts for the fact that, with hindsight, it often appears that collapsed civilizations are in fact accompanied by major ecological exhaustion as well.

In the models of civilization that we have used in our research, the crises are related to growth itself and to the nature of such growth in terms of the articulations of local/global relations. Emergent hegemony is based on a combination of military conquest, the transfer of wealth, and the development of export production.[4] A hegemon is a dominant actor within a larger group of polities—some allied, some competing—and a peripheral zone of lesser-developed or underdeveloped suppliers of raw materials and manpower. Although a number of works have stressed the importance of systemic limits in understanding decline (Tainter 1988; Yoffee & Cowgill 1988), they have not placed their analyses within a global systemic framework.

Hegemonic Shifts

Much of this cyclical argument is related to the reasons for and effects of hegemonic exhaustion and accompanying shifts in accumulation within global arenas. Although decline and accompanying shifts of hegemony are relatively slow processes, they also include sudden threshold phenomena. The shock of awareness is an important part of this, as illustrated by how the recent understanding that China has become a world center of production has produced innumerable panicky discussions about where the world is heading.

Chinese production as percentage of world production

Tractors:	83%
Watches/clocks:	75%
Toys:	70%
Penicillin:	60%
Cameras:	55%
Vitamin C:	50%
Laptop computers:	50%
Telephones:	50%
Air conditioners:	30%
TVs:	29%
Washing machines:	24%
Refrigerators:	16%
Furniture:	16%
Steel:	15%

The Chinese diaspora (30–50 million people) accounts for 75 percent of all foreign investment in China and controls 60–70 percent of the gross domestic product of Indonesia. China is rapidly approaching a position that was once occupied by the United States and before it Britain. This particular shift of the locus of production took place over a number of years, but thresholds of awareness occur quite suddenly. Recent reports in the media indicate the nature of such rapid change. All the following headlines appeared during a few weeks in April 2005.

Young street children in Chad recruited into Islamist groups

Shipments of children from Philippines a major industry

Micro-credits, a form of micro-financing common in the Third World, now being employed extensively in Europe

New York City for sale

Burnout a phenomenon linked to fear of conflict and the social stress of the work place

Euro-skepticism is on the rise all over Europe

Violence against women in "progressive" Sweden reported on in France as a scandal

China is making a major effort to repatriate Chinese researchers in other parts of the world with offers of high salaries and good working conditions.

China and India meet to establish alliance in which taking increasing global responsibility is a central issue.

What do such headlines reveal? Increasing disorder, violence, and dissonance in the West at the same time as there is consolidation in east and south Asia. The surprise that is often indicated in such reports is one that is very much the product of a lack of information concerning the context within which such events and transformations occur. Now it is of course true that a major crisis in the West would lead in turn to a world crisis that would cripple Asia as well since the latter is very much dependent on Western markets. But the trend is quite clear, one that consists in a shift in global hegemony, no matter how this may eventually strain the system to its absolute limit.

The Opacity of Strategic Social Operators

The examples here seem to indicate that major social change is cyclical in nature. At various levels of social organization we confront periodic expansions and contractions. In global systems this cycle logically implies the decline of older centers and the shift of wealth accumulation to new centers. We have argued that there is a high degree of determinism in the dynamics of global and even of smaller systems of social reproduction. One question that always arises is the degree to which such determinism actually exists. My argument is that this seems empirically to be the case and that it is so for reasons that have not always been researched in the social sciences, although well captured in certain works of literature, most powerfully in the work of Kafka on the way in which actors are imprisoned within social universes and cultural orders that are instrumental in the production of personal knowledge of the world. The immediacy of what is taken for granted lies in the fact that it presents itself as an existential/phenomenological reality. This is also a primary reason for the difficulty of overcoming the disastrous situations that humankind has often found itself confronting.

Survival is a short-term operation for most social actors, and the premises of survival are constituted within larger sets of assumptions about reality that are not often subject to real reflexive analysis about systemic conditions of material reproduction. Bourdieu suggested the importance of this phenomenon in discussing the notion of doxa, a set of assumptions that form the rules of the game and the shape of the playing field. Within the field of doxa there may be a multitude of positions and counterpositions, but they are all logically related to the invariant structures of the field itself.

The same notion was also touched upon by Marx when discussing the fetishism of commodities. The immediate appearance of the commodity can be said to conceal its "inner" or essential properties, that is, the social relations under which it is produced. This analysis can be extended to all dominant social relations in all social systems. In the tribal societies referred to above, the sacred chief is sacred because he (that is, his lineage) is able to produce more wealth than others, which implies that he has a closer relation to those who supply fertility, that is, the ancestors of the entire group. In the logic of this particular social order, closeness can be expressed only as kinship proximity, so that the chief is by definition the nearest descendent of the ancestors/gods and is thus himself sacred. It would make no sense to exclaim that this is an inversion of the real situation of control over other people's labor. In the same sense, the accumulation of abstract wealth, capital, in many ancient and modern forms of capitalism is a process that cannot be said to reflect underlying realities. Speculation creates a redistribution of access to the "real" resources of the world. It also generates inflation and may even slow down the growth process by increasing the ratio of fictitious value to real costs of reproduction. If the financial and/or nonproductive component of the process of reproduction becomes an increasing proportion of the latter, it appears in the "incorrect" form of declining productivity and "diminishing returns." Differential rates of accumulation also generate a differential gradient of costs of production so that

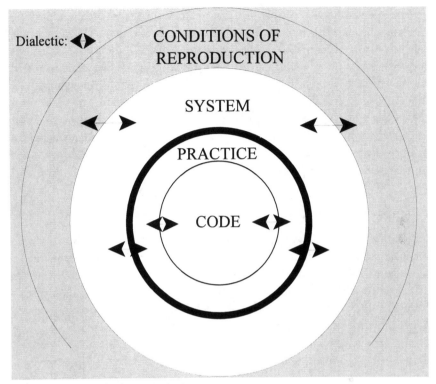

Figure 5 • Dialectic: fetish/practice/system.

a particular area becomes expensive compared to other, less-developed places (for example, the West's recent relation to China and India), that is, areas with lower overall costs of social reproduction. Capital, as accumulated wealth, does not contain within itself information concerning the relations of productivity in technological terms or about the conditions of its own reproduction over time. It is a fetish that fundamentally misrepresents significant properties of the reality that it organizes. Figure 5 attempts to capture the degree to which social orders do not learn, or at least the limits within which such learning might be said to occur. It is this framework that, I would suggest, accounts for the ultimate ubiquity of decline and for the logical tendency toward cyclical patterns in history, as well as for the experienced suddenness of the former.

Here again the notion suggested by Diamond that societies make choices, metaphorically or literally, concerning their own survival is grossly reductionist in the terms set out here. One must clearly identify the actors that could make such choices. There is no evidence that societies, small or large, are like subjects. On the contrary, one finds that there are dominant actors who are themselves caught in the webs of reproductive logics that escape their own intentionality and which, in fact, are rarely correctly cognized. This perspective on the history of humanity is a bit like *The Economist*'s evaluation of various national economies. Thus, when Asia was growing rapidly we were told that they were doing something very right, company flags and discipline, state intervention and the like, which we in the West ought to imitate. But when the crisis came, *The Economist*'s journalists turned around and blamed them for precisely too much state intervention, for corruption and waste, and called for reforms closer to the Western model. These journalists have always been saved by being anonymous, no authors ever appearing in their articles.

Alternative Scenarios

The catastrophe in New Orleans in 2005 is an excellent example of the complex process of accumulated contradictions and the decline of centrality in the center of a world-system. With some hindsight and without access to the actual activities involved in the collapse of the dikes and the flooding of this large city as well as its abandonment, it might easily be attributed to a more general phenomenon such as climate change, whether global warming due to human activity or to natural cyclical changes. On closer examination, however, we see a center under stress. The hurricane that struck the city did not itself cause the greatest damage. In fact the first reports were that New Orleans had escaped relatively unscathed. But then the dikes collapsed in strategic places, and the city was quickly flooded. The results were catastrophic, with hundreds of deaths (some predicted 10,000), and the question of why and whose fault it was immediately became media hype. If we were to look at the abandonment of the city and its destruction as archeologists, we might connect climate changes to the heating up of the Caribbean and the production of increasing numbers of hurricanes. Either anthropogenic global warming or natural climatic cycles could then be causal links to the decline of this urban area. If this were followed by the declining power of the United States, then climatic changes could be argued to be the cause of the decline of this major levee. The Thera syndrome would be perfectly replicated. The volcanic eruption of Thera, the dating of which is disputed but now is thought to be closer to 1640 B.C.E. than 1450 B.C.E., is said by some to have caused the decline of Crete via the combined result of a tidal wave that struck the north coast of the island and the spread of volcanic ash in the region that caused serious agricultural problems. There is no real evidence here, and this explanation of a decline spanning 200 years is a very weak argument, especially in the light of other more socially based accounts of the decline of Minoan civilization and its conquest by the Mycenians, accounts in which the changing balance of power between the Greek mainland and Crete is approached as an historical process that can be accounted for in terms of social systemic analysis.

Assuming that U.S. economic hegemony is on the decline, and has been for some time, the argument for climatic or natural catastrophic causes strikes me as misleading. It is of course true that nature is not reducible to the social, even if it is social strategies that largely determine the properties of nature that are relevant for the survival of human populations. It is also true that there is a significant articulation between social processes and the natural processes on which the social processes depend. This implies, however, that catastrophes entailing the destruction of cities and the large-scale loss of lives are more an expression of a social situation than a question of natural impact. It is increasingly clear that the reason for the flooding in New Orleans was related to a complex of factors that can be traced back to a decline in the state's capacity to deal with such problems. The factors involved were

1. Lack of coordination among agencies, from city and state government to federal;
2. Lack of available troops, owing to deployment in Iraq;
3. Lack of maintenance of the levees, although it was well known for years that this was a critical problem; and
4. Conflicts among different social actors over the years, for example, ecologists and government agencies, concerning the ecological impact of the levee complex on the "natural" environment.

These are social factors that led to what looked like a natural disaster. It is of course true that there was a major storm, which may have been indirectly related to the warming of the Caribbean, but the consequences of the storm in this particular case can be understood only in terms of the failure of state structures to deal with this natural phenomenon in a situation in which there was, in fact, adequate available knowledge of the consequences. There are a number of issues involved here. It is clear that the expansion of accumulative systems leads to increased stress on environmental systems. It seems to be generally accepted that global warming is a result of human activity, although it might be difficult to establish the actual causality involved. But the accumulation process also creates strains on the social system, which weaken its capacity to deal with human-induced natural catastrophes that might in other circumstances have been successfully controlled.

Notes

1. I was a doctoral student at Columbia from 1968 to 1972, when I finished my thesis, discussed in part below.

2. It should be noted that there is no evidence that the sources of tin dried up at the end of the Bronze Age, but the intensive warfare and collapse of trade would have made tin unavailable to the centers of bronze production.

3. Why this should be the case is not a part of our discussion here, but it is becoming increasingly clear from archeological research that accumulative dynamics play an essential role in all of human history. Even the notion that hunting and gathering societies represent stable equilibrium has been challenged for some time. It is based on the conflation of ethnographic examples, drawn from the marginal zones of larger social systems, with the archeological past.

4. Population growth is sometimes assumed as an independent variable in discussions of growth and decline. In the approach suggested here, population growth and population density are outcomes of other strategies of accumulation that lead to increasing rates of fertility and/or the import of labor.

Part II

Case Studies of Socioenvironmental Change in Prehistory

Agrarian Landscape Development in Northwestern Europe Since the Neolithic: Cultural and Climatic Factors behind a Regional/Continental Pattern[1]

BJÖRN E. BERGLUND

Cultural landscape dynamics reflect changes in an agrarian society and can be studied by means of paleoecological techniques and access to archeological and historical information. Holocene climate change is suggested to be an important environmental factor behind the step-wise development of the cultural landscape in northwestern Europe. Another factor influencing changes in agrarian technology and organization has been the availability of soil nutrients. Eight distinct human impact events (3900, 3500, 2500–2200, 1800, 800 B.C.E.; 500, 800–1000, 1300–1400 C.E.) are defined and compared with the paleoclimatic situation, as reconstructed from information on solar activity, tree growth at timber line, lake catchment erosion, and other proxy data. There is evidence of wide-scale synchronicity over much of northwestern Europe, but there is also local differentiation of landscape development. It is hypothesized that the agrarian society and landscape developed in a step-wise fashion, dependent on the interaction among technology, society, and the ecological capacity of the landscape, highly influenced by climate.

Mesolithic humans were adapted to the environment and its natural resources. The Neolithic food economy was based on a mixed diet, derived from cultivated crops and cattle breeding. Such expansive societies were more vulnerable to, and dependent on, the interaction of social and natural factors. Climate has been acknowledged as one of the main triggers of cultural development (for example, Lamb 1982, 1984), although its importance is debatable (for instance, Bell & Walker 1992; Roberts 1998; de Menocal 2001; Mannion 1991; Redman 1999; Zolitschka et al. 2003). It is thus important to explore the pattern of cultural expansion of agrarian societies and its possible relation to climate change (Chase-Dunn, Hall, & Turchin 2007). Northwestern Europe may be regarded as a marginal area for agriculture and is thus a suitable region for detecting expansions and regressions of agrarian societies.

The interaction between humans and environment in agrarian society is reflected in the cultural landscape. Vegetation and soil changes are recorded in lake sediments and bog deposits, and can be detected by paleobiological (for example, palynological), geochemical, geophysical, and other kinds of analyses (Berglund 2003[1986]; Roberts 1998). Agricultural expansion in a forested landscape leads to deforestation; in contrast, regression leads to forest regeneration. The general deforestation chronology of the Holocene is shown in Figure 1. A broad-scale deforestation/regeneration pattern has been recognized in northwestern Europe and discussed on the basis of numerous pollen diagrams (Berglund 1969, 1985; Berglund et al. 1996). In some interdisciplinary, regional projects, data on the forest history have agreed with archeological data (for example, Andersen 1995; Berglund 1991; Behre & Kucan 1994; Molloy & O'Connell 1991, 1995; Rösch 1992). The cultural landscape dynamics of an area in southern Sweden were demonstrated in the so-called Ystad Project, which is used as an example in this paper (Berglund 1991, 2000). Figure 2 shows four prehistoric landscape periods after 4000 B.C.E., each with initial settlement expansion and deforestation, followed by settlement restructuring and forest regeneration before the next expansion of open landscape.

Based on a screening of pollen diagrams from northwestern Europe (Berglund et al. 1996), eight time slices since 4000 B.C.E. have been selected as important periods in the development of the cultural landscape:[2] (1) 3900 B.C.E., (2) 3500 B.C.E., (3) 2500–2200 B.C.E., (4) 1800 B.C.E., (5) 800 B.C.E., (6) 500 C.E., (7) 800–1000 C.E., and (8) 1300–1400 C.E. These periods were ones of dynamic landscape development, in most cases characterized by deforestation and expanding agricultural land use. Periods 2, 6, and 8 are different from the others in the sense that they represent times of forest regeneration and reduced human impact. It has earlier been shown that there is concordance between the paleoclimate records and these major human impact events (Berglund 2003). However, one must bear in mind that climate records are heterogeneous, comprising long-term trends and prone to high-frequency variability. An accurate and precise chronology is crucial for these correlations. With these reservations, the human impact events are plotted against climate information from solar activity, a complex parameter affecting insolation as well as cloud formation (van Geel et al. 1999; Muscheler et al. 2003), tree growth at the timber line, and mineral magnetic data of selected varved lake sediments, with all climate data expressed on an annual time scale (Figure 3). The agrarian productivity was dependent on several factors, such as the length

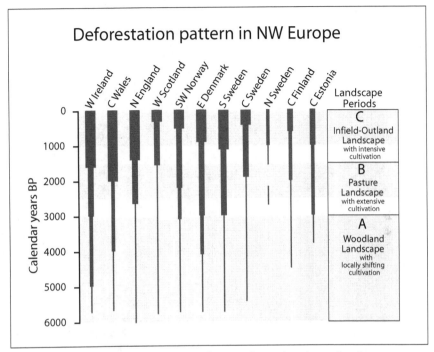

Figure 1 • Main trends of deforestation in northwestern Europe based on pollen diagrams along a transect from Ireland to Estonia (Berglund et al. 1996, Berglund 2000).

of the vegetation growth period, its temperature, and levels of precipitation. Winter conditions affected the storage of food, as well as the overall survival of humans and animals. Soil erosion is another complex parameter. In a forested landscape increased erosion is generally related to severe winters with late and intense snow-melting, whereas in an open landscape it may be connected with increased agrarian activity.

Human Impact Events

3900 B.C.E. (Early Neolithic Period)

This is a time marker horizon because of the regionally synchronous elm decline in northwestern Europe, which probably had a climatic cause (Birks 1986), even if the spread of a pathogen may have been the more proximate factor. It was followed by the first agricultural expansion, the so-called *landnam*, which has been interpreted as the introduction and expansion of an agricultural economy from central to northwestern Europe (Berglund 1985; Iversen 1941). Climatically, it was a dramatic period with low solar activity around 3900 B.C.E.

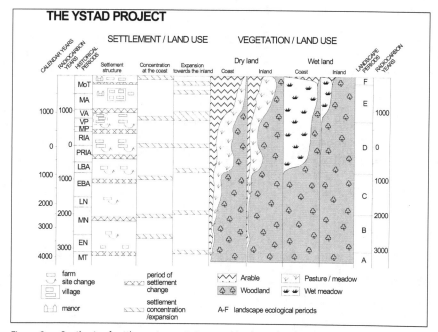

Figure 2 • Synthesis of settlement, vegetation, and land use development during the last 6,000 years in the Ystad area, South Sweden. Landscape periods A-F are defined on the basis of main changes in the cultural landscape dynamics (Berglund, ed. 1991, revised).

followed by a period of high solar activity, resulting in dry and warm summers for 300–400 years. In the Scandinavian mountains the tree limit reached its highest altitude and glaciers retreated. In the Baltic Sea, as well as in the North Sea, a rapid sea-level regression occurred, which must have influenced coastal settlements (Christensen 1995; Larsson 1990; Yu 2003). It is quite possible that this situation favored agricultural expansion in northwestern Europe, perhaps even globally (Sandweiss, Maasch, & Anderson 1999).

3500 B.C.E. (End of Early Neolithic Period)

A phase of forest regeneration in southern Scandinavia succeeded the landnam period. It has been interpreted as a time of settlement contraction, particularly in marginal areas. However, sparse settlement based on wood coppicing may have existed in these regenerated forests (Göransson 1986). The abandonment of farming on Ireland, combined with woodland regeneration, is typical of the period between 3200 and 2500 B.C.E. (Molloy & O'Connell 1995; O'Connell & Molloy 2001). Climatically, it was a period of low solar activity, leading to cooler

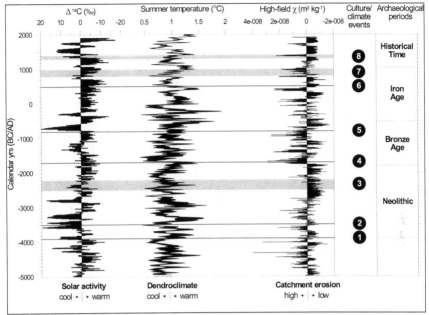

Figure 3 • Comparison of three proxy climate archives: Solar activity interpreted from carbon 14 measurements of tree rings (Stuiver et al. 1998), summer temperature interpreted from tree ring data derived from pine trees in Swedish Lapland (Grudd et al. 2002), and lake catchment erosion based on mineral magnetic analyses of annually laminated (varved) lake sediments from Lake Sarsjön, northern Sweden (Snowball, Sandgren, & Pettersson 1999). Eight culture/climate events discussed in this paper are indicated.

and more humid conditions. Tree growth was reduced, and glaciers expanded in the mountains. Lake levels rose, and bogs expanded at lower elevations.

2500–2200 B.C.E. (Transition Middle/Late Neolithic Period)

This was a time of gradual deforestation and agricultural expansion within central as well as marginal settlement areas. Climatically it was a period characterized by low solar activity in the beginning, but with higher activity toward the end. The mountain tree-limit descended, and glaciers expanded. High annual precipitation and cool conditions during this period are reported from central Europe (Zolitschka & Negendank 1997). In western Denmark, stock breeding expanded, possibly because of less favorable conditions for crop cultivation. Here, as well as in western Norway, open heaths expanded owing to heavy grazing (Andersen 1995; Kaland 1986; Kristiansen 1998; Odgaard

1994). Agriculture expanded northward along the Norwegian coast, as far north as the Lofoten Islands. In the Near East, a marked transition to a more arid climate at 2200 B.C.E. is associated with societal collapse (de Menocal 2001; Weiss 1997), which contrasts with the situation in northern Europe. Similar conditions have been reported from East Asia (Yasuda 2001).

1800 B.C.E. (Beginning of Bronze Age)

The beginning of the Bronze Age is associated with the expansion of agriculture and, in particular, pastures in Scotland and western Scandinavia. The distribution of numerous grave mounds from the Early Bronze Age in Denmark and southern Sweden is indicative of an open landscape at this time. Climatically, this is a transition phase from continental to oceanic climate, leading to decreased tree growth, expanding glaciers, and soil erosion. The rapid changes demonstrated in the annual tree ring data and the varved lake sediment records in Figure 3 have not yet been correlated with a corresponding change in the cultural landscape. This is a challenge for future research.

800 B.C.E. (Younger Bronze Age)

This was a very dramatic period with expanding agriculture and a remarkable expansion of pastures in eastern Denmark and southern Sweden. Similar expansion, sometimes described as the Late Bronze Age Landnam (O'Connell & Molloy 2001), has been documented in Ireland. This was also a period of significant climate change. High solar activity is recorded around 1000 B.C.E., leading to warm and dry conditions, but around 800 B.C.E. there was a short but distinct period of low solar activity. This event was one of the most remarkable climate changes during the Holocene, and its consequences for agrarian societies have been much discussed, particularly in Holland (van Geel, Buurman, & Waterbolk 1996; van Geel et al. 1999). A regression of agriculture has been documented in the coastal areas, which appears to have prompted human migrations and settlement restructuring. Such changes have not been recorded in southern Scandinavia, but there seems to have been an overall expansion of the open landscape after 800 B.C.E., including a colonization of marginal inland areas (Berglund & Börjesson 2002; Lagerås 1996).

500 C.E. (End of Migration Period)

This period was characterized by a severe regression of agricultural areas, pastures as well as open fields, in central Europe as well as in Scandinavia, followed by forest regeneration in these areas (Andersen & Berglund 1994).

Dendro-climatological time series reveal a strongly reduced tree growth around the year 530 C.E., probably as a result of cold summers (Figure 3). The indication of comparatively weak erosion may be a consequence of reduced human impact in the catchment (Figure 3). The period 480–540 is a time of strong turbulence in Europe, involving the collapse of the Roman Empire and the spread of the Justinian plague (Ambrosiani 1984).

800–1000 C.E. (Viking Period)

These two centuries are characterized by strong expansion of agriculture and settlements, including the establishment of villages and towns, in Scandinavia. There was even a need to colonize new areas outside old settlement areas, including mountain areas and more remote areas such as Iceland and southern Greenland. A prerequisite for this expansion was a favorable climate, and the period 800–1200 has been called the Medieval Warm Period (Lamb 1982, 1984). Solar activity was high, leading to a warm and dry summer climate. Tree growth increased and glaciers retreated in the mountains (Figure 3). The diagram in Figure 3 indicates strong erosion, probably because of increased agriculture in the catchment area. The favorable period came to an end around 1200, when the climate gradually entered a phase known in northern Europe as the Little Ice Age.

1300–1400 C.E. (Transition Early/Late Medieval Period)

This period was characterized by the regression of settlement and agriculture, particularly distinct in the sub-Arctic areas that were settled during the boom period, 800–1200 C.E. It was a critical period for people living on Iceland and Greenland. Climatically, this was the beginning of the Little Ice Age, with lowered summer temperature and increased precipitation and stormy weather (Grove 1988; Lamb 1982). Climate deterioration and overgrazing causing soil erosion, combined with social and economic regression, caused a population decrease on Iceland during the fourteenth century and complete abandonment of the Greenland settlements between 1350–1450 (Fredskild 1990). The settling of Greenland can be regarded as "a failed experiment" (Redman 1999), obviously a severe struggle against the climate for people not adapted to the Arctic environment, as were the native Greenlanders. The Black Death was another factor that caused depopulation and desertion of many settlements all over Europe in the fourteenth century. Indirectly, this favored the agrarian expansion that followed the crisis of the fourteenth and fifteenth centuries (Myrdal 2003).

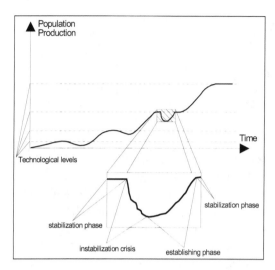

Figure 4 • (a, left) Mineral nutrient hypothesis behind the agrarian technology development, through critical ecological phases (Emanuelsson 1988). (b, page 115) Model for the long-term agrarian society development, through socioeconomical crises (Myrdal 1997, 2000, revised). Human impact/climate events 6–8 discussed in this paper are indicated.

Interacting Environmental Causes behind Agrarian Crises

Expansions and regressions of the agricultural landscape have here been described in relation to climate changes. Other environmental factors have certainly also been important. In the Neolithic period, sea-level changes influenced the availability of marine food resources. A reduction of these resources may have played a role in promoting an agrarian economy (Larsson 1990). Marine resources have always been important along the coasts, perhaps especially during agrarian regressions. However, the spread and welfare of human populations along coasts with conditions influenced by the North Atlantic Current (or Gulf Stream) may also have been associated with climatic changes.

Another factor of great importance for the long-term development of an agrarian economy is the quality of the cultivated soils, more specifically the available amount of mineral nutrients, which depends on the agrarian technology (Emanuelsson 1988; Welinder 1983). This has been an aspect of sociocultural development, influenced by innovations as they spread from the continent to northwestern Europe. Production crises caused by soil leaching and overgrazing may have played a crucial role in such technological and organizational changes. However, the recovery time from ecological production crises is assumed to be more lengthy than the period of climate changes that may have caused them. Overgrazing may have had negative consequences for the light soils of Jutland, in western Denmark, during the early Bronze Age (Kristiansen 1998) as well as on Öland, in southeastern Sweden, at the end of the Roman Iron Age (Enckell & Königsson 1979).

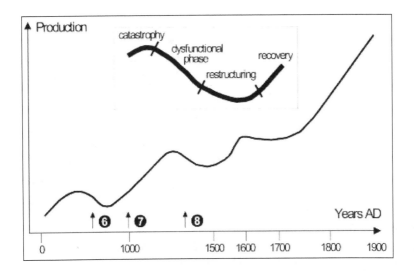

Conclusions: Landscape and Societal Development through Crises

The long-term development of the agrarian cultural landscape has been a step-wise process, as evidenced by paleoecological and archeological records. As early as the 1970s, the Swedish archeologist Stig Welinder presented a step-shaped model, in which an improvement of the agrarian technology was adopted in order to raise the production capacity of a landscape under pressure from a growing population (Welinder 1975, 1983). This model was inspired by the expansions and regressions of open landscape identified in Swedish pollen diagrams. Welinder's model was based on the hypothesis of the Danish economist Ester Boserup (1965, 1981), who proposed that population growth is a major factor behind agricultural development.

The Swedish plant ecologist Urban Emanuelsson elaborated this model in the direction of a "soil nutrient hypothesis," emphasizing that available soil nutrients have been a major factor in the development of an agrarian technology, involving, for example, soil preparation, fertilization, rotation systems, farm and village organization, and land mobilization (Emanuelsson 1988; Emanuelsson & Möller 1990, Figure 4a). The importance of soil nutrients for increasing crop production was also a major factor in the more recent agrarian development in the nineteenth century, when artificial fertilizers were introduced.

The economic historian Janken Myrdal has widened the perspective further by emphasizing the interactions among society, technology, and environment, conceptualized as a technological-social complex that changes through crises (Myrdal 1997, 2000). He has described such crises by defining different subphases (Figure 4b). The crises have prompted various changes serving to increase production. For the marginal areas in northwestern Europe—uplands, coasts, and other "poor" areas—there is evidence of such a step-wise development of agrarian society, dependent on the interaction between the technological-social complex and the ecological capacity of the landscape. Similar perspectives on the importance of crises, sometimes called "Dark Ages," have been expressed by other colleagues (for example, Zolitschka, Behre, & Schneider 2003).

Climate has thus played a major role as the background for this development, particularly in regard to the timing of changes. There is some evidence for this in the paleoecological, archeological, and historical sources, but we need to verify it further by creating new and well-designed interdisciplinary projects, focused on carefully selected regions and specific time periods such as the Migration Period or the Late Medieval Period. But we have to bear in mind that each time period is unique, which makes generalizations almost impossible. Nevertheless, this research is very challenging.

In this chapter, I have shown that there has been some synchronicity in the long-term expansion and regression of the cultural landscape and agrarian society in northwestern Europe. Marginal areas have been particularly sensitive. However, there have also been regional and local differences in the timing of these dynamic changes (Digerfeldt & Welinder 1988). Some colleagues have described large-scale expansion waves for all of "Afroeurasia" during the last 3,000 years (Chase-Dunn, Hall, & Turchin 2007). Whether the pattern in northwestern Europe can be linked to such "pulsations" is an open question.

Notes

1. Dr. Håkan Grudd provided digitalized dendro-data and Dr. Ian Snowball environmental magnetic data. Dr. Shiyong Yu assisted with the editing of the figures, and Dr. Snowball corrected the English text. I have had stimulating discussions with Dr. Snowball concerning paleoclimatic data and interpretations. I am most grateful for all this support.

2. The time scale in this paper is calendar years, based on a calibrated radiocarbon chronology.

CHAPTER 8

Climate Change in Southern and Eastern Africa during the Past Millennium and Its Implications for Societal Development[1]

KARIN HOLMGREN AND HELENA ÖBERG

Climatic records from equatorial eastern Africa and subtropical southern Africa have shown that both temperature and the amount of rainfall have varied over the past millennium. Moreover, the rainfall pattern in these two regions varied inversely over long periods of time. Droughts started abruptly and were of multidecadal to multicentennial length, and the changes in the hydrological budget were of large amplitude. Changing water resources in semiarid regions clearly must have had regional influences on both ecological and socioeconomic processes. Through a detailed analysis of the historical and paleoclimatic evidence from southern and eastern Africa covering the past millennium, one sees that, depending on their vulnerability, climatic variability can have an immense impact on societies, sometimes positive and sometimes disastrous.

Introduction

Global temperatures are currently rising. Regional climatic models predict considerable future changes in precipitation patterns and temperatures; the implications of these changes for ecosystems as well as for humans and their societies seem alarming. It is interesting, however, that while few doubt the potentially severe implications of these changes for humans and society, suggestions of similarly significant relationships between climate and humans in the past are often criticized as representing a simplistic climatic determinism.

It is now known that, even without human impact on climate, past climatic events have been abrupt and have lasted for decades to centuries. One example is the documented variations in lake levels in northern Africa during the past

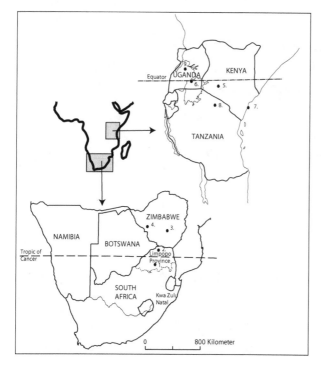

Figure 1 • Map over southern and eastern Africa showing sites discussed in text:
1. Cold Air Cave, Makapansgat Valley, Limpopo Province;
2. Mapungubwe;
3. Great Zimbabwe;
4. Khami;
5. Lake Naivasha;
6. Lake Victoria sediment-core site;
7. Malindi;
8. Engaruka;
9. Munsa.

10,000 years (Gasse 2000). The magnitude of these variations in lake level can be as great as 100 meters. Such changes must have implied huge changes in the water budget of the tropics. A Nordic example is the transition from a Medieval warm period to the so-called Little Ice Age, when sea ice increased and the Norse settlements in western Greenland became more or less isolated. These kinds of climate changes certainly must have affected societies, although it is unclear to what extent. There is a need to further explore the complex interactions between the different factors that cause changes in societal development.

With the growing number of high-resolution paleoclimatic data that provide fairly precise measurements of the timing, amplitude, and duration of past climate events, the potential to more accurately assess the role of climate in the development and the decline of human societies is increasing. Information on both societal development and climate history is increasingly accessible; it is now time to explore and thoroughly analyze the interactions between these processes.

If we can increase understanding of what role climate changes have played in the past, this could provide a basis for gaining a better understanding of the potential influence that future climatic changes might have on societies at global, regional, and local scales. Can it be argued that climate has been a major factor in societal change? Can we explain why climate appears to have been a determinant factor at some times and places, but not at others? Can this knowledge be applied to design more climate-resilient societies? Or can we conclude that climate always plays a subordinate role in societal development and that there is no need to worry about global warming or cooling?

This chapter discusses the interactions between climate and societies in two regions in Africa during the last millennium: subtropical southern Africa and intertropical eastern Africa. This type of analysis is now possible, thanks to the detailed regional climate series and the archeological and historical data available for both regions.

Southern Africa

Two detailed climate series are available from the Limpopo province, South Africa (see Figure 1). The series derive from precisely dated cave stalagmites, which have given a time resolution of about 10 years for the last millennium. The first series is a stable oxygen isotope record (Holmgren et al. 2003; Lee-Thorp et al. 2001) (see Figure 2). Peaks in the record indicate warmer, wetter climate, whereas troughs mean colder, drier climate. The other data series (Figure 2) is a temperature reconstruction based on an observed strong correlation between color changes in the annual growth layers of stalagmites and regional annual maximum temperatures (Holmgren et al. 2001). Peaks again indicate warmer conditions, troughs colder ones. The two records are independently derived and show a very consistent pattern of climate variability. The temperature reconstruction yields information about local temperatures, while the isotope reconstruction yields information about the regional pattern of relative changes in temperature and precipitation.

It is apparent that climate has fluctuated between warmer, wetter periods and colder, drier ones, with a quasiperiodicity of approximately 80 years (Tyson, Cooper, & McCarthy 2002) and with the shift between these two patterns often being fairly abrupt. A prolonged colder, drier period from 1500 to 1800 C.E., estimated as being around 1°C lower than present-day temperatures (Holmgren et al. 2001), corresponds to the Little Ice Age known from the high latitudes of the northern hemisphere. It can be noted that the present-day warming is not a unique feature in the Limpopo province during the last millennium.

The period from around 850–1290 C.E. was a time of agricultural expansion in the Shashi-Limpopo region, according to archeological and historical sources (Leslie & Maggs 2000). Communities expanded from the east (Zimbabwe) into the fringes of today's semiarid Kalahari. Agriculture and the trade in gold and ivory were important activities that contributed to the accumulation of wealth in expanding settlements (Huffman 1996, 2000; Parsons 1993).

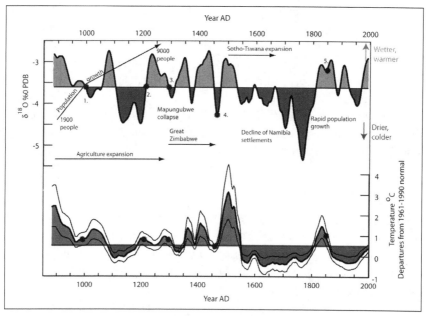

Figure 2 • Climate time series derived from analysis of stalagmites from Cold Air Cave, Makapansgat Valley, South Africa, together with historical information. The top series show δ18O variations reflecting relative changes in temperature and moisture, and the bottom series show temperature changes (with uncertainty intervals) in °C anomalies from 1961–1990 normal, as derived from changes in color in the stalagmite and its correlation to temperature (Holmgren et al. 2001; Tyson, Lee-Thorp, Holmgren, & Thackeray 2002). Horizontal lines denote the average of the period. The numbers denote: 1. shift of center from Schroda to K2; 2. shift of center from K2 to Mapungubwe; 3. fall of Mapungubwe; 4. fall of Great Zimbabwe; 5. *Difaquane*.

If we relate this period of agricultural development to the regional climate record (Figure 2), it might be concluded that societal expansion occurred through times of continuously shifting climate and that there is no relation between climate and societal development. However, by adding data on population growth from 900–1290 c.e. (Huffman 2000), we might instead conclude that the sudden collapse of the capital at Mapungubwe in 1290 c.e. was a result of the fact that population growth had reached a limit, above which this society became unstable. It could cope with the drier conditions around 1000 c.e. and 1100–1200 c.e., but when climate again deteriorated in 1290 c.e., the combination of high population, dry conditions, and water shortage led to the collapse of Mapungubwe (Hall 1987; Huffman 1996, 2000; Parsons 1993).

Viewing the Mapungubwe period in more detail (Figure 2), we note that the development of large centers of power and trade began around 900 c.e., when climatic conditions were favorable. The centers shifted within a small area of a few square kilometers, from a site called Schroda to the site K2 at 1030 c.e. and then from K2 to Mapungubwe at 1220 c.e. (Vogel 2000). These two occurrences of capital reorganization coincide with periods of climatic instability.

The fall of Mapungubwe was followed by the construction of a new center, the Great Zimbabwe, situated toward the east and along the southeastern escarpment, where the amount of rain is generally more favorable. Great Zimbabwe developed slowly at first, then more rapidly as climatic conditions improved. It survived one period of drought and then flourished, with a rapidly growing population, between 1400 and 1420 c.e., that is, through a period of wetter and warmer conditions (Figure 2). The collapse of Great Zimbabwe coincided with a rapid decline in precipitation and temperature around 1450 c.e. Water shortage and famines, in conjunction with political instability and a decline in trade, have been proposed as the causes for the abandonment of Great Zimbabwe (Parsons 1993).

The first Sotho-Tswana settlements in Eastern Botswana (Khami) coincide with a warm, wet pulse in climate at around 1475–1525. Large settlements in Namibia (Kuiseb River delta) were abandoned between 1460 and 1640 (Burgess & Jacobson 1984), while the expansion of the agropastoral Sotho-Tswana continued (Parsons 1993) in spite of harsh environmental conditions.

During the first half of the eighteenth century many communities in northeastern South Africa (the Natal–Zululand region) relied heavily on drought-resistant sorghum as a food staple. There were significant political changes among the northern Nguni people, including movements from the drier interior to the humid coast (Ballard 1986). Toward the end of the eighteenth century, increasing humidity and the adoption of maize as a staple crop probably contributed to the rapid increase of the number of settlements in the Natal-Zululand region (Huffman 1996; Maggs 1984).

The evidence from the climatic record of slightly drier conditions and decreasing temperatures in the early nineteenth century is matched in the historical records by mention of a prolonged drought, alternately called *Madhlatule, Difaquane,* or *Mefacane.* This was a period of wars and famines of such magnitude that there was a serious breakdown of social, political, and economic institutions among the Nguni agropastoralists, who experienced starvation and increased migration (Ballard 1986).

It is unlikely that the famines were directly caused by the drier conditions; more likely, the political instability, increasing number of people, and increased reliance on water-demanding maize, which had replaced the drought-resistant sorghum, resulted in an imbalance between people and resources. A slight change in climate would then suffice to trigger societal collapse. However, this was also the era when southern Africa's most powerful black state, the Zulu empire, was consolidated (Ballard 1986). It thus appears that the crisis stimulated the development of a new empire.

East Africa

Detailed records of hydrological changes that are based on lake sediments are available from Lake Naivasha, Kenya (Lamb, Darbyshire, & Verschuren 2003; Verschuren, Laird, & Cumming 2000) and northern Lake Victoria, Uganda (Stager, Cumming, & Meeker 1997, 2003; Stager et al. 2005) (Figures 1, 3). Peaks in the records indicate wetter conditions and troughs drier ones, as deduced from lake-level changes in meters (Lake Naivasha) and the abundance of shallow-water diatoms in percentage (Lake Victoria). A shorter temperature record, spanning the past 200 years, is available from stable isotope studies on corals outside the Kenyan coast (Cole et al. 2000).

Taking existing dating uncertainties into account, the records are fairly consistent, although the periods of dry and wet conditions are not equally pronounced at both sites. Whether this is due to different techniques of analysis or reflects regional climate variability is a question that needs to be investigated further. Again, it can be noted that climatic conditions have varied through time and that recent droughts, such as the one in the 1970s, have been preceded by much more severe ones in the past.

Archeological surveys show population expansion and the establishment of central settlements in western Uganda around 1000–1200 c.e. (Robertshaw & Taylor 2000), a period when the two lake records indicate region-wide dry conditions (Figure 3). The lack of accurate chronological control hinders us from deducing whether the centers were founded before or after the onset of dry conditions. The population, which practiced agropastoralism, continued to grow, but with short-term relocations of settlements until the fourteenth or fifteenth century (Robertshaw & Taylor 2000).

At the end of a dry period that has been identified from both lake records from around 1400 c.e., there occurred a famine known as the *Wamara* drought (1400–1412 c.e.) (Webster 1980). The Bacwezi Empire in western Uganda collapsed shortly afterward, around 1450 c.e., and settlements declined as a combined result of drier conditions, overgrazing, and diseases (Robertshaw & Taylor 2000; Taylor, Robertshaw & Marchant 2000). Following a shift to more humid conditions, new settlements were established in northern Uganda and

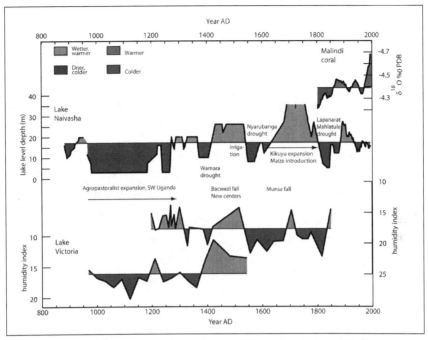

Figure 3 • Climate time series derived from analysis of lake sediments and corals, East Africa, together with historical information. Top: stable isotope variations in corals outside Malindi, Kenya, yielding relative temperature changes during the past 200 years (Cole et al. 2000). Middle: lake level changes inferred from sediments from Lake Naivasha, Kenya (Verschuren, Laird, & Cumming 2000). Bottom: humidity changes, inferred from diatom species composition in sediments from northwestern Lake Victoria, Uganda (Stager, Cumming, & Meeker 1997, 2003; Stager et al. 2005). Horizontal lines denote the average of the period. Peaks in the lake records indicate wetter conditions and troughs indicate drier conditions.

East Africa generally experienced a period of political stability and agricultural expansion. For example, a highly sophisticated irrigation system was developed in Engaruka in northern Tanzania, which today is a very dry region that cannot sustain a large population (Sutton 2004).

The next prolonged dry period that can be observed from the lake records is around 1600–1625 C.E. This climatic event appears related to a period that is known from oral traditions to have been one of extensive political instability, migrations, and famines, including the famine known as the *Nyarubanga* (1587–1589 C.E.) (Webster 1980). An extreme drought in the 1620s may have set processes in motion that later resulted in the fall of the capital at Munsa in Uganda in 1700 C.E. (Robertshaw & Taylor 2000).

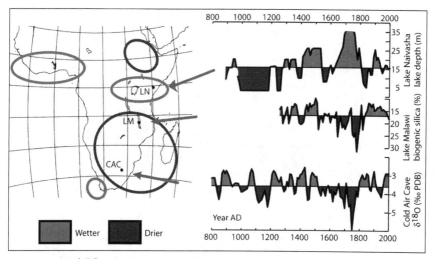

Figure 4 • Rainfall fluctuations in equatorial eastern and subtropical southern Africa, expressed as regional averaged standardized departure. Arrows show examples of inverse relationships for the twentieth century (Nicholson 2000).

The following period is characterized by humid conditions. In east Ukamba in Kenya, for example, large settlements develop, possibly encouraged by favorable environmental conditions, the Kikuyu people expand, and maize cultivation is initiated (Lamb, Darbyshire, & Verschuren 2003).

The third dry period indicated by the lake records is contemporary with a famine known as the *Lapanarat-Mahlatule* drought (1760–1840 c.e.) (Webster 1980). In this period, famine and short-term drought struck Ukamba and agropastoral production declined. One response to the harsh environmental conditions may have been trade in food staples between the Kamba and the Kikuyu (Jackson 1976).

Regional System

When considering the climatic records from southern and eastern Africa, on the one hand, and then comparing them with a third and geographically intermediate record, from Lake Malawi (Johnson et al. 2001), on the other, we find that the rainfall pattern in equatorial eastern Africa and subtropical southern Africa has often varied inversely (Figure 4) (Tyson et al. 2002). A similar pattern is evident in present-day weather. An El Niño situation induces wet conditions in East Africa but droughts in southern Africa. During La Niña, the opposite pattern prevails. Rainfall fluctuations throughout the twentieth

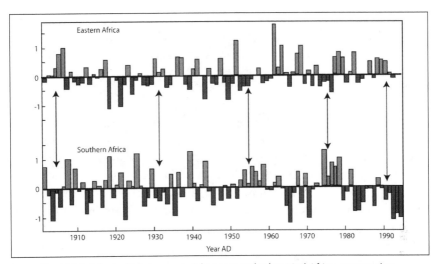

Figure 5 • Rainfall fluctuations in equatorial eastern and subtropical Africa, expressed as regional averaged standardized departure. Arrows show examples of inverse relationships for the twentieth century (Nicholson 2000).

century show the same pattern (Figure 5) (Nicholson 2000). The paleoclimate data reveal that this has been the case over long time periods throughout the past millennia.

It is thus tempting to speculate that this climatic gradient may have been one factor in the promotion of large-scale population movements from equatorial eastern Africa, at the time when the climate there was deteriorating, toward southern Africa, which was simultaneously experiencing favorable climatic conditions. This may have been the case at the end of the first millennium. The appearance of a new ceramic style (Huffman 1989) and linguistic affinities between some of the peoples of southern and eastern Africa have been interpreted as reflecting the first migration of Sotho-Tswana people into the southern region (Huffman & Herbert 1994; Iliffe 1995). The climatic gradient may have been one factor prompting the movement of populations from equatorial east Africa toward southern Africa.

Discussion

The climate system is a global system. The Earth receives heat from the sun, most of it at low latitudes. It is then redistributed to higher latitudes through a complex pattern of circulation via the atmosphere and the oceans. The causes behind climatic changes are multiple and include external factors, such as changes in astronomical cycles and in solar radiation, as well as internal factors, such as changes in atmospheric or oceanic circulation patterns, volcanism, and greenhouse gases. Some factors have a cyclic behavior, whereas others have a random character; some factors are well understood, whereas others are only poorly explained.

The climate system is thus a complex, dynamic global system that will continue to set the limits for life on Earth. Anthropogenically induced global warming will have major implications for future climate, but it is important to bear in mind that climate will no doubt change even without anthropogenic impact, on time-scales and magnitudes that do affect human life. With the increased understanding of regional and temporal patterns and causes behind climate processes, we are today faced with the challenging possibility of applying this knowledge in global physical planning as well as in local rural, coastal, and urban planning.

The data from southern and eastern Africa allow us to conclude that

1. Societal changes often coincide with climatic changes.
2. Climatic changes do not always result in societal changes—a stable society can survive severe climate conditions.
3. Climatic change is a common external trigger in societies suffering from internal instability. When periods of climate change coincide with periods of socioeconomic and political instability, this may result either in societal catastrophes or in new developments.
4. Climatic conditions that are favorable for agricultural or pastoral production have been an important factor in the rise of new and powerful centers of accumulation.
5. From the historical data, we can observe that adaptational strategies include
   a. flexibility in short- and long-term mobility and in the relocation of centers;
   b. flexibility in agricultural practices and in types of staple crops; and
   c. the possibility of controlling external trade.

To avoid having variations in climate trigger societal catastrophes, physical planners must consider the full range of climatic variability—natural as well as anthropogenic—in relation to social systems. For example, a society that is dependent on one type of crop, has limited access to trade, and is based on settlements on floodplains is more likely to be at risk than a society that has a choice of crops and good trading possibilities and that avoids building settlements in areas vulnerable to raised sea levels, heavy beach erosion, and so on. People at high risk in times of climatic change are, for instance, those living on floodplains, in coastal areas, and on mountains. The interconnected concerns with the world ecosystem and with social resilience thus constitute a complex challenge for decision makers, if sustainable development is to be achieved at global and local levels.

Note

1. This study has benefited from discussions within the SIDA-funded, Stockholm-based network PLATINA (People, Land and Time in Africa). The work presented here was funded by the Swedish Research Council. This chapter is a slightly revised version of a paper with the same title published in the journal *Environment, Development and Sustainability* (2006) 8:185–195. The paper is reprinted with kind permission from Springer Science and Business Media.

CHAPTER 9

World-Systems in the Biogeosphere: Urbanization, State Formation and Climate Change Since the Iron Age

CHRISTOPHER CHASE-DUNN, THOMAS D. HALL,
AND PETER TURCHIN

In Kurt Vonnegut's *The Sirens of Titan* a traveler from another solar system has crash-landed on one of the moons of Jupiter and is using his last bit of fuel to beam forces onto the Earth in order to send a message home. His efforts induce the Central Asian steppe nomads to behave in a way that causes successive Chinese states to build the Great Wall in the form of a script that appears from space as a rescue plea. This trope of distant forces affecting human history is an ironic tool in the hand of the fiction-smith who pokes fun at us for our hapless intentions. World-historians have hypothesized other powerful mechanisms by which macro-social processes may have been shaped by exogenous forces.

Since Ellsworth Huntington's *Climate and Civilization* there has been a growing literature on how spatial and temporal variations in rainfall, temperature, prevailing winds, and episodic weather extremes have influenced the course of history. Archeologists routinely invoke climate change as the explanation for social and cultural developments. As much more has been learned about the patterns of global weather these accounts have become more sophisticated. Brian Fagan's (1999) *Floods, Famines and Emperors: El Niño and the Fate of Civilizations* is a recent and compelling version. But instead of painting the humans as inert victims of powerful forces, Fagan argues that climate change has acted as the critical spur that pushed people to invent and implement radical new ways of interacting with nature and with one another.

Mike Davis's (2001) *Late Victorian Holocausts: El Niño Famines and the Making of the Third World* depicts how droughts caused by El Niños in the nineteenth century interacted with the rapid integration of peripheral regions into global markets in a context of colonialism and neocolonialism to bring about unprecedented huge famines and epidemic disease fatalities in Brazil, India, China, and the Philippines.

There is also an important literature about how human action may affect the climate. Much of this is focused on anthropogenic global warming in the twentieth century, but there is also a literature on how deforestation, irrigation, and other land-use patterns may have affected local weather in the past (for example, Chew 2001). A growing research tradition on urban ecology has discovered the phenomenon of the "urban heat island," an example of anthropogenic effects on the local weather (Gallo & Ower n.d.).

Here we present a theoretical and empirical framework for the study of human societies and their interactions with the biogeosphere on a millennial time scale. We begin by noting that the world-systems approach focuses on human interaction networks, which enables us to examine systemic combinations of very different kinds of societies. This makes it possible to study multicultural systems and core-periphery relations as cases that can display dynamics of social evolution. All world-systems display oscillations of expansion and contraction, or pulsations. These waves of expansion, now called globalization, have, in the last two centuries, created a single, integrated intercontinental political economy in which all national societies are strongly linked. This chapter investigates the pulsations of regional interaction networks (world-systems) in Afroeurasia over the past 3,000 years. The purpose is to examine the causes of a remarkable synchrony that emerged between East Asia and the distant West Asian/Mediterranean region but did not involve the intermediate South Asian region. The hypothesized causes of this synchrony are climate change, epidemics, trade cycles, and the incursions of Central Asian steppe nomads. This chapter formulates a strategy of data acquisition, system modeling, and hypothesis testing that can allow us to discover which of these causes were the most important in producing synchrony as the Afroeurasian world-system came into being.

One limitation of regional analyses has been the tendency to define regions in terms of homogeneous attributes, either natural or social. A major problem with both the civilizationist and cultural-area approaches is the assumption that homogeneity is a good approach for bounding evolving social systems. Even sophisticated approaches that examine distributions of spatial characteristics statistically must make quite arbitrary choices in order to specify regional boundaries on this basis (for example, Burton et al. 1996). We argue that heterogeneity rather than homogeneity has long been a pervasive aspect of human social systems. The effort to bound systems as homogeneous regions obscures this important fact. Spatial distributions of homogeneous characteristics do not bound separate social systems. Indeed, social heterogeneity is often produced by interaction.

The relationship between natural regions and human interaction networks has been important in cultural ecology, which stresses the ways in which local ecological factors condition sociocultural institutions. While useful for understanding small-scale systems, it is much less compelling in large world-systems because of the scale of interaction networks and the development of technologies that allow imposition of external logics on local ecologies. Some social evolutionists have argued that this means that social institutions have become progressively less ecologically determined (for example, Lenski, Nolan, & Lenski 1995). Rather, we argue that what has happened is that ecological constraints have now become global (Chase-Dunn & Hall 1998).

Spatially Bounding World-Systems

The world-systems perspective emerged as a theoretical approach for modeling and interpreting the expansion and transformation of the European system as it engulfed the globe over the past five hundred years (Wallerstein 2004). Chase-Dunn and Hall (1997, 2000, 2002) have modified the basic world-systems concepts to make them useful for a comparative study of very different kinds of social systems. Their scope of comparison includes very small intergroup networks composed of sedentary foragers (for instance, Burch 2005; Chase-Dunn & Mann 1998) as well as larger regional systems containing chiefdoms, early states, agrarian empires, and the contemporary global political economy.

The comparative world-systems perspective is designed to be general enough to allow comparisons among quite different systems. Chase-Dunn and Hall (1997) argue that different kinds of interactions often have distinct spatial characteristics and degrees of importance in different sorts of systems. They hold that the question of the degree of systemic interaction between two locales precedes the question of core-periphery relations, and that it is fundamentally an empirical issue rather than an assumption.

Spatially bounding world-systems necessarily must proceed from a locale-centric rather than a whole-system focus. This is because all human societies, even nomadic hunter-gatherers, interact importantly with neighboring societies. However, interaction networks, while always intersocietal, have not always been global. When transportation and communications occurred only over short distances, the world-systems that affected people were small.

Thus, Chase-Dunn and Hall use the notion of "fall-off" of effects over space to bound the networks of interaction that importantly impinge on any focal locale. The world-system of which any locality is a part includes those peoples whose actions in production, communication, warfare, alliance, and trade have a large and interactive impact on that locality. It is also important to distinguish between endogenous systemic interaction processes and exogenous impacts that may importantly change a system but are not part of that system. The fact that maize diffused from Mesoamerica to eastern North America need not mean that the two areas were part of the same world-system. Similarly, virgin soil epidemics are not necessarily evidence of a system. Interactions must be two-way and regularized to be socially systemic.

Chase-Dunn and Hall (1997) identify several different kinds of networks with different spatial scales:

1. Information Networks (INs)
2. Prestige Goods Networks (PGNs)
3. Political/Military Networks (PMNs)
4. Bulk Goods Networks (BGNs)

The largest networks are those in which information travels. Information is light and travels a long way, even in systems based on down-the-line interaction. These are termed Information Networks (INs). A usually somewhat smaller interaction network is based on the exchange of prestige goods or luxuries that have a high value/weight ratio. These are called Prestige Goods Networks (PGNs). The next interaction network comprises polities that are in alliance or at war with one another. These are called Political/Military Networks (PMNs). The smallest networks are those based on a division of labor in the production of basic everyday necessities such as food and raw materials. These are Bulk Goods Networks (BGNs). Figure 1 illustrates how these interaction networks are spatially related in many world-systems.

The spatial characteristics of these networks clearly depend on many things: the costs of transportation and communications, and whether interaction is only with neighbors or whether regularized long-distance trips are being made. These factors affect all kinds of interaction; thus the relative size of networks is expected to approximate the sequence shown in Figure 1. As an educated guess, for instance, we would suppose that fall-off in the PMN generally occurs after two or three indirect links.

Chase-Dunn and Hall (1997) distinguish between two types of core-periphery relations: core-periphery differentiation and core-periphery hierarchy. Core-periphery differentiation exists when two societies are in systemic interaction with each other and one of these has higher population density and/or greater complexity than the other. Core-periphery hierarchy exists when one society dominates or exploits another. These two types of relations

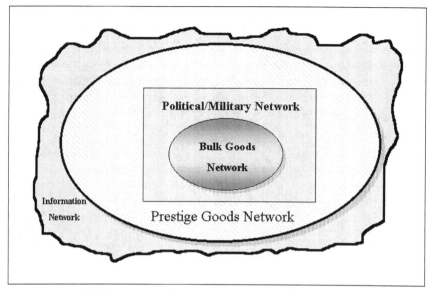

Figure 1 • Nested interaction networks.

often go together, but there are important instances of reversal (for example, the less dense, less complex Central Asian steppe nomads who exploited agrarian China [see Barfield 1989; Kradin 2002]). Hence this distinction is both theoretical and empirical. The question of core-periphery relations needs to be asked at each level of interaction designated above. It is more difficult to project power over long distances, and thus one would not expect to find strong core-periphery hierarchies at the level of Information or Prestige Goods Networks. Figure 2 illustrates a core-periphery hierarchy.

Core-periphery hierarchies are important in processes of social evolution because semiperipheral societies, those that are intermediate between core regions and peripheral hinterlands, are fertile locations for institutional innovations and frequently are the key actors that transform the developmental logic of world-systems, called "semiperipheral development" (Chase-Dunn & Hall 1997, Chapter 5). Semiperipheral marcher chiefdoms have conquered more senior core chiefdoms to form larger and more centralized complex chiefdoms, as have the better-known semiperipheral marcher states (for instance, Chin China, Assyria, Rome, and Islamic Arabia). Semiperipheral capitalist city-states (the Phoenicians, the Italian city-states, the Hanseatic cities, Malakka) were agents of commercialization in the interstices of tributary empires. In the modern world-

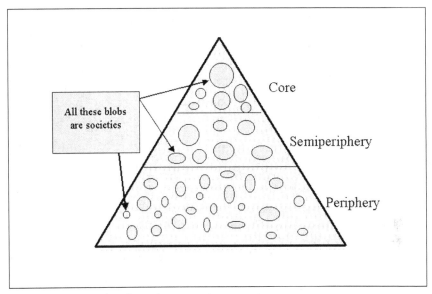

Figure 2 • Core-periphery hierarchy.

system, it was the semiperipheral and capitalist Dutch republic, then England, and then the United States that rose to hegemony and further globalized the world economy. Semiperipheral development is still an important pattern in the twentieth and twenty-first centuries (Chase-Dunn & Boswell 2002).

Recently Turchin (2003b:62) has pointed out that not all semiperipheries are "hotbeds" of marcher state development. Focusing specifically on the territorial dynamics of states, he has shown that large agrarian states ("empires") almost always originate in areas where frontiers of previously existing empires coincide with intense ethnic or cultural ("civilizational") fault lines. Two typical situations can be distinguished. One is a frontier between a large empire and a stateless (but not necessarily chiefdomless) hinterland. Such tribal war zones abutting imperial frontiers are notorious for their ability to produce aggressive expansionist states (examples: the Roman Empire and the Germans, the succession of Chinese empires and steppe nomads). The second situation is a frontier zone between two empires dominated by different exclusionary religions. For example, a number of European empires originated from the frontier between Islam and Christianity in Europe and Asia Minor (Castile-Spain, Austro-Hungary, Muscovy-Russia, and the Ottoman empires).

World-System Cycles: Rise-and-Fall and Pulsations

Comparative research reveals that all world-systems exhibit cyclical processes: the rise and fall of large polities and pulsations in the spatial extent and intensity of trade networks. Rise and fall corresponds to changes in the centralization of political-military power in a set of polities—an "international" system. It is a question of the relative size and distribution of power across a set of interacting polities.

All world-systems in which there are hierarchical polities experience a cycle in which relatively larger polities grow in power and size and then decline. This applies to interchiefdom systems as well as interstate systems, to systems composed of empires, and to the modern rise and fall of hegemonic core powers (for example, Britain and the United States). Although very egalitarian and small-scale systems such as the sedentary foragers of northern California (Burch 2005; Chase-Dunn & Mann 1998) do not display a cycle of rise and fall, they do experience pulsations.

All systems, including very small and egalitarian ones, exhibit cyclical expansions and contractions in the spatial extent and intensity of exchange networks. Different kinds of trade (bulk versus prestige goods) usually have different spatial characteristics and may exhibit different temporal sequences of expansion and contraction. Again, this is an empirical issue. In the modern global system large trade networks cannot get spatially larger, because they are already global in extent, but they can get denser and more intense relative to smaller networks of exchange. Much of what has been called globalization is simply the intensification of larger interaction networks relative to the intensity of smaller ones. Research on trade and investment shows that there have been two recent waves of integration: one in the last half of the nineteenth century and the most recent since World War II (Chase-Dunn, Kawano, & Brewer 2000). Whether rise-and-fall and pulsations are correlated in different types of world-systems is also an empirical issue.

Chase-Dunn and Hall (1997) have contended that the causes of rise and fall differ depending on the predominant mode of accumulation. One big difference between the rise and fall of empires and the rise and fall of modern hegemons is in the degree of centralization achieved within the core. Tributary systems alternate back and forth between a structure of multiple and competing core states, on the one hand, and core-wide (or nearly core-wide) empires, on the other. The modern interstate system experiences the rise and fall of hegemons, but these never take over the other core states to form a core-wide empire. This is the case because modern hegemons are pursuing a capitalist, rather than a tributary, form of accumulation.

Analogously, rise and fall works somewhat differently in interchiefdom systems because the institutions that facilitate the extraction of resources from distant groups are less fully developed in chiefdom systems. David G. Anderson (1994) has examined the rise and fall of Mississippian chiefdoms in the Savannah River valley. This cyclical process begins with a chiefly polity extending control over adjacent chiefdoms and establishing a two-tiered hierarchy of administration. At a later point, these regionally centralized chiefly polities disintegrate back toward a system of smaller and less hierarchical polities.

Chiefs have relied more on hierarchical control of kinship relations, ritual, and imports of prestige goods than have the rulers of true states. These chiefly techniques of power are all highly dependent on normative integration and ideological consensus. States developed specialized organizations for extracting resources that chiefdoms lacked: standing armies and bureaucracies. States and empires in tributary world-systems were more dependent on the projection of armed force over great distances than modern hegemonic core states have been. The development of commodity production and mechanisms of financial control, as well as further development of bureaucratic administrative techniques, has allowed modern hegemons to extract resources from faraway places with much less overhead cost.

The development of new techniques of exerting power has made core-periphery relations ever more important for competition among core powers and has altered the way in which the rise-and-fall process works in other respects. Chase-Dunn and Hall (1997:Chapter 6; see also 2000, 2002) have argued that population growth in interaction with the environment and changes in productive technology and social structure produce social transformations that are marked by cycles and periodic jumps. This is because the parameters of each world-system oscillate owing both to internal instabilities and environmental fluctuations. Occasionally, on an economic upswing, people solve systemic problems in a new way that allows for substantial expansion. We want to explain such expansions, evolutionary changes, and collapses in terms of systemic logic. That is the point of comparing world-systems.

The multi-scalar regional method of bounding world-systems as nested interaction networks outlined above is complementary to a multi-scalar temporal analysis of the kind suggested by Fernand Braudel. Temporal depth, the *longue durée*, needs to be combined with analyses of short-run and middle-run processes to allow us to fully understand social change. A key example of this is Jared Diamond's (1997) study of the original distribution of zoological and botanical resources. The geographical distribution of those species that could be easily and profitably domesticated explains a significant part of the variation regarding which world-systems were able to expand and incorporate

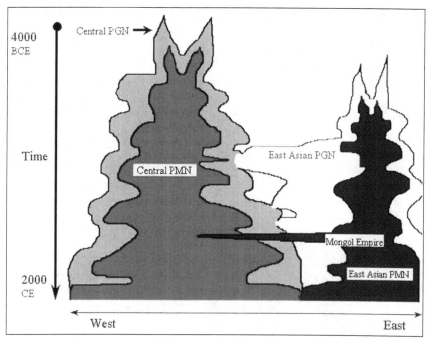

Figure 3 • East-West pulsations and merger.

other world-systems over the millennia. Diamond contends that the diffusion of domesticated plant and animal species occurs more quickly in the latitudinal dimension (East-West) than in the longitudinal dimension (North-South). Thus, domesticated species spread quickly to Europe and East Asia from West Asia, whereas North-South diffusion in both Africa and the Americas was much slower.

The diagram in Figure 3 depicts the process of integration of the East Asian and the West Asian-Mediterranean systems. Both the PGNs and the PMNs are shown, as are the pulsations and rise-and-fall sequences. The PGNs were intermittently linked and then more permanently joined. The Mongol conquerors linked the PMNs briefly in the thirteenth century, but the Eastern and Western PMNs were not permanently joined until the Europeans and Americans established Asian treaty ports in the nineteenth century.

Synchronization of Empires, Cities, and Demographic Waves

Earlier studies have used data on the sizes of both cities and empires to examine different regional interaction systems and the hypothesis that regions distant from one another were experiencing synchronous cycles of growth and decline (for example, Chase-Dunn & Manning 2002; Chase-Dunn, Manning, & Hall 2000). Frederick Teggart's (1939) path-breaking world-historical study of temporal correlations between events on the edges of the Roman and Han Empires argued the thesis that incursions by Central Asian steppe nomads were the key to East-West synchrony. An early study of city-size distributions in Afroeurasia (Chase-Dunn & Hall 1997:222–223) found an apparent synchrony between changes in city-size distributions and the growth of largest cities in East Asia and West Asia-North Africa over a period of 2,000 years. That led us to examine data on the territorial sizes of empires for similar synchrony, which we also found (Chase-Dunn, Manning, & Hall 2000). Chase-Dunn and Manning (2002) have reexamined the city-size data using constant regions rather than PMNs to see if the East-West synchronous city growth hypothesis holds when the units that are compared are somewhat different. Their results confirm the existence of East-West city-growth synchrony.

Here we present a new analysis of East-West synchrony that uses overall population estimates compiled by McEvedy and Jones (1978). They note a synchrony between East Asia and the Mediterranean area in periods of regional demographic growth and decline during the late first millennium B.C.E. and during the first millennium C.E. Interestingly, McEvedy and Jones (1978:345–346) reject the idea that climate change may have caused this synchrony in favor of a hypothesis of parallel and connected technological and organizational change.

We have computed the partial correlations, controlling for year to remove the trend, of population levels from 1000 B.C.E. to 1800 C.E. among three regions. We stop at 1800 C.E. because the trend becomes exponential after that and would drown out earlier, middle-range variations. What we want to know is whether or not the middle-term ups and downs—what we have called growth versus decline phases—are synchronous or not. We examine four regions: East Asia, South Asia, West Asia-Mediterranean, and Europe.[1] These are the same constant regions that Chase-Dunn and Manning (2002) used to study the synchrony of city growth versus decline phases.

Table 1 shows the partial correlation coefficients of population change estimates for four Old World regions. These have been de-trended in two ways to allow us to look for synchronous growth-decline oscillations across regions. We eliminate the years after 1800 C.E., when most of the regions were undergoing geometric growth rates, and compute the interregional correlations as a partial correlation, controlling for year, which should remove the long-term trend.[2]

The results in Table 1 are somewhat surprising. There are statistically significant partial correlations among all the regions despite our efforts to remove

Table 1 Interregional partial correlations of population change, controlling for year, 1000 B.C.E.–1800 C.E. (population estimates from McEvedy & Jones 1978)

	West Asia-Mediterranean	East Asia	South Asia	Europe
West Asia-Mediterranean	1	.81 (26)	.60 (26)	.79 (26)
East Asia		1	.88 (26)	.95 (26)
South Asia			1	.92 (26)
Europe				1

the long-term trend. The correlation between East Asia and the West Asian-Mediterranean region is higher than that for cross-regional partial correlations of either city or empire size (.81), but it is not as high as some of the other coefficients in Table 1. Curiously, the correlations between Europe and both East Asia and South Asia are very high (.95, .92). The lowest correlation is between West Asia and South Asia (.60), and the correlation between Europe and the West Asia-Mediterranean region is also relatively low, considering that these two "regions" overlap geographically.

It is possible that these high correlations are partly due to the rather coarse temporal resolution of the population estimates that we have extracted from graphs produced by McEvedy and Jones (1978). Our data set is organized in one-hundred-year intervals, a temporal resolution that smooths out most of the growth/decline fluctuations that we are trying to study. Unfortunately, McEvedy and Jones do not present enough detail about the evidence they used to produce their graphs. Figure 4 presents the demographic data in graphical form for the same four regions.

Examination of Figure 4 shows both the long-term trends and the shorter-term variations, though these have been smoothed by the low temporal resolution just discussed. What we see is a long hump that starts slowly in 1000 B.C.E. and winds back down to a low point around 600 C.E. in all the regions except South Asia. In South Asia the slump does not appear. This is the East-West synchrony noted by McEvedy and Jones. After about 600 C.E., all the regions go up again, but then the patterns partly diverge. The East Asian rise is early and steeper. All the regions except South Asia display a partly synchronous decline after the twelfth century. East Asia has another decline in the seventeenth century, and this is also a period of slow growth in Europe and decline in West Asia, but South Asia continues to grow. The West Asian-Mediterranean region does not partake in the rapid population growth that sweeps the other regions after the fifteenth century.

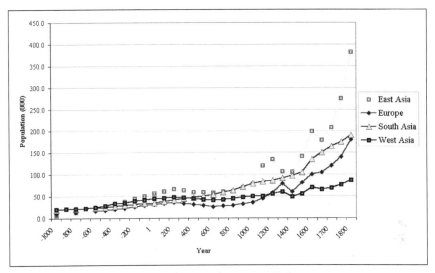

Figure 4 • Regional population growth (McEvedy & Jones 1978).

A rather similar result is obtained by a different approach to the data presented by McEvedy and Jones. First we plot everything on the log-scale, which makes the patterns much easier to see. The log-plot (Figure 5a) makes it clear that the South Asian "data" are mostly extrapolation, being very close to a straight line on a log-scale. Of course, all McEvedy and Jones's data are to a certain degree extrapolation, but it looks like the South Asian data are the most conspicuous case.

We do not want to simply correlate the population numbers between different regions directly, because they are all affected by the same long-term, evolutionary trend. Rather, we have chosen to difference each series, that is calculate $\Delta Y - Y(t+1) - Y(t)$, where $Y(t)$ is log-transformed population number at time t. This is a particularly appropriate procedure in this case, because it yields something known as the *realized per capita rate of change*, the standard quantity that population ecologists calculate. Plotting these differenced log-transformed numbers (rates of change) produces Figure 5b. Cross-correlation coefficients among different regions are given in Table 2.

The results confirm the initial impression that South Asia tends to fluctuate on its own (with all the caveats about these data), whereas the rest are cross-correlated with one another. An additional observation is that the highest correlations are between West Asia and Europe or East Asia, respectively, which makes sense, given the central location of West Asia. Of all regions, West Asia is also the most correlated with South Asia (although the correlation is not quite statistically significant).

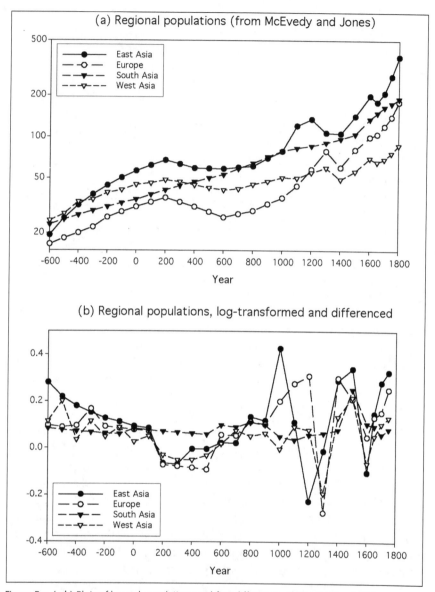

Figure 5 • (a-b) Plots of logged populations and first differences of logs (McEvedy & Jones 1978).

Table 2   Correlations among logged and differenced population scores (boldface italic indicates those significant at the $P < 0.05$ level)

	East Asia	Europe	South Asia	West Asia
East Asia	1	*0.465*	0.247	*0.570*
Europe	*0.465*	1	0.139	*0.767*
South Asia	0.247	0.139	1	0.372
West Asia	*0.570*	*0.767*	0.372	1

The "Moran Effect" in Population Ecology

The cyclical aspects of climate change lead easily to hypotheses about how these may cause certain cyclical (or at least sequential) phenomena in human affairs. This is especially the case when cycles from distant regions appear to be synchronized. Population ecologists model population dynamics of species within adjacent and distant "patches" to explain how predator-prey relationships, food availability, and migration affect the cycles of population growth and decline. P.A.P. Moran's (1953) study of the population cycles of the Canadian lynx led him to formulate what has become known as the "Moran effect"—the idea that synchronized exogenous shocks to local oscillating systems will cause them to come into synchrony even when the exogenous shocks do not themselves display much periodicity (see Chapter 5 and Turchin & Hall 2003 for a more detailed account). Population ecologists usually have climate change in mind as the most likely source of exogenous shocks.

The important implications of the Moran effect for our problem of the causes of synchrony are that any exogenous shock can bring oscillating systems into synchrony even if the temporal features of the exogenous variable are completely different from the temporality of the local oscillating systems. A meteor impact could reset local systems and put them into synchrony. Turchin and Hall (2003) point out that the best situation for the empirical study of synchrony requires exact measurement and fine temporal resolution, and also many oscillations and many different cases of oscillating systems in order to disentangle different plausible causes of synchrony. These are daunting requisites for our single case of East-West synchrony. We argue, however, that sufficiently accurate and temporally fine data can be feasibly assembled to make it possible to sort out the major causes of East-West synchrony.

Comparable other instances of distant systems that come into weak contact with one another can be found. Within the Old World, the Mesopotamian and Egyptian core regions were interacting with one another by means of prestige goods exchange from about 3000 B.C.E. until their PMNs merged in 1500 B.C.E. Chase-Dunn and Hall (2001) have already examined this case for synchronicity, but have not found it, although the data on Bronze Age city and empire sizes are crude with regard to temporality and accuracy.

The Moran effect implies that synchrony occurs easily because a single exogenous impact that resets systems with similar endogenous oscillations will bring them into synchrony. But if this is true we would expect to find more synchrony than we have found up to now. Population ecology also usually finds greater synchrony in patches that are close to one another than in those that are more distant, but this is not what we find in Afroeurasia. The South Asian system, intermediate between East and West, seems to be marching to its own drummer.

Modeling Climate Change Effects on Population

Patrick Galloway (1986) models the way in which climate change can affect human population growth. He argues that it was climate change that caused the synchrony of demographic cycles noted by McEvedy and Jones (1978). Galloway's model is depicted in Figure 6.

Galloway's model is entirely plausible and could easily be amended to include effects on city growth and empire-formation. But for this model to account for synchrony across regions the changes in temperature (and other climatological variables) would need to also be synchronous, or else there would have to at least be an initial strong climatological shift that affected all the regions during the same period. The only way to sort this out is to obtain indicators of climate change in or near the regions we are studying in the relevant time periods. Knowledge about the climate change record in Greenland will not settle the question, because despite global connections, climate change is ultimately local. Our effort to gather the relevant climate change data has only just begun.

There are a few other questions regarding this model that need to be attended to. On the one hand, where agriculture is marginal and the frost-free season approximates the growing season, such as in many mountainous areas, slight cooling would make agriculture impossible, at least until crops with shorter growing season are introduced. On the other hand, slight warming would make more land available and existing land more productive. This would enhance food production and increase populations. Where conditions are volatile—again not unusual in mountainous areas or desert fringes—there could be considerable fluctuation. As Turchin (2003a) argues, such conditions themselves created strong pressures for change and experimentation. In other

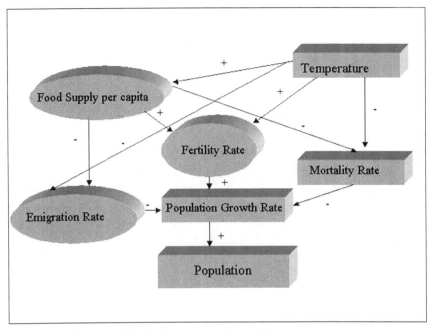

Figure 6 • Galloway's (1986) climate and population model.

areas, such as much of Africa, West Asia, and South Asia, slight increases in temperature would have the opposite effect. A rise in average temperature would make agriculture impossible, whereas a slight cooling would make more land available and available land more reliable. Thus, the effects of climate change depend on what kind of change and on preexisting marginal conditions.

This conclusion suggests another set of reasons why marginal areas that are frontiers or boundaries between biome regimes are hotbeds of change. Volatile conditions force populations in such areas to be more flexible. Also, such areas often serve as a "coal miner's canary," signaling approaching climate changes already when they are quite small.

A Comprehensive Model of the Causes of Interregional Synchrony

We can now propose a comprehensive model of the plausible causes of East-West synchrony. The purpose of complex causal modeling is to allow us to discover the relative strengths of different causative mechanisms by examining the logical implications of the posited relations and operant parameters. Figure 7 depicts a complex causal model that contains the hypothesized factors resulting in the East-West synchrony discussed above. This model can be translated into a

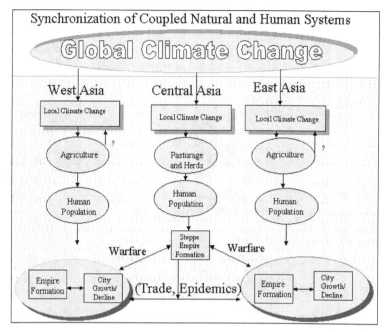

Figure 7 • Comprehensive East-West synchrony model.

complex system of structural equations and estimated parameters that allow us to examine the conditions under which causation can lead to synchrony. In future work, we plan to combine this theoretical exercise with an effort to improve our empirical knowledge of the population sizes of cities, the territorial sizes of empires, and climate change over the past 3,000 years (cf. Pasciuti & Chase-Dunn 2002). By approaching the problem through both induction and deduction we hope to be able to estimate the relative strengths of the different possible causes of East-West synchrony. The outcome should be a better understanding of the way in which human social systems have interacted with biological and geological processes in world history.

Notes

1. The West Asia/Mediterranean region includes the whole Mediterranean littoral so as to encompass the whole interactive city system that originated in West Asia and spread to the Mediterranean with Etruscan, Greek, and Phoenician migration and the emergence of the Latin cities. Thus Europe and the West Asian-Mediterranean region are geographically overlapping.

2. De-trending with a partial correlation for year assumes that the temporal relationship is linear, whereas it may be an accelerating trend. It is possible that this linear de-trending does not remove the entire millennial trend.

CHAPTER 10

Eurasian Transformations: Mobility, Ecological Change, and the Transmission of Social Institutions in the Third Millennium and the Early Second Millennium B.C.E.

KRISTIAN KRISTIANSEN

In this article I explore the origin and nature of the social and economic processes that in later prehistory transformed the Eurasian continent from a large but enclosed marginal region into a highly dynamic and mobile interaction zone connecting eastern and western Asia. The basic components in this process were the adoption of a nucleated family structure suited for expansion, incorporation, and the transmission of mobile wealth, in combination with the formation of an agropastoral economy based on herding, wagons, and mobile property. This led to an ecological transformation that created open steppelike environments from northwestern Europe to east of the Urals. By the end of the second millennium B.C.E. these historical processes had transformed Eurasia into a vast interaction zone for mobile, warlike pastoral nomads, linking eastern and western Asia to a common historical pulse.

Mobility and Ecological Transformation

Today it can be stated with some certainty that the third and early second millennia B.C.E. was a period of major social change over wide areas in Eurasia (Kuzmina 2002; Sherratt 1997), and further that this change was in part linked to a complex pattern of interaction, ranging from travel and small-scale population movements to large-scale migrations. It was based on the formation of a new economy and a concomitant social and religious order with a tremendous capacity for expansion and incorporation. Regional series of C14-dating define the beginning of this major expansion within a very narrow time span during the early part of the third millennium B.C.E. This interpretation is supported by new evidence from sciences such as ecology and metallurgy.

Recent developments in strontium isotope analysis of teeth and bone are producing new compelling evidence of the movement of individuals in later prehistory (Ezzo, Johnson, & Price 1997; Grupe et al. 1997; Price, Grupe, & Schröter 1998; Montgomery, Budd, & Evans 2000; Price, Manzanilla, & Middleton 2000). Also, physical anthropological evidence testifies to a change of population in some regions, such as Denmark and Poland in the third millennium B.C.E. (Dzieduszycka-Machnik & Machnik 1990; Petersen 1993). A population taller than previous Neolithic peoples enters the scene and accounts for a general rise in population from the late third millennium onward. In Denmark, the average height of males increases by 7 cm from the Megalithic period of the late fourth millennium to the early Bronze Age of the late third millennium B.C.E.

A second area of new research concerns the ecological and economic transformations taking place in the steppe and forest steppe regions. Here recent paleobotanical research and C14-datings of buried soils under barrows have revealed the early formation of grasslands and steppe environments, and their systematic exploitation (Anthony 1998; Kremenetski 2003; Shislina 2000, 2003). During the third millennium B.C.E., the Yamna tribal groups (2800–2350 B.C.E.) practiced small-scale pastoral herding, moving locally between summer and winter pastures, using four-wheeled vehicles. Rich grasslands and higher humidity than today supported this economic transformation and its widespread geographical expansion, even into the Balkans and the Carpathians and Hungary, but also toward the east (Ecsedy 1994; Kalicz 1998; Kuzmina 2002). Figure 1 illustrates the two major cultural complexes in the early third-millennium expansion of pastoral farmers in the western steppe and temperate Europe: the Yamna groups around the Black Sea, and the Corded Ware/Battle Axe and Single Grave Cultures in central and northern Europe.

This was a pioneering phase of expansion. Wooded areas were still preserved in the river valleys, as evidenced in burials and wagons (Shislina 2001:357ff). The Catacomb Culture groups (2500–1900 B.C.E.) saw the further development of a pastoral economy based on sedentary settlements and long-distance herding and trade. It corresponded to the formation of a more hierarchical, metal-producing society with a wide distribution, also toward the eastern steppe. Periodical ecological stress and soil destruction, caused by overgrazing, is evidenced. Seasonal migrations and herding now extended across the whole ecological zone (Shislina 2001:259f). Although one can hardly generalize from these discoveries in the Kalmyk steppe, they suggest a widespread development when we consider the similarity of the archeological record throughout the steppe region.[1] It implies that, by the beginning of the second millennium

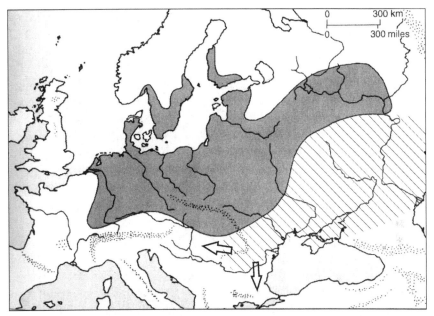

Figure 1 • Distribution of the new agropastoral economies with family barrows during the third millennium B.C.E. To the west we find the Corded Ware/Single Grave Culture, and in the Pontic steppe we find the Yamna Culture. Together they formed a common cultural complex that shared social and religious institutions, and possibly also varieties of Proto-Indo-European languages.

B.C.E., pastoral economies were widespread in the Pontic zone (Anthony 1998). The osteological evidence confirms that cattle were dominant (more than 50 percent), especially big-horned cattle, followed by horse and sheep. Sheepherding was linked to textile production for clothing and cloth, which played an increasingly important role in the new Bronze Age economies of the third and second millennia B.C.E. (Shislina, Golikov, & Orfinskaya 2000). Pigs, however, played an insignificant role, because they need forests to roam in (Chernykh, Antipina, & Lebedeva 1998:Abb. 10–11; Morales & Antipina 2003:Table 22.3). What we see is a development from localized herding to true pastoralism with sedentary centres of production that unfolded and reached a climax after 2000 B.C.E., for instance, in the Sintashta Culture (Zdanovich & Zdanovich 2002) and the Srubnaya/Timber Grave Culture. Agriculture played a minor but increasing role through time as supplementary production (see Bunyatyan 2003; Gershkovich 2003; Morales & Antipina 2003; Otroschenko 2003; Pashkevich 2003).

Thus, from the Pontic region to the Balkans, central and northern Europe, the third millennium B.C.E. saw the expansion of a new type of agropastoral economies. These societies shared many traits in economy and burial ritual, such as the construction of *tumuli* over graves and the predominance of individual burials (Yamna, Corded Ware, Battle-Axe, and Catacomb Cultures). They also employed ox-drawn, four-wheeled wagons (Burmeister 2004). Recent paleobotanical evidence has made it clear that the third millennium B.C.E. represents the formation of open steppelike environments that apparently served as pasture for grazing animals from the Urals to northwestern Europe (Andersen 1995, 1998; Kremenetski 2003; Odgaard 1994). The mobile lifestyle is exemplified by the use of mats, tents, and wagons, which are sometimes found in burials (Ecsedy 1994). Some have called this a "barbarization" or decline of the Neolithic (Kruk & Milisauskas 1999; Rassamakin 1999:125 ff, 154). It followed after a period in the fifth to fourth millennia, when stratified societies with copper metallurgy were developing in the Balkan-Carpathian region, only to collapse or be transformed during the later part of the fourth millennium B.C.E. (Chernykh 1992:Chapter 2; Sherratt 2003). Stretching from the Romanian Black Sea coast to the north-east of the Dniester-Dnieper Rivers, the proto-urban communities of the Tripolje Culture during this period created a barrier toward the west. It represents what Mallory has called the first of three fault-lines to be passed in order to explain the expansion of Indo-European languages. These proto-urban communities, which also employed some form of primitive script (tokens), were organized around fortified settlements with two-storey houses arranged in concentric circles, the largest settlements extending 100–400 ha and containing 5,000–15,000 people (Videjko 1995). Each community with satellite settlements would hold some 6,000–20,000 people, and a local group of several communities between 10,000 and 35,000 people. Their interaction with steppe communities and later abandonment or transformation into pastoral groups from the late fourth millennium onward is still a matter of debate (Chapman 2002; Dergachev 2000; Manzura 2005), but it opened up for a westward expansion of the new social and economic practice into central and northern Europe.

Approximately at the same time, during the middle to late fourth millennia B.C.E., the Caucasian region rose to prominence as a metallurgical center of production, and from 3200 to 1800 B.C.E. there developed a Circum-Pontic metallurgical province, including Anatolia, that received most of its metal from the huge mines in Caucasia (Chernykh 1992; Chernykh, Avilova, & Orlovskaya 2002). Around the centers of production and distribution in the northern Caucasus there emerged a series of stratified societies, burying their dead in impressive and richly furnished *kurgans* (Rezepkin 2000). The

Maikop Culture, as it is called, integrated local and foreign influences from northern Mesopotamia (Stein 1999). Sometimes they would contain imports (for example, decorated silver vessels) not even present in the centers, such as the famous Maikop burials from the late fourth millennium Uruk expansion (Chernykh 1992:Chapters 3–5, Figures 17 and 31; Sherratt 1997). In some chiefly burials we find a Mesopotamian royal symbol, a copper arm ring with protruding ends, daggers, and swords (Rezepkin 2000:Tafel 13ff.). Here, in the chiefly *kurgans*, we find the earliest four-wheeled wagons from the mid-fourth millennium B.C.E. (Trifonov 2004). The new social and economic organization was also adopted in the southern steppe from 3000 B.C.E. onward, where it proved highly dynamic.

The third area of new research is in the field of metallurgy and absolute chronology. E. N. Chernykh and his colleagues have carried out a long-term research project that has made it possible to identify different metallurgical provinces during the third and second millennia B.C.E. (Chernykh 1992; Chernykh, Avilova, & Orlovskaya 2002; Chernykh & Kuzminykh 1989). In recent years, work has been conducted in collaboration with Spanish colleagues to detail this evidence, especially the ecological impact of large-scale mining in the region (Díaz del Rio et al. 2006; Chernykh, Antipina, & Lebedeva 1998). The mining area of Kargaly in the Urals produced huge amounts of copper during the Bronze Age (an estimated 150,000 tons), which was distributed over the whole steppe region (Chernykh 2002). Deforestation was an immediate result but must have been compensated for by imports of wood from further away. Huge smelting and production sites in the mountains are packed with cattle bones from meat consumption. It suggests an intensive production and exchange of food and metal, indicating a widespread division of labor between steppe societies and mining societies. Recent paleobotanical research has demonstrated that the area was completely deforested already during the Bronze Age (Diaz del Rio et al. 2006). It is thus reasonable to assume that much of the copper was distributed in raw form and later remelted at centers such as Sintashta.

In the beginning of the second millennium B.C.E., from about 1800 B.C.E., the Circum-Pontic Metallurgical System expanded geographically to include the whole of Eurasia (Chernykh 1992:Chapter 7; Chernykh, Avilova, & Orlovskaya 2002). It was based on highly stratified centers of production and distribution such as Sintashta, with a ruling warrior elite using two-wheeled chariots and living inside heavily fortified settlements, from which they controlled the region. It also included a widespread adaptation of metallurgical know-how, and the opening of new mines. The Andronovo Culture (Figure 2) represented this eastward expansion of the new political economy, including two-wheeled

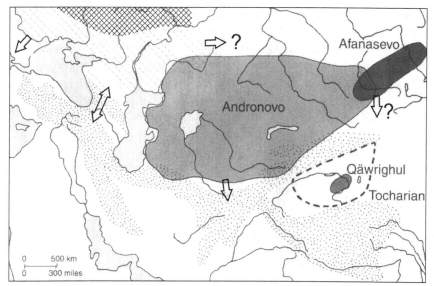

Figure 2 • Distribution of mobile Bronze Age cultures of the Eurasian steppe in the late third and early second millennium B.C.E. The map shows the distribution of the Andronovo Culture of the early second millennium B.C.E., and also some isolated late third-millennium satellite expansions toward the east, resulting in the Afanasevo Culture and the Bronze Age cultures of the Tarim Basin to the southeast, forming a bridge to China. I have added the Yamna culture to the west, from which the Andronovo Culture originated, through the transformations that took place in the Sintashta Culture east of the Urals.

chariots (Kuzmina 2000; Mallory 1998) and corresponds to Mallory's second fault line. To the south, the Andronovo Culture bordered the desert oasis cultures of more complex societies and started to interact with them (Hiebert 2002). This cultural border represented Mallory's third fault line, which was crossed sometime during the early second millennium B.C.E. (Shislina & Hiebert 1998). Thus, in all probability, the Andronovo communities to the south were the driving force behind the conquest of India and the formation of the Indo-Iranian language and culture (Hiebert 1999). At the same time, in the Caucasus, the opening of trade with Anatolia and Assyrian merchants once again led to the formation of highly stratified chiefdoms or proto-states, which buried their dead in richly furnished chamber tombs under large barrows, in the so-called Trialeti Culture (Puturidze 2003), strongly influenced from the Near East (Rubinson 2003). It can now be demonstrated that the Old Assyrian trade systems in Anatolia were more extensive than has been thought so far, extending north to the Black Sea for copper and far west in Anatolia as well

(Barjamovic 2005). From here trade linked up with important coastal sites such as Troy, where inland Anatolian trade and maritime Aegean trade converged and extended either into the Black Sea or inland through Thrace (Leshtakov 1995:Figure 2.2). The Old Assyrian merchants were able to exploit the new Bronze Age world-system by trading tin from Asia, probably Uzbekistan (Parzinger & Boroffka 2002), and selling it with a profit in Anatolia, several thousand kilometers away from its source.

In the beginning of the second millennium, the Pontic zone and eastern Eurasia was thus in a position to interact with southern regions in Anatolia, Greece, and the Iranian plateau on an equal basis. Eastward expansion had also established connections with the Bronze Age chiefdoms of China, where two-wheeled chariots appeared during the second millennium B.C.E. (Kuzmina 1998). There are also indications that these highly stratified societies had a surplus not only of metal and horses, but also of warriors. Migrations were soon directed both toward the southeast, into the Iranian plateau and India, and toward China in the east (Mallory & Mair 2000), as well as the Carpathians and the Aegean (Drews 1988).

To summarize, during the third millennium B.C.E. there emerged a new social and economic order in Eurasia. Widespread travel, seasonal transhumance, and some migrations accompanied these changes. By the mid-third millennium B.C.E., a common complex of ritual and social institutions was employed from the Urals to northern Europe within the temperate lowland zone (Kristiansen 1989; Prescott & Walderhaug 1995). It laid the foundation for later developments in social and economic complexity within the same regions during the first half of the second millennium B.C.E., to which we shall now turn.

The Expansion of the Chariot and of Warrior Aristocracies

With the introduction of the chariot, the composite bow, the long sword, and the lance, warfare took on a new social, economic, and ideological significance from the beginning of the second millennium B.C.E. This was reflected, for instance, in burial rituals where chiefly barrows became a dominant feature. A new class of master artisans emerged to build chariots, breed and train horses, and produce and train the use of the new weapons. This package of skills was so complex that it demanded the transfer of artisans, horses, and warriors in order to be properly adopted. Once adopted it changed the nature of society, because it introduced a whole series of economic and social demands, as well as a new ideology of aristocracy linked to warfare and political leadership. The warrior aristocracies and their attached specialists changed Bronze Age societies throughout Eurasia and the Near East.

The expansion of warrior aristocracies and chariots occurred so rapidly that it is impossible to trace its origin with archeological dating methods. What we can show, however, is that it spread as a package, and we can also demonstrate its impact on local societies. I shall briefly discuss how it spread, that is, whether through warfare or through travel and trade, but first we need to establish its geographical expansion.

To identify this new institution and its geographical impact, I have chosen to map the cheek pieces employed for the horses. They can be found in burials where the horses were buried with the warrior and the chariot, but they are also found in settlements. In Figure 3 we see the distribution of three interregional networks of travel, trade, and possibly conquest. This initial expansion of the chariot complex took place along three regional trajectories: a steppe tradition employing bone bits with circular cheek pieces extending from the Urals to the Carpathians, a Near Eastern/East Mediterranean tradition employing bronze bits of similar type as used on the steppe, and an East-Central European tradition employing antler cheek pieces. Horse bits were part of a warrior/chariot package that included new types of long swords, bows and arrows, and lances with a similar distribution. The three traditions meet in the Aegean and in the Carpathians. This area established regional links with the eastern Mediterranean and northern Europe. The new chariot warrior aristocracy expanded along these regional trading links to northern Europe (David 2001; Engedal 2002; Kristiansen 1998a:Figure 191; Larsson 1999a, 1999b), and possibly to the eastern Mediterranean, if the latter area had not already been reached from the Near East. The three kinds of cheek pieces are further unified by a specialized style of waveband decoration linked to these objects, which are mostly foreign to the local tradition (David 1997).

The distribution of this new package thus suggests the expansion of a new institution that was adopted throughout Eurasia and the Near East. In the initial phase, that is, early second millennium, it was still unified by a number of common traits, including the specialized waveband decoration and also the use of and trade in large, well-bred steppe horses of the kind recovered in early Mycenaean burials at Dendra (Payne 1990). As it demanded the transfer of new skills, craftsmanship, and horses, we have to envisage the migration of small groups of warriors, craftsmen, and horse breeders that were welcomed at the chiefly courts along the networks just described.

Parts of their training program for chariot horses is described in the famous Hittite Kikkuli text from the middle of the second millennium B.C.E. (Raulwing & Meyer 2004). The occurrence of identical or nearly identical objects in the Carpathians, Mycenae, and Anatolia indicates that direct personal contacts and long-distance travel were involved in the creation and expansion of the new

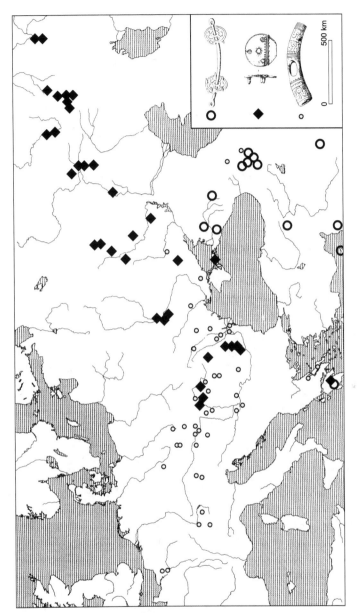

Figure 3 • Distribution of the three major types of bits in the chariot complex in Eurasia and the east Mediterranean during early- to mid-second millennium B.C.E., demonstrating the existence of three interregional networks, which converged in the Aegean and the Carpathians (based on Boroffka 1998 and Penner 1998).

social institutions. We cannot exclude that conquests were also a part of the scenario in some regions, particularly where the package appears "intrusive," for example. the emergence of shaft-grave dynasties with links to the steppe region both in terms of burial ritual and anthropological type (Angel 1972; Manolis & Neroutsos 1997; but cf. Day 2001).

Textual evidence from Anatolia, Egypt, and the Near East describe this period as one of disruption. Whether or not one wishes to agree with Robert Drews (1988) about the coming of the Greeks, he nonetheless points to a series of interrelated historical changes in the Near East during the eighteenth to sixteenth centuries B.C.E. They were linked among other things to the spread of the Indo-European "chariot package," which demanded both skilled specialists and the import and training of horses from the steppe. It coincides with disruptions and social changes, including conquest migrations over large areas: the Kassites in Mesopotamia, the Aryans in India, the Hyksos in Egypt, a new chiefly dynasty in Mycenea (the B circle), and Indo-European-speaking peoples emerging in Mittani texts and other sources from the Levant and Palestine. In all these cases we are dealing with rather small groups of warriors and specialists linked to the ruling elite. "The new rulers are in most cases a dominant minority, constituting only a tiny fragment of the population. This was especially true of the Aryan rulers in Mitanni and the Aryan and Hurrian princes in the Levant; it seems also true of the Kassites in Babylon and the Hyksos in Egypt. The Aryan speakers who took over Northwest India may have gone there en masse but were nonetheless a minority in their newly acquired domain" (Drews 1988:63).

It is obvious that these major historical events are interrelated and had far-reaching implications in central and northern Europe. However, after this initial period of interaction between the steppe, the Near East, and central and northern Europe, new routes of exchange rose to dominance. Disruption in the Carpathian *tell* cultures and the expansion of Mycenaean power into the western Mediterranean prompted new patterns of interaction, for example, between the Tumulus Culture in southern Germany and southern Scandinavia between 1500 and 1300 B.C.E.

Thus, after 2000 B.C.E., long-distance trade and movement of warriors and other specialists linked the societies of Eurasia from the Urals to Mesopotamia to the Aegean and Scandinavia. This corresponds to the spread of warrior aristocracies and the light, two-wheeled war chariot (Anthony 1995; Kristiansen 2001). It transformed not only warfare but also the social and religious institutions from Scandinavia to Mesopotamia and later also India, as evidenced in contemporary written sources. These changes represented a new level of social complexity, but were based on the previous social and religious framework, spreading along established routes of travel and exchange. There is much to suggest that the Indo-European languages accompanied these historical processes, beginning in the third millennium B.C.E., as the social and religious institutions reconstructed for Proto-Indo-European societies are identical to the institutions indicated in the archeological record (Anthony 1995; Kristiansen 2005; Sherratt 1999). The chariot complex and the institution of a warrior aristocracy can be archeologically documented from Scandinavia to India, and so can the religious concept of the Divine Twins (Kristiansen 2004; Kristiansen & Larsson 2005:Chapter 5). Other traits cover only some parts of this huge geographical area. An item of specific interest is the phallic-shaped stone mortar, distributed from the Black Sea region through Caucasus, the eastern steppe, and the Iranian plateau (Boroffka & Sava 1998). It originated in the steppe during the third millennium B.C.E., but its distribution linking the Pontic steppe with the Iranian plateau is during the early to middle second millennium B.C.E., that is, during the same period as the conquest migrations to India along the same route. Because it is well known from the Rig Veda that Soma was created using a stone mortar, we can in all probability now trace the origin and spread of this central ritual idea.

The Origin of the Family, Personal Property, and Gender Divisions

I have demonstrated that there is mounting archeological and other evidence for major transformations in the third millennium B.C.E., but with antecedents in the late fourth millennium originating in the Caucasus region and in the Pontic steppe. These historical changes were linked to the rise of proto-state societies and urban life in Mesopotamia and the Near East, which required long-distance exchange relations in order to maintain access to a number of essential goods such as copper, tin, and later on also horses. The so-called Uruk expansion of the late fourth millennium B.C.E. (Algaze 1989) established such new links, circulating copper from the Caucasus in exchange for new types of prestige goods and technological expertise (Dolukanov 1994:326ff; Sherratt 1997). Stein (1999) has demonstrated how the Uruk expansion transformed local societies, generating ranked chiefdoms in the Caucasus (Maikop Culture).

The early city-states of Mesopotamia had developed new patterns of trade and exchange that required appropriate concepts regarding property and the transmission and accumulation of wealth. This in turn entailed a new economic and legal definition of family and inheritance (Diakonoff 1982; Postgate 2003; Yoffee 1995). These new concepts were selectively adapted to different and less complex social and economic environments in the Caucasus and beyond, which led to the formation of new institutions based on a concept of rank linked to movable, personal property, mainly in the form of prestige goods and herds of animals. The new patterns of social organization were ritually manifested in a type of *kurgans* with individual burials and rich deposits of personal grave goods. They later also influenced societies on the steppe and even south of the Caucasus, for example. the Kura-Araks Culture (Dolukanov 1994:301ff, Figure 6.18; Kohl 2001; Rothman 2003). The latter represented a new type of socioeconomic network that appears to have monopolized production and distribution of metal in the Levant and Mesopotamia. They may in fact represent those Indo-European-speaking groups that were later mentioned in written sources under various names such as Hurrians and Hittites.

I thus propose that the transmission of new patterns of social organization from the city-states of the south during the Uruk expansion, involving altered definitions of family, property, and inheritance, facilitated the formation of a mobile, agropastoral society in the steppe region and beyond. It focused on the monogamous extended family as a central social and economic unit, based on a patrilineal Omaha kinship system (see discussion in Kristiansen & Larsson 2005:Chapter 5; Rowlands 1980), favoring the accumulation of mobile wealth through expansion and exogamous alliances, and its transmission between generations. The individualized *tumulus* burials, furnished with these very same symbols of wealth, represented the ritualized institutionalization of these new principles, now also transferred to the land of death. They correspond to a specific religious cosmology that developed into a complex religious system by the second millennium B.C.E., when it is manifested in written sources (Kristiansen & Larsson 2005:Chapter 6).

Another important institution that was introduced from the early city-states to their peripheries in Anatolia and Caucasus was that of warriors and organized warfare under royal or chiefly command. In the Eurasian societies of the third millennium B.C.E., the ideal of the male warrior was associated with the institution of chiefly leadership (Vandkilde In press). It was materialized in the ubiquitous, carefully executed war axe in precious stone, copper, silver, or gold. We can now begin to see the contours of a more complex division of social roles and institutions (Hansen 2002; Müller 2002). Specialists, such as the metal smith, can be identified in burials, and ritualized, priestly functions are also indicated in grave goods. A complex society of warriors, priests, specialists, and herders/farmers is emerging, albeit in embryonic form. The new set of social roles and the new rules of kinship and inheritance of property and mobile wealth also brought stricter and more differentiated definitions of gender roles. Male and female identities are strictly defined in burials (Häusler 2003), and the universal adoption of the family burial covered by a *tumulus* can be seen as the ritual formalization of the gendered, monogamous family.

Conclusion: The Formation of the Eurasian Interaction Zone and the Mobile Warrior Societies

The formation of the Eurasian interaction zone known to us from the Iron Age onward as the Silk Road originated in the long-term social and ecological transformations described above. During the third millennium B.C.E. they mainly affected the western steppe area, as well as central and northern Europe, whereas from the second and early first millennia B.C.E. they also included the eastern and southeastern steppe. This second expansion was a result of connections already established with the city-states and kingdoms of Anatolia and Mesopotamia. By the end of the second millennium these processes had transformed Eurasia into a vast interaction zone for mobile, warlike pastoral nomads, linking eastern and western Asia to a common historical pulse. As recognized by Philip Kohl (2003:21): "Major transformations in the prehistory of Eurasia were marked by fundamental developments in the production and exchange of materials basic to the reproduction of and consolidation of societies stretching from the Eurasian steppes to the ancient Near East and northern Europe. Whatever model one adopts, this certainly was an interconnected world." Periodical expansions through conquest migrations into neighboring regions of eastern Europe, Anatolia, and the Near East sometimes brought long-term historical effects, while at other times not. Innovations in warfare, however, were often linked to such periodic conquest migrations.

These macro-historical processes were accompanied by micro-level transformations in social organization. The third millennium B.C.E. saw the formation and expansion of the monogamous family (*kurgans*, individualized family burials), herd inheritance, and patrilineal, Omaha-type kinship systems throughout Eurasia, symbolically expressed through new, formalized burial rituals. The concept of personal property and its accumulation and transmission within families was derived from Mesopotamia. Adapted to a steppe environment and mobile pastoralism, it generated new economic dynamics leading to demographic expansion, migrations, and new social institutions of leadership linked to warfare and the accumulation of mobile wealth. In the early second millennium B.C.E., new innovations in warfare and metallurgy (for example, the chariot, weapons, tools) allowed warrior groups to establish more coercive forms of power relations and exploitation. It led to the formation of complex warrior societies, ruled by war leaders and priests with their dependent specialists. Herders and farmers were now emerging as distinct social groups ruled by the elite. This archeological trajectory corresponds to the reconstruction of Proto-Indo-European society proposed by historical linguists and sociologists. During the first half of the second millennium B.C.E., these warrior societies engaged actively with the emerging city-states of Anatolia and the Near East, and in a series of conquest migrations alternating with trade they expanded toward China, India, and into the Aegean. In the process, they also transformed the organization of warfare throughout Eurasia, which over the next several centuries was based on chariotry, later followed by mobile warriors on horseback. The warrior societies of the steppe corridor connecting Europe and the Far East, historically known as the Silk Road, were thus established and over the next three millennia remained a central factor in the history of western Asia.

Note

1. Based on paleobotanical work carried out during the last ten to fifteen years, it can now be stated that during the third millennium huge areas from the Urals to northwestern Europe were transformed into open grasslands. The transformation is very well documented in a number of case studies (Andersen 1995, 1998; Kristiansen 1989). This massive deforestation was caused by a new economic strategy of pastoral herding with some agriculture. It thus represented a social and economic transformation on a large interregional scale. Yamna Culture, Corded Ware, Beaker, and Single Grave Cultures all shared this economic strategy (but with local cultural variations), and a similar cosmology linked to single burials, mostly under low mounds along river valleys or other ecological zonations. The formation of this open environment in northwestern Eurasia held a huge potential for large-scale interaction that was not fully exploited until the systematic introduction of metallurgy (bronze).

CHAPTER 11

Climate, Water, and Political-Economic Crises in Ancient Mesopotamia and Egypt[1]

WILLIAM R. THOMPSON

Despite widespread concerns about contemporary global warming, climate considerations do not currently warrant a great deal of attention in Old World archeology. Culture and ideology seem to fare much better in an era more inclined to emphasize differences between and among societies. Yet the current ambivalence toward climate as an explanatory variable may be sacrificing an important key to ways in which ancient systems behaved, both similarly and differently. For instance, the first two areas to develop in the Old World, Mesopotamia and Egypt, differed from each other tremendously. Mesopotamia was politically polycentric, early to urbanize, and taken over by successive waves of people who had moved into the area from adjacent hinterlands. Egypt became politically unicentric fairly early on, was slow to urbanize, and was comparatively more successful at resisting outsider takeover bids through the second millennium B.C.E. Despite some early Mesopotamian influences on Egypt, their cultures, religions, political ideologies, and languages were quite different. Although unlike in many ways, the two earliest systems did share something that might be termed "political-economic rhythm." The parallels in the timing of the changes of successive regimes and periods of greater and lesser turmoil in the two ancient Near Eastern centers are quite remarkable. Cultural and ideological differences cannot account for these similarities. To the extent that climate change can contribute to explaining these similarities, climate appears to have been a particularly significant parameter in the functioning of the ancient southwest Asian world (Chew 2001).

It is not difficult to find possible linkages between specific events and changes in the climate. But even if it is safe to say that environmental change can be linked without much doubt to a few well-known examples, the question remains whether we can relate climatic deterioration systematically (as opposed to episodically) to regime transitions, center-hinterland conflict, and the behavioral tempo of the first large-scale experiments in societal complexity. Moreover, is it possible to demonstrate even further that similar climatic deterioration experiences in Mesopotamia and Egypt led to similar societal problems at roughly the same time? If both questions can be answered positively and successfully, it should be obvious that invoking a climatic factor need not lead to environmental determinism. Even if the two systems faced similar environmental problems at roughly the same time, their general responses were not identical. Otherwise, their differences in organizational strategies and belief systems would have not been so pronounced. Climate changes can create opportunities and challenges, but they need not dictate the outcome.

Hypotheses (and indicators) on climate change, river levels, regime transitions, economic prosperity, trade collapse and reorientations, and center-hinterland conflict are derived from a simple model of general processes and then applied to Mesopotamia and Egypt for the period 4000–1000 B.C.E. Four of five hypotheses receive substantial support. A strong case can be made for linking water scarcity problems systematically to conflict, the fall of governmental regimes, and the collapse of trading regimes. Various Mesopotamian and Egyptian cultural innovations may also be traceable to environmental change. Thus, the effect of climate change was not merely that of an occasional catastrophe or gradual drying. Climate effects persisted throughout the duration of the ancient world. They helped foster the emergence of the ancient civilizations in the first place and then played a key role in their demise. The influence of climate change in the period between the origins and the end of the ancient world also appears to be highly significant and persistent.

The Argument

The argument to be developed here is certainly not that all problems in a social system can be blamed on the weather. Nor is the argument really reducible to a straightforward "climate-produces-problems"-type of explanation. In the ancient world, climate was a contextual factor that arguably influenced a large number of other important processes such as agricultural prosperity, state-making, governmental legitimacy, population size, size of urban labor force, religion, trade, warfare, and so forth. Climate was particularly critical to the dynamics of carrying capacities in the ancient world. The easiest generalization to make is that turmoil of various sorts was more likely to develop when carrying capacity was threatened or exceeded. Climate, therefore, can be linked fairly easily and fundamentally to intra-elite and center-hinterland conflict in systems in which economic survival is vulnerable to environmental deterioration. And what system is not vulnerable to some degree? However, fringed by Saharan deserts in the west, Arabian deserts and the Indian Ocean in the south, the Mediterranean and Syrian deserts in the north, and mountains in the east, the ancient southwest Asian region appears especially vulnerable to periods of extensive drought. In that respect, the fragility of the system to environmental deterioration was quite pronounced, but it was not unique. Comparable situations can be found in, for instance, the American southwest (LeBlanc 1999) and even Polynesian islands (Kirch 1984).

Climate discussions are hardly novel. Three items are needed to add something new to the debate. First, we need a model that locates climate change within the nexus of a network of interactive societal processes. Some effects of climatic deterioration are direct, whereas others are more indirect. If we are not proposing a simple, bivariate relationship between climate and conflict, how might we expect its manifestations to be best revealed? Just how extensive (or superficial) are these manifestations thought to be? Second, we need data on the processes and relationships that the model suggests are most worth examining empirically. Finally, we need explicit tests of hypotheses derived from the model. Granted, hypotheses about ancient system processes are not easily tested. The data are incredibly recalcitrant when they exist in the first place. But the effort should be made. Otherwise, it will be difficult to evaluate the relative accuracy of the model's hypotheses in terms other than face validity or logical rigor. Given the academic unpopularity of climatic explanations (see, for instance, Tainter 1988), attempts at empirical substantiation are especially indispensable.

The Model

A prime mover in the model is water availability, which is predicated, in turn, on climate change.[2] These two variables were especially critical for ancient systems, it is argued, because they were agrarian economies highly vulnerable to changes in precipitation and temperature. A second reason is that these early societies emerged in river valleys and were highly dependent on a predictable flow of water in the rivers around which their agrarian activities were organized.[3] Climatic deterioration affected the reliability of the amount and even the location of water in these central rivers. A third reason is that the appearance of the earliest Old World civilizations was initially favored by climate, that is, before the genesis of societal complexity (urbanization, writing, organized religion, governmental coordination), and their development then strongly influenced by climatic deterioration. The assumption is that the packages of societal complexities that did emerge might have developed quite differently in the absence of climatic deterioration.

The amount of water in the central rivers (for example, the Tigris-Euphrates and the Nile) influenced how much land could be cultivated. An abundance of water meant more land could be cultivated. Scarcity led to a contraction in the amount of land under cultivation, crop failures, famine, and increased interest in irrigation practices. As river levels dropped, several things happened. Human settlements that had been widespread in wetter times were abandoned as villages that now found themselves too far from a water supply became untenable. Some of their population was dislocated toward areas that still had access to water. Local population density in the latter areas increased as a consequence. In southern Mesopotamia, the surviving population centers thus grew into cities. In southern Egypt, population concentration near the Nile increased. The size of the labor force, swollen with economic refugees from dryer areas, expanded. Economic specialization became both more possible and more necessary. So, too, did agricultural intensification, the construction and maintenance of irrigation infrastructure, and the building of temples and monumental architecture (pyramids, ziggurats). More complex divisions of labor, greater population density, and more public goods increased the need for coordination, thereby expanding the role of bureaucratic and governmental managers.

Not everyone chose to move to these expanding concentrations of people. A different type of economic specialization occurred as some people chose to concentrate on raising herds of livestock in less populated zones. Finding pasture for these animals meant seasonal migrations. The distinction between sedentary and nomadic populations became greater as a consequence.

Thus, urbanization, nomadism, centralized religion, government, writing, and intensified trade were outcomes of these processes. The urbanization proceeded, particularly in Mesopotamia, from the concentration of population around a few nuclei where the population had once been more widely dispersed. Millennia-old trading networks expanded to meet the increased demands of larger, denser, and richer communities that invariably developed in areas lacking critical basic commodities such as wood and copper. Religion became more important as the environment became less predictable. Ways of communicating with the gods in the hope of obtaining better weather became an increasingly centralized activity. A variety of other activities needed coordination. Agricultural labor, irrigation management, surplus food storage, dispute adjudication, and defense were some of the most prominent. Bureaucrats were needed to count the number of laborers and slaves, the number of bowls necessary to feed them, taxes, and commodities exchanged between communities. Writing developed from these mundane accounting practices. Governments developed from coordination and supervision practices designed to enhance economic productivity, suppress domestic disorder, expand the community's access to resources, and protect the community from external attack.

Then as now, governments were evaluated for their ability to fulfill their coordination and protection responsibilities. They were no doubt also blamed for climate-induced economic deterioration, even if there was not much that could be done about it. That too has not changed much. In periods of severe economic deterioration, governmental legitimacy could be expected to suffer. Hungry populations were more likely to protest and riot. Unpaid armies were more likely to rebel. Provincial governors were more likely to act more autonomously from a weakening central government.[4] Political organization, in general, cycled back and forth between relatively centralized and decentralized conditions. One implication of decentralization was a weakened resistance to incursions from tribes inhabiting the hinterland, who were attracted to the river valleys (and the cities located in them) by the survival problems they were experiencing owing to climatic deterioration. To add to their already mounting problems, the probability of hinterland incursions increased as the central cities became more vulnerable to attack.

Several different types of warfare developed in the ancient civilizations. On the one hand, cities needed protection from bandits, nomads, and unwanted refugees. Walled cities developed in response. Ambitious political leaders would also go on the offensive to demonstrate their vigor and right to command by attacking groups outside the city walls who were perceived as threats. The threats were often real in the sense that the attacks from the center responded to tribal pressure on outlying farms or extended trade routes. Many of these offensive raids could be expected in the early years of a new reigning monarch, as both internal and external demonstrations of legitimacy and fitness to rule. The soldiers used for these purposes were recruited from the urban labor surplus and from hinterland populations brought under central control.

As cities became states, inter- and intrastate conflict also became more probable. Intrastate conflict was inherent to the cycle of political centralization and decentralization mentioned above. The states also needed cultivable land, access to raw materials not available at home, and secure trading networks. Expansion of the state to achieve these goals increased the probability of conflict with other states that were also expanding in the same direction, or with states whose territory or spheres of influence were being encroached on. A deteriorating environment would make these interstate frictions all the more threatening. Contrary to contemporary myths, sovereignty issues did not first emerge in the 1648 Treaty of Westphalia. They emerged thousands of years before in the Sumerian city-state system, the conflicts between Upper and Lower Egypt and their neighbors and, subsequently, in the conflicts of successive empires in the Near East.

Central to this argument is the fact that water was more readily available in the Near East prior to the fourth millennium B.C.E. The availability of water initially encouraged the expansion of human populations in the region, particularly in the river valleys.[5] When precipitation and river levels declined, subsequent water scarcities prompted the development of new adaptive strategies leading to the accelerated emergence of nomadic-sedentary divergence, urbanization, writing, government, religion, and state-making. Climate change did not determine what transpired. There were a host of possible responses, many of which were pursued. The most successful strategies, however, involved the development of cities and states. Climate change may not even have been necessary for these developments to occur. Some early concentrations of population such as Catal Huyuk and Jericho emerged prior to the general deterioration in Near Eastern climate. But climate change accelerated the development of multiple, interactive processes to new levels of intensity. Where once populations had been more dispersed, larger and more concentrated centers began to emerge and persist, which entailed a number of implications for other societal processes. Subsequent climate changes continued to shape the trajectories of these evolving societies, for example, the emphasis on conflict among elites and between center and hinterland.

Five hypotheses, derived from the model outlined above, are tested in this investigation:

H1: Periods of economic decline in the ancient world were systematically associated with periods of deteriorating climate and diminished water supply.

H2: Periods of trade collapse in the ancient world were systematically associated with periods of deteriorating climate and diminished water supply.

H3: Regime transitions in the ancient world were systematically associated with periods of deteriorating climate and diminished water supply.

H4: The most significant center-hinterland conflicts in the ancient world were systematically associated with periods of deteriorating climate and diminished water supply.

If any of the first four hypotheses are supported by the empirical data, it stands to reason that crises involving economic and political turmoil are likely to overlap. To the extent that these crises do overlap, societies and governments are likely to be overwhelmed by a deteriorating environment over which they have decreasing control.

H5: The conjunction of significant political and economic crises in the ancient world were systematically associated with periods of deteriorating climate and diminished water supply.

Indicators

Hypotheses 1 through 5 require systematic information on economic fluctuations, trade collapse, regime transitions, center-hinterland conflict, and environmental change. Data for these variables are not readily available, but indicators can be constructed.

Economic Fluctuations

Frank and Thompson (2005) have characterized each century between 4000 and 1000 B.C.E. as predominantly prosperous or depressed. These characterizations are based on an extensive survey of the appropriate historical and archeological discussions relating to 15 zones within Afro-Eurasia. The Mesopotamian economic fluctuations tend to cluster with prosperous centuries becoming less common over time. Relatively prosperous centuries characterized the 3800–3300 and possibly the 2700–2300 periods. Only two economically prosperous centuries are indicated after 2300. Periods of contraction occurred in 4000–3800, 3200–2900, 2300–2100, 2000–1900, 1600–1400, and 1200–1000, although one might extend some of the contraction periods if the "mixed" centuries are treated as years of limited growth.

The Egyptian record did not mirror the Mesopotamian sequence exactly, although one could describe Egyptian economic history as similarly susceptible to clustering. A long period of economic expansion characterized the 3800–2300 era. Prosperity returned in the 2000–1700 period. The other centuries are coded as mixed or periods of contraction. Although the century-to-century comparisons do not reveal a close correlation, Mesopotamian and Egyptian economic fortunes were similar in at least one important respect. Both demonstrate concentrations of prosperity in the fourth through mid-third millennia. Subsequent years are more prone to economic stagnation or decline.

Trade Collapse

Thompson (2001a, 2001b, 2006) has surveyed the emergence of southwest Asian trading networks from the eighth millennium B.C.E. to the end of the Bronze Age. There were three evident periods of trade crisis, reorientation, or collapse in the ancient world: around 3200–3000, 2200–2000, and 1200–1000. The maximal period of collapse came toward the end of the second millennium, with a reorientation farther to the west and then back to the east in the first millennium B.C.E. The earlier two crises, 3200–3000 and 2200–2000, did not reach the scale of the 1200–1000 dark age. The emphasis in the former periods was more on gradually finding replacements for imports and exports that had become difficult to sustain.

Regime Transitions

If the historical reconstruction of ancient regimes in Mesopotamia and Egypt is characterized by a fair degree of consensus, there are differences of opinion about the precise number of years to assign to each period in the sequence. The differences, however, do not seem so great that the adoption of a particular chronology would threaten validity. I have found use for Baines and Yoffee's (1998) schedule, which is based on fairly recent periodization principles.[6]

Center-Hinterland Conflict

An enumeration of ancient southwest Asian center-hinterland conflicts (Thompson 2002) unfortunately does not lend itself readily to treatments as time series. The most significant periods of conflict can be reduced to the following short list. In the Mesopotamian case, there was first the movement of Trans-Caucasians and Amorites toward the end of the fourth millennium, followed by Gutian attacks in the 2100s, and then the Amorite attacks in the 2000s, which led to a number of Amorite dynasties and rulers in the Old Babylonian period. The Kassite takeover in the 1500s, in the wake of a Hittite attack on Babylon, was the next major hinterland incursion, and many consider it a terminal blow to Mesopotamian attempts at centralization. Nevertheless, yet another round of hinterland incursions into Mesopotamia began with the increase of Aramaean pressures toward the end of the second millennium.

In the Egyptian case, there were three major bouts of hinterland attack. In the first intermediate period (2150–1980), the incursions came from the west and the east. The threat in the second intermediate period (1630–1520) led to a Hyksos takeover of parts of Egypt from the west. The Sea Peoples came from the north and northeast, along with attacks from Libyan allies attacks in the late 1200s and early 1100s. The Libyan pressure continued into the third intermediate phase (beginning 1070) and led ultimately to the Libyan Pharaonic dynasties. Since the Sea Peoples' attacks and the third intermediate period blend into one another, the third cluster of hinterland incursions translates into a 1200–1000 time span.

Conjunction

Hypothesis H5 requires that the indicators for the first four hypotheses have the same timing. It might be worth looking at every possible combination, but to simplify the current analysis, it should suffice to single out situations in which at least three of the four types of political-economic crisis were present simultaneously (that is, in the same century) in order to qualify as a conjunction.

Climate

Butzer (1995:138) draws attention to what he calls "first-order anomalies" of general atmospheric circulation. Three pan-Near Eastern "dry shifts" are identified as having occurred around 3000, 2200, and 1300 B.C.E. He notes that these dry shifts were not manifested at exactly the same time in Egypt and Mesopotamia. Fairly abrupt shifts in Nile flood levels were registered around 3000, 2250, 1850, and 1200. Protracted periods of low Mesopotamian rainfall, as registered in Lakes Van and Zeribar sediment layers and pollen traces, occurred around 3200–2900, 2350–2000, and 1300–1200.[7]

In a generally arid area, the two crucial weather dimensions that come immediately to mind are rainfall and temperature. There are different precipitation zones in southwest Asia (for instance, precipitation currently tends to increase as one moves away from Arabia in a northeasterly direction; see Nissen 1988:59). The most useful information is provided by Fairbridge and colleagues (1997). Based on an analysis of geological information, they are able to generate a sequence of cool/warm and wet/dry alterations that characterized southwest Asia, albeit subject to various subregional qualifications. If we convert this information into our focus on centuries, ancient southwest Asian periods of dry and warm climate were 3250–2900 (although perhaps less dry in Egypt), 2700–2345, 2200–1650 (described as a period of widespread desiccation), 1650–1400 (the desiccation continued but not as severe as in the immediately preceding period), and 1200–1000.

One would also wish more information on other climate factors such as wind forces and directions or even dew levels, which can make some difference in dry-zone agriculture, but it is doubtful that very much more detailed information is likely to be forthcoming. One exception, that may prove to be a rather major one, is river level data. Both Mesopotamia and Egypt were centered on river systems, and much of their harvest volumes and transportation opportunities were governed by the volume of water flowing through the Tigris-Euphrates and Nile rivers. As it happens, we have some reconstructed information on river volume that is easier to interpret than data we have on temperature and precipitation.[8]

In the case of the Tigris and the Euphrates rivers, the pattern is one of precipitous declines in water levels from 3500 to 2900 B.C.E., 2500 to 2000 B.C.E., and 1300 to 1100 B.C.E. In between these phases are periods of increasing water levels, but they never return to the levels of 4000 B.C.E. until early in the first millennium. The Nile pattern is similar but not identical to the Mesopotamian trajectory. Nile levels cascade downward from 4000 B.C.E. to intermediate troughs in 3800, 2900, and very low troughs in 2000 and 1200–1100 B.C.E. The river level was falling between 4000 and 3800, 3300 and 2900, 2500 to 2000, and 1600 to 1200, although one can argue that the repercussions of each successive fall would have been more serious than the preceding one(s) because the levels were becoming successively lower. In this analysis, the information on declining river levels is merged with the periodization of warm and dry climate, adding up to a picture of pronounced climate deterioration.

Data Analysis

If we simply arrange the timing of the various cycles and look for overlap, a casual evaluation of the hypotheses is possible. Periods of economic contraction and trade collapse (hypotheses H1 and H2) virtually never occur in the absence of decline in either climate or river level. Almost every regime change (hypothesis H3) in both Mesopotamia and Egypt after 3300 B.C.E. occurred in a phase of environmental deterioration. The one exception is the beginning of the first Early Dynastic phase in Mesopotamia, which commenced 40 years before the weather turned warmer and dryer and some 250 years before the river levels began to decline. It seems fair to say that increased probability of regime transition also appears to be associated with environmental deterioration.

Hypothesis H4 ties climate change to the major episodes of center-hinterland conflict. While it would be unreasonable to thus try to account for every single hinterland incursion, the major ones appear in conjunction with climate deterioration. The Akkadian takeover occurred after a long bout of warm and dry weather and in the middle of a half-millennium-long decline in Mesopotamian river levels. Gutian and Amorite pressures at the end of the third millennium are especially troublesome toward the end of the same 500-year river level decline and at the beginning of the driest interval in the ancient world. The Kassite takeover occurred in the beginning of the warm and dry interval that immediately followed the phase of "widespread desiccation." The Aramaean pressures became increasingly intense in another period combining declining river levels and dryer climate.

The same periods, by and large, coincide with Egypt's three intermediate phases and the attack of the Sea Peoples. In the first intermediate period, tribal pressures on the margins are manifested in both the east and the west toward the end of a 500-year decline in Nile river levels. The Hyksos takeover, evidently in response to pressures farther east, occurred toward the end of the "widespread desiccation" period. The initial Sea Peoples' attack, again responding in part to climatic problems throughout the eastern Mediterranean, came towards the end of another long decline in river levels. Subsequent attacks by Sea Peoples and Libyans took place as climate again had become warmer and dryer.

A significant proportion of conflict is about resource scarcities. People desire more of some commodity than is readily available. Competition over resources ensues, presumably with levels of intensity roughly commensurate with the level of scarcity. Without doubt, water was one of the more valuable commodities in ancient southwest Asia, but it was more than just a valuable commodity. It was also critical to economic growth, prosperity, governmental legitimacy, and survival, whether one was a sedentary farmer, a goat-herder in the mountains, a desert nomad, or a monarch. Kings were blamed when water was in short supply. Long periods of drought therefore threatened governmental legitimacy. Drought, particularly if extended over a number of years, would have had to influence the resources that states could mobilize for protection purposes, just as it affected what was available to eat. Conflicts between states and cities over contested water resources and cultivable land, however, would have multiplied as the commodity in question became even more scarce. Mountain and desert tribes had little recourse but to move toward whatever areas still possessed water when their own habitats became too dry to support them. If water levels in the Mesopotamian and Nile rivers are our most unambiguous indicators of environmental deterioration, they would predict maximum political-economic crisis, other things being equal, toward the ends of the fourth, third, and second millennia (3300/3100, 2200/2000, and 1200/1100 B.C.E.)—that is, when we should expect the most center-hinterland conflict. We do in fact find considerable unrest and turmoil in these periods. In addition, the hinterland attacks became increasingly formidable, especially after the second half of the second millennium, when they were instrumental in diffusing horse-drawn chariots to Mesopotamia and Egypt.

Nevertheless, merely looking at data that sometimes overlap is not an especially rigorous methodology. While we can sense that some of the relationships between economic and environmental decline appear to be supported by the data, there are also periods of environmental decline in which there is no corresponding political-economic decline. We need to ask whether political-economic crises are relatively more common in the presence of environmental deterioration than in its absence. Table 1 summarizes information on five cross-tabulations associated with each of the five hypotheses. Here we discover that, despite appearances, economic decline is not systematically related to deteriorating climate. Economic contraction may be more common in years of poor environment, but only marginally so.

Table 1 Testing five hypotheses on environmental deterioration and political-economic crisis

		Deteriorating Climate and Declining River Levels		
		Absent	*Present*	*Total*
(1) Economic		24 centuries	10 centuries	
Deterioration	absent	(.585)	(.526)	34 centuries
	present	17 (.415)	9 (.474)	26
	total	41	19	60
chi square = .184	*p* = .668			
(2) Trade Collapse	absent	37 (.902)	11 (.579)	48
	present	4 (.122)	8 (.421)	2
	total	41	19	60
chi square = 6.362	*p* =.012			
(3) Governmental				
Regime Change	absent	29 (.707)	9 (.474)	38
	present	12 (.293)	10 (.526)	22
	total	41	19	60
chi square = 3.052	*p* =.081			
(4) Center-Hinterland				
Conflict	absent	36 (.878)	11 (.579)	47
	present	5 (.122)	8 (.421)	13
	total	41	19	60
chi square = 6.844	*p* =.009			
(5) Three of Four				
Problems Occurring				
Simultaneously	absent	36 (.878)	11 (.579)	47
	present	5 (.122)	8 (.421)	13
	total	41	19	60
chi square = 6.844	*p* =.009			

If hypothesis H1 is not supported, the other four hypotheses can be said to pass the chi square test. Trade collapses (37 percent versus 10 percent), regime changes (53 percent versus 29 percent), center-hinterland conflict (42 percent versus 12 percent), and the conjunction of multiple crises (39 percent versus 14 percent) are much more likely to occur in years of deteriorating climate and declining river levels than in years of improving climate and rising river levels. But climatic deterioration does not systematically lead to social crisis. Treating the crises separately, only regime changes are more likely than not in centuries of deteriorating climate and declining river levels, and even this case is close to a 50–50 probability. In reference to the other types of crises, they are somewhat more likely *not* to occur even in years of deteriorating environment. However, the simultaneous occurrence of multiple types of crises is more likely than not in the presence of environmental deterioration.

Mesopotamia and Egypt, while highly dependent on central rivers, do not represent identical ecological niches. Declining water levels in southern Mesopotamia initially may have helped boost Uruk to the lead among Sumerian cities, as new land became available in the south. But continuing decline in water levels may have been another matter. Something of the reverse happened in Egypt, with new land becoming available for cultivation in the northern delta area and less in Upper Egypt (in the south), but this shift probably occurred over a longer time period than that which took place in Mesopotamia. Nor did the two centers of the ancient world share the same type of political evolution. Egypt was moving toward unification as southern Mesopotamia was moving into a period of competing city-states. The shock brought on by a declining water level could certainly lead to different kinds of repercussions. Conceivably, it could have contributed to the relative decline of Uruk's leadership in Sumer by heightening intercity conflicts. At the same time, it could have presented an opportunity to coercively unite northern and southern Egypt, particularly if conquering the north had become more attractive to the south because of the environmental changes.

But information about water supply is not sufficient to account for all of the regime transitions and the major center-hinterland conflicts. Some phases of deterioration were warmer and dryer than others. Fairbridge and associates (1997) identify the long period 2205–1410 period as one of intense desiccation that only slowly gave way to something resembling the regular pattern at the end of the fifteenth century B.C.E. If environmental deterioration has an impact on a number of variables, including the ability of the center to organize resistance and the ability of the hinterland to survive in their natural habitats, it stands to reason that such an extended period of aridification would be even more damaging than the normal fluctuations between warmer and cooler periods. Therefore, it should not be surprising to find center resistance virtually disintegrating after several centuries of desiccation, which simultaneously propelled hinterland populations toward the cities situated along the central rivers of Mesopotamia and Egypt. The interacting cycles of climate, river levels, political-economic concentration, and center-hinterland conflict became less sustainable as key parameters such as agricultural productivity were substantially altered.[9]

In contrast, the Egyptian end of the ancient world managed to continue to function cyclically, but not without some radical rearranging of its elements. Unification (for example, the first Egyptian centralization) took place in the context of falling Nile flood levels and increasing aridity. The Old and Middle Kingdom polities took advantage of rising river levels and periodic soil renewal. The New Kingdom effort not only had to work against falling Nile levels and, eventually, a return to dry conditions; it was also assaulted by hinterland people from throughout the eastern Mediterranean area. The Libyan threat was greater than ever before, in part because they were in turn being displaced by migrants from other parts of the Mediterranean world.[10] The collapse of the ancient world in the last centuries of the second millennium B.C.E. was not simply the result of climate change; climate change in the Middle East, Europe, and Central Asia appears to have been a significant factor in generating extensive turmoil and population movements throughout the eastern Mediterranean area. Unlike the Hittites, the Egyptians were able to survive this turmoil and fend off the invasions of the Sea Peoples (see, for instance, Nibbi 1975; Sandars 1978).[11] Yet their victory over the Libyans proved only temporary. Subsequent dynastic efforts at centralization were undertaken in Egypt, but they were carried out by people of hinterland origin and later by even more distant foreigners.

The greatest danger in constructing an explanation that assigns great significance to environmental deterioration would be to suggest that people and social systems behaved as if they had no choice in how to respond to weather and water problems, and that the outcomes were predestined. Nothing of the sort happened in the ancient world-system, as the many differences between Mesopotamian and Egyptian behavior (see Baines & Yoffee 1998; Trigger 1993) during this period illustrate. Climate and water availability were only two of the key variables necessary to reconstruct how the ancient southwest Asian system emerged and then collapsed. However, the available evidence suggests that the interaction of climate and water availability with other key variables was pervasive. Economies did not immediately contract or governments immediately fall when confronted with deteriorating environments. Continuing deterioration, however, did lead to contraction, the collapse of trading networks, and the demise of political regimes.

Similarly, hinterland peoples did not attack the center as soon as the temperature rose or water levels declined. A division of labor between center and hinterland first had to evolve. Migrations to hinterland areas from other areas occurred. The first concentrations of power in Sumer and Egypt enjoyed the advantage of limited hinterland resistance, a condition, along with abundant water, that became more and more rare with successive regimes. Nor could the successive regimes be assured of continued access to a material foundation for political-economic concentration. In Mesopotamia, agrarian resources diminished in response to these regimes' attempts to cope with fluctuations in the water supply, that is, through irrigation-induced salinization. However, early political-economic regimes did benefit from climatically encouraged population concentrations, a process that continued but not at the same rate.

Sometimes the center was able to resist the attacks from the hinterland, sometimes the hinterland overwhelmed what remained of the center.[12] Gradually, however, the capacity of the center to resist not only the assault of mountain and desert tribes, but also the uneven succession of environmental cycles, diminished. The power of the center to revive and to reorganize itself also diminished, and the system collapsed. This did not mean that a reconcentration of innovation and resources was out of the question. Rather, it meant that such a reconcentration would be more likely to occur somewhere else. In the case of the ancient world-system, somewhere else turned out to be centered in the northern littoral of the Mediterranean (Greece and Rome), as well as in China.

In sum, the point is not that climate or hinterland attacks were responsible for the demise of successive regimes in the ancient Old World. However, if the data on climate, river levels, trade interruptions, regime transitions, and hinterland attacks should hold up as reasonably accurate, they appear to be highly correlated. Deteriorating climate and decreasing river levels were associated with significant increases in conflict between the center and the hinterland. Collapses and reorientations of trading networks were most likely in the context of a deteriorating environment. Major regime changes also appear to be highly correlated with changes in climate and river levels. The conjunction of multiple types of crises was more probable in times of environmental problems. Correlations are not the same as causation, but the hypothesized reasons for the correlations are not implausible, and they do suggest causation. These findings indicate that neither climate nor hinterland clashes with the center should be relegated to the periphery of archeological explanations. They have interacted with each other as well as with a wide range of other variables and processes over long periods of time. We need to continue the investigation and mapping of these interactions as best as we can in order to explain how the ancient southwest Asian system, and others like it, worked.

Notes

1. This paper represents a highly abridged version of Thompson (2003).
2. The model that is sketched here is based on arguments found primarily in Bell (1971, 1975) and Hole (1994). Bell explicitly states that her argument is also applicable to Mesopotamia, even though she confines her own analyses to Egypt. Hole's argument is explicitly restricted to the Ubaid-Uruk transition in Mesopotamia prior to 4000 B.C.E.
3. Butzer (1976:108) has described Egyptian economic history as "primarily one of continuous ecological readjustment to a variable water supply."
4. Vercoutter (1967:280) argues that since Egypt was 35 times as long as it was wide, natural conditions made centralized authority desirable, whereas, in practice, geography made intermittent dismemberment probable.
5. According to Butzer (1976:86), the Egyptian population quadrupled in the 1500 years preceding the establishment of the Old Kingdom.
6. This is not the last word on the subject, however. Algaze and colleagues (1998) and Joffe (2000) discuss some of the implications of the most recent revisions in the Mesopotamian sequence. These revisions have the effect of extending the Uruk phase farther back in time, thus addressing a period not given much attention here.
7. At the same time, these "anomalies" suggest causation at a scale greater than the local or even regional weather systems. Whereas Egypt and the Indus shared a common denominator in the African monsoon (Weiss 2000), Mesopotamian river levels are predicated on Anatolian precipitation. Therefore, similar climate problems in Mesopotamia and Egypt at roughly the same time, especially in conjunction with such problems even outside southwest Asia, suggest world-level climate change.
8. The source for the river level data is Butzer (1995:133), who refers to his series as "inferred" volume flows but unfortunately does not discuss his specific approach to inference. The Nile plot, however, resembles Butzer's (1976:31) plot of East African lake levels which feed into the Nile, which suggests that the Tigris-Euphrates reconstruction is based on Anatolian lake data. Obviously, the data are not as solid as we might prefer, but it is unlikely that superior alternatives for river level estimations will be forthcoming in the near future. Cf. Algaze (2000) for an argument that the attributes of the ecological niche of southern Mesopotamia enabled that area to be the first to take the lead in developing "complex civilization." Butzer (1976:23) also notes that the 7000–4000 B.C.E. rise in Mediterranean levels, due to melting glaciers and precipitation, transformed the northern third of the Egyptian Nile delta into swamps and lagoons.
9. Jacobsen and Adams (1958) discuss two major episodes of salinization for the period in which we are most interested. The first one was in 2450–1750 B.C.E.,

and a second occurred between 1350 and 950 B.C.E. Crop yields began to decline by 2100 B.C.E. without ever recovering in ancient times.

10. The attack of group X on group Y often minimizes the full scope of activity that was involved. Often, group X was set in motion by an attack or pressure from group Z. This is one of the hazards of delineating the boundaries of a system too narrowly. The ancient world was in contact directly and indirectly with areas normally considered outside its boundaries. This is also a problem when looking for climate implications under the southwest Asian lamppost. Weather patterns in the Ukraine and southern Russia have implications for southwest Asia if they set off southern tribal migrations into the Balkans, Anatolia, and Iran that, in turn, prompt incursions into the core of the ancient world-system. Gerasimenko (1997) depicts the 2500–1000 B.C.E. era as one of strong aridification, peaking around 1500 but continuing into the first millennium B.C.E. Krementski (1997) identifies a serious and rapid climate shift around 2650–2350 B.C.E., which caused the collapse of agricultural communities in the southwest Ukraine and Moldova areas. Gerasimenko posited an earlier arid period at 4100–3800 B.C.E., but both authors describe the fourth millennium and the first half of the third millennium as generally cool and wet, favoring sedentary agriculture.

11. It is sometimes argued that Mesopotamia was sheltered from the destruction at the end of the Bronze Age because of its location, but it seems just as likely that by that time it was simply less inviting. However, Kassite Mesopotamia had its own Elamite problems roughly at the same time.

12. Butzer (1997) also observes that centers can destroy themselves via imperialism or internal conflict, with or without environmental deterioration.

Ages of Reorganization[1]

GEORGE MODELSKI

Dark ages is a familiar, if undertheorized, term of world history. In this chapter, I propose to generalize that concept and to reinterpret it as "ages of reorganization." I do this by viewing the two major periods of past "dark ages" as phases in the millennial thrust toward the formation of a world community, being one of a cascade of processes that make up world-system evolution (Devezas & Modelski 2003).

This reconceptualization allows us to see contemporary developments as the onset of another millennial age of readjustment, understood also as a world-system mechanism of self-organization. It is a means whereby the negative features of earlier developments—those of the preceding ages of accumulation and concentration—can be reined in, as it were automatically, to contain the dangers that they harbor.

I propose to take up these themes, opened up by Sing Chew in two recent papers (2002a, 2002b), and will proceed, in response, to review the following questions:

1. How robust is the concept of "dark ages"?
2. Have "dark ages" been recurrent features of world-system history?
3. Are there grounds to assume the workings of an evolutionary process?
4. Have we already entered the modern "age of reorganization"?

How Robust Is the Concept of "Dark Ages"?

Two millennium-long stretches of world history could be described as "dark ages": on following the collapse of the Sumerian, Harappan, and also Mycenaean civilizations, and a second one, following the decline and fall of the Han and the Roman empires. Such dark ages stand in sharp contrast to those preceding them, the ages of concentration, that were marked by population growth and

180

strong urban and economic expansion, as well as by rising inequalities. That concentration in turn put heavy pressures on the environment. But the dark ages that followed, while punctuated by extensive population movements and social disorder, were also characterized by systematic adjustments in the form of a cessation of economic growth, a relaxation of pressures on the environment, and a measure of redistribution of wealth and power.

The concept of a dark age is well embedded in the public mind, both in the metaphorical sense, and in reference to remembered historical experience. The entry for "Dark Ages" in the fifteenth edition of *Encyclopaedia Britannica* (1975) neatly summarizes the contemporary understanding of it:

> **Dark Ages**. A term employed from about the 18th century to denote the early medieval period of western European history; specifically it referred to the time (476–800) when there was no emperor in the west; or, more generally, to the period between c. 500 and c.1000, marked by frequent warfare and a virtual disappearance of urban life. It is now rarely used by historians because of the unacceptable value judgment it implies. Sometimes taken to derive its meaning from the fact that little was then known about the period; its more usual and pejorative sense was of a period of intellectual darkness and barbarity. It has also been used to describe a similar period (11th to 10th centuries BC) in the history of ancient Greece.[2]

The *Britannica* entry treats the term *dark ages* as a well-known, but also contested, expression. Let us highlight three of its characteristics:

1. It is a well-established concept. Catalogs show a number of books using it as a title. Historians have employed it, albeit cautiously, for maybe two centuries, and continue to use it, subject to qualifications. It is crisp and suggestive, and it has recently proven capable of being extended into the realm of environmental concerns.

2. It is a descriptive concept first applied to the period that in the classical era followed the collapse of the Western Roman empire. It was then extended to the centuries that followed the demise of the Mycenaean civilization at the close of the ancient era. It is now also used in relation to events in ancient Egypt, Mesopotamia, and South Asia. However, it primarily represents the description of a local region rather than a statement on the condition of the world system.

3. It is a concept with a judgmental edge. It is closely linked to the idea of civilization, because it is hard to think of "dark ages" before cities and writing. In the paradigmatic case of Rome we have the center of a regional

civilization apparently threatened by, and succumbing to, the onslaught of the "barbarians." In other cases, too, a "dark age" connotes conditions prevailing in what should be the center of the world system, rather than in its hinterlands, which are only expected to be "shrouded in darkness."

These characteristics make "dark ages" an interesting concept, with a fine pedigree, and they highlight important local problems, capable of arousing some attention. We should give them careful scrutiny but might also ask: what is their relationship to the general trajectory of the world system? Are they more than a descriptive reference to periods of "troubles" experienced by some societies at particular times? Are these "important phases in world system history," as Sing Chew (2002b:218) declares? What might justify projecting such historical events into the future of the modern world system?

Testing for Systemic "Dark Ages"

Can we demonstrate the existence of dark ages by an analysis of systematic data on world urbanization and world population? I shall attempt to do this by employing the "World Cities" database (see below), subject to one overriding premise: that world-system history over the long haul of millennia may be understood as a sequence of "ancient," "classical," and "modern" eras. This periodization is now commonplace among students of world history (though views might differ as to the precise dating), but it is worth being explicit because each era has its own special characteristics and is in some way more complex than its predecessor.

Can we discern, in each of these eras—ancient, classical, and modern—a phase that might be labeled "dark" in the light of the record of urbanization? We might recall that the *Britannica* entry cited above mentioned "virtual disappearance of urban life" as one principal distinguishing characteristic, the other being frequent warfare. Can we identify recurrent such phases in the available information on the history of world population?

I have put these questions to the "World Cities" database, the product of a collection effort underway since the mid–1990s and previously reported in a number of partial reports at conferences and on the Internet. Inspired by the work of Tertius Chandler, this database differs from Chandler's in that it does not attempt to cover all the world's cities but documents only those that might be regarded as the most important in each of the three eras.

The criterion of selection for the "World Cities" database is the population estimate for each city at a given point in time, on the premise that the most important cities are most likely to be those with the largest populations. The importance of the city is of course a function of its position in the world system, its contribution to the institutional structure of the system. For ancient-era urban centers, the effort is made to identify all those that have more than 10,000 inhabitants. For the classical era, the threshold is 100,000. For the modern era, our search criterion is much higher than Chandler's, viz. a population of one million. We posit that trends in world cities are representative of world urbanization at large.

Included in the collection are data from the earliest beginnings of the system of world cities, in the mid-fourth millennium B.C.E., and then at one-century intervals since 2500 B.C.E., right up to the year 2000, for which information was culled from the *U.N. Demographic Yearbook*. The database thus contains information on about 500 urban centers distributed over five millennia, with a total of about 1,000 individual data points. The entire project has now been assembled under one cover as *World Cities: 3000 B.C.E. to 2000* (Modelski 2003), together with a commentary and some analysis of propositions bearing on world-system evolution.

Tables 1 and 2 supply the basic information for answering the questions we have posed regarding dark ages (for fuller data, see Modelski 2003).

The number of world cities expanded between 3000 B.C.E. and 2000 B.C.E., and between 1000 B.C.E. and 1, but remained stationary or declined in subsequent periods. The same goes for the world population, which expanded between 3000 and 2000 B.C.E. and between 1000 B.C.E. and 1, but remained stationary between 2000 and 1000 B.C.E., and between 1 and 1000.

In the ancient world, the collapse of Sumer and Harappa after 2000 B.C.E. was offset by an increasingly wide distribution of cities after 1500 B.C.E. In the classical world, expansion continued to year 1, followed by a subsequent

Table 1 Estimated number of world cities and size of world population in the ancient and classical eras (from Modelski 2003:92, 216, column 2)

World Cities (number)					
	3000 B.C.E.	2000 B.C.E.	1000 B.C.E.	1	1000
Ancient	10	22	16		
Classical			4	25	25
World Population (million)					
	3000 B.C.E.	2000 B.C.E.	1000 B.C.E.	1	1000
Ancient	14	50	50		
Classical			50	254	255

Table 2　Regional distributions of world cities in ancient and classical eras (from Modelski 2003:38, 59)

Ancient World Cities (10,000+)					
	3000 B.C.E.	2500 B.C.E.	2000 B.C.E.	1500 B.C.E.	1000 B.C.E.
West Asia	10	18	16	4	3
Sumer	8	13	11	—	—
Mediterranean		2		8	9
South Asia		2	6		
East Asia				3	4
Total	10	22	22	15	16

Classical World Cities (100,000+)					
	1000 B.C.E.	500 B.C.E.	1	500	1000
East Asia	1	8	9	5	6
South and SE Asia		1	6	1	4
Mediterranean	2	5	8	8	4
West Asia	1	2	2	2	10
The Americas				3	1
Total	4	16	25	19	25

period of no growth or contraction, until growth in West Asia regained the level reached in year 1.

The following paragraphs summarize the conclusions that can be gleaned from these data.

1. Table 1 shows that urban growth (that is, concentration) occurred in the first millennium (between 3000 and 2000 B.C.E.), whereas overall zero growth was characteristic of the second (after 2000 B.C.E.). In actual numbers, this means that the system of ten "world cities" in 3000 B.C.E. expanded in number to 22 in 2000 B.C.E. but then shrank to 16 by 1000 B.C.E. The same pattern holds for the classical period, though in a slightly stronger form: a rise from four major (100,000+) cities in 1000 B.C.E. to 25 in the year 1, but still the same number (25) an entire millennium later. Here we have the first *prima facie* case for a "dark age" both in the ancient and the classical worlds, showing up as a no-growth period. This is not a case of systemic deurbanization; cities did not disappear, just stopped expanding. Urban life continued albeit dispersed, and at a slower pace. The basic phenomenon that we can identify

here is the cessation of growth. Through the prism of urbanization, and at the systemic level, the two dark ages represent periods of stasis.

2. Lest we dismiss this first basic finding as an exception, or aberration, we see it confirmed in the second part of Table 1, in the figures on world population.[3] Here again we observe growth in the initial millennium of the ancient era (3000 to 2000 B.C.E.), followed by no growth in the next one. Data for the classical era are better. The first millennium (1000 B.C.E. to 1) shows a sharp rise, from 50 million in 1000 B.C.E. to 254 million one thousand years later. The second, however, shows no growth whatever beyond the level attained in year 1.[4] Although the case is less strong for the ancient era, for which few firm data are now available, they show a similar trend. This means that both the data sets in Table 1, that is, the data on world urbanization and on world population, converge. When population expands, cities grow; when population stops growing, cities stagnate or decline. Here is the second basic characteristic of the two "dark ages": they are periods of zero growth in population.

3. A finer-grained picture of the two eras may be gleaned from Table 2, which shows regional distributions of world cities. It indicates that the quantitative stasis characteristic of the two "dark ages" does not mean lack of movement, or change. In the ancient world, the most striking illustration is the disappearance of Sumer (in southern Mesopotamia) and of the Indus Valley culture (in South Asia), balanced by the onset of urbanization in the Mediterranean and East Asia, the two growth centers of the classical world.

Sumer was the original "heartland of cities" of the ancient world. In 3000 B.C.E., Sumer accounted for eight out of ten world cities, the remaining two (in Iran and Northern Mesopotamia) also being Sumer-influenced. After 2300 B.C.E., the city-states of Mesopotamia lost their independence to the empire of Sargon of Akkad. In 2000 B.C.E., Sumer still held one-half of the total, and the other important group, in the Indus Valley, was still linked to Sumer. But Ur III collapsed under the pressure of the Elamites and the Amorites (for example, Hammurabi), and in the 1740s B.C.E. disaster struck the south. To quote a recent study (Postgate 1992:299), during the subsequent dark ages in Mesopotamia, "we are confronted with an absence of written information," and "there is a consistent absence of archeological remains at the southern cities." The Sumerian language died, and its civilization came to an end, while a similar fate befell the cities of the Indus Valley. The Hyksos, believed to be Amorites, established themselves in Egypt and, in an episode for which records are sparse, controlled it until they in turn were expelled, in an effort that launched the New Kingdom. At the same time, urban life was emerging in the Mediterranean (Crete, Mycenae) but collapsed after 1200 B.C.E., inaugurating what in the twentieth century has often been described as the Greek "dark ages," with abundant evidence of destruction and depopulation, but also of Greece's transformation, to use a felicitous expression, from "Citadel to Polis."[5] While Egypt remained an island of urban life, its once-powerful New Kingdom faltered, the Hittite empire collapsed, and Babylon came under attack from Aramean desert tribes that had settled in Syria. Almost all the centers of the world system were now under severe pressure from the hinterlands.

In the classical era, urbanization spread to all the major world regions. The general story of the second "dark age" is not restricted to any one region in recounting the decline and fall of empires. Contrary to a widely held impression, imperial structures were not the dominant organizational force of premodern history. The great urban expansion of the first classical millennium was the product of networks of autonomous societies stretching across Eurasia, East Asia, and the Mediterranean. The empires that emerged toward the close of this millennium—Han in China, Rome in the West, and Maurya (somewhat earlier) in northern India—no more than consolidated the growth of the preceding centuries.[6] It was the collapse of these empires that animated the dark ages of the classical world, and paradigmatically so in Europe. That collapse was due as much to the inherent weaknesses of their far-flung, over-stretched, and undemocratic organization[7] as to the ascendancy of the hinterlands. The intrusion of the Huns and the Germanic and other tribes into the Mediterranean world, culminating in the sack of Rome (C.E. 410, 455), have become emblematic of the image of "barbarians at the gates." But similar processes were also at work in South Asia, where the Kushans, a clan of Yue Qi nomads, established a wealthy domain that supplanted the post-Mauryan world, and in China the late Han dynasty disintegrated under conditions of peasant rebellions and military coups, leading to what historian Jacques Gernet has called the "Chinese Middle Ages." The imperial capital Luoyang was sacked twice, in 190 C.E. by a military adventurer whose army comprised large numbers of "barbarians," and in 311 by a Xiongnu ruler. This left the field open to "barbarian" rule in northern China but sparked a cultural boom in the south.[8]

In the seventh and eighth centuries the Arab armies brought down the Sassanian empire of Persia and severely weakened that of Byzantium, besieging Constantinople itself in 674 and 717. The Arabs came out of the desert hinterlands of the Fertile Crescent and proceeded to build a Moslem community *(Ummah)* in the central portion of Eurasia. At a time when Europe was experiencing its "dark ages," the world of Islam was flourishing.[9]

By the end of the classical era, we find the four main Eurasian regions assuming quasidistinct identities, each with its own urban center. The overall level of urbanization is basically unchanged; zero growth, however, did not mean stability but entailed significant turmoil consequent upon the decline of the established centers and empires in combination with opportunities for shifts in power, new alliances, and population movements. It is not at all obvious from the last column in Table 2 that the next (modern) surge of urbanization and population growth would occur in Europe, but it does make it appear likely that such a surge would rapidly spread to all of the world's major regions.

An Evolutionary Process

What are the findings of this empirical analysis of dark ages? Having searched four millennia of world history for systematic data on world urbanization and population, we cannot escape the conclusion that the evidence suggests an evolutionary process.[10] In the first place, it indexes social change on the scale of the world system—call it world community formation, integration, or socialization. Over *la longue durée*, moreover, it shows urbanization gaining both in geographical extension and in complexity, moving from smaller to larger cities serving a population that grows by orders of magnitude. Over the same span of time, the urban or "civilized" way of life has been selected for, at the expense of its nomadic, tribal, or rural alternatives. Some fundamental innovations have been launched and adopted worldwide: cities and urbanism; literacy, information storage, and time management; and the experience of solidarity on scales larger than blood lines or face-to-face contact.

We also find that the process of world social integration is not simply a matter of marching up a linear slope of progress. It is a learning process that includes periods of growth as well as of pause. On the one hand, some periods undoubtedly display characteristics suggestive of "dark ages." In particular, the second millennium of each era (second millennium B.C.E., first millennium C.E.) feature zero growth in urbanization and world population, that is, two dimensions that are crucial to world-system organization, a condition that would suggest stability, if not necessarily stagnation. On the other hand, each of these two millennia also manifests great structural changes, evoking evolutionary processes. In world perspective, we observe no general deurbanization, population decline, or overall loss of evolutionary potential. That is why, while bearing in mind that the "dark" appellation might be appropriate regarding certain identifiable "local" or regional situations, in the wider perspective we cannot describe the world system as moving through unequivocally "dark" phases. The world system has not exactly passed though dark ages, although it has experienced some localized "dark spots."

In sum, what we see is a long-term social process of world proportions, with 1,000-year long periods featuring zero growth, but also important transformations: for without the dark ages, could we have had classical Greece or modern Europe? How do we conceptualize these ambiguous periods?

In an earlier Lund conference paper (Modelski 2000:38), I proposed that the evolution of the world community has entailed a four-phase learning process with 1,000-year long phases, a process that can be characterized as one of world community formation, or socialization:

> The evolution of the human community . . . is not a process of linear expansion but one of persistent tension between the pressures for innovation . . . and the demands for equality that are the operative conditions of every community. Innovations produce concentrations of metropolitan power . . . often centered on opulent cities and brilliant empires. Forming in opposition to them are the hinterlands . . . that from time to time organize themselves to effect a system leveling. . . . It is hypothesized that major phases of concentration, a millennium in length, alternate with equally significant intervals of hinterland assertiveness. . . .

This alternation of millennial phases of concentration with phases of "reorganization" (see Table 3) can be viewed as a mechanism of self-organization (using the term in the sense proposed by Eric Jantsch [1980] in *The Self-Organizing Universe*). The oscillations are mechanisms of social leveling but also of environmental balancing. The data on urbanization and population offer strong confirmation of such long-term fluctuations.

The alternation of millennial phases of concentration and redistribution characterizes the process of social integration at the level of world system.[11] We postulate a human propensity to cooperate that tends to bring about the evolution of forms of cooperative action, even at the global level. The four millennial phases in the ancient and classical eras that we have just reviewed can be seen as steps in the creation of several regional matrices of cooperation, frameworks within which large-scale cooperative action can develop. As we have seen, four city-based networks of interaction did emerge toward the close of the classical era: in East Asia, around the Kaifeng-Hangzhou axis; in South Asia, between Kannauji, near the Ganges, and the Chola capital of Thanjuvur, in the south; in the Moslem world, from Baghdad to Cairo; and in Europe, centered on Constantinople.

Table 3 Alternation of phases of concentration and reorganization in world system integration

Year	3000 B.C.E.	2000 B.C.E.	1000 B.C.E.	1	1000	1850	2900
Period	Regional solidarities				Global community		
Phase	Concen- tration	Reorgani- zation	Recon- centration	Reorgani- zation	Concen- tration	Reorgani- zation	Recon- centration

Over a period of some four millennia, we thus observe the formation, at the world level, of networks of regional solidarities. These involved at various times extensive trade linkages, vast political structures including empires, and wide-ranging religious communities. In the classical world, empires were linked to the spread of religious communities, as in Asoka's espousal of Buddhism in the Mauryan era around 250 B.C.E.; followed by Kanishka's Kushan patronage (around 100 C.E.) that propelled it toward East Asia; Constantine's embrace of Christianity in the Mediterranean world (312 C.E.); the "great religious fervor" in "Buddhist" China in the "middle ages" (Gernet 1982:172); and the Islamic empire founded by Arab cavalry. Accompanying these changes, also, were of course the dissemination of knowledge and technologies, particularly of the military kind, together with the intensification of long-distance commerce.

Periods of reorganization tended toward eroding concentration and enhancing leveling. But these ancient and classical times were a "rough world" of uncertain order and pervasive insecurities, lacking in consensus on basic rules and institutions. In these "rough" conditions of the ancient and classical worlds, the catalysts of readjustment were nomads of the deserts, steppes, and forests, who proceeded to impose their rule on the faltering centers by force of arms, seizing new lands, power, wealth, and social positions. The ages of reorganization saw few contests among central powers but many assaults on power centers from the hinterlands. Complementing their military strength was the exhaustion of the centers, both material resource exhaustion (as in degradation of soils, deforestation, and pollution) and human exhaustion (through epidemics, manpower shortages, and lack of adaptability).[12] The question we can now pose is if such conditions are likely to resurface once again, in the modern era of the world system?

A New Age of Reorganization?

What reasons have we for anticipating another age of reorganization? Table 4 shows the past millennium as another period of concentration. From small and slow beginnings, close to being aborted by thirteenth-century Mongol-induced devastations, the expansion of world cities entered a spurt in the eighteenth century that took them from four "million-plus" cities in 1800 to almost 300 only two centuries later. This is an unprecedented growth rate that probably cannot be sustained for much longer, if only because world urbanization has already reached 50 percent of the world population. The same trend is evident in world population, which, according to the United Nations projection of 1999 that is used in the table, is expected to approach a plateau by 2100. Both these trends, urbanization and world population, are thus approaching a peak about a millennium after the closing of the classical age. Their peaks may or may not be sustainable, but much greater concentration seems unlikely beyond that point. The empirical projections support the theoretical prediction that the process of world community formation (what I have also called "socialization") is entering, or has entered, another age of reorganization.

In turning our gaze toward the future, we need to sharpen our dating scheme. We have so far operated with millennial (1,000-year long) time spans, and at such scales, an error margin of one or even two centuries might be tolerable. We should add, too, that this millennial interval is no mere matter of operating with round figures, although this may seem a legitimate criticism. In the cascade of evolutionary processes that is founded on generational turnover, with an average of some 30 years per generation, the four phases of world integration are each postulated to extend over 32 generations, that is, on the average, around 1,000 years (Devezas & Modelski 2003:18ff). This interval thus has theoretical as well as empirical support.

Empirical data provided in Table 4 indicate that the twentieth century was indeed marked by spectacular spurts both in urbanization and population that appear similar to those in the centuries around 2000 B.C.E. and around the year 1, even though the most recent rate of growth is the highest ever. But these long-term world-systemic trends must also be understood as synchronized with shorter-range, global processes such as K-waves, long cycles of global politics, and possibly also democratization. For these shorter sequences of events, the mid-nineteenth century suggests a turning-point, with say 1850 as the "start" of a new era (as shown in Table 3).[13] That would suggest that a new age of readjustment has now been underway maybe for over a century and a half and will continue its course until the latter part of this millennium. Setting the "start" of modern "reorganization" at 1850 does not mean that zero

Table 4 World cities and world population in the modern era (from Modelski 2003:74, 216, column 7)

Year	World cities (1 million+ inhabitants)	World population (million)
1000	1	310
1500	1	500
1800	4	980
1900	16	1650
2000	363	6161
2100	?	9460

growth must already have begun. In fact, the momentum of concentration may be expected to continue for a while and was exceptionally powerful in the twentieth century. But countervailing forces are now mobilizing, starting with new ideas, new ways of looking at the world.

The modern Age of Reorganization will be different from the ancient and the classical ones, in that the world system now shows higher capacity for problem solving, including problems of readjustment and redistribution. Knowledge about the functioning of global processes is at a decidedly higher level, making an informational blackout on the model of the earlier dark ages hard to imagine. The bounds of solidarity are in the process of extending to all of humanity, institutional structures at the global level are gaining ground, and the economic surpluses available for global action are becoming significant.

If, in the earlier four millennia, the basis for world order was expansive regional solidarities, the following four millennia would be more than enough to ensure the formation of an integrated world community. Within such a framework, problems of redistribution should appear manageable, even for a world whose cities and population have ceased to expand. It would also be a "nicer" world to live in than those plagued by fear of the "barbarians at the gates."

The most substantial promise of a "nicer" world lies in democratization, combined with the IT Revolution, and the onset of global governance. These are processes that have been registering substantial advances in the past millennium. The practices of democracy are now well entrenched in a number of nation-states, and by 2000, over one-half of the world's population lived in democracies, a condition greatly favored by a parallel rise in urbanization. But democracy needs to be seen not just as a matter of electoral machinery and constitutional engineering; it needs to be recognized as a condition of leveling that extends to all spheres of social life. The conditions of democratic life at the scale of the world system are yet to be realized, but they are aided by the rapid spread of information, which suggests the very antithesis of "dark ages," and advances in global governance. These are huge challenges but ultimately inescapable, for only on a democratic foundation can a secure world order be constructed that is adequate to the challenges of a new age of readjustment.

Implications for World Environment

If an "age of reorganization" can indeed be anticipated, what are the chief implications for world environment?

1. "Reorganization" is a long-term mechanism of self-organization in the world system. Problems and imbalances of the ages of concentration—that is, those that create and empower the center—have in the past twice been corrected by the forces generated by such ages of reorganization, and they are likely to be so again.

2. This analysis predicts an approaching limit to urbanization and world population growth, which would alleviate pressures on the environment, though on a scale of centuries.

3. The modern age of reorganization is unlikely to assume the form of a generalized, systemic "dark age" (barring a "nuclear winter") because of ongoing processes of globalization. The Information Revolution, the evolution of democratic practices, and improved global governance make it likely that problems of readjustment will find resolution in a manner more acceptable than those experienced in the ancient and classical eras.

Notes

1. This is a revised version of a paper prepared for the Lund conference on "World System History and Global Environmental Change," which bore the title "Ages of Redistribution." The present title conveys more accurately the main thrust of this contribution. A different version of this chapter also appears in the journal *Nature and Culture*.

2. This entry is repeated, in a slightly abbreviated form, in *The New Encyclopaedia Britannica*, 1998 edition, 3:888.

3. For the historical series of world population data derived from the United States Bureau of the Census, see Modelski (2003), Appendix 5.

4. The data for the years 1 and 1000 are from the world population series by Jean-Noel Biraben (1979, cited in Modelski 2003). A more recent United Nations

Table 5. "Dark Ages" in World History

Ancient	Duration	Authors	Why "Dark"
Ancient Egyptian	2200–1700 B.C.E. 1700–1550 B.C.E.	Bell *AmJArch* 1975	Floods, famines
Post-Sumerian	2000 B.C.E. –1400	Postgate Weiss	Amorites Economic collapse Salination
Post-Harappan	1900–1000 B.C.E.	Kenoyer	Ghaggar-Hakra dries up Civic disorder Sumerian collapse
Post-Mycenaean	1200–700 B.C.E.	Snodgrass Thomas & Connant	Destruction Depopulation Drought
Classical	**Duration**	**Authors**	**Why "Dark"**
Post-Western Rome	500–1000 B.C.E.	Buckle Oman	Imperial collapse
Post-Han	200–600	Gernet	Imperial collapse
Post-Mayryan	50–300	Smith Ch.3	Sakas, Kushans
Post-Gupta	600–1000 B.C.E.	Smith 190	Ephtalite Hunas
Post-Mongol (Central Asia)	1200–1500 B.C.E.		Devastation
Post-Mayan	800–	Webster 2002	System collapse

     estimate is 300 million in year 1 and 310 million in the year 1000. The figures for China are the best documented, because they are based on censuses that have survived in official histories; they indicate a population size that basically remained unchanged for one thousand years.

5. Carol Thomas and Gary Connant (1999) argue that classical Greece could not have developed without the preceding "dark age," and wonder whether that expression refers to conditions actually prevailing ("a lengthy, severe and widespread cultural depression") or to "our own ignorance of them."

6. In year 1, empires controlled 18 of 25 world cities; by 500 C.E., they held sway over only 8 out of 19, and in 1000, 6 out of 25 world cities (Modelski 2003).

7. As Robert Wright (2000:134) comments, "by the time the barbarians descended on the western Roman Empire *en masse*, it deserved to die."

8. Jacques Gernet (1982:172,181) regards as "inaccurate" comparisons between the incursions of the "Five Barbarians" of the fourth to sixth centuries in northern China and the invasions experienced a little later in Europe. He argues that,

unlike the Huns in the West, who were true nomads, the Chinese "barbarians" had already been much sinicized, and that no link can be established between the Huns (in the West) and the Xiongnu (in East Asia). Gernet's point is valid regarding the Huns, but not for the Germanic tribes, who had been interacting with the Romans for several centuries. China continued to be exposed to intrusions from the steppes until the fourteenth century.

9. The center of the world city system nucleated in West Asia (Sumer) at the opening of the ancient era and returned to West Asia (Baghdad) at the close of the classical era. The "flourishing" of cities in the Moslem world around 1000 C.E. did no more than restore the world city system to its size one thousand years earlier.

10. It is, however, only one in a "cascade" of world system processes, including what I elsewhere refer to as the world economy process, the political active zone process, and the world system process (Devezas & Modelski 2003:18–24; Modelski 2000:37–43).

11. Such phases are to be understood as overlapping rather than as sharply demarcating. Yes, we did enter an age of reorganization in the mid-nineteenth century, but that is not to say that at that time a bell rang, and a no-growth period set in. Rather, what I postulate is the slow start of a millennial learning process best described by an S-curve that has an initially slow take-off but that gradually builds up to a stronger movement. The driving force of "reorganization" or "readjustment" is the social movement of democratization, a process that in its institutional form may reach the bulk of the world population by the end of the century. That would create the social force for increased redistribution, and for structural change in global governance, in the next century. At the same time, the momentum of the age of concentration will continue for some time to come. World population is not expected to level off before the end of the century, and urbanization must reach some kind of equilibrium in the same time-frame. More generally, an overall no-growth regime may not be expected to set in more fully for another century or so.

12. This is an endogenous account of the process of reorganization; it leaves aside such exogenous forces as earthquakes and non-anthropogenic climate change.

13. The mid-nineteenth century (1850) marks both a new period of the world economy and a new phase of global political evolution.

CHAPTER 13

Sustainable Intensive Exploitation of Amazonia: Cultural, Environmental, and Geopolitical Perspectives

BETTY J. MEGGERS

Whereas growing concern over the environmental and social consequences of global warming and globalization is stimulating biologists and archeologists to collaborate in identifying the impact of climatic fluctuations on cultural developments in the past, the existence of any intrinsic or intermittent limitation on cultural complexity is a controversial issue among anthropologists working in Amazonia. One faction argues that indigenous societies "did not adapt to nature, but rather they created the world they wanted" and that they "figured out successful and efficient ways to sustain large and dense populations, produce surpluses, and manage wastes" (Denevan 2001; Erickson 2003; Heckenberger 2002; Neves 1999–2000). This group cites the existence of a town of 200,000 to 400,000 at the mouth of the Tapajós (Woods in Mann 2002), a population of a million on Marajó Island (Roosevelt 1991) and "civilizations of considerable complexity, possibly even protostates" in the Guianas (Whitehead 1994). The other faction points to inherent environmental limitations on human carrying capacity and provides archeological and ethnographic evidence for prehistoric settlement and social behavior similar to that of surviving traditional societies (Clark & Uhl 1987; Meggers 1996; Robinson & Bennett 2000).

Resolution of this conflict has more than academic significance. The rapid depletion of natural resources elsewhere on the planet, accelerating human population growth, and increased technological sophistication make the relatively undeveloped resources of Amazonia increasingly attractive to landless immigrants and international corporations. If permanent settlements larger than Manaus were supported by local subsistence resources in the past, their existence needs to be documented rather than assumed.

Environmental Limitations

The poverty of Amazonian soils and the compensating adaptations of the vegetation to edaphic and climatic constraints have long been recognized. Weischet and Caviedes (1993) identify an "ecologically decisive difference with far-reaching consequences" between Amazonian rainforests and extratropical forests; namely, most of the nutrients and all the calcium are stored in the biomass in the former and in the soil in the latter. Soil properties that cannot be markedly altered by humans are (1) poor weatherable primary mineral content, (2) low cation exchange capacity, and (3) high mineralization rate of organic matter. Soil acidity, aluminum toxicity, inability to fix phosphorus, intense leaching, imperfect drainage, and nutrient poverty are additional constraints (Fearnside and Filho 2001; Leopoldo 2000; OEA 1974; Serrão 1985; Sombroek 1984). The biota have overcome these obstacles by rapid degradation of organic debris, recycling, and storage of the nutrients in the vegetation. Retrieval is maximized by interspersal of plants with different nutrient requirements, which also inhibits the spread of pathogens.

Although annual deposition of sediments eroded from the Andean headwaters renews the fertility of soils on the *varzea* (floodplain) under ideal conditions, "the higher fertility does not automatically translate into a higher potential for agricultural yield" (WinklerPrins 1999). The inception, rate, duration, and magnitude of annual inundation fluctuate, major deviations are unpredictable (Santos 1982), and crop loss in some regions has been estimated at one year in four (Barrow 1985). In short, "with the present traditional forms of cultivation, the cost-benefit comparison is not significantly better than with equivalent forms of cultivation on the Terra Firme" (Petrick 1978:39–40).

The principal evidence in support of dense sedentary populations is the existence of patches of anthropogenic black soil (*terra preta*) along the Amazon and many of its tributaries. Its composition differs from the adjacent soil in higher contents of calcium, magnesium, potassium, phosphorus, and carbon, lower content of aluminum, low nutrient leaching, higher water retention, high cation exchange capacity, and high proportion of organic matter. Although the specific process of formation is uncertain, there is general agreement that it develops from the disintegration of habitation refuse, and this assessment is supported by the nearly universal presence of fragments of pottery (Lehmann et al. 2003). Agricultural productivity is greater for some crops, but fertility is too high for manioc, enhances weed production, and declines with continuous cultivation (Hiraoka et al. 2003).

Archeological Evidence

The perishable composition of all other cultural remains makes fragments of pottery discarded in habitation sites the only significant form of evidence. Fortunately, pottery is among the cultural traits subject to evolutionary drift with resulting possibilities for reconstructing prehistoric settlement and social behavior. Realization of this potential depends on collecting unselected samples of adequate size from the surface or stratigraphic excavations and using uniform criteria for their classification. The trends in each excavation establish the direction of change, and excavations with compatible types, trends, and relative frequencies are interdigitated to produce a seriated sequence. Sites that fit into the same seriation identify an endogamous community and define its territory. Samples that cannot be interdigitated identify earlier, later, or contemporary communities associated with the same or a different ceramic tradition (see Meggers 1999 for details). Applying this methodology to habitation sites on the *terra firme* and along the *varzea* permits establishing their magnitude and permanence.

Territories
Classification of the pottery from 35 *terra firme* sites on the lower Tocantins in southeastern Amazonia produced five seriated sequences distinguished by differences in the presence, relative frequencies, and trends of the undecorated and decorated pottery types. Plotting the distributions of the sites identified contiguous territories with permanent boundaries that correlate with physical changes in the river and associated differences in the composition, seasonality, and productivity of fishing and in the methods of capture (Figure 1). This correlation has been identified both archeologically and ethnographically elsewhere on the *terra firme* and suggests that maximization of adaptation to one set of riverine conditions was not equally effective in another, making reciprocity a more effective strategy than invasion (Meggers 1996; Miller et al. 1992; Simões & de Araujo-Costa 1987).

Village Permanence
Wide separation between successive levels of the same excavation in a seriated sequence implies abandonment and reoccupation of the location sampled. The magnitude of differences in the radiocarbon dates from consecutive levels in the same excavation at RO-PV–35 on the Jamarí in southwestern Amazonia, and the noncontemporaneity of dates from the same depth in different parts of the site indicate that the surface area cannot be assumed to correspond to a single continuously occupied village (Figure 2).

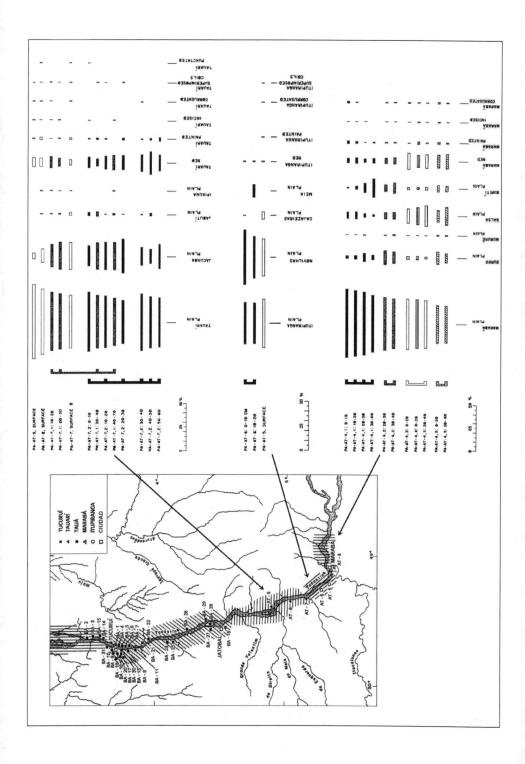

Figure 1 • (opposite) Seriated ceramic sequences of the Tauarí, Itupiranga, and Marabá phases on the Tocantins, the easternmost tributary of the lower Amazon. The vertical bars at the left connect consecutive levels of stratigraphic excavations, which establish the directions of change. The differences in the trends and relative frequencies of the pottery types require construction of three seriations defining endogamous territories. The boundaries correlate with differences in riverine topography and aquatic fauna, seasonal fluctuation in productivity, and methods of exploitation (revised from Simões & de Araujo-Costa 1987).

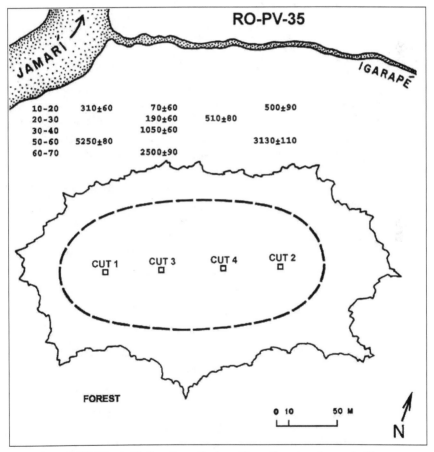

Figure 2 • RO-PV–35, a habitation site on the Jamarí in southwestern Amazonia. The horizontal and vertical discrepancies in radiocarbon dates from four stratigraphic excavations support seriational evidence for multiple episodes of reoccupation by small villages rather than long-term occupation by a large population (courtesy of Eurico Th. Miller).

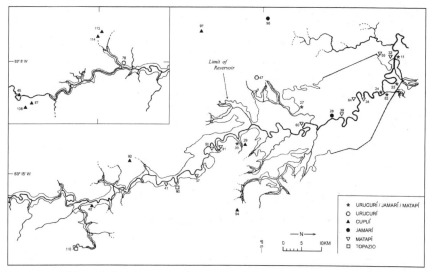

Figure 3 • Of the 45 habitation sites on the Jamarí with stratigraphic information, 26 were occupied during a single phase. Only six were occupied throughout the entire sequence, and the remainder were occupied successively by two phases. As a result, the number of sites increased through time, giving the misleading impression of high population density (courtesy of Eurico Th. Miller).

Village Contemporaneity

The assumption that the patches of *terra preta* along Amazonian rivers represent contemporary villages is also incompatible with the archeological evidence. For example, survey along the Jamarí identified five ceramic phases representing three successive periods of occupation between 200 B.C.E. and European contact. All belong to the same ceramic tradition and differ in the trends and relative frequencies of the pottery types. Of the forty-five habitation sites with stratigraphic information, twenty-five were occupied during a single period and only six were occupied during all three periods (Figure 3). When reoccupation occurred, it was usually adjacent to rather than on top of the previous refuse, increasing the surface dimensions of the site. As a consequence, the number and dimensions of sites increased through time, giving a misleading impression of the density of settlements and the magnitude of the population (for example, Kern et al. 2003).

Archeological surveys along the lower Xingú (Perota 1992), the upper Essequibo in southern Guyana, on the Rupununi savanna and adjacent Brazil (Evans & Meggers 1960; Ribeiro 1999), along the Ventuari, Manipiare

(Evans, Meggers, & Cruxent 1960), and the upper Orinoco and Casiquiare in Venezuelan Guiana (Cruxent & Kamen-Kaye 1950; Wagner & Areuelo 1986; Zucchi 1991) have all identified endogamous territories with boundaries that correlate with changes in riverine resources and reoccupation of sites with resultant increase in their area. No permanent settlements, social stratification, or other evidence of proto-states has been encountered in the Guianas or elsewhere on the *terra firme*.

No information on settlement pattern is available from the Santarém region, but surveys along the lower Madeira (Simões & Lopes 1987) and the left bank of the Amazon east of Manaus have also identified endogamous territories and village movement (Simões & Correa 1987; Simões & Machado 1987). The most extensive survey on Marajó was conducted along the Camutins in the center of the island. Excavations in 34 mounds indicated that each elite burial mound was associated with five to six habitation mounds, giving an estimated population of about 2,000. The presence of dams, weirs, and ponds suggests that fishing was a major subsistence resource (Schaan 2004). Like eastern Marajó, the region is unsuitable for agriculture, but it is covered with dense stands of palms including *Mauritia flexuosa*. Starch from the trunks is the principal carbohydrate source among the Warao in the Orinoco delta and may have played the same role among the Marajoara (Meggers 2001).

Ethnographic Evidence

The accuracy of the archeological interpretations is supported by the existence of the same settlement and social behavior among contemporary indigenous communities that preserve their traditional behavior. Although ethnographers rarely provide such data and many groups have abandoned their indigenous way of life, endogamous territories with permanent boundaries, matrilocal residence, frequently moved villages, reoccupation of sites by the same community, and avoidance of sites occupied by previous groups have all been reported.

Territories
Contiguous territories bisected by rivers and occupied by endogamous communities have been reported among the Akawaio (Figure 4; Colson 1983–84), Achuar (Uriarte 1985), Cubeo (Goldman 1966), Siona/Secoya (Vickers 1983), Kalapalo (Basso 1973), and Yukpa (Ruddle 1974). Boundaries are stable and often coincide with rapids or tributary creeks or are separated by unoccupied zones. Exploitation of resources is restricted to the community and rights are respected or defended by supernatural sanctions rather than warfare (Århem 1981; Conklin 2001; Descola 1994b).

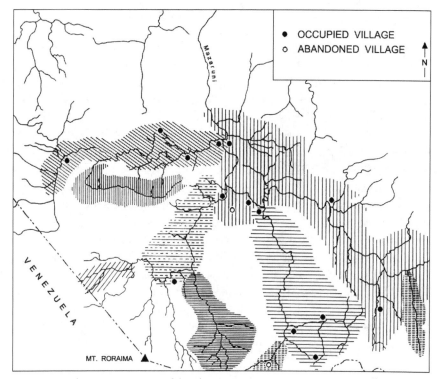

Figure 4 • Endogamous territories of the Akawaio in west-central Guyana, showing the same pattern of bisection by the river and boundaries at tributaries reconstructed for the prehistoric communities on the Tocantins (after Colson 1983–84).

Village Movement

Villages are moved on the average every five to ten years, when the house begins to deteriorate, local game is depleted, or land in the vicinity suitable for gardens is exhausted. Reoccupation of their own former village sites has been reported among the Akawaio (Butt 1977), Kalapalo (Basso 1973), Siona/Secoya (Vickers 1983), Piaroa (Zent 1992), and Huaorani (Rival 1996). Avoidance of habitation sites of earlier populations has been documented for the Kalapalo (Basso 1973) and Tukanoans (Reichel-Dolmatoff 1996). Both these traits are intelligible in the context of the widespread practice of burial in the floor of the house (Århem 1981; Basso 1973; Butt 1977; Descola 1994b; Gallois 1981; Reichel-Dolmatoff 1996; Vickers 1989; Zent 1992). This situation makes it doubtful that *terra preta* sites were cultivated by Pre-Columbian groups.

Carrying Capacity

Whereas some ethnographers consider that contemporary Amazonians underexploit their subsistence resources "to a considerable degree" (Descola 1994a) and estimate that a population several times larger could be sustained (Allen & Tizón 1973; Århem 1976; Lizot 1980; Wagley 1977), this optimistic assessment is not shared by their informants. The Machiguenga fear subsistence failure and practice a wide variety of risk-avoidance behavior (Baksh & Johnson 1990). The Achuar consider the daily gardening routine risky in spite of its high productivity and take ritual precautions (Descola 1989). Some groups refrain from exploiting certain edible tubers, reserving them as "famine foods" (Lizot 1984; Price 1990; Schultes 1977). Contemporary indigenous and *caboclo* communities consider the floodplain unreliable and generally plant subsistence crops on higher ground (Baksh & Johnson 1990; Parker et al. 1983).

Similar concern is reflected in reproductive behavior. The Tapirapé have an "ironclad rule" that no woman may have more than three children, and no more than two of the same sex (Wagley 1977); the Siona/Secoya ideal is four offspring four to six years apart (Vickers 1989). If a Cashinahua woman had a child more frequently than every three to four years, older women harassed her husband for being a sex fiend (Kensinger 1995). Abstinence, contraception, abortion, and infanticide are widespread. Although it has been argued that protein is not a limiting factor for humans (Nietschmann 1980; Vickers 1984), this view is contradicted not only by the existence of a wide variety of temporary and permanent taboos on consumption of various species and by rotation of hunting zones (Figure 5) but also by estimates of sustainable

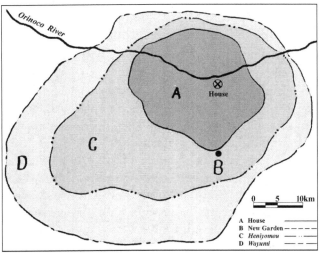

Figure 5 • Hunting territories of a Yanomami community in southern Venezuela. A, One-day individual hunt; B, Temporary camp; C, Four to five-day communal hunt; D, Annual sojourn of the entire community during several weeks (after Good 1987, Figure 16.1).

A House
B New Garden
C *Heniyomou*
D *Wayumi*

Table 1 Sustainable population density estimated from carrying capacity of hunting and agriculture compared with that recorded among contemporary Amazonian groups.

Sustainable Carrying Capacity		
0.2/km²	Robinson & Bennett 2000:24 (hunting)	
0.2/km²	Hill & Padwe 2000 (hunting)	
<1/km²	Milner-Gulland et al. 2003:351 (hunting)	
<0.2/km²	Phillips 1993:30–31 (gathering)	
0.24/ha	Fearnside 1990:195 (soil)	
<0.8/km²	Clark & Uhl 1987:13 (soil)	
Contemporary Human Density		
1.5/km²	Yukpa-Yuko	Ruddle 1974:28
0.087/km²	Piaroa	Zent 1998
0.08/km²	Achuar (inland)	Descola 1994b:61
0.44/km²	Achuar (riverine)	Descola 1994b:61
0.9–1.8/km²	Runa	Irvine 1989:225
<1/mile²	Ye'kwana, Yanomamo	Hames 1980:33
0.2/km²	Siona-Secoya	Vickers 1991:77
0.5/km²	Huaorani	Mena et al. 2000:58
0.025/km²	Waorani	Yost & Kelley 1983:192
0.03/km²	Aché	Hill & Padwe 2000:56
0.03/km²	Tucanoan	Jackson 1994:386
0.03/km²	Machiguenga	Johnson 1989:215
0.24–0.29/km²	Yanomama	Lizot 1980:65
0.2/km²	Ka'apor	Balée 1994:2

hunting. Combining observations of species density in unhunted sites, estimates of sustainable harvest for preferred species with different life spans, actual harvest rates in hunted sites, and natural predation offtake rates indicates that sustainable harvest of game in tropical forests rarely exceeds 200 kg/km² and is probably around 150 kg/km². Per capita consumption of ± 25 kg indicates that the maximum sustainable human density in most *terra firme* forests is ca 0.2/km². The similarity between this estimate and the population densities observed among indigenous communities is unlikely to be coincidental (Table 1). Its correlation with carrying capacity is also indicated by the environmental degradation that follows increased village size, sedentism, and abandonment of traditional behavior (Simões & Correa 1987; Descola 1981; Eden 1974; Gross 1983; Henley 1982; Kane 1995; Stearman 1990; Triana 1987; Yost 1981).

Climatic Fluctuation

Amazonia is subject not only to minor fluctuations in the inception, intensity, and duration of annual rainfall but also to unpredictable long and short-term droughts during episodes of El Niño that have significant impacts on subsistence resources (Nelson 1994; Tian et al. 1998). During the minor 1912 event, fires burned continuously for several months in the north, killing thousands of rubber gatherers. During the 1926 event, extensive fires affected the entire lower Negro region, causing great destruction to the fauna and heating streams sufficiently to kill fish (Carvalho 1952), while the combination of low maximum and low minimum water level on the Amazon at Manaus caused exceptional decimation of the aquatic biota (Soares 1977). During the 1972–1973 event, fire destroyed the gardens of a Yanomami community, forcing the people to abandon their village and adopt a hunter-gatherer way of life until normal conditions returned (Lizot 1974). During the 1983 event, all weather stations reported rainfall 70 percent below normal (Nobre & Renno 1985). During one day in February, discharge near the mouth of the Trombetas was 47m^3 in contrast to the long-term average of 2,100 m^3 (Molion & de Moraes 1987).

The disruptive impact on indigenous populations of four mega-Niño events during the past two millennia is documented by discontinuities about 500, 1000, 1200, and 1500 C.E. in the archeological sequences from lowland Bolivia, the Jamarí, the lower Xingú, Marajó, and the lower Orinoco (Figure 6; Meggers 1994). In each region, an earlier phase that had existed for several hundred years was replaced by a later one of the same or a different ceramic tradition, implying the failure of risk avoidance measures sufficient to cushion against briefer episodes of drought. A pollen core from Lago Ararí on Marajó shows a correlation between fluctuations between forest and savanna vegetation and discontinuities in the archeological sequence (Meggers & Danon 1988). A layer of eolian sand 8 to 20 cm thick on the surface of Teso dos Bichos testifies to the magnitude of the dessication in the vicinity at the time of its abandonment (Roosevelt 1991).

The archeological evidence for repeated fractionation and dispersal of human populations is supported by the linguistic and genetic distributions. Amazonian linguistic diversity is not only the highest in the Americas, but the geographical distributions of the major families are more heterogeneous than in any other part of the world. The correlation between lexico-statistical

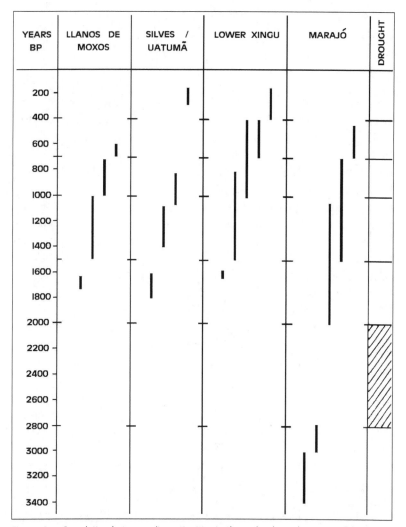

Figure 6 • Correlation between discontinuities in the archeological sequences from northeastern Bolivia, the Jamarí, the lower Xingú, Marajó Island, and the lower Orinoco, and mega-Niño episodes around 500, 1000, and 1500 c.e., reflecting the catastrophic impact of severe drought on well-adapted human populations.

dates for separations in the major language families and radiocarbon dates for the archeological discontinuities provides an explanation (Dixon & Aikhenvald 1999; Meillet 1952; Renfrew 2000). Dispersal is also reflected in the consensus among geneticists that "the pattern of genetic relationships and genetic diversity . . . is consistent with the hypothesis that evolution in South America proceeded by a process of fission-fusion leading to isolation of subpopulations with subsequent genetic differentiation" (Salzano & Callegari-Jacques 1988; Ward et al. 1975).

Geomorphological, sedimentological, and hydrological studies conducted along the middle Amazon above and below the mouth of the Negro indicate that the *varzea* reached its present extent only after sea level stabilized, giving it a maximum antiquity of 5,000–6,000 years (Irion, Junk, & de Melo 1997). It has been suggested that the present vegetation was not established until about 2000 years ago (Behling 2002).

Historical Evidence

Although advocates of the existence of large permanent settlements along the Amazon and in the Guianas support their interpretation with the descriptions by Carvajal and other sixteenth- and seventeenth-century explorers, historians warn against trusting their accounts (Alés & Pouyllau 1992; Hemming 1978; Henige 1998; Meggers 1993–1995; Silverberg 1996). They stress that "the mentality of the conquistador was peculiar to him and emerged from his unique historical formation. . . . These Europeans . . . wrote stories with themselves as the heroes and the Other as antagonist and background. They wrote stories for self-justification and glory; it was not necessary to portray the places they went and the people they saw accurately—just that they do it convincingly. Unfortunately for archeology, they succeeded" (Galloway 1992).

Contemporary maps demonstrate how little the explorers knew of the geography of the rivers. Raleigh's map of Lake Parima, the locus of El Dorado, reputed to be so large it took three days to paddle from one end to the other, looks like a gigantic centipede. Although no one ever saw it, the lake appeared on maps from 1599 (Figure 7) to 1808, constituting "by far the biggest and most persistent hoax ever perpetuated by geographers" (Gheerbrant 1992).

Discussion

Advocates of the existence of dense sedentary populations throughout Amazonia after 1 c.e. assume that "the size and depth of Amazonian Dark Earth are directly associated with population size of the settlement and settlement duration." Although they recognize that "as forests around the settlements were gradually turned into gardens, fields and orchards, firewood would be imported from longer distances" and that the amount of palm fronds required for thatch would have been "staggering," they dismiss the significance of these constraints (Erickson 2003). A review of the ethnographic and archeological literature offers a different perspective.

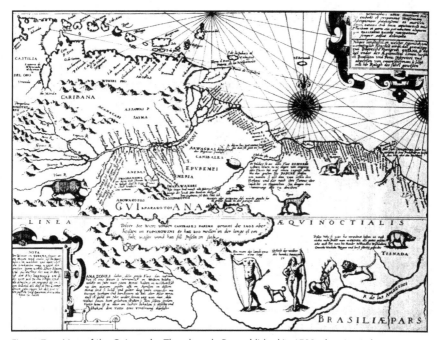

Figure 7 • Map of the Guianas by Theodore de Bry published in 1599, showing Lake Parima, the presumed location of the "great and golden city of Manoa." Although dozens of expeditions searched for it in vain, the lake continued to appear on maps until 1808 (Alexander 1976).

Among the Barí, a single communal house required 750,000 fronds from 125,000 palms collected from 40 km² (Beckerman 1977). The thatched roof of a typical Pumé house consumed 13,498 fronds, which had to be replaced every two to three years. Scarcity of palms in the vicinity is a factor in the abandonment of the house among the Achuar (Descola 1996) and Ka'apor (Balée 1994). These data are incompatible with the satisfaction of the requirements of a city of 200,000 at Santarém for thatch and firewood during several hundred years. It is noteworthy that scarcity of firewood alone has been proposed as a trigger in the collapse of Classic Copán (Abrams et al.1996), Cahokia (Lopinot & Woods 1993), and Mesa Verde (Johnson, Kohler & Cowan 2005).

Another way to assess the credibility of the Amazonian settlement sizes is by comparison with sites with monumental architecture. Wherever detailed spatial and temporal data have been obtained and environmental resources have been taken into consideration, peak population estimates have been reduced substantially. In Mesoamerica, new occupational data on Copán reduce the population during the early Classic below 10,000 (Paine et al.

1996), and measurement of the internal floor space of potential residences and the capacities of associated cisterns at Xculoc in Campeche "suggest that most estimates of Maya population made during the past twenty years need to be examined" and reduced 30–50 percent (Becquelin & Michelet 1994). The maximum productivity of arable land places the sustainable population of the central Andes in 1542 at under two million (Shea 1976), and the population of Egypt during the Greco-Roman period has been estimated at not more than six million (Hassan 1994). Reevaluation of settlement data and subsistence productivity indicates that Cahokia was occupied by "no more than several thousand people, certainly not tens of thousands of them" (Milner & Oliver 1999). The contrast between the impressive physical remains in these regions and the scattering of pottery fragments representing the more substantial populations postulated to have existed in Amazonia is notable.

Conclusion

Hunter-gatherers arrived in Amazonia at least 13,000 years ago (Meggers & Miller 2003). During subsequent millennia, they acquired comprehensive knowledge of the biota, culminating about 3000 B.C.E. in the establishment of semisedentary villages supported by shifting cultivation. By 200 B.C.E., the population density, settlement, and social behavior characteristic of surviving traditional communities had been adopted throughout the lowlands. The achievement of sustainable exploitation of rainforest resources is reflected in the close agreement between their typical population density of 0.3/km² and independent estimates of 0.2/km² for sustainable carrying capacity.

Five hundred years after the first Europeans described large cities and complex social organization in Amazonia, their existence continues to be accepted by anthropologists in spite of the absence of archeological evidence. By contrast, the impossibility of intensive agriculture is increasingly documented by soil experts and validated by the failure of modern efforts to achieve sustainable production. Rather than assume that the prehistoric population found a way that we have yet to discover to overcome the inherent environmental constraints, we need to abandon "the lingering myth of Amazon empires" (Foresta 1991) and reconcile the archeological and environmental evidence. This reconciliation is not only crucial for understanding prehistoric cultural development, but for designing sustainable programs for modern use of the region.

CHAPTER 14

Regional Integration and Ecology in Prehistoric Amazonia: Toward a System Perspective[1]

ALF HORNBORG

This chapter discusses the significance of a regional system perspective for the ongoing debate on the extent of social stratification and agricultural intensification on the floodplains and wet savannas of Pre-Columbian lowland South America. It concludes that the emergence of Arawakan chiefdoms and ethnic identities in such environments after the first millennium B.C.E. signifies the occupation of a niche defined in terms of both ecology and regional exchange, but also that it transformed both these kinds of conditions. In these processes, ethnicity, social stratification, economy, and ecology were all recursively intertwined.

The reconstruction of Amazonian prehistory raises issues of general theoretical interest for our understanding of the emergence of domestication, sedentism, and social stratification in several parts of the prehistoric world. The focal questions seem almost universally the same: What kinds of social processes are signified by the appearance of domesticates, permanent settlements, long-distance exchange, and evidence of status differentiation? How are the geographical distributions of various elements of material culture—such as ceramic styles or subsistence technologies—related to ethnolinguistic or other divisions recognized by prehistoric populations, and what do these divisions in turn signify? The comparatively high feasibility of tracing ethnoarcheological continuities in the Amazonian material provides more compelling foundations for interpretation than are usually accessible in the archeology of "Neolithization,"[2] and the similarities in the material record are significant enough to warrant consideration of possible parallels with other areas. I believe that generalization may indeed be possible at the abstract level of questions such as: What is the relationship between material culture, language, and ethnic identity? What is the relationship between ethnicity, economy, and ecology? What is the relationship between trade, social hierarchy, kinship, sedentism, and intensification of resource use?

Economy, Ecology, and Ethnicity in a Regional Perspective: The Significance of Trade

Until recently, anthropological attempts to account for cultural variation in Amazonia in processual terms have resorted to notions of environmental determinism, diffusion, or migration, or to combinations of these factors (Brochado 1984; Lathrap 1970; Meggers 1971; Meggers & Evans 1957; Myers 2004; Nordenskiöld 1930; Oliver 1989; Schmidt 1917; Steward & Faron 1959; Wilson 1999; Zucchi 1991, 2002). The challenge for a renewed concern with diachronic, cultural processes in a regional perspective is to take due account of earlier concerns with ecology, diffusion, and migration while acknowledging more subtle and intangible factors such as politics, exchange, identity, and the autonomous logic of symbolic systems emphasized by most modern anthropologists.

The best way to go about this, I believe, is to begin by assuming that cultural and linguistic variation in Amazonia has been generated through continuous, dynamic interaction among ecology, economy, and ethnicity (Figure 1). Various natural environments have afforded particular populations different options regarding subsistence, economic specialization, and exchange with other groups, while these economic activities in turn have modified the environment as well as provided foundations for ethnic identity construction. Viewed as a regional system of exchange, Amazonia as a whole already in the first millennium B.C.E. had developed a differentiated political-economic structure in which the geographical positions of specific populations contributed to shaping the various roles that they came to play within this larger system. It must nevertheless be emphasized that the indigenous groups (Figure 2) engaged in this exchange should not be viewed as passive recipients of impulses from either their economic or ecological environment but as agents creatively developing their own cultural responses to the economic and ecological niches that were available to them. It is precisely their status as agents or *subjects* that obliges us to include ethnic identity construction and historical self-consciousness as a central factor in our account. Ethnic identity is a product of the dialectic between externally attributed and internally experienced qualities, often closely interwoven with traditional modes of subsistence and the specific kinds of

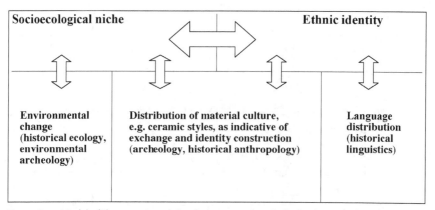

Figure 1 • Model of the recursive relation between socioecological niche and ethnic identity construction, indicating the main categories of traces left by such processes in prehistory, and the different academic fields required to recover them.

landscapes within which they are conducted (Barth 1969). "Ethnogenetic" processes (cf. Hill 1996a; Renfrew 1987) thus implicate ecology and economy as well as culture, language, politics, and history.

The point of departure of any account of the ecology of Amazonia must be the fact that it harbors the greatest contiguous rainforest in the world (approximately 5 million square kilometers) as well as the world's most voluminous river (with a flow of water five times greater than the Congo and twelve times the Mississippi). The area is habitually described as composed of 98 percent *terra firme* (older, poorer, and slightly more elevated land) and 2 percent *várzea* (fertile, periodically inundated floodplains along the shores of major rivers). The ecology of the Amazon Basin is actually much more diverse and complex than suggested by this simple distinction (cf. Moran 1993), but the fertile, sedimentary soils of the *várzea* in any event seem to have been a scarce and coveted resource for prehistoric populations. Intensive cultivation of maize and peanuts may have been conducted on the floodplains already in the first millennium B.C.E. (Oliver 2001:65–66; Roosevelt 1993). In addition, these same riverbanks offer the richest abundance of fish, turtles, manatees, and other aquatic resources. Historical sources indicate that the floodplains were densely populated and intensively exploited when the first Europeans traveled down the Amazon River in 1542, mentioning a series of huge settlements obeying a paramount chief, extensive cultivation, and numerous turtle corrals (Carvajal 1934; Porro 1994). Archeological excavations in the vicinity of Santarém and Manaus have confirmed significant prehistoric population densities, but the actual size of individual settlements is a contested

Figure 2 • Indigenous groups (1–17) and archeological sites (18–30) mentioned in the text. (Darker shaded areas = elevation over 1000 m). 1. Achagua (Arawak); 2. Amahuaca (Pano); 3. Campa/Asháninka (Arawak); 4. Chibcha/Muisca; 5. Chipaya; 6. Conibo (Pano); 7. Mojo (Arawak); 8. Omagua (Tupí); 9. Otomac (Arawak); 10. Palikur (Arawak); 11. Piro (Arawak); 12. Quijos; 13. Shipibo (Pano); 14. Taino (Arawak); 15. Uru; 16. Yaminahua (Pano); 17. Yanesha/Amuesha (Arawak); 18. Açutuba; 19. Altamira; 20. Belterra; 21. Chavín de Huántar; 22. Chiripa; 23. Cuzco; 24. Hupa-iya; 25. Juriti; 26. Kondurí; 27. Santarém; 28. Tiwanaku; 29. Valdivia; 30. Wari.

issue. Anna Roosevelt (1993:274) believes that some sites may have had tens of thousands of inhabitants; however, Betty Meggers (1992:35–36) considers such concentrations ecologically unfeasible.

The occurrence of complex, stratified societies along the main rivers of prehistoric Amazonia should not be reduced to a direct reflection of the fertility of their floodplains. These rivers were simultaneously the main arteries in a continent-wide trade network, the extent of which we have only begun to appreciate. Access to rare prestige goods from remote areas were, here as elsewhere, an important foundation for ritual and political-economic authority.

Such authority, in turn, was what enabled chiefs to maintain densely populated settlements and persuade their followers to intensify the exploitation of natural resources (Heckenberger 2002:118).[3] Although most of this trade undoubtedly consisted of organic plant and animal products that had no value for Europeans and quickly decomposed in the tropical climate, leaving no traces either in the historical or the archeological record, there is plenty of early historical as well as archeological evidence for such long-distance exchange throughout Amazonia.

Although inferences from historical evidence about precolonial conditions are always risky, the complex ways in which many of these trade relations reflect long-established and altogether *indigenous* demands and consumption patterns often suggest time depths antedating 1492. For instance, green stone amulets (called *muiraquitã* on the lower Amazon and *takourave* in the Guyanas) were traded for gold objects and other products from the Vaupés, Orinoco, and Roraima (Boomert 1987; Whitehead 1994:38). These amulets were often shaped like stylized frogs and may have been connected with a frog cult in eastern Amazonia (Whitehead 1993:295–296).[4] From three main manufacturing areas—coastal Surinam, the lower Amazon (Nhamundá-Trombetas-Tapajós), and the Virgin Islands—they were traded widely and used, for instance, as prestigious ornaments in women's necklaces and as a medium of elite ceremonial exchange, including brideprice and death compensation (Boomert 1987:36–41). Representations of what may be *muiraquitã* on ceramics from Santarém, where many such amulets have been found, suggest that they may also have been used as ornaments on women's headbands (Gomes 2001:141).

Historically, three extensive trade networks converged on the central Orinoco *llanos* (Hill 1996b:149–150; Spencer 1998:109). From the north and east, Caribs came to trade blowguns, arrows, baskets, arrow-poison (*curare*), dyes, and pearls for shell beads (*quirípa*), turtle oil, smoked fish, gold, and salt. Arawaks traded forest and savanna products for gold, salt, and cotton textiles from the Chibchan chiefdoms in the northern Andes, and in the south they traded, for example, gold and *curare* for *quirípa*, turtle oil, and smoked fish. Shell beads (*quirípa*) were used both as prestigious ornaments and as a medium of exchange. They were particularly in demand among Arawak-speakers such as Achagua in the Orinoco area and were still being produced in the beginning of the nineteenth century by the Otomac in Uruana, central Orinoco, where people from all over the *llanos* regularly came to trade (Gassón 2000:595). Notable in all this trade is the occurrence of foodstuffs such as smoked fish and turtle oil. The high population densities and intensive food production along the floodplains should in part be understood against this background. Significant portions of the fish, turtles, and even cassava were evidently produced for export (Whitehead 1994:36).

The significance of regional trade networks for the formation and reproduction of economically and ecologically specialized ethnic groups can hardly be overestimated. In eastern Peru, the salt cakes traditionally produced by the Campa of the sub-Andean *montaña* have served as a medium of exchange along the trade routes reaching deep into Amazonia (Renard-Casevitz 1993, 2002:131–136). Arawak-speaking groups such as Campa, Mojo, and Piro regularly visited the Inca capital, Cuzco, to trade forest products such as medicinal herbs, birds, and tropical hardwoods for Andean metalwork and other highland products. Chiefs—for example, among the Conibo and the Cocama—based their power in part on their access to objects of silver and gold obtained from Cuzco through Piro traders (Taylor 1999:199). Different lowland groups specialized in specific kinds of products. Arawaks in the area were known for their cotton textiles with decorative motifs or feathers woven into the fabric, canoes, and pearls, whereas Panoans were known for their painted pottery, mats, hammocks, and gourds (Renard-Casevitz 2002:133). Such trade to this day reinforces ethnic boundaries while institutionalizing their transgression and cementing interethnic alliances. The Arawak-speaking Yanesha (also known as Amuesha) recognize as "real human beings" (*acheñ*) not only other Arawaks such as Campa and Piro but also riverine Panoans such as Shipibo and Conibo. Among the qualities that qualify them for inclusion in this category are their proclivities to drink manioc beer and to wear the *cushma* (Ibid.). Piro count both Campa and Yanesha as "people like us"; however, marginalized Panoans such as Amahuaca and Yaminahua are classified as "wild Indians" who walk about naked and eat raw, unsalted food (Gow 2002:155). Such moral barriers within the lowlands were generally more difficult to overcome than the ethnic boundaries distinguishing highland and lowland groups with a mutual interest in trade. Along the eastern slopes of the Andes, there has for several centuries been lively interaction between people of the mountains and the lowlands, for instance between the Quechua and Aymara and the Campa, Piro, and Mojo in southern Peru and Bolivia, between the Quijos and the Omagua in Ecuador and northern Peru, and between the Chibcha (or Muisca) and the Achagua in Colombia (Gassón 2002; Kurella 1998; Lovén 1928; Oberem 1974; Renard-Casevitz, Saignes, & Taylor-Descola 1986; Taylor 1999:199–201). From Colombia to Bolivia, the primary agents of this trade have often been Arawak-speakers.

Linguistic Distribution and Societal Structures

The distribution of Arawakan languages suggests a pattern of expansion along the very barriers that surround and separate other linguistic families: the Orinoco, Río Negro, Amazon, Ucayali, Purús, and Madeira Rivers, as well as the *llanos* of Venezuela and Bolivia and the coastal areas of Guyana (cf. Heckenberger 2002:105–106). Considering the discovery of pottery near Santarém dating from the sixth millennium B.C.E. (Neves 1999:219; Roosevelt et al. 1991), however, we see that it is unlikely that the highly productive floodplains and aquatic resources in these areas would have been unoccupied prior to the Arawakan expansion beginning in the second millennium B.C.E. Whether earlier populations were displaced by or incorporated into the Arawakan network, the linguistic distribution maps suggest that the Arawakan expansion created ethnic wedges that contributed to the geographical demarcation of other, spatially more consolidated linguistic families such as Carib, Tukano, and Pano. In some cases, it is even possible to detect how a wedge of Arawakan languages has split a previously united language family, as in the case of the Panoan groups on either side of the Arawaks along the Purús and Madeira (cf. Erikson 1993:55). The dispersed pockets of Arawakan dialects that have been documented along the river systems from the lower Orinoco to the upper Madeira appear to be the remains of a contiguous network of Arawak-speaking societies that in prehistoric times spanned the entire extent of western Amazonia. In view of their role in integrating regional exchange, these Arawak-speakers should be viewed not so much as ethnic "wedges" as the social "glue" of ancient Amazonia.

Although a recent and authoritative summary of Amazonian linguistics (Dixon & Aikhenvald 1999a) advocates extreme skepticism with regard to higher-level genetic groupings, several studies have suggested various degrees of affinity among the four most important language families in Amazonia: Arawak, Tupí, Carib, and Gê. To the extent that there is a foundation for any of these studies, it would lend support to the hypothesis that at least these families are to be seen as products of regional ethnogenetic processes rather than as traces of migrations from other parts of the continent. The significance of ecological factors in such processes deserves also to be considered. Betty Meggers (1982, 1987) has suggested that drought-related fluctuations in the extent of forest vegetation have contributed to the geographical distribution of different language families, some of whom (for example, horticulturalists such as Arawak, Tupí, Pano, and Carib) were originally confined to distinct forest refugia but subsequently expanded, at the expense of savanna-dwelling hunter-gatherers, with the recovery of the rainforest as the climate grew more humid. Dixon's Punctuated Equilibrium model similarly implies that linguistic families such as Arawak, Carib, and Tupí, prior to the "punctuation" represented by the adoption of agriculture, originated as the result of relative confinement within specific geographical zones (Dixon & Aikhenvald 1999b:17). However, ecological factors can be assumed to be significant for the distribution of, for instance, Arawak (wetland agriculturalists) and Gê (hunter-gatherers of the dry savanna) without any reference to paleoclimatic fluctuations or to ecologically induced isolation. On the contrary, an anthropological perspective on the formation of ethnolinguistic identities would emphasize ecologically induced *interaction* rather than isolation (Barth 1969). The geologically recent expansion of Arawak-speakers along floodplains and wet savannas from the *llanos* of Venezuela to the *llanos* of Bolivia over the course of a millennium and a half (cf. Heckenberger 2002:106–107) suggests the systematic exploitation of an existing socioecological niche, in intensive interaction with the populations of other such zones, rather than reflecting post-Pleistocene changes in biogeography or long periods of homogeneous, egalitarian "equilibrium." Furthermore, as studies in historical ecology show, the relation between ecology and cultural identity cannot be a matter of one-way causality, when the biophysical environment is continuously transformed by human activity.

A convincing account of the genesis of ethnolinguistic divisions in prehistoric Amazonia needs to recognize the recursive relation between ecological and economic specialization within regional exchange systems, on the one hand, and ethnic and cultural creativity, on the other (Figure 1). The various cultural traits and institutions that enabled Arawak-speakers to integrate long-distance trade networks in ancient Amazonia should be understood not only as prerequisites but also as *products* of these exchange systems. Cultural patterns do exhibit a certain degree of autonomy and inertia, acknowledged in notions such as "ethos" or "tradition," but rather than replace environmental determinism with cultural essentialism, we should ask how the cultural creativity of the proto-Arawak may have constituted a response to the economic niche afforded them by the opportunities of riverine trade. Instead of treating either ecology or culture as an independent variable, a more dynamic ethnogenetic perspective can illuminate the emergence of cultural traits in a regional and historical perspective, by focusing on the historical structures of regional exchange systems rather than ecology or culture in themselves. Viewed from a regional perspective, as Hill (2002:229) observes, the proto-Arawakan territories around the Içana and Guainía Rivers in the northwest Amazon were actually "centrally located" in relation to the riverine connections between the Orinoco and Amazon Basins. If this was indeed the area in which Arawakan traits and institutions originally developed, it is not difficult to imagine a close connection between their cosmopolitan "ethos" (cf. Santos-Granero 2002) and their role as long-distance traders. As this contagious cultural "ethos" reproduced and entrenched itself along the trade routes, however, it would be misleading to represent its diffusion in terms of the movement of "peoples."

Considering the rapidity and the apparent ease with which indigenous populations along the Río Negro were able to adopt the Nheengatú "trade language" and European utensils in the colonial era, as well as a great number of other Amazonian examples of language shifts and interethnic cultural adoptions (cf. Aikhenvald 1999), we might find it puzzling that we should continue generally to think about Pre-Columbian cultural processes in terms of reified "peoples" migrating across the Amazon Basin. Nheengatú is to this day spoken as a first language by some populations on the upper Rio Negro (Jensen 1999:127). In view of its conspicuously riverine distribution pattern, we see that there is a distinct possibility that the Arawakan language family (that is, proto-Arawak) similarly originated as a "trade language" among a wide network of bi- or multilingual societies in prehistoric Amazonia (cf. Schmidt 1917). An influential and contagious "Arawakan" identity seems indeed to have been founded on a fairly coherent, if provisional, constellation of traits, including language and ceramic style, but this possibility does not allow us to draw any conclusions on population movements. Rather than continuing to reproduce the billiard-ball model of migrating, essentialized "peoples" pushing one another across the Amazon Basin and thus generating our linguistic and archeological distribution maps, we should be asking ourselves what prehistoric linguistic and stylistic diffusion could tell us about communicative processes within a pan-Amazonian system of exchange relations.

Traces of Intensification

To dissociate the Arawakan "ethos" (Santos-Granero 2002) and its various stylistic markers from the notion of a biologically delineated population is not to stop asking questions about material processes in Amazonian prehistory. Whichever genes they may have carried, the Arawak-speaking potters of the floodplains in the first millennium B.C.E. were engaged in a process of social transformation that also had major ecological repercussions. The tropical landscape still carries imprints of these transformations, even if they are generally invisible to the untrained eye. A fundamental example of such imprints are the dark, anthropogenic[5] soils that in Amazonia are known as *terra preta de índio* and that occur along most larger rivers (Denevan 2001:104–110; Glaser & Woods 2004; Lehmann et al. 2003; Petersen, Neves, & Heckenberger 2001). These black (*terra preta*) or dark brown (*terra mulata*) soils are less acidic and contain more humus, nitrogen, and phosphorus than surrounding soils and are appreciated by both indigenous and non-indigenous farmers for their high fertility. *Terra preta* occurs in patches or as contiguous zones along the shores of major rivers, normally varying between 1 and 100 hectares in extent, with an average around 21 hectares. Some sites, however, are considerably larger, measuring 500 hectares at Santarém, 350 hectares at Juriti, west of Santarém, and 200 hectares *terra preta* plus 1,000 hectares *terra mulata* at Belterra, by the Tapajós (Denevan 2001:105). Sites are typically elongated in shape and run parallel to riverbanks, for instance at Altamira, on the Xingú (1.8 km x 500 m, 90 hectares), and at Manacapurú, near Manaus (4 km × 200 m, 80 hectares). A recent survey maps almost 400 sites in Brazil alone (Kern et al. 2003). The deposits may be up to two meters in depth. Most researchers agree that *terra preta* has been formed in connection with dense, sedentary, and extended human habitation, indicating more permanent and often larger communities than those that have been documented ethnographically in Amazonia.[6] It has been proposed that the black soils (*terra preta*) are the result of human habitation, whereas the dark brown soils (*terra mulata*) are former agricultural land (Herrera et al. 1992:102, ref. to Andrade; Petersen, Neves, & Heckenberger 2001:100). *Terra pretas* are usually associated with artifacts such as pottery, whereas *terra mulatas* are not (Kern et al. 2003:73). The most fertile (black) "anthrosols" appear to be the result of a continuous deposition of household garbage, ashes, feces, urine, bones, shells, and other organic materials.

Terra preta begins to form at roughly the same time along the larger rivers in Amazonia a few centuries B.C.E. At Hupa-iya, near Yarinacocha, by the Ucayali River in Peru, the oldest deposits of *terra preta* have been dated to 200 B.C.E. At the large site of Açutuba on the lower Río Negro, *terra preta* may have begun to form around 360 B.C.E. (Petersen, Neves, & Heckenberger 2001:97, 100). In view of postulated correlations between ceramics and linguistics (Heckenberger 2002; Lathrap 1970; Zucchi 2002), the abundant finds of Barrancoid ceramics at both Hupa-iya and Açutuba, as at other sites with *terra preta* along the Amazon (cf. Myers 2004:91), could be mustered in support of the hypothesis of an Arawak-speaking population on the intensively cultivated floodplains from at least 500 B.C.E. up to its identification as such by Europeans. These anthrosols indicate a population density that could not have been sustained with the current (shifting) agricultural practices of indigenous people in the area (Oliver 2001:73; cf. Roosevelt 1993). The evidence suggests that the floodplains of Amazonia in the first millennium B.C.E. experienced an unprecedented concentration of human population in conjunction with significant economic intensification and that these material processes were part and parcel of complex new social formations associated with what we have referred to as an "Arawakan" culture and identity.

Another lasting imprint of complex social systems and economic intensification in Amazonia was made by the various kinds of earthworks that have been identified in association with Pre-Columbian settlements and cultivation systems. The most conspicuous of these are the extensive drainage systems that have been discovered in the seasonally inundated wet savannas (*llanos*) of Bolivia, Colombia, and Venezuela and in other waterlogged areas (floodplains, deltas, coastal zones, lake shores, marshes) in the Guyanas, highland Colombia, Ecuador, Peru, and highland Bolivia (Denevan 2001:215–290; Parsons 1985). In these widely separate areas, a similar method of drainage was employed, the basic idea of which was to construct artificially raised fields to protect the crops from periodical inundations. Such raised or ridged fields have been given various names in different parts of South America, but a commonly used, non-English name is the Spanish *camellones*, which was applied already in the sixteenth century by Spaniards in the Orinoco *llanos* and in highland basins of Colombia and Ecuador. It was also used at least by 1674 for the famous *chinampas* of the Aztecs in Mexico, which appear to belong to the same agricultural tradition. The term *camellones*, which refers to camel humps, was obviously invented by the Spaniards after 1492 but is used to this day in the Beni area in Bolivia (Denevan 2001:217, 220, 237–238, 252). Raised fields had several functions in addition to drainage, including soil aeration, reduction of root rot, increased nitrification, pest reduction, reduction of acidity, moisture retention (in the ditches), enhancement of fertility by application of muck from ditches, facilitation of weeding, facilitation of harvest, and increase in soil and water temperatures (Ibid.:220).

It was not until the 1960s that researchers began to grasp the significance of these methods of cultivation in South America, following William Denevan's discovery and exploration of extensive areas of prehistoric *camellones* in the Llanos de Mojos in Beni, Bolivia. Earlier scholars who had mentioned cultivation on "mounds" or "platforms" in various parts of South America include Alfred Métraux in 1942 (having probably received the information from Erland Nordenskiöld), Max Schmidt in 1951 (Schmidt 1974), and Carl Sauer in 1952 (Denevan 2001:218). Schmidt had perceived a connection between "mound cultivation" in the Llanos de Mojos, the Titicaca Basin, the Antilles, Marajó Island, and other areas of South America, and Sauer also recognized in these mounds a pattern characteristic of the New World tropics. The only historical information on the ridged fields in Beni that Denevan was able to locate, however, is a note by two Jesuits from 1754, and the only modern researcher who had previously observed them personally was Erland Nordenskiöld in 1916 (Ibid.:217). The reason why these fields emerged from obscurity in the 1960s is that the patterns they create are clearly visible from the air but difficult to discover on the ground.

Similar systems of cultivation have subsequently been reported from the *llanos* of Venezuela and Colombia, coastal areas in the Guyanas, river valleys and waterlogged basins in the highlands of Colombia and Ecuador, the Guayas Basin in coastal Ecuador, the Casma Valley on the north coast of Peru, and the Titicaca Basin on the border between Peru and Bolivia. Their occurrences in the highlands as well as the lowlands undoubtedly reflect an ancient exchange of ideas between the two areas. Their shapes and proportions vary, but there are individual fields in the Orinoco area that are over 1 kilometer long, some in Beni that are 25 meters wide, and some by the San Jorge River in Colombia that are 2 meters high. Raised fields can occur over very extensive areas, particularly in the Titicaca Basin (120,000 hectares), the lower Sinú River and the Mompós area between the Cauca and San Jorge Rivers in Colombia (90,000 hectares), the Guayas Basin (50,000 hectares), and the Llanos de Mojos in Beni (at least 6,000 hectares). In addition to *camellones*, the Beni area features a great quantity of artificial mounds, causeways, and canals. Most of these earthworks in the Llanos de Mojos are located between the Beni and the Mamoré Rivers, tributaries to the Madeira. Ridged fields have also been reported from forested areas southwest of these *llanos* (Denevan 2001:247).

By multiplying the known acreages of raised fields with experimentally established figures for productivity, we can estimate how large were the populations they could have sustained. Experimental cultivation of raised fields in the Titicaca Basin has yielded up to 16 tons of potatoes per hectare. Such harvests would theoretically be able to sustain almost 40 people per hectare cultivated land (Denevan 2001:220–222, 272; Erickson 2000:336). Experimental fields in Mojos have yielded 25 tons of manioc and 2 tons of maize per hectare (Denevan 2001:222, 252). Irrespective of the level of optimism in terms of nutrient yields, however, these estimates should always be tempered by the recognition that a significant portion of the harvests would have been used for feasting and brewing manioc beer rather than pure subsistence. In fact, judging from historical and ethnographical documentation of indigenous consumption patterns throughout much of South America (cf., for example, Gastineau, Darby, & Turner 1979; Goldman 1966:86), we see that it is likely that such "ceremonial" consumption may have been a major incentive for agricultural intensification in the first place. The domestication and consumption of manioc and maize in South America have undoubtedly from the very start been implicated in the maintenance of social reciprocities ranging from local kinship obligations and trade partnerships to chiefly redistribution. The taste for manioc or maize beer should thus not be underestimated in our understandings of prehistoric agricultural intensification in Amazonia.[7]

Again, various kinds of evidence suggest an "Arawakan" ethnolinguistic identity as the common denominator of these widely dispersed but apparently related cultivation systems. When the Europeans arrived, the *llanos* of Bolivia,

Venezuela, and Colombia as well as the Antilles and coastal Guyanas had for a long time been inhabited by Arawak-speakers. Historical sources mention mound cultivation using digging sticks among the sixteenth-century Taino of Hispaniola and the eighteenth-century Palikur on the northeast coast of Brazil (Denevan 2001:227; Renard-Casevitz 2002:140–141). The ridged fields in the Llanos de Mojos of Bolivia were probably constructed by the Arawak-speaking Mojo using similar methods. Excavations of *camellones* in Venezuela have yielded ceramics that Alberta Zucchi attributes to Arawak-speakers expanding north along the Orinoco after 500 C.E. (Denevan 2001:226; Denevan & Zucchi 1978). The Andean chiefdoms in highland basins in Colombia, Ecuador, and the Titicaca area all maintained close interaction with various ethnic groups in the adjoining lowlands, prominent among who were Arawak-speakers. Donald Lathrap (1970:162–163, 169–170) has interpreted the prehistoric societies of the Guayas Basin in western Ecuador as an extension, by way of an unusually accessible segment of the Andean highlands, of Amazonian cultural traditions. In his view, the *camellones* of the Guayas Basin are remains of the Milagro culture from 500 C.E., whose pottery (funerary urns, appliqué decoration, and so on) are reminiscent of Santarém, Kondurí, and other ceramic styles from the lower Amazon. Lathrap (Ibid.:169) also associates the raised fields in the San Jorge Basin in Colombia with funerary urns with Amazonian affinities. Finally, he adopts Kingsley Noble's hypothesis that an early population of the Titicaca Basin, today represented by the Uru and the Chipaya, were Arawak-speakers with roots in the lowlands (Ibid.:72, 74). This view appears to have been endorsed by several influential linguists, including Greenberg, Suárez, and Migliazza (cf. Campbell 1997:189; Ruhlen 1987:373). Clark Erickson has suggested that the earliest raised fields in the Titicaca Basin were built by the ancestors of the Uru around the beginning of the Chiripa period 800–200 B.C.E. (cf. Denevan 2001:273); David Browman (1980:117) has also identified the Chiripa culture with the ancestors of the Uru and Chipaya.

It would thus be possible to argue that, from the beginning of the first millennium B.C.E., more or less all occurrences of raised fields in Pre-Columbian South America may have been associated with an "Arawakan" sphere of influence. The apparently simultaneous appearance of ridged fields in areas as widely apart as northern Colombia and the Titicaca Basin around 800 B.C.E. does not support the notion of migration as a significant factor in the distribution of this system of cultivation. The earliest dates are from the Guayas lowlands of Ecuador, where Valdivia-type pottery associated with raised fields suggests a time depth going back to around 2000 B.C.E. (Parsons 1985:155). Other dates from various parts of lowland South America include the Beni area around 1 C.E., the Guyanas 200 C.E., and the Orinoco 500

C.E. (Denevan 2001). Like the sequence of pottery dates, this chronology should not be interpreted in terms of a process of migration but in terms of the diffusion of an agricultural technique along a continent-wide network of wetland agriculturalists integrated by intense social exchange and a common ethnolinguistic identity. We might even suggest that the finds of riverside *terra preta* and marshland *camellones* are complementary manifestations of this same social network, each reflecting the conditions of both cultivation and preservation along the rivers and in the *llanos*, respectively. Ridged fields suggest the adaptation of intensive agriculturalists to wetland environments of a more predictable nature than the major Amazonian floodplains, where the annual floods are much more violent. However, as Lathrap (1970:29–30, 39, 160–161) has proposed, the idea of artificially raised fields may well have been inspired by the natural series of sedimentary ridges created by such floods along the rivers, since it was precisely these natural ridges that were intensively farmed by the populations on the floodplains.

Conclusions

The complex distribution maps tracing the linguistics, ethnography, and archeology of Amazonia represent a daunting jigsaw puzzle. Anthropologists and archeologists have long been struggling with the challenge of finding intelligible patterns behind the patchy indications of cultural diversity. Some have sought clues in the natural environment, others in historical processes or an autonomous, semiotic logic of culture. In this chapter, the analytical platform that I have chosen as a point of departure is that of regional and interregional *exchange systems*. Exchange systems are ecologically, historically, and culturally *conditioned*, but they simultaneously generate tangible ecological, historical, and cultural *consequences* (Figure 1). They thus constitute a theoretical juncture where different scientific perspectives and levels of analysis can be integrated in recursive, nondeterministic ways. The geographical distribution of natural resources, territorial boundaries, and cultural patterns of consumption are all factors of significance for the development of exchange systems, just as, again, the trajectories of exchange systems are of significance for environmental change, politics, and cultural identities. It is often precisely these three aspects of prehistoric social change—that is, patterns of resource use, power structures, and delineation of cultural boundaries—that we most urgently want to reconstruct, particularly in our attempts to understand the driving forces behind transitions to sedentism and agricultural intensification on different continents.

In South America, expansive exchange networks have previously been postulated as underlying the diffusion of, for instance, the Chavín art style (cf.

Burger 1992; Lathrap 1971) and the Quechua language (Schwartz & Salomon 1999:457; Stark 1985:181; Torero 2002:91–105), neither of which is believed primarily to have involved demic migration. In this chapter, I have suggested that a similar interpretation can be applied to the spread of Arawakan languages and certain aspects of material culture and agricultural practices that tend to appear in conjunction with them. This interpretation can be based on at least six types of argument:

1. It is well known that many and sometimes widespread language shifts (for example, to Nheengatú) have occurred in Amazonia without involving migration.
2. The areas outside their homeland in the northwest Amazon that first adopted Arawakan languages were, with the probable exception of the upper Xingú, already fairly densely populated by that time.
3. Arawak-speakers are historically and ethnographically known throughout their range to have been active traders, often along the very rivers that have been postulated as their primary migration routes.
4. Arawak-speaking groups are also historically and ethnographically known to have practiced extensive intermarriage with other ethnolinguistic groups.
5. Arawakan languages spoken in different areas often show more structural similarities to their non-Arawak neighbors than to one another (Aikhenvald & Dixon 1998).
6. Attempts to find correlations between Amazonian languages and genes have been conspicuously unsuccessful (Cavalli-Sforza, Menozzi, & Piazza 1994:341).

The archeological evidence suggests that floodplains and wet savannas (*llanos*) in various parts of lowland South America in the first millennium B.C.E. experienced the emergence of a new kind of expansive and densely populated societies characterized by extensive ethnic alliances and power hierarchies based on long-distance trade and intensive exploitation of both terrestrial and aquatic resources. The intensification of resource use should be understood partly in direct relation to trade, as some of it seems to have been production for export, partly in relation to a rising need for surplus production generated by the consumptive demands of the elite, the craft specialists, and the demographically more concentrated settlements. These "demands" should in turn be understood only partly in terms of subsistence, because a significant proportion of the product would have been allocated to ceremonial consumption of, for example, manioc or maize beer.

This sociocultural pattern may originally have crystallized among Arawak-speaking populations inhabiting the border zone between the Amazon and Orinoco Basins, an area that had long seen a lively trade and high density of interaction between different ethnic groups. The familiarity with rivers and river traffic initially favored the rapid expansion of Arawak-speakers downstream along the Orinoco and the Río Negro, which was based as much on alliance-making and the ethnolinguistic assimilation of other groups as on actual population movements. With time, the expansive inertia of the "Arawakan ethos" as described above was more or less dissociated from the distribution of biologically definable populations. Successively more distant groups farther on along the waterways continued to gravitate toward the prestigious new way of life and its rewards and obligations; became a part of the "Arawakan" network; adopted its language, ceremonies, and patterns of consumption; and finally served as its missionaries in a continuous outward movement that spanned a millennium and a half and most of the continent of South America. This continent-wide network absorbed and disseminated new cultural traits from the groups thus "Arawakized" while maintaining a recognizable core of "Arawakan" features including language, pottery styles, and ceremonial life. In several cases, it is difficult to ascertain whether traits were adopted from neighboring groups or part of an original cultural luggage. This fluidity or readiness to absorb new elements is a general hallmark of ethnogenetic processes, but a more remarkable aspect of Arawakan ethnicity is the extent to which a recognizably coherent constellation of core features has been able to reproduce itself over such vast areas and over such long periods of time (Hill & Santos-Granero 2002). A conclusion that suggests itself is that this particular constellation of traits was uniquely well fitted to the task of integrating the regional exchange system of prehistoric Amazonia.

The process described above has ecological as well as political and cultural aspects. Earlier attempts to account for prehistoric intensification in Amazonia and elsewhere have generally chosen to emphasize one of these aspects at the expense of others. It would be misleading, however, to imagine that the process in any significant way was "determined" either by ecological conditions, political aspirations, or cultural idiosyncrasies. All these aspects should rather be viewed as expressions of a more general, socioecological logic. The process of "Neolithization" that we can discern in Amazonia during the first millennium B.C.E. is fundamentally a *regional systemic phenomenon* in the sense that it is a crystallization of a given set of geographical, historical, and cultural conditions. This *systemic* character is reflected, for instance, in the observation that "something new" occurred simultaneously in the last few centuries B.C.E. over vast areas of Amazonia, a manifestation of which was larger and more sedentary settlements with the capacity to generate *terra preta* (Neves et al. 2003:29; Petersen, Neves, & Heckenberger 2001:101). Abrupt changes can also be detected in several sites in central Amazonia around 700 C.E. (Neves et al. 2004). When juxtaposed and correlated, such local cultural discontinuities may prove to be associated with the integration and transformations of continent-wide exchange networks. Thus, for instance, the main period of consolidation of the Arawakan trade network appears largely to coincide with the so-called Early Horizon (1000–200 B.C.E.) in the Andes, defined by the diffusion of the lowland-oriented Chavín style across the Andean crest, and the most significant period of reorganization (reflected in major stylistic discontinuities over much of Amazonia) with the collapse of the highland polities Tiwanaku and Wari around 1000 C.E.

The set of relevant systemic conditions for such synchronized developments would include the geographical distribution of natural resources such as turtles, shells, or green stone, as well as cultural constellations of symbolically and sociologically constituted demand for such products, from the Andean demand for feather mantles and hallucinogenic plants to the central Amazonian demand for frog-shaped amulets (cf. Boomert 1987:34–36). Systemic conditions also include the specific geographies of navigable rivers and cultivable floodplains, as well as the distances to, and the historically given political conditions in, other parts of the continent such as the Andes and the Caribbean. Finally, we must count among these crucial conditions the culturally specific motives of traders and chiefs along the rivers, which necessarily implicate prehistoric political economy, kinship systems, and marriage rules. Just to give a brief example of these last factors, we could mention the use of green stone amulets and shell beads as brideprice among various groups in the Amazon and the Orinoco Basins (Boomert 1987:37; Gassón 2000:589).

On all continents, ecology and climate have obviously influenced the cultural development of human populations and their opportunities to engage in long-distance exchange and economic specialization. But it is equally obvious, I would conclude, that geographically extensive systems of exchange and interaction have for millennia exerted crucial influence not only on the formation of local cultural identities, consumption patterns, and economies but concomitantly also on the ecosystems in which these culturally constituted economies operate. It is this socioecological recursivity that so often continues to elude us in our struggles to comprehend the relation between nature and society.

Notes

1. I am grateful to the University of Chicago Press for permission to use a much abridged and adapted version of my article "Ethnogenesis, Regional

Integration, and Ecology in Prehistoric Amazonia," previously published in *Current Anthropology* 46(4):589–620; © 2005 by the Wenner-Gren Foundation for Anthropological Research. This work, as part of the European Science Foundation EUROCORES Programme OMLL, was supported by funds from the Swedish Research Council and the EC Sixth Framework Programme under Contract no. ERAS-CT–2003–980409.

2. The term *Neolithic Revolution,* or *Neolithization,* is misleading in several ways, but the prehistoric processes which it denotes—that is, the intensification of resource use based on domestication of plants and animals, and the emergence of stratified societies—constitute real challenges for archeological research, not least because such processes on different continents seem to share certain similarities. By "Neolithization" I here do not mean the *origin* of crop cultivation, which by this time had already occurred in Amazonia for several millennia (Heckenberger 2002:118; Neves et al. 2003:34; Oliver 2001:65–66), but a relatively sudden intensification of agriculture in conjunction with the emergence of sedentary, densely populated, and stratified societies. It is important to recognize the gradual domestication of food plants such as manioc as a process distinct from, and generally much earlier, than "Neolithization" in this sense. Following traditional usage, however, authorities such as Donald Lathrap have characterized the Amazonian domestication of manioc as a first step in the "Neolithic Revolution" of the New World (cf. Neves 1999:225).

3. In indigenous Amazonia, in particular, many anthropologists have confirmed Pierre Clastres's (1987) observation that the standard response to any pretence of authority is to walk away and set up a new village elsewhere. To understand the emergence of stratified societies in Amazonian prehistory, we thus need to reconstruct the outlines of integrative ideologies capable of counteracting such centrifugal forces. The ceremonial life of contemporary Arawakan groups in the northwest Amazon (cf. Hill 2002) does suggest such an ideological system, embedding social hierarchy in compelling constructions of inclusive, ethnic identities ultimately founded on familiar notions of consanguinity.

4. The color green, frogs, and water in much of Amazonia symbolize femaleness and fertility (Boomert 1987:36).

5. Experts disagree on whether Amazonian Dark Earths were deliberately created as a "technology" of agricultural intensification (Myers 2004; Myers et al. 2003) or merely an unintentional artifact of long-term human occupation (Balée 1992:42; Neves et al. 2003:44). Considering recent research on Amazonian Dark Earths, and following Denevan's (1992) observation on the excessive labor requirements of shifting cultivation using stone axes, many now agree that shifting cultivation became prevalent in Amazonia only after the European introduction of metal axes, implying that Pre-Columbian horticulture in Amazonia was generally of a

more permanent character (Denevan 2004; Mora 2003; Myers 2004:74; Myers et al. 2003; Neves et al. 2004:44).

6. A notable exception is Betty Meggers, who attributes extensive areas of *terra preta* to discontinuous occupation by small groups (for example, Meggers 1992).

7. It has long been common among archeologists to refer, like Ester Boserup, to population growth as the explanation of agricultural intensification and increasing social complexity (cf. Lathrap 1970). Rather than view population growth as an independent variable, however, we should ask which sociopolitical factors lie behind the emergence of larger and more sedentary concentrations of population (cf. Gassón 2002:295; Petersen, Neves, & Heckenberger 2001:101). In Amazonia, it is particularly evident that community size depends on the ability of political and ritual leaders to integrate greater concentrations of people, which in turn relies on ideological factors such as ethnicity, kinship, and a hierarchical cosmology. These ideological factors of integration must nevertheless continuously be supported at a symbolic *and* material level through ceremonial feasting, generally focused on the consumption of manioc or maize beer (cf. Gassón 2003; Goldman 1966:86; Renard-Casevitz 2002:128) and the redistribution of rare prestige goods (cf. Gassón 2002:292; Heckenberger 2002:117–118). The latter two activities are archeologically reflected in agricultural intensification and long-distance trade, respectively. It is thus only to be expected that sites with evidence of intensive agriculture tend to be strategically located along riverine trade routes (cf. Herrera et al. 1992; Kern et al. 2003; Mora 2003). The ceremonial consumption of beer is also abundantly reflected in finds of ceramic brewing and drinking vessels (Lathrap 1970:54–56, 85–86, 88, 100–101, 183). Once major investments in agricultural intensification and sedentism have occurred, of course, a factor that could provide powerful incentives for further demographic concentration is warfare (Heckenberger 1996:203).

Part III

Is the World System Sustainable? Attempts toward an Integrated Socioecological Perspective

The Human–Environment Nexus: Progress in the Past Decade in the Integrated Analysis of Human and Biophysical Factors[1]

EMILIO F. MORAN

I. Introduction

The Earth continues to be treated with little thought for the future. More and more species are going extinct. Wetlands are disappearing at a rapid rate, endangering the migration routes of birds. Even our closest primate relatives are finding less and less of their habitat left standing to ensure their survival. The story goes on. There is little concrete strategic policy that incorporates the development of a sustainable Earth system as a practical objective. Yet, that is exactly what we must establish. Without a conscious exercise dedicated to the objective of ensuring the sustainability of the world's ecological systems, our days on this planet are numbered.

Humans, as a distinct species, have been on this planet a very long time. What is not widely recognized is that in the past fifty years we have changed nearly every aspect of our relationship with Nature. Yes, the Industrial Revolution began some three hundred years ago, and we have been gradually increasing the effects we have on the Earth since then (Turner et al. 1990). And, in the past 10,000 years, in various times and places, we have had considerable effect on the local and the regional scale (Redman 1999). But never before has our impact had planetary-scale consequences, and that is what we are having trouble understanding. As a species we tend to think and act locally; however, for the first time in human evolution we have begun to have a cumulative, global impact.

Our impact in the past fifty years has no equivalent in our entire history as a species (see Figure 1). In the past fifty years we have seen not only an exponential increase in carbon dioxide but also ozone depletion and nitrous oxide concentrations in the atmosphere, losses in tropical rainforests, frequency of natural disasters, and species extinctions. The same can be said for fertilizer consumption, damming of rivers, water use, paper consumption, the number of people living in cities, and the number of motor vehicles. Although we see a few cases of nations and regions with a growing middle class and improved

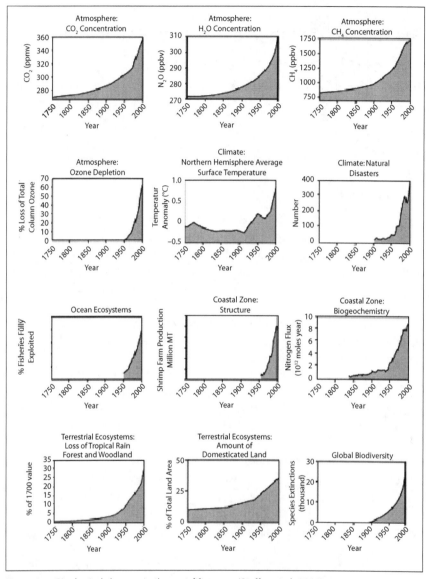

Figure 1 • Biophysical changes in the past fifty years (Steffen et al. 2004).

living standards, more often than not in the past twenty years we have seen a decline in the living standards of the poor and the middle class, with the gap growing and the concentration of wealth becoming as pervasive as the loss of species.

The exponential increase in environmental change is tied to two factors: the increase in human population and changes in consumption habits. Indeed, one must think of these two factors in tandem. One Euroamerican citizen consumes twenty-five times the resources that one average citizen from India, Guatemala, or other less developed countries does. So, while birth rates have declined to replacement level or even below in developed countries, these populations continue to impact the Earth's resources far more than do the billions of people in developing countries. Both "the North" and "the South" have a huge impact on Nature, and if we want to leave an Earth worth living in to our children, both the North and the South will need to change how they go about their business. Yet, changing business-as-usual— "culture," worldview, and such—is easier said than done.

Whether in the North or the South, specific societies have deeply ingrained cultural and historical traditions that have both positive and negative elements that facilitate and hinder our capacity to respond to the current crisis in the Earth system. Looking at North American and European society, we can speak positively of the democratic institutions that are in place, which provide an effective mechanism for citizens to respond to information provided to them, whether about schools, politics, or the environment. This is all to the good. Yet, how do we explain the lack of responsiveness in the United States to the growing evidence for a global environmental crisis? Side by side with our democratic institutions, the United States has a culture of individualism, with a much greater value given to capital accumulation as a measure of a person's worth than in almost any other society. These cultural values tend to sway a great portion of the citizenry against environmental regulations, seeing them as costly and thus likely to increase taxes on individuals, and to raise the cost of environmental goods and services. Even the promotion of public transportation as a response to reducing fossil-fuel emissions is opposed by many on the grounds that it limits personal freedom, despite the costs to the country (in terms of dependence on foreign oil supplies) and the globe (in terms of emission of Earth-warming gases).

This example can be paralleled by many other countries. Each will have a slightly different twist to it: a product of the historically contingent nature of human affairs. Other countries may lack, for instance, democratic institutions with a capacity to mobilize the populace, but they may have enlightened rulers who respond quickly to evidence for environmental crisis: witness the rapid reforestation of China in the past twenty years, following decades of deforestation. The pace of the reforestation has been without equal in the world, despite the many economic constraints faced by China and its vast population. In short, there is no one answer to finding environmentally appropriate solutions to the current global environmental crisis. Human agents in specific places need to work within the constraints and opportunities provided by their physical, social, economic, and cultural setting. We are all responsible for the condition of our planet, by our action and by our inaction.

II. Can One Conceive of Ecosystems without Human Agents?

Ecologists have a tendency to blame human agents for our current crisis. However, doing so does not begin to move us toward solutions. Human agents are part of the problem, but they are the only ones who can alleviate the current crisis. Fortunately, we know one thing: human agents are eminently self-interested and capable of amazing self-organization when properly motivated and led. So, if we are so capable of looking after ourselves, and to organize to achieve our goals, why are we in the current crisis? I think the answer lies in our evolutionary tendency to think primarily of local territories, even though our contemporary capacity to use resources from far and distant places has grown enormously. We still have not been able to internalize the consequences of our contemporary consumption of environmental resources from throughout the world, and we have not developed effective ways to get information and feedback on what the impact of our consumption has been. In other words, economic globalization has been very effective at using global resources but not in giving consumers the information they need to make a decision on whether they want to have that kind of impact. This is a systemic failure that must be corrected if we are to begin to be able to respond to our current environmental crisis. Without feedback from our consumption actions, we will continue to act irresponsibly. That has not always been the case in how we use resources.

In the past, human agents went out from their communities to gather needed resources to sustain their population at a very local level. We must recall that for most of our experience as a species, we were hunter-gatherers. The range of hunter-gatherers was fairly limited, and when they overused resources they were forced to move considerable distances until they could find another territory, not occupied by others, to sustain them. As hunter-gatherer populations increased, they found themselves running into other bands, and perhaps experiencing conflict with them. In short, it was preferable in many cases to limit the group's consumption to sustainable levels, rather than face a very uncertain future access to distant and possibly dangerous territories.

Even with the advances in control made possible by domestication of plants and animals, human agents could experientially understand how the local land and water responded to their agricultural management. What was happening in China was of no interest to those living in Europe or Africa. Products came from relatively close distances and anyone could assess whether they were putting themselves at risk.

Those familiar ways of adjusting our behavior to existing resources are now completely changed for much of the human populations on Earth. Today, whether in China, Germany, Argentina, or the United States, human agents are provided with coffee from Brazil; bananas from Honduras, Philippines, or Gabon; fish from oceans on the other side of the world; and powdered milk from places unspecified on the can labels. The human consumer has no way to know how much forest was cut to grow that coffee, which people were displaced to make room for those banana plantations, which fish stock was depleted, or which smallholder was displaced for that dairy farm. In short, we have a disconnection between what we use on the Earth and the consequences of that use for people and nature (cf. Moran 2006).

If we are to begin to move toward a sustainable Earth system, we must begin by building an awareness of what we do—no matter where it might be—and to reflect on whether that is an impact that we want to have. Just as consumer movements have, after much effort, succeeded in having many products labeled by corporations as to their nutritional and caloric content, we need to begin to require that products indicate where they come from and to post, in public sites on the Internet, environmental impact statements that show the products' ecological consequences.

III. Human Agency: Individuals Making a Difference

A fine line exists between endowing individuals with agency, or the ability to take decisions and actions, and ignoring actual people altogether. Ecologically, we have tended to do the latter. In many major texts and popular books, we read about how people do this to the environment, or degrade that landscape, or pollute these rivers. Just as the socialist literature treated the workers as *Lumpenproletariat*, or an aggregate proletarian mass, so does modern analysis deal with how people treat the environment, not recognizing the diverse ways that people in fact act toward their physical surroundings. But in giving individuals the attention they deserve, and in trying to understand their actions, we can also fail to see the patterns in their actions. After all, human agency takes place within an environmental and social matrix, and individuals are members of social groups with shared economic, cultural, and political interests. Thus, in ensuring that we give individual human agents their due, we must balance this attention with a concern for how many other agents share similar values and make similar decisions with given cumulative impacts.

It is appropriate to consider how human agency can make a difference, and how social movements can make an even greater difference. Individuals, as members of given societies, do not represent the entire society but some segment of it characterized by a specific economic position, education, and political linkages. When individuals act they commonly represent the interests of those parts of the social fabric within which they are embedded, but on occasion they rise above those contexts and represent wider interests. Time and again we see evidence of how an individual through his or her actions can change how we think about the world and how we can act on it.

In short, human agency does make a difference, whether expressed as ideas or in action. Until 1985 there were hardly any stories in major magazines or newspapers about Amazonian deforestation, even though there had been a growing discussion of it in scientific journals and plenty of research attesting to the rapid rates of forest destruction. But the appearance of an interview with Tom Lovejoy in the *New York Times* in 1985 overnight mobilized the considerable resources of the press and other media, and over the next decade there was an exponential growth in the number of stories in major newspapers and magazines, which resulted in considerable international pressure on Brazil to stop the subsidies that were fueling the deforestation.

So, it seems that we need to have an accumulation of information over an extended time, gradually shaping into a picture that instigates concern in some quarters and action by some individuals. When such action is associated with some notable event or overwhelming evidence, it appears that public response can result in remarkably rapid and effective mobilization. But this will not happen if individual agents do not take the considerable risks involved in trying to change business-as-usual and to advocate a significant shift in how we do things. Change is resisted by all complex systems largely in self-defense and because it can be very costly if the change proves unnecessary or wrong-headed. Thus, human political and economic systems, like ecological systems, resist changing their basic patterns until there is overwhelming evidence that something fundamental has happened that requires a shift in the structure and the function of the system, if it is to survive. Are we there yet? Do we have overwhelming evidence?

IV. Overwhelming Evidence

Figure 2 illustrates what is happening in terms of demographic variables, which should be reason for concern. Population has been increasing rapidly since 1750, but it is really only since 1950 that the exponential nature of this growth has become manifest, showing very little sign of subsiding in the next thirty to forty years. By that time the human population will be in excess of

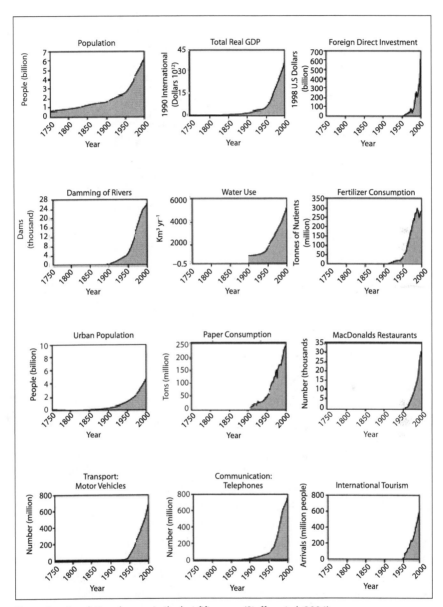

Figure 2 • Population changes in the last fifty years (Steffen et al. 2004).

10 billion (it is now about 6 billion). Total Gross Domestic Product, foreign direct investment, damming of rivers, water use, fertilizer consumption, urbanization, paper consumption, the number of motor vehicles, and the number of telephones have also all jumped exponentially since 1950.

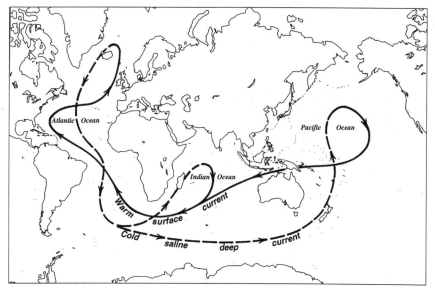

Figure 3 • Oceanic conveyor belt (adapted from Broecker 1991).

Similarly synchronous trends can be observed on the Earth-system side
(see Figure 1): CO_2 concentrations, N_2O concentrations, CH_4 concentrations,
ozone depletion, northern hemisphere average surface temperatures, the
number of natural disasters, loss of fisheries, increase in nitrogen fluxes in coastal
zones, loss of tropical rain forests and woodlands, amount of land dedicated to
cultivation, and number of species gone extinct have all jumped exponentially
since 1950.

In short, the simultaneous and interconnected nature of these changes
in human ecological relations since 1950 suggest that human activities could
inadvertently trigger abrupt changes in the Earth system. The most troubling of
all would be the triggering of a disruption in the oceanic conveyor belt, which
regulates the world climate (see Figure 3 and Broecker 1991). Simulations show
that increases in greenhouse gases can trigger changes in the North Atlantic
circulation, yielding scenarios resulting in rather dramatic collapses. We know
already that the Atlantic thermohaline circulation (THC) reorganization can be
triggered by changes in surface heat and in freshwater fluxes, and that crossing
thresholds can result in irreversible changes of ocean circulation (Rahmstorf
& Stocker 2003). Our current situation with regard to CO_2 alone, not to
mention all the other gases, is well above the recorded experience of the past
500 million years as recorded in the Vostok Ice Core (see Figure 4).

Once we begin to operate well above any recorded levels, not just for
one but for many measurable parameters, the question has to be asked if we

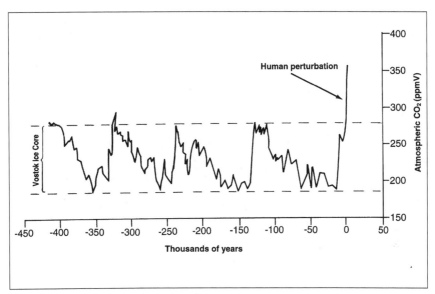

Figure 4 • Vostok ice core (adapted from Steffen et al. 2004).

have begun to play a game with the survival of our species on planet Earth. Do we recognize that business-as-usual is a sure guarantee of the end of life as we know it? Do we recognize our own contribution to it? Or are we so self-satisfied in our own material success that we cannot recognize overwhelming evidence when we see it? In the answer to these questions lies the likelihood of our having a future in a world worth living in.

V. Progress in the Integrated Study of Human–Environment Interactions

Over the past decade a series of international efforts have made considerable contributions to understanding the dynamics of coupled human–environment systems. The International Geosphere Biosphere Programme (IGBP) constitutes a network of scientists who have focused their attention on Earth-System Science, first by addressing global atmospheric circulation and climate change, then terrestrial ecosystems, hydrology, and modeling. These scientists in 1988 approached the social sciences community to engage their interest in addressing questions of the human dimensions of such global changes.

The science of global environmental change has, arguably, been responsible for the discovery of the rapid and large-scale accumulation of CO_2 in the atmosphere and the concern that this process will trigger global climate changes whose consequences could threaten the planet. Research quickly identified land-use and land-cover changes as a major element of the global carbon cycle, both as source and sink (Houghton et al. 1983; Moore et al. 1981; Woodwell et al. 1983). This turned research interests toward the human alteration and conversion of landscapes, especially forests, agricultural lands, and grasslands, which increased or reduced carbon in the atmosphere. In addition, suggestions on how to balance the carbon cycle identified land cover as a candidate for helping explain the so-called missing carbon sink, with recent evidence pointing to such land changes as the regeneration of forests on abandoned agricultural lands as well as changes in ecosystem production owing to longer growing seasons and fertilization by CO_2 and nitrogen (Goodale et al. 2002; Schimel et al. 2001). Using these questions as points of departure, global environmental change research subsequently expanded to include a broad array of human-induced changes in the structure and the function of the Earth system, including ecosystems and their services and biodiversity (Daily et al. 2000; Lubchenco 1998; Raven 2002), in which land change plays a fundamental role. Recent evidence points to the importance of regional-to-local climate change as driven by land change (Kalnay & Cai 2003), and the emergence of sustainability science (Schellnhuber et al. 2004; Kates et al. 2001) represents yet another strong interest in land change, with strong policy implications (Turner et al. 2001).

A crucial element in the past decade has been the land-use and land-cover change program. Land-cover changes are complex processes that are discontinuous rather than smoothly even over time and space. Change is often triggered by sudden shock events that cascade throughout vast areas. Land cover will follow different temporal trajectories of change as a result of the differential uses to which the land is put, and we see evidence for high spatial heterogeneity in patterns of land use at the local level. We can see both land-use intensification and extensification occurring side by side in the same region, which makes it wrong-headed to suggest simple trajectories from extensive to intensive use, as we had done earlier in the social sciences.

Researchers on land use and land cover have focused a lot of their effort in the past decade on identifying the "drivers" of land-use and land-cover change. Examination of 152 studies of tropical deforestation indicated complex interactions and contradictory conclusions. Simple answers that we have turned to, such as the roles of population growth, poverty, and other drivers of land degradation, prove to be affected by other factors, such as social institutions, in ways that are at times surprising. Population proves to be important, but less so than national objectives for agricultural development and the expansion of roads, technology, and infrastructure. The comparative study of these cases shows that we have dealt rather simplistically with demographic factors. Demographic change is not necessarily a shift from high to low mortality and fertility regimes (referred to as the demographic transition) but is more likely associated with the breakdown of extended families into a greater number of households and the consequences of more households for consumption behavior.

The study of a large number of cases also shows that there are distinct regional pathways to tropical deforestation and other land-use and land-cover changes. In Latin America, especially Amazonia, a phase of colonization is followed by infrastructure improvements, logging, and the expansion of ranching and pasture development. In contrast, changes in Africa and Asia are driven more by timber concessions and large-scale plantations, and in the case of Southeast Asia by intensive, high-density migration projects focused on commercial cultivation displacing native peoples.

Cross-cutting these pathways are the many processes of globalization that amplify or reduce the impact of such forces. Rapid land-use changes tend to be associated with the incorporation of regions into global markets and capital and information flows. When such incorporation occurs, local processes and relationships can be eclipsed by external drivers that bring about devastating impacts on local social and political processes. It can also change the biodiversity in a region by forcing a market-driven specialization of production to fit global standards or expectations. Yet, we know that this does not always happen: witness the recent expansion into urban-industrial areas of products previously restricted to the Amazon hinterland, such as the consumption of *açaí* (*Euterpe oleracea*) in Rio de Janeiro and São Paulo, and soon also in Europe (Brondizio In press).

Significant interest exists in improving our understanding of the drivers of land change and recognizing their complexity and variation beyond the general factors of demand for resources from increasing population and levels of consumption. Significant headway has been made, including the social causes of deforestation and arid land degradation (for example, Archer 2003; Indrabudi, de Gier, & Fresco 1998; Moran 1993; Reynolds & Stafford Smith 2002; Robbins 1998; Sierra & Stallings 1998; Walker et al. 1999); the role of institutions in land-use decisions (for instance, Klooster 2003; Lambin et al. 2001; Ostrom et al. 2002; Turner et al. 2001); and understanding the reciprocal relationships between population and land change (for example, Crews-Meyer 2001; Döös 2002; McCracken et al. 1999). Significant gains have also been made in how to link social with physical processes using remotely sensed data and in nesting data and studies from local to regional to global scales (for instance, Fox et al. 2002; Turner et al. 2001; Moran & Brondizio 2001; Walsh & Crews-Meyer 2002), including a means of comparing different land classifications used in various studies (Di Gregorio & Jansen 2000; McConnell & Moran 2001).

Our understanding of the role of population growth has also changed. From thinking that more people always meant less forest, a growing number of cases suggest that forests can persist under high population densities (for example, Moran & Ostrom 2005; Ostrom et al. 2002). The role of communities and institutionalized rules of management plays a critical role in such cases, emerging from a variety of sources, among them scarcity of the valued good (Laris 2002). Studies have shown how political and economic structures constrain individual choices about management of land resources (for instance, Archer 2003; Robbins 1998). Cultural traditions and land tenure rules are critical in influencing how land can be used and by whom (Tucker 1999). A notable advance has been the growing use of orbital Earth-observing satellites linked to ground research to address regional to local issues of land change (Fox et al. 2002; Liverman et al. 1998; Walsh & Crews-Meyer 2002; Wood & Porro 2002), contributing novel insights to the interpretation of land-cover change on topics rarely addressable with any accuracy at global or regional scales, for instance, land change in areas undergoing urbanization (Seto & Kaufmann 2003) and stages of secondary succession and their management (Brondizio et al. 1994, 1996; Moran et al. 2000).

In short, research over the past decade on land-use and land-cover change is making increasingly productive use of case studies by linking them to regional and global modeling exercises that challenge past simplifications, and in more nuanced regional and global understandings of pathways of change that not only capture the complex socioeconomic and biophysical drivers of land-use change but also account for the specific human–environment conditions under which these drivers operate. But none of this will matter if we fail to imbue all of it with a stronger sense of why it matters.

Note

1. I wish to thank the Lund conference organizers for the opportunity to present these views before a superb audience and for the comments received since then. The first part of this chapter is elaborated into a full-length book, *People and Nature*, published by Blackwell Publishing in 2006. The work reported in the second half of the chapter reflects the collective efforts of many people in the global-change community (see Gutman et al. 2004). It also reflects many years of field research by me and my colleagues, made possible by numerous funding agencies: NSF, NOAA, NASA, and NIH. None of these colleagues or funding agencies, however, is responsible for the views expressed herein. They are the sole responsibility of the author.

CHAPTER 16

In Search of Sustainability:
What Can We Learn from the Past?[1]

BERT J. M. DE VRIES

> Concepts of past cultures have probably changed as much in the last thirty years as have ideas of the earth system. The two massive data sets await reconciliation. (Gunn & Folan 2000:227)

Over the last decade, the idea of *sustainability* and *sustainable development* has gradually become a modern equivalent of, and complement to, the Declaration of Human Rights, which inspired so many people shortly after the devastating Second World War. Respected business and government leaders have embraced the concept and hailed it as the foremost challenge for the twenty-first century. Inevitably, this concept has been widened to the extent that it now accommodates a large variety of interpretations, objectives, and proposals. These are intertwined with personal and collective values and perceptions, which are in turn rooted in millennia of developments that shaped human experiences, knowledge, technical skills, social arrangements, and psychological traits.

It seems logical to ask whether we can learn something from the past in our search for the roots of unsustainable human–nature interaction.[2] Moreover, in the past few decades a large amount of new scientific research results have become available, in particular from undertakings such as the IGBP PAGES and the BIOME 6000 projects. There is need for an overview. In addition, novel insights and tools exist for a more in-depth, model-based understanding of the past that can help to synthesize various disciplinary data, concepts, and theories into a more coherent and transdisciplinary framework.

In this chapter, I reflect on some of the lessons learned from a three-year project sponsored by the *Hollandsche Maatschappij der Wetenschappen in Haarlem* in celebration of its 250th anniversary (de Vries & Goudsblom 2002).

The project resulted in a book with contributions from scientists from different backgrounds: archeology, history, sociology, geography, biology, engineering, and climatogy. The aim was to sketch in a broad and impressionist way some key empirical and theoretical findings about the evolution of socionatural systems. Three broad questions are addressed: What can we learn from recent paleoclimate and paleovegetation reconstructions? Which insights have been gained from emerging, computer-based techniques such as the modeling of complex adaptive systems? Which concepts and theories now dominate the "Grand Narrative" of socionatural system evolution? In no way can I claim completeness, however, either in the sense of covering all the relevant research or in the sense of considering all the integrating approaches.

Early Humans: The Threats and Opportunities of a Changing Environment

As part of Global Change research, and in particular the IGBP and HDP networks and the PAGES and BIOME 6000 projects (www.pages.org), a large stream of satellite and field data is being generated that allows (re)construction of present and past climate and vegetation characteristics. In some regions, it has been possible to make rather detailed reconstructions of past climate and vegetation, as well as of people's diets and diseases, based on investigations of ice cores, tree rings, sediments, stones, and bones. As a consequence, new and refined hypotheses have been proposed for the transitions from hunting-gathering (that is, foraging) to more sedentary societies.[3] In the first stages of this agrarianization process, human groups were confronted with changes in their environment.[4] Some had a catastrophic immediacy, such as earthquakes; others were slow but no less relentless, such as changing courses or drying of rivers and changes in climate (temperature, precipitation) and vegetation. They presented threats as well as opportunities, risks as well as challenges.

These human groups were basically dependent on their natural environment and would have responded to signs of local resource scarcity with migration into new areas with better opportunities or attempts at increasing control of plants and animals. In the latter case, the interaction between humans and their natural environment was intensified, leading to a more sedentary life and significant innovations in behavior, technology, and social organization. Which route was actually chosen in this agrarianization process, that is, from gathering of wild plant-foods to crop production (horti-/agriculture) or from hunting to protective herding and the raising of livestock (pastoralism), depended to a significant degree on climate and biogeography.

Before approximately 13,000 B.C.E., almost all the interior of southwest

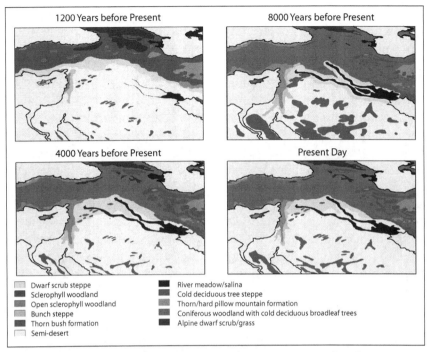

Figure 1 • Vegetation change in the Near East over the past 12,000 years, based on recent observations and reconstructions (Marchant & de Vries 2002). The maps do not take into account the sea-level changes in this period.

Asia was covered by steppe and desert-steppe, dominated in part by grasses such as perennial feather grass. The steppe vegetation probably offered local foragers a diverse array of wild plant foods that could provide all the necessary ingredients for a healthy human diet. Some of these foods have relatively low energy costs of processing and thus a high "net" caloric value for humans. Recent data from pollen diagrams seem to confirm the views of Boserup (1966) and Sahlins (1972) that the life of early hunter-gatherers may not have been so bad.

Climatic and other environmental changes were almost certainly powerful forces in the shift to agriculture and possibly also to animal domestication, mainly through changes in the distribution and the composition of vegetation. The prevailing current view is that agriculture probably originated at least 12,000 years ago in the so-called Levantine Corridor, near the Jordan valley lakes, in the form of the domestication of cereals and pulses (cf. Figure 1). Within a millennium, there was also domestication of pigs, goats, and sheep (domestication of dogs preceded agriculture).

It is hypothesized that hunter-gatherer populations survived in small refuges. The steppe vegetation started to become richer across the Fertile Crescent as a consequence of climate change. Wild cereals and grasses spread and were followed by oak-dominated woodlands. This landscape permitted a much higher gross yield of food and, hence, a larger carrying capacity for human beings.

As so often happens, these changes led to other changes that were neither intended nor anticipated by the people who initiated them. In a self-reinforcing causal loop, the agrarianization process was accelerated by an increasing climatic seasonality and unpredictability. Forest expansion reduced the open range and encouraged territoriality and domestication of animals through the protection and propagation of local herds (Hole 1996). Birth-spacing was probably reduced as people became less mobile, yielding higher fertility rates and increasing sedentism. This in turn led to the need for further increases in harvests. There were also counterforces, however. The intensified exploitation of locally available resources (soil, water, trees) accelerated processes of degradation such as soil erosion. Mortality may also have risen, since micropredators would have become more abundant with rising temperature and because of more intense human-animal contact. Figure 2 shows a causal loop diagram (CLD) from system dynamics: it is a condensed way of presenting some major dynamic factors in the agrarianization process.[5]

According to this narrative, agriculture, animal herding, and the use of trees for wood and fodder became a more rewarding strategy than foraging because the dry cool steppe was generally a region of low mean energy yield per unit of area, compared to, for example, the later moist woodland steppe with its grasses and wetlands. Agrarianization was thus in part a response to deteriorating conditions for foraging. It led people irreversibly into a spiral of higher population density and more working hours. Once established, the agrarian way of life gradually replaced foraging almost everywhere.

There were also early agropastoral economies outside the Levant, for instance in the semiarid areas surrounding the Iranian Plateau around 8,000 B.C.E.[6] The recognition of the very early, probably independent origin of agriculture in China has been one of the important recent archeological discoveries. Other places in Asia and the Americas have probably been the locus of ancient and independent beginnings, too. The transition processes have sometimes been successful and enduring; in other cases they have been truncated by complex interactions of environmental change and social responses.

Many narratives have been written about human–environmental histories; less common are attempts to reframe such narratives into formal models.

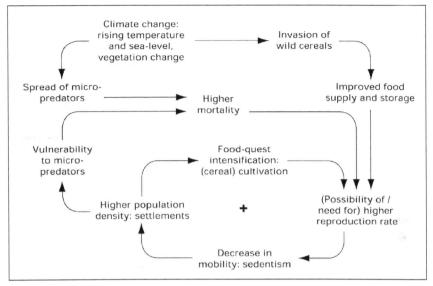

Figure 2 • A causal loop diagram (CLD) presenting some major dynamic factors in the early agrarianization process.

An example is the global simulation of the Neolithic transition (de Vries, Thompson, & Wirtz 2002; Wirtz & Lemmen 2003). It traces the spread of agriculture against the biogeographical background as reconstructed from a limited set of paleoclimate data. The simulation uses an algorithm of adaptive dynamics from evolutionary biology. Although highly formalized, the model does provide a framework to explore systematically the biogeographical setting for socioecological development and can reveal gaps in our knowledge of those regions that are sparsely investigated by scientists or for other reasons offer a small amount of finds. It can also be used to investigate the impacts of climate change, for instance the socioeconomic difficulties in Mesopotamia, Egypt, and the Indus Valley during the dry period around 2200 B.C.E., which was almost certainly caused by climate change (Yasuda & Catto 2004; Wirtz 2005). One question arising from these simulations is whether commonly attested worldwide patterns of human–environment interactions during the Holocene period can be generated from a deterministic rule system. Given that parameters, initial values, and evolutionary equations do not carry site-specific modifications, the model is global and generic and can link theories of the macro-evolution of humanity to specific archeological and paleobotanical observations and hypotheses.

The Rise of Social Complexity:
Environmental Risk and Social Organization

The natural environment provided the background against which the first steps of agrarianization were taken. A concurrent process was the unfolding of social complexity. Archeological and historical research can help us understand the balance between "nature" and "culture" in the rise and fall of empires. Did human-induced environmental change play a significant role in the rise and decline of social complexity? Can variation in the environment explain the nature of social organization? To what extent was the perception of environmental resources and risks a major determinant of how social complexity evolved? In answering these questions, we should beware of simple environmental determinism: reality is more complex than many anecdotes suggest. Referring to the "triad of basic controls" proposed by Elias, Goudsblom and colleagues (1996) distinguish among dangers coming (1) from the extrahuman world—droughts and floods, wild beasts and pests, earthquakes and volcanic eruptions; (2) from interhuman relationships—hostile neighbors, invading warriors; and (3) from intrahuman nature—mismanagement owing to negligence, ignorance, lack of self-restraint or discipline. Indeed, it is the interface between inter- and intrahuman interactions and environmental change that may provide the most significant insights into socioecological system evolution.

Environmental Feedbacks and Risks

Did people experience the impacts of human-induced changes in the natural environment? There is much evidence indicating that intensified exploitation of the local resource base caused environmental change. In some cases it was local and directly visible. Although the extent and mechanisms are still debated, there is general agreement that environmental deterioration in the form of salinization, deforestation, and other human interferences with natural processes has played a role in the collapse of many of the great empires. Such environmental change has also operated over larger spatial and temporal scales, and more indirectly. For instance, climate reconstruction and simulation experiments suggest that land-clearing in the Roman period affected climate and caused a shift toward drier conditions (Reale & Shukla 2000).

If environmental change occurred as a consequence of human activities, how would people have responded? This is a much harder question to answer. One may conceptualize the issue in terms of the control and dependency loop shown in Figure 3. The rise of social complexity is closely related to the efforts to control the natural environment. A large and stable food surplus, and an adequate means and infrastructure for distributing it, were a precondition

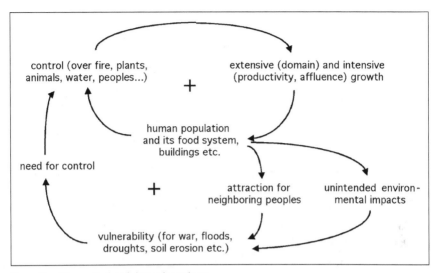

Figure 3 • The control and dependency loop.

for the rise of urban settlements. The necessary increase in productivity of land and labor required investment, that is, stored labor efforts or "capital goods." Tools were produced and terraces and canals were built. In order to provide protection, distribute food, and trade, defense works, storage rooms, roads, and transport equipment had to be constructed. To legitimize social stratification, large palaces and temples were built, which also required a significant surplus.

This process of intensification increased the food surplus; it also improved the management of short-term risks related to recurrent meteorological events, such as those related to variations in rainfall. It also introduced new risks and vulnerabilities. Capital goods were particularly susceptible to deterioration or destruction. The new techniques and practices introduced unknown longer-term environmental impacts and could, with an improper or incomplete understanding of environmental processes, accelerate detrimental feedback loops.[7] Learning to cope with such longer-term and more erratic events is more difficult. Vulnerabilities often became visible only when the system came under internal and/or external stress. The longer-term consequences of such a loss of resilience and the erosion of coping capability could include invasions by other peoples, destruction by raiders, disappearance of survival skills, and the like.

Increasing Social Complexity

The increase in social complexity occurred partly in response to the need to procure food, water, and shelter from an exacting and unpredictable natural environment. Using a functionalist framework, we could argue that the increase in social complexity expressed itself in social stratification as a way to combine technical and organizational skills with social coherence; in specialization in certain skills in order to permit and sustain higher and more diverse production; and in trading as one of the strategies to reduce risks of famine and war. An urban–rural divide started to develop, with larger variations in population density. Thus, complexity manifested itself in increasing spatial interaction and demographic, socioeconomic, and cultural heterogeneity.

The roles of priests and soldiers were clearly related to the risks that early agrarian communities were faced with (de Vries & Goudsblom 2002; Goudsblom, Jones, & Mennell 1996). Priests mediated between ordinary people and the extrahuman world, but they also played a pivotal role in inducing the self-restraint required for a farming life of hard work and for the exigencies of food storage and distribution. Harvest feasts and sacrifices are social institutions to manage the cycles of frugality. The interdependency of peasants and warriors was also strong, the former needing the latter for protection and the latter the former for food.

Social Change Mechanisms as Part of Socioecological Evolution

Archeologists have tried to achieve an in-depth understanding of past processes of social organization, sometimes applying principles of system dynamics (for example, Flannery 1972). Increasing differentiation and specialization of subsystems (segregation) and increasing linkages between the subsystems and the highest-order controls (centralization) are seen as driving forces of several sociocultural mechanisms such as the rise of special-purpose institutions and the overruling of lower-order controls by higher-order controls. Such systemic phenomena could develop into "pathologies," causing stress that might erode a system's resilience and accelerate disintegration. Several historical examples illustrate how such sociocultural "pathologies," in interaction with natural environmental dynamics, can cause stagnation and decline (Flannery 1972). Colonialism and resource exploitation in modern low-income countries also provide examples.

Some archeologists have stressed the role of interaction between ecological diversity and the exchange of goods and information.[8] Peer-polity interactions were part of the rise of socionatural heterogeneity and as such part of the evolution of socioecological systems. Quite a few environmental histories testify to the importance of warfare, competitive emulation, symbolic entrainment, innovation dispersal, and exchange of goods for the way in which humans interacted with their natural environment (Renfrew & Cherry 1985). For instance, warfare—itself possibly induced by resource scarcity—was a perennial phenomenon in the early civilizations of the Middle East and Greece and often led to accelerated deforestation:

> During campaigns, wood foraging parties were sent out. An extreme example was at the siege of Lachish, in 588 B.C.E., by Nebuchadnezzar, King of Babylon. After 2,500 years, layers of ash several meters thick still remain, higher than the remains of the fortress walls. The hills for miles around were cleared of trees. The wood was piled outside the walls and fired. Day and night sheets of flame beat against the walls until eventually the white-hot stones burst and the walls caved in (Thirgood 1981:58–59).

Another common consequence was a decline in population, which could temporarily alleviate the pressure on the forests. People seeking refuge in mountainous areas often turned to pastoralism, which could further degrade the environment if it led to intensive grazing. Competitive emulation may have been a factor in the decline of some megalithic cultures, with Easter Island a prominent example.[9]

Collapse and Diminishing Returns

When decline threatens, societies have had a variety of responses. Expanding trade, technical and social innovations, changing environmental management practices, migration, and conquest, or a mix of all these have sometimes postponed, sometimes reverted, and sometimes accelerated the processes of decline and collapse. When societal collapse occurred, new shoots on the tree of human civilizations were given a chance. Explanations of the collapse of civilizations can be categorized into three groups:[10]

1. Resource- and environment-related changes, fully exogenous or partly endogenous, in the sense of human-induced;
2. Interaction-related changes in the form of conquest or other, less dramatic forms of invasion; and
3. Internal changes in sociopolitical, cultural, and religious organization and worldview, diminishing the adequacy of response to external events.

This classification matches Goudsblom, Jones, & Mennell's (1996) categories of extra-, inter- and intrahuman change. On the basis of historical examples such as the decline of the Roman Empire, Tainter (1988, 2000) proposes that the diminishing returns of adding societal complexity is the root cause. Increasing complexity, then, can be a strategy to solve societal problems such as diminishing productivity, but it can in turn lead to increasing costs for energy, labor, and so on in order to reproduce the institutions necessary to

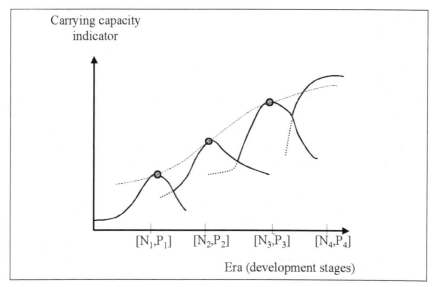

Figure 4 • Transition cycles in the process of extensive and intensive growth (that is, geographical and economic expansion).

deal with the complexity. The need to control information and energy flows in turn affects how the environment is perceived and used. An open question is whether the declining marginal returns on further investment were more of a consequence than a cause of rising complexity (Leeuw & de Vries 2002). In all likelihood, the problem is best understood as a "vicious circle." In any case, the capacity of institutions to have requisite variety—or be "clumsy," to use Thompson's phrase (de Vries, Thompson, & Wirtz 2002)—is an essential aspect of a system's capacity to transform itself structurally, that is, of its resilience.

Modeling Transitions, Adaptations, and Perspectives

Transition Dynamics

Accounts of the development of socionatural systems are often based on quantitative reconstruction, but they rarely use simulation models. Ecology, demography, and the more generic approach of system analysis have attempted to deepen our understanding by developing integrated population–economy–environment models. A well-known example is the logistic growth curve, along which a population increases either smoothly or with overshoot-and-collapse cycles successively approaching some maximum carrying capacity. Using the ecological image of "filling a niche," we could view human evolution as a series

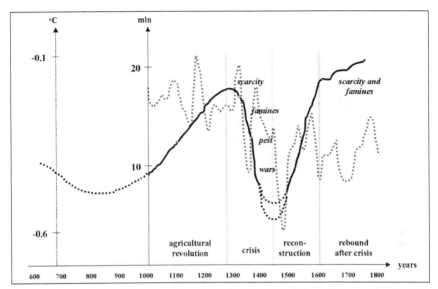

Figure 5 • Expansion and decline in a socionatural system: population in France and average Northern Hemisphere temperature relative to the period 1961-1990 (IPCC 2001; Mazoyer & Roudart 1997).

of transition processes toward higher numbers and activity levels (Figure 4). Each transition had its peak, beyond which contradictions among prevailing technologies, institutions, and belief systems became too strong, and decline set in. Often, although sometimes after a considerable delay, a new transition process would begin, in which both spatial scale and complexity emerged in new configurations with new potentialities.[11]

An example of such a series of transitions, derived from medieval France, is illustrated in Figure 5, which portrays the human population trajectory between 1000 C.E. and 1800 C.E. Detailed analyses of agricultural practices and techniques reveal an increase in potential population density (Mazoyer & Roudart 1997). In early medieval times (900 C.E.), Europe could support an average of <30 persons/km², with wide local fluctuations. This gradually rose to a European average of 30–80 persons/km² around 1250 C.E. Then a series of famines and wars set in, possibly related to rather sudden drops in temperature (the dotted curve in Figure 5). The fall in population liberated large amounts of productive land. After the crises, with improved fertilization strategies and tools (for example, the horse-drawn plough), the population quickly recovered to a new plateau with a sustainable density of up to 160 persons/km². This period in European history is a dramatic illustration of a cycle of expansion and decline where both natural and social forces are simultaneously at work.

Complex Systems Modeling

A next step is to use more advanced modeling techniques in combination with the massive data-sets which have become available from satellite and other monitoring. Such techniques—such as cellular automata, multi-agent simulation (MAS), and complex adaptive systems (CAS)—will acknowledge the fact that complex socio-natural systems are constantly undergoing structural transformation, during which thresholds, non-linear behavior, and feedback loops generate a unique series of interconnected, irreversible events. Causes and effects operate at various temporal and spatial scales, each with their own dynamic characteristics, and a simulation should be path-dependent, either from nonlinearities or stochastic processes, or both. Instead of a single attractor, as in the simple logistic growth process, there would be several stable attractors toward which a process will tend (see, for instance, Kaufmann 1995 for a biological, Scheffer et al. 2001 for an ecological, and Geels 2002 for a technological system equivalent).

The availability of powerful simulation tools has stimulated a focus on modeling individuals with their motives, habits, rules, and forms of cooperation and conflict. The resulting "multiagent" models are interpreted as virtual "worlds" that can deepen our understanding of past and present "real" worlds, because they supposedly resemble them in useful respects. Under certain circumstances, they may exhibit a remarkable capacity for self-organization. One of the more detailed and interesting analyses along these lines has focused on the Pueblo III period in the Mesa Verde region during the final 400 years of pre-Hispanic agricultural society (Kohler & Gumerman 2000). It is based on what the authors call "first principles of human adaptation": the minimization of energy expenditure, a population growth responsive to resource conditions, and the possibility of subsistence intensification.

In general, there are three very important and related roles that models can play in such research contexts. The first is to suggest hypotheses that can be tested by other means. The second is to examine the effects of different kinds of behavior, such as the exchange of maize, that are difficult or impossible to observe directly in the archeological record but that ought to have measurable effects, for example, on settlement behavior, which *can* be detected archeologically. Finally, there is the sense that we get much closer to an explanation of phenomena such as settlement behavior when we can generate it from a small set of rules, boundary conditions, and low-level agents, than when we derive statistical, system-level correlations between, for instance, agricultural productivity and the density of households.

Conclusion: A Theory of Ecocultural Dynamics?

In the past decades, ecological observations have led to several interesting theories that may help us understand socionatural systems. Ecosystem succession is conceptualized as determined by two principles: exploitation, in which rapid colonization of recently disturbed areas is emphasized ("r-strategists"), and conservation, with an emphasis on the slow accumulation and storage of energy and materials ("K-strategists"). Empirical observations suggest that two additional processes are needed to adequately explain ecological change (Gunderson et al.1997; Holling 1986). One is a stage during which tightly bound biomass and nutrients that have become increasingly susceptible to disturbance—overconnected, in system terms—are released. The resulting debris is then reorganized in a series of soil processes, which makes the nutrients available again for a renewed cycle of exploitation. The complex system is reduced to detritus and then undergoes renewal through low-level energy enclaves, which are the seeds for rapidly expanding pioneer communities.

Such an "ecocycle theory" is best approached as a conceptual framework with heuristic value. It might be seen as analogous to a "cultural theory" (Thompson, Ellis, & Wildavsky 1989) building on the work of anthropologist Mary Douglas (1970), who categorizes societies according to their position along two axes: "group" and "grid." The group axis represents the existence of a collective, shared set of values; the grid axis the degree of ranking and stratification in a society. The resulting four combinations can be generalized as ways of structuring the relationship not only among humans but also between humans and nature. They are the hierarchist (high on both), individualist (low on both), egalitarian (high in group, low in grid), and fatalist (low in group, high in grid).

Within each category, there will be quite different judgments about technology, environmental risks, and the distribution of prosperity between now and the future and between here and elsewhere. Each position tends to correspond to a particular view of the world, following its own rationality. The *hierarchist* places the emphasis on control and expertise in order to guarantee stability within a world of limits (procedural rationality), resembling the mature K-strategist in ecosystems. The *individualist* tends to see and grasp opportunity, out of the conviction that the world is inherently abundant (economic rationality). Its ecological equivalent is the pioneer community with its r-strategists. These two constructions of the natural and social environment can be represented by hierarchical state-empires versus market-oriented trade regimes. Just as ecocycles acknowledge two additional stages, so does cultural theory propose two additional perspectives. The *egalitarian* emphasizes the fragility of nature and the probability of irreversible destruction. The *fatalist* experiences the world as determined by pure chance.

The four worldviews interact dynamically, and none of them can exist without the other three (Thompson, Ellis, & Wildavsky 1989; De Vries, Thompson, & Wirtz 2002). Change often happens when one worldview becomes overly dominant and rigid. For instance, excessive hierarchism leads to legalism with ever lower marginal returns, containing the seed of decline and eventual disintegration. Extreme individualism leads to conflict and marginalization, which generates a desire for social stability and justice. Egalitarianism, arising from the desire to purify society from extortion and greed, can, if pursued to its extremes, be converted into sectarian self-righteousness and religious wars. Fatalists, finally, tend to be at the disposal of the other three, as converts for the egalitarians, cannon fodder for the hierarchist, or cheap labor for the individualist. Both the "ecocycle theory" and Douglas's cultural theory share a formal congruity with the theory of collapse proposed by Tainter, based on ecological and economic notions of increasing instability and subsequent decline of complex hierarchical systems.

Throughout history, egalitarian forms of organization sustained themselves in the "fringes" of religious-military and trade empires. From an environmental sustainability point of view, these egalitarian forms of organization may be associated with what has been called "common property regimes" (Ostrom 1990). Some groups have developed institutions that have survived droughts, floods, epidemics, and economic and political turmoil. Most of these regimes were in highly variable and uncertain environments and resource systems. These groups have "designed basic operational rules, created organizations to undertake the operational management of their common property regimes, and modified their rules over time in light of past experience according to their own collective-choice and constitutional-choice rules" (Ostrom 1990:58). Such self-organizing groups solved the problem of commitment and mutual monitoring without resorting to centralized power exercised by external agents or to competitive market institutions. Perhaps this is what conscious and explicit simplification could lead to if the bads of overcomplexification begin to outweigh the goods. Maybe it is in these "fringes" that real-world resilience and sustainability is hiding.

Notes

1. I wish to thank the contributors to the *Mappae Mundi* project and in particular Joop Goudsblom, Jodi de Greef, Sander van der Leeuw, and Kai Wirtz. The editors are grateful to Frank Hole for providing them with comments on this chapter.

2. Here I talk about socionatural or socioecological systems to indicate the complete context of humans living in their natural environment. As to sustainable development, the definition of the Brundtland Commission is still a useful one: meeting the needs of the present without compromising the ability of future generations to meet their own needs (WCED 1987).

3. At this stage, human groups had already mastered the control of fire, which should be considered as a *sine qua non* for the onset of agrarianization (see Goudsblom 1992).

4. We use the word "agrarianization" to emphasize that the shift to agriculture was a gradual intensification of the relationship among groups of humans, their environment, and one another, rather than a "revolution."

5. This way of presenting system dynamics is similar to what is called "figurational dynamics" by some sociologists.

6. Agrarian settlements also spread over the entire Plateau itself, in areas with accessible surface water (Christensen 1993).

7. See, for instance, Janssen, Kohler, & Scheffer (2003) for a model-based hypothesis on how a "sunk cost" effect of investments may lead to wrong decisions.

8. In Mesoamerica, Blanton et al. (2003) found ecological diversity to be a key element in understanding state-market interactions.

9. See, for example, Anderies (2000) for a discussion on the mechanisms behind the collapse of Easter Island culture.

10. Based on Tainter (1988), who lists them under eleven headings.

11. Turchin (2003) attempts to formulate these dynamic processes in a mathematical model, using ethnic center-periphery gradients, autocatalytic allegiance processes, and elite cycles as driving forces.

CHAPTER 17

Political Ecology and Sustainability Science: Opportunity and Challenge

SUSAN C. STONICH AND DANIEL S. MANDELL

This chapter is a comparative evaluation of the frameworks of "political ecology" and "sustainability science" in terms of their capacity to understand and address dynamic human–environmental interactions (also referred to as human–environmental relations, or human–natural systems), including those related to global environmental change. This assessment includes a brief intellectual history of "political ecology" within the context of significant shifts and transformations in social science approaches to understanding human–environmental relations in the Post World War II period. Among earlier approaches to this field are "human ecology" and "cultural ecology"; more recent frameworks include "political ecology" and "sustainability science." The chapter points out several important trends, especially those related to the emergence and considerable expansion of "political ecology" as a dominant approach to the study of human–environmental relations. Although political ecology has flourished, its intellectual coherence as a field of study and its potential scholarly contribution have been the subject of contentious debate. Several serious issues remain unresolved. Despite continuing questions, we contend that recent trends in studies of human–environmental relations present both a window of opportunity and a challenge to social scientists engaged in such efforts. A key purpose of this chapter is to explore ways to enhance the participation of social scientists in the new paradigm of "sustainability science."

The Emergence of Sustainability Science

Zoologist Jane Lubchenco called for "a new social contract for science" in her 1997 Presidential Address to the Annual Meeting of the American Association of The Advancement of Science, published in revised form the following year in *Science*. Her proposal reads in parts like a manifesto for social science research: acknowledging humans as an overwhelming "new force of nature" that needs to be understood (1998:492). Hence, "integration of the human dimensions of . . . global changes with the physical-chemical-biological dimensions is clearly needed" (Ibid.). But, as she notes, human dimensions of "scientific" problems are usually given short shrift. As Lubchenco argues, apprehending "the current and growing extent of human dominance of the planet will require new kinds of knowledge and applications from science—knowledge to reduce the rate at which we alter the Earth systems, knowledge to understand the Earth's ecosystems and how they interact with the numerous components of human-caused global change, and knowledge to manage the planet" (Ibid.:494). Unfortunately, even studies of the human dimensions of environmental problems, such as vulnerability to climate change, have maintained a traditional science, or "environment first," strategy (National Research Council 1997; Stonich 2001). Thus they have failed to produce these new kinds of knowledge and applications so urgently needed to understand, conserve, and manage resources.

Lubchenco conveys the need to balance among "science/environment first," "society first," and policy-oriented strategies, integrating "research across all disciplines" (Lubchenco 1998:495). She emphasizes the importance of an understanding of society and, consequently, the involvement of social scientists. Furthermore, she calls for "more effective bridges between policy, management, and science, as well as between the public and private sectors" (Ibid.). Thus, not only does Lubchenco's call for a new social contract for science suggest a leading role for social scientists, but also her vision statement recognizes the vital role of applied work and an active engagement between academics and practitioners.

More recently, Kates and colleagues (2001) published a manifesto, also in *Science*, proclaiming the emergence of "sustainability science" and claiming to provide new orientations for science in response to the growing divide between science and "the preponderantly societal and political processes that were shaping the sustainable development agenda" (Ibid.:641). Embraced by "international scientific programs, the world's scientific academies, and independent networks of scientists," sustainability science demonstrates efforts by the scientific community to respond to the problems that Lubchenco presents. Notably, Robert Kates and William Clark served as co-chairs for the National Research Council's Sustainability Transition Study, as well as for the National Research Council's Board of Sustainable Development (with Kates as Vice Chairman), so they are well-positioned to speak for the U. S. National Academies. In *Our*

Common Journey, they describe sustainability science as integrating biological, geophysical, social, and technological systems research in place-based science (National Research Council 1999:280–285). Thus, sustainability science "seeks to understand the fundamental character of interactions between nature and society" in a way that "encompass[es] the interaction of global processes with the ecological and social characteristics of particular places and sectors . . . integrat[ing] the effects of key processes across the full range of scales from local to global" (Kates et al. 2001:641). In addition to looking at the full range of scales, sustainability science aims to understand temporal complexity, including lags between causes and effects and degrees of inertia and urgency of various processes; functional complexity, such as the fact that certain effects may have numerous and disparate causes; and the multiplicity of views regarding "what makes knowledge usable within both science and society" (Ibid.). Furthermore, Kates and colleagues have established several key issues, framed as "core questions," for sustainability science to examine: the dynamism of nature–society interactions, "long-term trends in environment and development," vulnerability and resilience, whether "scientifically meaningful 'limits' or 'boundaries'" can be defined for warning of risks, incentive structures, "operational systems for monitoring and reporting," and systems integration of "research planning, monitoring, assessment, and decision support" (Ibid.).

Sustainability science is very much oriented to applied research and developing applications of a scientific understanding of nature–society interactions. Its considerations and core questions reveal this bias toward applied work, which is understandable given that sustainability science originated from experiences with sustainable development (Kates et al. 2001:641). Thus, a major objective of sustainability science, coming out of the *Friibergh Workshop on Sustainability Science* (2000), is to reconnect "scientists, practitioners, and citizens in setting priorities, creating new knowledge, evaluating its possible consequences, and testing it in action." To date, the major social science proponents of sustainability science have been geographers, especially Robert Kates and Roger Kasperson, both of whom are deeply involved in human dimensions of global change research including risk and vulnerability. Although sustainability science has yet to be addressed as directly from other social science perspectives, we argue that other disciplines are fertile and essential ground for its development. In particular, the field of applied anthropology is perhaps most ready to involve "the public at large to produce trustworthy knowledge and judgment that is scientifically sound and rooted in social understanding" (Ibid.). Moreover, sustainability science recognizes the arbitrary nature of the boundary between scientific research and application, particularly the fact that "they tend to influence and become entangled with each other" (Kates et al. 2001:641).

Sustainability science offers a framework for uniting the efforts of academic and applied social scientists. Yet, as an open (multiscaled and multidimensional) and engaged view of science, sustainability science also holds promise for a reconciliation of science with society, in other words, with views of multiple discourses of sciences (Nader 1996), environments and environmentalisms (Little 1999), ecologies (Scoones 1999), and natures (Escobar 1999). As a matter of fact, a two-page statement from the *Friibergh Workshop* (2000) determined that

> by structure, method, and content, sustainability science must differ
> fundamentally from most science as we know it. Familiar approaches to
> developing and testing hypotheses are inadequate because of nonlinearity,
> complexity, and long time lags between actions and their consequences.
> Additional complications arise from the recognition that humans cannot
> stand outside the nature-society system.

However, the reconciliation of science and society remains unlikely if social scientists choose to dismiss this potential paradigm shift in the sciences and do not actively engage in its development.

To live up to its promise, sustainability science must realize a new social contract, rather than simply reorient away from a "science first" perspective. But rather than starting from scratch, sustainability science purports to "improve on the substantial but still limited understanding of nature-society interactions gained in recent decades" (Ibid.). Curiously, substantial research on nature–society interactions in the social sciences, particularly political ecology, is absent from discussions of sustainability science. Yet, applied and policy-oriented studies within a political ecology framework have made significant progress in addressing the stated concerns of sustainability science in regard to land use and degradation (Blaikie & Brookfield 1987), hazards and disasters (Blaikie 1994; Hewitt 1983; Oliver-Smith & Hoffman 1999), impoverishment and environmental destruction linked to development strategies (Painter & Durham 1995; Stonich 1993), tourism (Stonich 2000), and protected areas (Walker 2005). As a matter of fact, the literature of political ecology is extensive enough to question whether sustainability science proposes anything new.

The Growth of Political Ecology and Sustainability Science

Recently, political ecology has become an increasingly dominant approach to the study of human–environmental relations in the contemporary social sciences. Although having its intellectual roots in the earlier and cognate fields of human

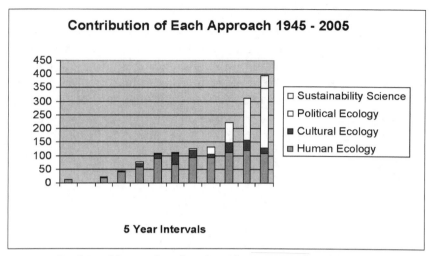

Figure 1 • Trends in publication of "ecological" articles 1945-2005, by number of articles (source: Web of Science, Social Science + Humanities + Biophysical Sciences Databases. Accessed 13 March 2006. www.library.ucsb.edu).

and cultural ecology, it has overshadowed its predecessors to a great degree. Although this trend is complex, it has been deftly and humorously captured by Patricia Townsend (2000) in the subtitle of her recent text, *Environmental Anthropology: From Pigs to Policies*. As a way to measure this trend, Figures 1 and 2 summarize the results of a search of the *Web of Science* for the number of articles published in major peer-reviewed social science, biophysical science, and humanities journals between 1945 and 2005. The same search was done for the keywords "human ecology," "cultural ecology," "political ecology," and "sustainability science." Figure 1 shows trends in the number of publications using each approach during the period. Figure 2 presents trends in the relative percentage contribution of each approach to the total number of publications during each five-year period. First, Figure 1 obviously reveals a significant overall increase in the total number of articles using an "ecology" approach, from thirteen articles in the 1945–1950 period, to 395 articles in 2001–2005. Figure 1 also clearly demonstrates the momentous rise in the number of articles using a political ecology approach since 1985, as well as the emergence and importance of "sustainability science" between 2001 and 2005. Figure 2 more clearly reveals the growing importance of political ecology compared to the cognate fields of cultural and human ecology. Between 2001 and 2005, articles using "political ecology" as a keyword constituted 55 percent (218) of the total number of articles (395), compared with 27 percent (107) for

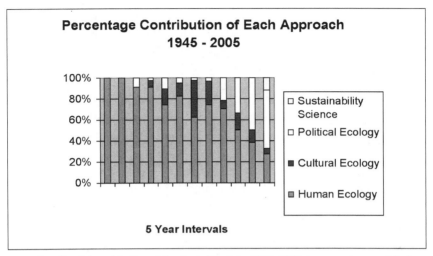

Figure 2 • Trends in publication of "ecological" articles 1945–2005, by percentage contribution to total for five-year interval (source: Web of Science, Social Science + Humanities + Biophysical Sciences Databases. Accessed 13 March 2006. www.library.ucsb.edu).

human ecology and 6 percent (22) for cultural ecology. The first articles to appear using sustainability science as a keyword did not appear until 2001, but by 2005 made up 12 percent (48) of the total number of articles, that is, twice the percentage contribution of its predecessor cultural ecology. Further analysis of the search results demonstrated that the majority of the journals, in which "political ecology" was used as a keyword, were classified under the broad subject categories of Geography (37 percent of articles), Anthropology (18 percent), Environmental Studies (15 percent), Sociology (11 percent), and Political Science (10 percent). Specifically, the five journals in which the greatest number of these articles appeared were *The Annals of the Association of American Geographers*, *The Professional Geographer*, *Human Ecology*, and *Human Organization*. The publication pattern for articles using "sustainability science" as a keyword is quite different. In this case, the largest percentage of articles appeared in journals classified as "Multidisciplinary Sciences" (24 percent), 18 percent in "Environmental Sciences," 16 percent in "Ecology" journals, 10 percent in "Environmental Studies," and 10 percent in Geography journals. The major publications included *The Proceedings of the National Academy of Sciences*, *Science*, *Current Science*, and *Global Environmental Change—Human and Policy Dimensions*. It is important to note, however, that the authors of the majority of these articles are social rather than natural scientists (particularly geographers).

A thorough presentation of the intellectual history of political ecology is beyond the scope of this short chapter and can be found in several recent reviews (for example, Neumann 2005; Paulson, Gezon, & Watts 2003; Peet & Watts 1996; Stonich 2001; Zimmerer & Bassett 2003). Political ecology emerged as part of a broader critique of cultural ecology, risk-hazard studies, and ecological anthropology that began in the 1970s and stemmed from the apolitical and micro-level analytical traditions of these fields. This critique was centered on the perceived neglect of the political dimensions of human–environmental interactions, the preoccupation with homeostatic processes, and the conceptualization of human communities as relatively autonomous and homogeneous. Many discussions of the genealogy of political ecology start with Eric Wolf's use of the term in critiquing "cultural ecological and ecological anthropological approaches to the study of Alpine ecology" to stress "the theoretical need to situate local ecological realities within the broader political economy" (Stonich 2001). Several strains of political ecology have since emerged, all concerned with "the many ways in which power and politics affect and are affected by ecology and the biophysical environment" (Ibid.). Some political ecologists, such as Escobar (1999), take a constructivist approach. But as Vayda and Walters (1999) argue in "Against Political Ecology," such an emphasis may result in a "politics without ecology" and may "diminish the concern for the material issues and practice that first provoked the emergence of political ecology" (Stonich 2001). Others, including most of the above-cited authors, have tried to integrate politics and ecology, that is, "the cultural/social construction of the environment with a meaningful and comprehensive analysis of the environmental construction of the social and the cultural" (Ibid.), or, to put it another way, "environment first" and "society first" perspectives.

Trends in Political Ecology

Several developments in political ecology speak for its potential integration with sustainability science as a means of furthering understanding of crucial human–environmental relations. These include a significant growth in the number of social scientists who study human–environmental relations, especially those related to social and environmental change; a greatly increased focus on the asymmetrical distribution of the costs and benefits of such changes, especially a growing number of studies of risk and vulnerability; greater attention to human–environmental systems in disequilibrium rather than in equilibrium; significantly expanded multi- and interdisciplinary research efforts, initially within the social sciences but more recently encompassing the biophysical/natural sciences as well; the creation of theoretical and methodological approaches aimed at linking various kinds of scales (for example, geopolitical, ecosystem, spatial, temporal) at different levels and at linking human dimensions and biophysical factors; and finally, greater attention to contemporary real-world problems, including a commitment to integrate academic research with practice, to address social/environmental justice, and to become engaged in policy-relevant work (Neumann 2005; Stonich 2001).

Political Ecology: Unresolved Issues and Debates

Although political ecology has boomed, several continuing concerns remain unresolved that may affect the potential contributions of the field, including more collaboration with sustainability scientists. Among the most important of these issues is that political ecology has become so diverse in terms of theoretical perspectives, concepts, and methodologies that it lacks unity as a coherent field of study (Stonich 2001). While political ecology may represent an emerging research agenda, neither past developments nor recent trends are theoretically integrated, and it remains to be seen where existing convergences and tensions may lead. Current trends and new directions in political–ecological research reveal significant tensions between material and idealist perspectives that are linked to possibly irreconcilable differences between scientific and poststructural/postmodern positions. Another of the most persistent and serious debates revolves around whether or not political ecology has become "environmental politics" rather than "ecology," that is, the familiar question, "Where is the Ecology?" It is ironic that a field that developed in part as a critique of "ecology without politics" has now been accused of becoming "politics without ecology." Prompted by the critique, "Against Political Ecology," published by Vayda and Walters, mentioned above, this debate remains the most serious point of contention for both proponents and opponents of political ecology (see Paulson, Gezon, & Watts 2003 and Walker 2005 for recent and contrasting perspectives on this issue). In our opinion, the unfortunate belief by proponents of sustainability science that all political ecology has become "politics without ecology" is the most serious obstacle to the integration of political ecology and sustainability science. Finally, a serious criticism often made by more "scientifically" oriented researchers is that, because most political–ecological studies have tended to focus on understanding social and environmental changes within the context of local ecologies and histories, studies remain restricted in their applicability and unable to contribute to the creation of broader theories. While this is a serious concern, one of the major thrusts of recent political–ecological studies is aimed precisely at the rigorous methodological integration of local-level studies within broader contexts and various scales (Neumann 2005).

Enhancing Collaboration between Political Ecology and Sustainability Science

Like sustainability science, some (but certainly not all) political ecologists have attempted to integrate human dimensions and biophysical factors into their research. In addition, political ecologists have been investigating nature–society interactions for some time—far longer than "sustainability science" has existed. Developing a sustainability science without building on political ecology's accomplishments—and learning from its difficulties—is tantamount to reinventing the wheel when the situation demands new and more integrated theoretical frameworks. Lubchenco (1998) points to the "urgent and unprecedented environmental and social changes" and the "immediate and real challenges" presently confronting science and human communities throughout the world. Likewise, the *Friibergh Workshop* report (2000) avows that the need for this "understanding of the complex dynamic interactions between society and nature" is urgent, "so that the alarming trend towards increasing vulnerability is reversed." Because integrating research across disciplines is a major and common goal of both sustainability science and political ecology, it behooves sustainability scientists to take heed of political ecology and political ecologists to make their research known to—and seek collaboration with—sustainability science. As Lubchenco passionately contends, given the urgency and the dire necessity of addressing global social and environmental problems, all scientists, including anthropologists, geographers, and other social scientists who can bring the needed insight of balancing "science first" and "society first" perspectives, should find new ways to cooperatively engage in analyses of nature–society interactions.

Perhaps a fruitful place to start building collaborations between political ecologists and sustainability scientists are studies of risk, vulnerability, and resilience, which are major foci of both approaches. In part, political ecology emerged as a critique of risk-hazard-vulnerability studies, as discussed by Blaikie and Brookfield (1987) in *Land Degradation and Society*, one of the foundational works on political ecology, and this topic has remained a major focus of political–ecological research. This is also one of the core questions specified in the agenda for sustainability science, "What determines the vulnerability or resilience of the nature-society system in particular kinds of places and for particular types of ecosystems and human livelihoods?" (Kates et al. 2001:641). As Hewitt (1995) has pointed out, a vulnerability perspective offers a corrective to the mechanistic emphasis that "science/environment first" perspectives have put on disaster research. Clark et al. (2003) have defined vulnerability "as the risk of adverse outcomes to receptors or exposure units (human groups, ecosystems, and communities) in the face of relevant changes in climate, other environmental variables, and social/economic changes," encompassing dimensions of exposure, sensitivity, and resilience. Derived from studies of hazards, disasters, and climate change, vulnerability studies take diverse approaches, as shown elsewhere (Stonich 2001), including biophysical (Browder 1989), human–ecological (Moran 1990), political–economic (Kelley & Adger 2000), postmodern/constructionist (Tierney 1999), and political–ecological (Stonich 1993, 2000). Unlike the biophysical approach, which maintains the "science first" perspective, or the political–economic and postmodern approaches, which neglect biophysical factors, the political–ecological approach is most appropriate to sustainability science because

> it is interdisciplinary . . . centers on cross-scale linkages . . . attempts to link social structure, human agency, and the biophysical environment . . . has the potential to integrate environment-first, society-first, and policy oriented studies . . . [and] can demonstrate and lay out the differential vulnerability of human groups by class, ethnicity, gender, time, age, spatial location, and/or other relevant categories. (Stonich 2001)

The political ecology approach stresses the dynamic interaction of the social and biophysical factors that lead to vulnerability.

Initial studies of vulnerability as part of sustainability science are likely to continue to focus on disaster and climate change research, since practitioners in these fields have already accepted and incorporated the concept. But vulnerability and resilience need to be investigated in all dynamic nature–society interactions, that is, all situations involving the social management and use of resources, particularly, as is often the case, the differential access to and control over resources. In other words, sustainability science must turn its focus back on development. In particular, development is a nexus for the intersection of sustainability science, political ecology, and vulnerability studies (Stonich 2000).

CHAPTER 18

No Island Is an "Island": Some Perspectives on Human Ecology and Development in Oceania[1]

THOMAS MALM

During a conference in 1992—arranged by UNESCO and its international council for island development, INSULA—a number of specialists within different disciplines suggested as the first of its conclusions that the Earth is like an island in space and that its brittleness is most clearly reflected on small islands in the oceans (Bouamrane 1993). In the same year Bahn and Flenley published their book *Easter Island, Earth Island,* where they argued that Easter Island with its largely depleted natural resources could be seen as a microcosmic warning about what may happen to our entire planet. Since then, this perspective has been frequently recurring in popular as well as scientific discourses on environmental issues (for example, Diamond 2005; McDaniel & Gowdy 2000; Redman 1999).

The purpose of this chapter is to question to what extent the analogy of the Earth and islands with finite natural resources is valid, considering such aspects as human migration, trade, and carrying capacity. On the one hand, the striking aspect of human life on the islands of Oceania—which will be used as examples in the following pages—is not that the inhabitants were isolated. Most of them had no or few contacts with people in Asia or America, but there were complex sociocultural inter-island networks, and practically every inhabitable island had been settled by sea-voyaging people hundreds or even thousands of years before the era of European exploration and the emergence of the modern world system (see, for example, Kirch 2000). Today, of course, it would be even less apt to characterize these islands as isolated, finite "planets," because they have become parts of a *global* system of migration and resource flow. The basic perspective suggested here is instead that the worst tragedy, as far as human island populations are concerned, is not isolation but increasing integration into a much larger economic system.

Islands and the Concept of Carrying Capacity

In 1911, twenty-five reindeer were put ashore on a small island off Alaska. For the next twenty-six years the population grew nearly exponentially, until there were over 2,000 reindeer on the island. They badly overgrazed their food supply, primarily lichens, and the population crashed so that only eight animals were left in 1950 (Pianka 1978:114).

What this example illustrates could be summarized with the concepts of "carrying capacity" and "overshooting." In short, carrying capacity can be defined as the upper limit on the long-term population size that an environment can support. This concept is connected to the fundamental ecological principle that no population can grow exponentially without sooner or later reaching a point where it is "overshooting" the resource base, that is, encountering difficult environmental conditions or shortages in its means for reproduction. As a consequence, unless the average actual rate of increase is zero, it either decreases until becoming extinct or increases so as to lead to the extinction of other populations.

Because they are so clearly geographically finite, the islands of the world's oceans provide excellent conditions for the study of such processes. Particularly following the publication in 1967 of *The Theory of Island Biogeography* by MacArthur and Wilson, islands have received considerable attention by ecologists and other scientists who seek natural models for population growth and regulation.

Thus, if a canoe load of, say, twenty-five persons arrived to the Hawaiian archipelago in 400 C.E. and their descendants proliferated at an annual rate of 2 percent—which is below that of several Pacific islands in recent times—the size of the population by the time of Captain Cook's arrival in 1778 would not have been a few hundred thousand (as it actually was), but 2.32×10^{13} people (Kirch 1984:102), or more than 4,000 times the present size of the entire world population!

One name that immediately comes to mind in this context is Thomas Malthus, who concluded in the late eighteenth century that whereas human population has a tendency to grow geometrically—or, as we now say, exponentially—agricultural production of food grows only arithmetically. This means that population growth tends to outstrip the productive capabilities of land resources. The Malthusian perspective suggests that because of limitations in food production, "positive" checks such as famine and increased mortality, or preventive ones such as postponement of marriage and limitation of family size, work to reduce population growth back to zero or minus (see Malthus 1960). Although such limiting factors certainly are important, a major problem with

Malthus's discourse is that he assumed food productivity to be *fixed*. In the case of the reindeer being confined to their island, such was indeed the case, because when there were no more lichens to eat they could not do anything about it and had to starve, but for human beings, as we know, the situation is quite different. We have at least the potential ability to *try* to plant, grow new types of crops, intensify agriculture, preserve food, import food, practice birth control, move away, and so forth. This is the reason why cases such as the reindeer on their island and the prehistory of Hawaii are not directly comparable.

Still, such comparisons are often made. Within modern theoretical ecology, any habitat can be analytically regarded as an "island" if it is, somehow, *isolated* (see, for example, Gorman 1979). Depending on the species, this approach could apply, for instance, to a desert oasis, a mountain peak, a valley, a pond or a deep cave—even an animal can be an island to the parasites inhabiting it. Some years ago, two Swedish scholars (Sörlin & Öckerman 1998:13) stated in a book, the title of which translates as "Earth an Island," that the sea, for people just as for plants and animals, functions as a *barrier* against the rest of the world. This is true, however, only if the people who wish to reach or leave the island do not have any boats or rafts—and this has certainly been an exception rather than a rule throughout the prehistory and history of coastal or island peoples. (Today, of course, airplanes often make them even less isolated.)

To return to the "Easter Island, Earth Island" model, one might get the impression that the consensus is that by the time of European contact, the resources of Easter Island, including the forests (Flenley 2001), had been depleted by the once prosperous inhabitants to the extent that they no longer could build large canoes and migrate to other islands. Without trees, neither would they have been able to transport those huge stone statues that have made the island famous. However, aside from the fact that we do not have any data regarding the extent to which logs were needed for the transportation of statues (see Heyerdahl, Skjølsvold, & Pavel 1989), it is by no means certain that the trees disappeared mainly as a result of logging. It is quite possible that an extended drought transformed the landscape of the island into a barren wasteland (Hunter-Andersson 1998; McCall 1994).

Nunn (1993, 2003) argues that a rapid cooling of temperatures in the Pacific Basin around 1300 c.e. and a climate change that perhaps lasted for a century might have had severe impacts on the environment of Easter Island and could have contributed to societal breakdown. For example, the fall in sea level, perhaps as much as 1.1 meters, may have damaged the near-shore marine ecosystems, and the fall in water tables would have caused many crops to yield less well. Inevitably, he writes (2003:224), "the carrying capacity of many islands was abruptly exceeded, societies fragmented, and there was conflict between various human groups competing for the diminished pool of available resources." Thus, there is no conclusive evidence to suggest that the depletion of resources simply was a result of population growth and a lack of ecological insights, such as implied by Ponting (1991:7) when he states that the people, "aware that they were almost completely isolated from the rest of the world, must surely have realized that their very existence depended on the limited resources of a small island. After all it was small enough for them to walk round the entire island in a day or so and see for themselves what was happening to the forests. Yet they were unable to devise a system that allowed them to find the right balance with their environment."

Ponting's conclusions about what the people "must" have realized are not self-evident at all. Today, no logging company that is cutting down a rainforest could possibly defend its actions by referring to the gods or spirits as being able to bring back the trees, but when we talk about a premodern society such as Easter Island we cannot assume that ecological ignorance was implied by what Bahn (2001:65) describes as a "boundless confidence in their religion to take care of the future." As argued by Nunn (2003:226), "there is abundant evidence that environmental changes of extraneous causation *forced* island peoples to alter a whole range of lifestyle options" (emphasis added).

Catton (1980:215) states that by the time that Easter Island was first reached by Europeans in 1722, the population "had declined to an estimated 3,000 or 4,000, from a maximum that was probably at least twice that [. . .]. Mortality continued to exceed births, and the entire population of the island was down to 155 persons by 1866." However, whatever major crisis there may have been previously appears to have been over by 1722, and it was not as a result of this crisis that the people were drawn close to extinction but because of the Peruvian slave trade in the 1860s and the introduction of epidemic diseases (including those transmitted by repatriated slaves) as well as emigration to the islands of Tahiti and Mangareva (Maude 1981:194). As a matter of fact, for the 140 years between 1722 and 1862 there is no clear evidence of any major decline in population. There might even have been a slight *increase,* because Maude (1981:192,194) estimates the number to have been 4,126 in 1862. The following year, after 1,407 slaves had been taken, the number ought to have been over 2,700, but it actually dropped to around 1,740 (Ibid.). Métraux (1940:43) writes that the reason for this was that repatriated slaves, who were brought to the island, "carried with them the infection of smallpox which in a short time decimated the rest of the population. The casualties caused by the epidemic are said to have been in the thousands." At the least, they would have been around 1,000.

Despite Ponting's statement that the people had not been able to find a balance with their environment, it is quite possible that the population of around 4,000 *was* the average population size, given the environmental limitations after 1300 C.E., which, after all, allowed the cultivation of bananas and root crops as well as the breeding of chickens. When Cook visited the island in 1774, he described its produce as sparse but "all excellent in its kind" and stated that the sweet potato was the best he had ever eaten (Beaglehole 1961:349). In any case, despite the popularity of the analogy with an isolated planet in space, no one could possibly know what would have happened if the people had been left alone on Easter Island. It is not unthinkable that their chiefs could have negotiated peace among the competing factions or that a more sustainable agriculture and fishing could have evolved. Be that as it may, the point here is that although a number of plant and animal species had become scarce or extinct, perhaps owing to human action and most likely with climatic changes as aggravating factors, the big tragedy from the 1860s and throughout the nineteenth century occurred because the island was *no longer* like an isolated "planet."

The same could be said about Nauru. In their book *Paradise for Sale,* McDaniel and Gowdy (2000) use this island as an example of what might happen to our planet, concluding that "Nauru is a window through which one can see global trajectories into disaster. . . . The story of Nauru is the story of all of us." Is it? The reason why Nauru has become barren is that its phosphate (guano) has been exploited, to be used as fertilizers overseas, a fact that is certainly not due to a local process in isolation but to conditions far beyond it, that is, a demand on the world market. The "paradise" could be "for sale" only because there were buyers somewhere else. Obviously, from such a perspective, the analogy between Easter Island or Nauru and the "Earth Island" would be apt only if extraterrestrial beings were introduced into the picture.

Alternative Perspectives on Population and Carrying Capacity

Nunn (1993) has presented an alternative view of the relationship between carrying capacity and population growth, according to which carrying capacity can be quite variable and highly mutable in response to climatic changes. Naturally, the number of organisms—including human beings—that can be supported in a given area depends in part on factors such as temperature and precipitation.

If we consider people, their lifestyle, exploitation of natural resources, and other factors seen in relation to fluctuations in world market prices for their products and other changes in their economic relationship to other societies, we realize that the "crisis point" is not at all self-evident. Similarly, it is because of a changed lifestyle and imports of fattening food from overseas that obesity and cardiovascular diseases have recently become a tremendous problem among people on some of the most densely populated islands in the world. On quite a few islands, in fact, we find that as the population has grown, people have not begun to starve but have acquired more and more fattening food to eat, because their relatives move overseas and send money and goods (including food) back home (Crocombe 2001:77–79; Thaman 1982).

If major ambiguities in our analyses are to be resolved, we must specify if they are local, regional, or global "densities" that we are analyzing, and how a population's resource territory is delineated, and one must avoid regarding the human population as being fixed in space.

Let us consider the words of Tongan anthropologist Epeli Hau'ofa (1994:156–157), who writes that what he calls a "sea of islands," Oceania, "is neither tiny nor deficient in resources." It was that way, he argues, "only as a condition of the colonial confinement that lasted less than a century in a history of millennia." What has happened since the 1960s, in particular, is that many people from the islands "have broken out of their confinement" and are now "moving around and away from their homelands. . . . They are once again enlarging their world, establishing new resource bases and expanded networks for circulation." Therefore, this island world "certainly encompasses the great cities of Australia, New Zealand, the United States, and other countries too. It is within this expanded world that the extent of the people's resources must be measured." Thus, in addition to *local* population, resources, area, and climatic changes, that is, factors that we would focus on in studies of animals and plants, there is here another factor that has to be taken into account. This is the *global* network and its flows of migrants, aid, trade, and money transfers. Any "crisis point" here is a quite different matter from what could be summed up in simple models like those that we find in textbooks on ecology, and that often have been applied to human societies. It is evident that we need to look at the often problematic relationship between human populations and natural resources without any preconceived notion of a once and for all fixed local carrying capacity.

What, for instance, does "globalization" imply for contemporary Oceania? It is quite clear that for the daily life of its people, "globalization" has had two very different consequences. First of all, people in Oceania are of course in various ways affected culturally and economically by the global flows of ideas, money, and commodities. Second, and perhaps more surprisingly, the island communities are not limited to the people who live on the islands but are increasingly becoming characterized by what Bertram and Watters (1985) have called "transnational corporations of kin." They include a diaspora of relatives who have moved to or even been born in places overseas but who are still to a large extent emotionally and economically tied to island society. The latter has been particularly well documented for Polynesians, who are generally very collectivistic and usually regard themselves and all relatives as part of their extended families, no matter where they happen to live (Ritchie & Ritchie 1979:25). By the beginning of the new millennium, there were about 750,000 Polynesian immigrants and their descendants in the United States, New Zealand, and Australia plus another 5,000 and 1,000 in Europe and Asia, respectively, whereas there were only 536,000 in Polynesia, excluding Hawaii and New Zealand (Crocombe 2001:69). We do not know how the diasporic people will feel about their ties to the home islands after a few generations abroad (cf. Brown 1998), but for the contemporary situation, at least, it could be argued that more than half the members of Polynesian society live *outside* the Polynesian territories.

It is true that space for people to live, grow their food, and build their houses was very limited on many of the islands of Oceania. It was hardly the size of the islands that made them attractive to the colonial powers. With very few exceptions, neither was it their natural resources. In fact, after some 350 years of European exploration, until the latter half of the nineteenth century, there was almost no interest at all among the world's most powerful nations in establishing colonies among the smaller islands of Oceania. It simply seemed bad business to send government representatives to islands that had so little economic interest to offer. What they could offer visiting ships in the way of provisions, copra, sandalwood, and nacre could be obtained by trading and without establishing any colonial rule. Therefore, they were long merely interesting as idyllic stopovers for ships along the routes between the continents where much more profitable colonies could be established.

To take just one example (Toullelan & Gilles 1992), several years before Tahiti and its neighboring islands became a French protectorate in 1842, their queen and British missionaries had asked the government of Britain to annex these islands, but they encountered not the slightest interest. When the islands finally did become annexed it had nothing to do with natural resources but was a result of French and British missionary rivalry. These islands had actually been a French protectorate for almost fifty years before they became a colony. Until the 1960s and the beginning of the nuclear testing program, it remained a more or less noncolonized colony with at most around 2,000 Frenchmen. To this very day, the French "overseas territory" now known as French Polynesia has in fact cost France much more than it has yielded in terms of income. Thus, despite the world's largest exports of black pearls, total export revenues from French Polynesia covered only about 15 percent of the costs of imports by the late 1990s (ITSTAT 1998:334, 339), whereas the remainder was financed mainly by French aid. For Oceania, this is by no means an unusual trade "balance." In 1998, for instance, the Kingdom of Tonga imported nine times as much as it exported, in terms of monetary values, and until a local brewery was established there, the value of its dominating export, bananas, was almost equal to the annual costs of importing beer (Malm 1999:344).

One could argue that, with very few exceptions, the small island nations have very little hope of surviving economically only on their natural resources. How little they can export is quite evident from the fact that one of their most important sources of national income is *stamps,* many of which are sold only to philatelists and never used for mail. Starvation may not be a problem, but rather the fact that many of the Oceanian peoples have acquired what Walsh and Trlin (1973:50) call "a champagne taste on something less than a beer income."

Geostrategic Location and Independence as Economic Assets

If they have so few natural resources, and if it is generally a matter of moving much more capital and commodities *to* the islands than away from them, why then do the United States still keep Guam and American Samoa as "unincorporated territories," why is Easter Island the "Fifth Region of Chile" with Valparaiso as capital, and why does France still insist that French Polynesia is one of its "overseas territories"?

The islands of the Pacific are most of all of interest because of their *geostrategic* location among Asia, Australia, and the Americas. It is important to the great powers just to be represented there, directly or (like the United Kingdom) indirectly. One might wonder how this is possible in the "postcolonial era." The simple answer is: money. As pointed out by Poirine (1995:45–80), *aid* is actually often just another word for *rent.* Money and goods are sent to the people on the islands in the hope that they will live like happy consumers without causing trouble for the governments that wish to be represented there. This could explain why American Samoa, with its strategic location in the central part of the South Pacific, receives five times more aid than does the independent and much poorer western part of Samoa. In the French territories, the aid per capita is 366 times higher than the average in developing countries (Ibid.). Consequently, during the whole post-World War II period, arguments for independence in French Polynesia have repeatedly been met with rhetorical questions about how life there would become if France would abandon the islands and leave it to the people living there to finance everything that they have become accustomed to (see Danielsson & Danielsson 1986).

There has been a strong incentive for France to retain its islands as a nuclear testing ground. Thus, for three decades (1966–1996), French Polynesia was characterized by the economy of the atomic bomb.

The benefits of "geostrategic location" and "environmental load displacement" are a function of remoteness and isolation. It is difficult to imagine any other reason than the remote and "isolated" location of the Marshall Islands for the United States to pay them (in 1989) at least US$ 56 million for being allowed to deposit 23 million tons of waste there (Crocombe 2001:32), for the United States and the United Kingdom to have conducted 122 nuclear tests in Micronesia, or for France to have carried out 193 tests on the Tuamotu Islands to the east of Tahiti (Ibid.:590). There is nothing else about these islands that would make them particularly well suited for nuclear tests than their distance from the main population centers of France. These are the kinds of circumstances that generate problems of "environmental justice." If these tests were to pollute the environment and cause cancer among Polynesians, which many critics claim that they indeed have done (for example, Danielsson & Danielsson 1986; de Vries & Seur 1997; Johnson 1984), this would pose no major political threat in France, as it would not affect the majority of voters there.

For many years it was believed that the French nuclear tests would cease only if French Polynesia became independent. However, international negotiations and Glasnost did result in the tests coming to an end in 1996, but these islands are still a part of France, and their inhabitants even have EU passports. Is independence a politically realistic option?

One answer could be framed in terms of what has happened to other former colonies that already *have* become politically independent. In the 1980s, Bertram and Watters (1985, 1986) coined the term MIRAB—an acronym for migration, remittances, aid, and bureaucracy. These factors are still often seen as determining the development of the Pacific microstates (cf. Poirine 1998). These nations remain dependent, for their welfare, on people moving overseas to earn money. Money as well as goods sent home means a lot for the island economies, and aid is necessary for building hospitals and buying medical equipment. In addition, government officials can receive salaries, in a situation where there is so very little in the way of other jobs, especially for all those who have left the rural communities and outer islands to move to town or the main island. Today, we know that the picture is much more complex, not only because of factors such as tourism and the boom in pearl cultivation but above all, perhaps, because the island nations are becoming increasingly efficient at earning money from their independence.

Independence is often presented as a democratic right, but very few people seem to have realized that independence in itself is an economic asset that can generate much more income than can any other resource in the islands (Crocombe 2001:362–378). It is only because of small countries like Tuvalu that Japan could go on killing whales, because when the countries around the Pacific voted about this, 9,000 Tuvaluans had as much of a say as 1.2 billion Chinese. Similarly, because of its independence, Tonga has earned large amounts of money from selling passports to rich people in Hong Kong who feared that they would not be able to travel when communist China took over (see Bain 1993:160–167). There have even been attempts to grant an Australian biotechnical company the exclusive right to the Tongan gene-pool, in order to provide it with DNA and blood samples with the purpose of improving research on cancer and cardiovascular diseases (Hornborg 2002).

Many of these countries are now established as so called "offshore finance centers," "international trust centers," or "asset protection centers" (Crocombe 2001:363–367). For example, in Vanuatu, although only 0.2 percent of the population were involved in business of this kind, such financial activities have been estimated to account for 12 percent of the GNP (Barrett 2000). In such "centers" one can launder money, stow away capital, or register ships to avoid certain regulations. Attractive domain names on the Internet can be leased from these independent nations, who all have their own internet abbreviation (such as *nu* for Niue). The "Small Islands States Group" of Cook Islands, Kiribati, Nauru, Niue, and Tuvalu has demanded that international airlines should pay fees every time they fly over the sea territories that make up the exclusive economic zone of these island nations in the central parts of the Pacific. In the same vein, who would have imagined that Tonga would become number six among the world's satellite nations? As an independent nation, close to the equator, Tonga could claim the right to some orbital slots in space, so as to lease them out to big TV stations with the ambition to reach viewers all over the world. Finally, to handle all these new ventures in globalization, the island nations have expanded their state bureaucracies. Thus, the largest buildings in the capital of one of the poorest countries, Samoa, are no longer churches (as used to be the case in most Pacific capitals) but a six-storey government building and a seven-floor national bank, both built with aid money. In contrast, the hospitals in the islands are generally in poor condition.

Aid monies as well as remittances are used mainly for consumption. As a result of newly acquired tastes, there is a diminishing interest in what local resources there actually are. The story behind this is a long and complex one, which cannot be told here, but the material results are fairly easily observable by any visitor to the islands. Today, there are even island nations that import coconuts. Not only is imported coconut cream sold in many stores, but in Tonga I was told in 1988 that coconuts were imported in order to keep the coconut oil mill running. The Tongan islands are practically covered with palm trees, but the prices paid for coconuts and copra were so low compared to the money sent from relatives overseas that almost no one bothered picking up the coconuts anymore, except for domestic use or the small quantities for sale at the fruit and vegetable market. The new patterns of resource use often have detrimental environmental consequences. For instance, Tonga has earned a lot of money exporting squash pumpkins to Japan, but this has involved the use of great quantities of pesticides, leaking down into the aquifer and contaminating precious sources of freshwater. The Tongans have largely used the money to buy imported food, cars, and other commodities, which have brought further environmental problems such as how to dispose of increasing volumes of solid waste. Hills of garbage are now to be found on many islands once known for their pristine remoteness.

Conclusion

I have argued that the analogy between the "Earth island" and oceanic islands is not at all as apt as is often suggested. There is no conclusive evidence to suggest that the population of Easter Island would have become extinct if it had remained isolated. More or less all the negative trends in health and environment in Oceania are consequences of the islands *no longer* remaining isolated from a much larger economic system. The population of Easter Island became almost extinct because of slave trade and introduced diseases. That overeating has become a much greater problem in Polynesia than starvation, that numerous nuclear tests have been made there, that remittances sent home by relatives are used in ways that generate increasing health problems as well as problems of garbage disposal, and that more aid money is spent on impressive government buildings than on much needed hospitals—all these trends exemplify how incorporation in the world system continues to pose greater threats than isolation does.

I have argued, also, that the Oceanian diasporas living overseas illustrate that a "society" is not synonymous with people living in a certain place (cf. Sahlins 1994). In ecological terms this means that the boundaries of population and habitat do not coincide. Any analysis of the human ecology and development of contemporary Oceania must be made in light of the historical background and the relationship between the islands and the modern world system. This is a quite different framework of analysis than that suggested by the "Earth island" analogy. Thus, it is of fundamental importance to realize that, in our globalized world, *no island is an island.*

Note

1. Several of the views presented here are based on my fieldwork and travels in Oceania, particularly between 2000 (including a stay on Easter Island) and 2005, supported by Sida/SAREC, Magnus Bergvall's Foundation, The Society for Science in Lund, The Royal Academy of Humanistic Sciences in Lund, and the Elisabeth Rausing Memorial Foundation. I thank Ron Crocombe, Epeli Hau'ofa, Futa Helu, and Bernard Poirine for inspiration, and Alf Hornborg for many valuable comments on the manuscript.

CHAPTER 19

Infectious Diseases as Ecological and Historical Phenomena, with Special Reference to the Influenza Pandemic of 1918–1919

ALFRED W. CROSBY

Our germs, like our wheat and rice and goats and horses, are the creations, albeit unintentional in this case, of given societies at given times. As those societies grow and shrink in numbers, expand and contract geographically, shift from hunting and gathering to agriculture, flow into cities or desert them, travel on foot or by sailing vessel or jet planes, change diet, change sexual mores, have or cease to have contacts with various kinds of animals, and so on, they alter the environments of microorganisms and thereby change the characteristics of infections. These changes call for historical interpretation just as much as developments in politics, economics, or religions.

For almost all of the hundreds of thousands of years of the genus *Homo* on this planet, among the most important of its characteristics has been small numbers,[1] geographical dispersal, and epidemiological divergence. Roger Lewin, paleoanthropologist, estimates that 30,000 years ago in southwestern France and northern Spain a group of 50 humans would have needed more than 300 square miles to sustain themselves (Clark 1997:30-31).

Another of the characteristics of *H. erectus* and its successors, most especially *H. sapiens*, was to solve problems by migration, to adapt to population pressures, food shortages, drought, flood, war, diseases, and what-have-you by migrating, by substituting geographical movement for other means of coping. By at least 50,000 years ago, we humans had trekked from Africa to Australia, and we were the most widely distributed large land animal on the globe, and yet we hadn't even found America. We did that from 14,000 to 40,000 years or so ago, depending on which expert you listen to.

We have been hunters and gatherers for more than 90 percent of our time here, the majority of us without permanent residency. In all that time, we had no crowd diseases because we had no crowds. We suffered some but not all the diseases currently associated with parasitic and commensal creatures such as rats, because we were often on the move and had no permanent dwellings: a lot of our hangers-on couldn't keep up with us. We suffered few diseases associated with polluted food and water because, again, we were usually on the move, leaving most of our sewage and garbage behind.

I am not trying to paint a prehistoric Eden. Prehistoric people died young, had internal parasites, had lice, and were nibbled on by insects constantly, all of which certainly carried microorganisms. They must have had diseases, such as tuberculosis, that can survive long periods in the body, but they didn't have a good many of the infectious maladies that have dominated our epidemiological history for the past few thousand years. They didn't have the infections that either kill or produce long-lasting immunity, that is, the diseases that race through populations the way forest fires race through forests, using up fuel quickly and burning themselves out—for example, smallpox and measles. Furthermore, because many humans were moving into frontier regions where humans had never lived before (for example, America, Madagascar, Hawaii), they often left important parasites and pathogens behind and met up with few new ones adapted to invading their bodies.

Relative to what came later, the relationship between humans and micropathogens was characterized by a sort of rough and ready stability and, at least as significantly, of geographical divergence. Infections we had, but they were usually of a local character.

What I am saying here is that humanity was protected against many infections not so much by genetically acquired immunological defenses as by their small numbers and their movements. Humanity had, vis-à-vis infection, hedged its bets: a few thousand folks over here with this infection, a few thousand over there with that infection, and a minimum of contact between the two groups, leads to no pandemics for the same reason that you can't have a forest fire without forests. Humanity was not genetically prepared for the environment that it started creating ten or so thousand years ago. It is a major irony that humans are not well adapted to the environment that they have created.

One of the most important inventions of all time was agriculture, around 10,000 years ago. It appeared in at least seven different locations in both the Old and New Worlds. When humans became farmers, they radically changed the way they lived and thereby the environments of the microorganisms they sheltered and provisioned. Humans increased in numbers and settled down in permanent villages and cities. There was a heavy price to pay in the advent of diseases characteristic of dense populations.

Nature abhors solid stands of a single species—whether wheat, cattle, or humans—and tries vigorously to cut them back by mobilizing predators, both macro- (wolves, lions, cougars) and micro- (smut for wheat, *rinderpest* for cattle, and a whole assemblage of diseases for humans).

Farmers were sedentary. They lived elbow to elbow and right on top of their accumulating wastes. There have been vastly more rats and *E. coli* since civilization appeared than before. Until the last two centuries, cities were demographic sumps, sustained in population more by immigration from the countryside than by local births.[2] Farming populations could produce surpluses and support sedentary elites that coveted distant commodities and increasingly engaged in trade. In doing so, they acquired exotic goods intentionally and exotic diseases unintentionally. Epidemics show up early in the Old Testament and similar documents.

Such happened in the New as well as the Old World but accelerated faster in the latter. For the historian of disease, the most important thing Old World peoples did was to domesticate a number of animal species, to maintain them in dense herds and flocks, and to live amid these unnatural concentrations. Amerindians had domesticated dogs, some fowl, guinea pigs, but only one herd animal, the llama, and that only in the Andean region. Old World peoples had dogs, cats, several kinds of fowl, horses, cattle, goats, sheep, pigs, and so on. Amerindians provided the world with about one-third of its important food plants, but they did not do at all well as animal domesticators. Therefore, Old World peoples—Europeans, for instance—had a great advantage over Amerindians in their access to high-grade food, many kinds of fibers, fertilizer, leather, bone, speed of movement, and power to move heavy objects.

The price they paid for this was heavy. By sharing environments with animals in order to utilize their services, Old World peoples found themselves also sharing diseases with them. Hunters and gatherers live *among* animals but live intimately *with* few. Farmers live intimately with a number of species and lived much more so in the past. I refer you to a passage in *Christ Stopped at Eboli* by physician Carlo Levi, whom Mussolini exiled up into the hills of Calabria to dwell among farmers who lived much as they had for millennia. The peasants' houses were one-room affairs, kitchen, bedroom and all, with people sleeping on a giant bed and animals living underneath. As Dr. Levi leaned over the bed to examine a patient or to give an injection, he recalls how his "head touched the hanging cradles, while frightened pigs and chickens darted between my legs" (Levi 1948:120–121). What more perfect an environment could a flu virus ask for?

Different infections and strains thereof have been acquired from different animals in different places at different times. *The Iliad* starts off with an epidemic among the Greeks laying siege to the city of Troy. The pandemics of pustular fevers that swept through the Roman Empire in the first centuries C.E. may have been smallpox and/or measles, originally acquired from livestock. As of May, 2003, it seems that the Chinese taste for civet meat has brought us SARS.

Improvements in transportation technology made their most horrendous contribution to epidemiological history when they enabled humans to build transoceanic empires and trading companies. By the end of Europe's Middle Ages, several technologically advanced societies of the world had developed watercraft capable of purposeful (not just accidental) and repeated transoceanic voyages. Of these peoples, the Europeans were the most ambitious commercially, politically, and evangelically. Their square and lateen-rigged vessels were a good deal smaller and not more seaworthy than China's junks, but were owned and directed by men who were eager to pursue their ambitions outside Europe. They were also, collectively speaking, among the world's most diseased people. Europe's cities, specifically her ports, were hotbeds of infections from all over the Eastern Hemisphere. In the sixteenth century, Western Europe's ships created the first "globalized" disease pool.

When does flu, to pick one disease, come into this picture? That is hard to say. Documentation on even the most visually spectacular diseases, such as smallpox, is ambiguous. For a disease as vague and fuzzy symptomatically as influenza, tracing the path back to its original appearance is impossible. If we associate flu with the domestication of pigs and chickens, then it could have appeared 4,000 years ago. One medical historian chose 1387 as the birthdate for the first recorded flu epidemic in Europe. There are more respectable claims for sixteenth century epidemics—1510, 1557, 1580—but we can't be sure about the debut of flu until the eighteenth century, when there were three unambiguous pandemics in Europe. One surfaced in Astrakhan and Moscow in April of 1729, rolled west through Germany and France and England, and hitched a ride across to Boston, Massachusetts, in October of 1732. It showed up in Mexico also.

This was the first of a series of flu pandemics blamed on Russia. There may be something to that theory, because Peter the Great, Russia's great westernizer, built St. Petersburg on the Gulf of Finland to increase contacts with the West, which of course would work in both directions. There was another flu pandemic from Russia in 1732–1733 that got all the way to North and South America, and another, often credited with being the first really big pandemic, in 1761–1762, that spread from Siberia all over Europe.

The pandemic of 1781–1782 was the most widespread and dramatic for a century to come. Contemporaries guessed that two-thirds of Rome's inhabitants fell ill, three-quarters of Munich's, and even greater proportions of all who lived in Great Britain. Morbidity was high, but mortality was low, as in all the flu pandemics thus far.

The nineteenth century was the age of population explosion and steam. Steamships and railroads in practice diminished the size of the world. They globalized disease as they globalized commerce. The most famous examples of this globalization were the cholera pandemics, which rolled across and around the world. So did flu pandemics, which attracted much less attention because their mortality rates were so low but killed many more because their morbidity rates were so high. There were flu pandemics in the 1830s and 1840s, but these were mild compared to the big one in 1782. Then, for another generation, there was nothing more than the usual sputter of local flu epidemics.

The 1889–1890 pandemic came as a complete surprise. It first appeared in western Siberia and Kazakhstan, perhaps among the herders there. It showed up in Moscow and St. Petersburg in October, in Finland in November, in Germany and Italy in November and December, and jumped the Atlantic about the same time, surfacing in Boston and New York in December. The United States was ribbed with railroads by this time, and the pandemic exploded in New Orleans and San Francisco in early January of 1890.

The 1889–1890 pandemic killed more people than did cholera or any other pandemic in the nineteenth century, but it was not seen as a major disaster. Its mortality rate was low and the number of deaths high only because the morbidity rate was so high. Diarists in European cities estimated that one-third to one-half of the population fell ill. The age distribution of the deaths was as it had always been, low among young and middle-aged adults.

The current threat of SARS reminds me of the next influenza pandemic, in 1918–1919. The latest meticulous analyses by demographers put the toll, at a minimum, at 25 million dead, and the demographers don't flinch when the suggestion of 50 million is offered. The "Spanish flu," as it was improperly nicknamed in 1918, killed more people faster than the deadliest war, yet not because it was as lethal to the individual sufferer as a bullet or a bomb but because it spread rapidly and affected a very great number of people. By a conservative estimate, a fifth of the human species suffered the fever and aches of influenza in 1918 and 1919, and serological evidence indicates that the great majority of those who did not suffer the discomforts of flu had subclinical forms of the disease.

The most bizarre characteristic of the 1918 flu was that the majority of the people it killed were not, as usual, the very young and old but people from about fifteen to forty years of age, that is, those in the prime years of life. Plausible but not definitive answers as to why have been offered.

To exemplify the course of this pandemic, let me briefly recount what happened in San Francisco. The startling news of the September morbidity and mortality rates in Boston, the first of America's Atlantic ports to be hit by the pandemic, reached San Francisco several weeks before the pandemic itself, but the skepticism and confusion of public health officials and political leaders, and the ignorance and apathy of the general population, stalled preparations to combat the Spanish flu. As the pandemic rolled westward, San Francisco concentrated on the marches and other public gatherings of the Fourth Liberty Loan Drive, enhancing the rapid spread of communicable diseases. When the first person sick with the new flu (a traveler from Chicago) got off the train in late September, the city of the Golden Gate was just beginning to focus on the threat to its well-being.

Full preparations—dividing the city into districts, each with its own medical personnel, telephones, transportation, and supplies, and creating emergency hospitals in schools and churches—were not completed until November, after the worst days of the flu's siege of San Francisco. Should the city's leaders be condemned because they moved too slowly? Perhaps, but the situation was unprecedented and a little incomprehensible even to health professionals, and public ignorance and inertia precluded preparations involving any inconvenience to large numbers of people.

The factors that overruled all others during the pandemic were its velocity and virulency. To illustrate, the San Francisco Hospital, rated as the finest in the state, with the best trained and disciplined staff, earned the dreadful honor of being the city's isolation ward for pneumonia patients during the pandemic, and it came within a hair of failing. Seventy-eight percent of its nurses fell ill and it is a safe guess, considering the devotion to duty characteristic of the staff, that many of the "healthy" nurses ought to have gone to bed as well. During the course of the pandemic, the San Francisco Hospital admitted 3,509 cases of respiratory disease, and 26 percent of them died.

In October the city tried every remedy that had been used on the East Coast to slow the advance of or to cure the Spanish flu. All schools and places of public entertainment were closed. Thousands of citizens were inoculated with totally useless and possibly dangerous antiflu vaccines imported from the East Coast or whipped up locally.

The San Francisco Board of Supervisors passed a law making the wearing of masks obligatory in all public places, and on October 22 the *San Francisco Chronicle* announced: "WEAR A MASK and Save Your Life! A Mask is 99 percent Proof against Influenza." For the next month the great majority of San Franciscans obeyed.

On Armistice Day, November 11, a wildly enthusiastic crowd swirled up and down Market Street and spilled over into the rest of the city, the ecstatic celebrants surrealistically swathed in white masks. Happily, the masks seemed to work. So did the vaccines and all the other amulets that San Franciscans were clutching to shield themselves from sickness and death. In November, for reasons of its own, the flu slackened, and the number of cases declined dramatically. On November 21, every siren in the city shrieked the message that the moment for unveiling had come, and the masks came off amid general scenes of hilarity and triumph. A war had been won and a deadly disease defeated in the same month.

Barely two weeks later, the number of new flu cases began to move upward again. The chief of the Board of Health expressed the hope that they were mostly misdiagnosed colds, but soon an avalanche of new cases, 5,000 in December alone, confirmed the fear that the Spanish flu was back for round two.

The most memorable features of round two in San Francisco were what can normally be expected of an anticlimax: apathy and foolish antics. Medical authorities again trotted out their vaccines, but this time the audience showed little interest. The city government again made masks compulsory, but this time against a stiff opposition of Christian Scientists, civil libertarians, merchants who were worried that masks were discouraging Christmas shopping, and people who were simply fed up with masks, flu, and everything else. One of the last group sent the head of the Board of Health a bomb. It didn't go off.

The most effective opponents to the masks were experts in such matters from various public health departments. They pointed out that there seemed to be no consistent difference in morbidity and mortality between communities that adopted the mask and those that did not. The San Francisco politicians noted, as one supervisor put it, that 99.5 percent of the city's citizens opposed the compulsory mask law. On February 1, 1919, the masks came off officially. They had come off in fact some days before.

San Francisco, a city of 550,000, had made widespread use of all known preventatives and remedies for influenza and pneumonia and had enforced ordinances for the control of the pandemic that were as stringent as any implemented in any of the larger cities of the United States. Still, thousands of her citizens had fallen ill and 3,500 had died. Its record was not very different from that of Boston, the first city to be struck in America. In San Francisco, as elsewhere, nearly two-thirds of those who died of flu and pneumonia were between the ages of 20 and 40.

One is reminded of what Surgeon General of the United States Army, Victor Vaughan, wrote about the peak weeks of the 1918 pandemic: "At that moment I decided never again to prate about the great achievements of science. . . . The deadly influenza demonstrated the inferiority of human invention . . ." (Robert Kenner Films 1998).

What does history tell us about pandemic influenza? One, that the flu ye shall always have with thee. Since 1700, we have had three to five full-scale pandemics every century. Two, that flu pandemics do not correlate with large-scale human behavior such as wars. Three, long pauses without big pandemics—for example, 1847–1889—are followed by big, punishing pandemics. We haven't had a big one since 1968.

What does scientific and scholarly research have to tell us about the special nature of the 1918 flu? A great deal, but not why it was such a killer. The 1918 flu was a singularity. A few astronomers, Sir Fred Hoyle of the University of Wales being the most famous, have claimed meaningful correlation between the "inferior conjunction of Venus" and the first outbreak of flu in 1918. There has also been some talk of new viruses driven into our atmosphere by comets. The U.S. Center for Disease Control politely called the theory "intriguing."

My one certainty is that pandemics will be with us far into the future, whether AIDS or SARS or something even newer. Pandemic flu will certainly be back, no matter how many chickens we kill in Hong Kong or elsewhere to stop it. We need better global surveillance, and we have to learn how to develop appropriate vaccines and distribute them faster. We have to be ready with trained personnel in the right places, along with enough beds, and so on. The experience of the San Francisco Hospital in 1918–1919 proves that improvization is not the best path to dealing with pandemics. We need to be ready for the next pandemic, be it influenza or whatever. It is inevitable.

Notes

1. Demographer Massimo Livi-Bacci (1992:31) estimates that 12,000 years ago there were only about 6 million of us, that is, less than the population of a number of cities today.
2. We may be headed for such conditions again in the giant metropoli of the Third World: Mexico City has a bigger population than Denmark, Norway, and Sweden combined.

CHAPTER 20

Evidence from Societal Metabolism Studies for Ecological Unequal Trade[1]

NINA EISENMENGER AND STEFAN GILJUM

Since the 1990s the concept of societal metabolism has gained broad acceptance within the scientific community as a framework for analyzing society–nature interactions. The analytical tool used to operationalize the concept, material flow accounts, calculates the biophysical exchange relationships of a socioeconomic system, usually a nation state, with its natural environment. World-system theory, in contrast, deals with global social change and the interaction between nations. It is concerned with the historical development of the world economy and its political and economic structures and processes.

The concept of societal or industrial metabolism was first formulated by Ayres and Simonis (see Ayres 1994) and became established in the 1990s (Fischer-Kowalski & Haberl 1993, 1998). It approaches socioeconomic systems as systems that exchange materials and energy with the natural environment in order to build and maintain socioeconomic stocks. To operationalize the concept, material flow accounts (MFA) were developed to account for the material flows between societies and their natural environment or between different socioeconomic systems. Economy-wide MFA is modeled on national accounts but uses weight rather than monetary units, that is, metric tons. From MFA aggregated indicators can be derived that calculate the environmental pressures caused by societies (Daniels & Moore 2001; EUROSTAT 1999; OECD 2000).

MFA is a well-established tool with a first step toward methodological harmonization supported by the Statistical Office of the European Union, which resulted in a methodological guide (EUROSTAT 2001). Besides local approaches, which in recent years have become an emerging field of research (Grünbühel et al. 2003; Krausmann 2003; Singh & Grünbühel 2003), MFA is at present mostly applied on the national level. During the past decade, several economy-wide material flow accounts have been produced, mainly for industrialized countries but also some for developing countries.[2]

Looking at the results of these studies, one overarching trend is observable: countries tend to develop from a metabolic profile where they are mainly exchanging materials with their natural environment to a pattern of increasing exchange of raw materials and other commodities with other socioeconomic systems through international trade. Thus, trade relations and integration into world markets strongly shape metabolic patterns and options for sustainable development of national economies. In order to understand national material flow patterns it is therefore necessary to consider the global processes that countries are embedded in. World-system theory analyzes exactly these issues of global social change, observing the roles of and links among different countries and regions (Wallerstein 1974–1980).

The environmental problems generated by socioeconomic processes have generally not been much considered in world-system theory (Roberts & Grimes 2002). Only in recent years have attempts been made to integrate environmental issues. These studies have focused either on specific material flows such as hazardous wastes (Roberts & Grimes 2002) and greenhouse gas emissions (Burns, Byron, & Kick 1997) or on single economic sectors such as mining (Roberts & Grimes 2002). However, none of these efforts has dealt with society–nature interactions from a systemic perspective, and thus no full understanding of global socioeconomic processes and their effects on society–nature interactions has been developed so far. We think that an integration of world-system theory and the concept of societal metabolism could contribute to a better understanding of exactly these issues (Eisenmenger 2002). The framework of social metabolism approaches society–nature interactions in a systemic and comprehensive way, which facilitates analytical links to socioeconomic processes. World-system theory, however, offers long-term and detailed insights into the social dimensions of the world economy but lacks an adequate understanding of its biophysical dimension.

Societal Metabolism and the Role of Trade

Discussions about the shortcomings of economic accounts as indicators of social welfare are well known. Besides the limited explanatory power concerning social issues, national economic accounts do not tell us anything about the effects on natural systems caused by economic processes (Samuelson & Nordhaus 1995). The concept of social metabolism was thus developed to provide information on environmental pressure induced by societal processes.

The concept of social metabolism (Ayres 1994; Fischer-Kowalski 1998;

Fischer-Kowalski & Haberl 1993) refers to materials and energy exchanged between societies and their natural environment. Studies of societal metabolism thus embrace the overall material turnover of a social system and analyze it by balancing material inputs, outputs, and stock changes. Material inputs are resource extractions from the natural environment within a specified territory as well as imports from other socioeconomic systems. Within a given social system, these inputs are transformed and used in production processes and final consumption, finally leaving the social system again either to the natural environment in the form of wastes and emissions or as exports to other socioeconomic systems.

To operationalize this concept, an analytical accounting tool called "material flow accounting" (MFA) was developed. Methodological assumptions in MFA follow those in economic accounts as far as possible, in order to maintain close analogy between these two accounting systems. The units reckoned with in MFA are metric tons. Thus, material flow data can be compared to economic accounts and provide a comprehensive biophysical picture of socioeconomic processes (Daniels & Moore 2001; EUROSTAT 2001). A first step toward methodological harmonization was supported by EUROSTAT and resulted in a methodological guide (EUROSTAT 2001).

Increasing globalization has been accentuating an international division of labor, in which countries specialize in exporting specific materials and commodities on international markets. This trend toward intensification of trade relations is visible in material flow studies (EUROSTAT 2002; Weisz et al. 2004). Increasing specialization within the world economy encourages relocation of material-intensive production processes from industrialized countries to less-developed countries in the global South, thus improving the internal environmental performance of richer countries. Some scholars have provided empirical evidence for this trend (Fischer-Kowalski & Amann 2001; Giljum & Eisenmenger 2004; Muradian & Martinez-Alier 2001b; Rothman 1998).

An increasing number of empirical studies suggest that current levels of resource extraction from nature and disposal of wastes and emissions back to nature is not sustainable in the long run, particularly in the Northern industrialized countries (UNEP 2002; WWF et al. 2004). "Sustainable development" should thus imply a decrease in the total amount of natural resources extracted and used. Through processes of outsourcing of material-intensive production, industrialized countries are able to reduce the consumption of materials used within their domestic territory and seemingly "dematerialize" their economy without changing their lifestyles and consumption patterns. Developing countries, however, tend to intensify their domestic resource extraction without increasing their material standard of living. Analysis on a global scale shows that absolute "dematerialization" has not yet been achieved (De Bruyn & Opschoor 1997). Studies on these topics were conducted by Muradian and Martinez-Alier (2001a), who analyzed North-South trade patterns for nonrenewable resources; Fischer-Kowalski and Amann (2001), who compared the material imports and exports of selected countries in the core versus periphery; and Giljum and Eisenmenger (2004), who discussed the distribution of environmental goods and burdens generated by North-South trade.

In the current discussion about "sustainable development," we face two important challenges: (1) sustainable use of resources and (2) equal distribution among social groups and between generations. These goals are contradicted by a global division of labor, where some countries engage primarily in resource extraction and bear the environmental burdens caused by these material-, energy-, and land-intensive processes but do not profit from extraction either in terms of domestic consumption or of economic profits from exports. Material flow accounting can illuminate these problems from a biophysical perspective.

World-System Theory and Its Links to Material Flow Accounting

World-system theory (WST) was originally formulated by Immanuel Wallerstein (1974–1980) and developed into a theoretical framework with many research applications and different specializations among the involved scholars (cf. Frank & Gills 1993; Goldfrank 2000; Shannon 1996). Social, political, and economic relations among nation states play an important role in WST analyses of social change. The adequate unit of analysis in these studies is therefore not the nation state but the global system (Goldfrank 2000; Wallerstein 1974, 1974–1980). This world-system is characterized by a dynamic of its own, with special mechanisms through which nation states are positioned vis-à-vis one another. The notion of societal metabolism conceptualizes the links between social and natural systems. Society–nature interactions can be conceived as material or energy flows or as the social colonization of nature, that is, transformations of natural processes for the purpose of making them useful for society (Fischer-Kowalski & Haberl 1998). Socioeconomic features such as cultural preferences, lifestyles, technologies, trade relations, and so on shape these society–nature interactions. MFA studies can add a biophysical perspective on the global division of labor and unequal exchange among countries or regions in the world-system.

Adding a Biophysical View to the Economic and Political Dimension of the World-System

The world-system is integrated by a single economic market but can consist of several political systems. Based on historical developments, Wallerstein's analysis differentiates two kinds of world-systems: world economies and world empires. The latter are integrated by a common political system with one political core. In a world economy, however, economic processes integrate a system that is more inclusive than any political structure. Thus, a world economy integrates different productive structures located in various geographical zones as well as several competing political systems with different degrees of power (Goldfrank 2000). According to Wallerstein, a unique feature of the current world economy is that it has existed for 500 years without transforming itself into a world empire.

Wallerstein thus distinguishes between a political level and an economic level, on which diverse processes can occur independently of one another and where the relevant actors can be quite different. The economic level is characterized by a global division of labor, which generates a functional differentiation of the geographical regions involved. Trading partners cannot maintain their economic activities without the exchange that goes on between them (Wallerstein 1974–1980). In addition to the economic level, Wallerstein identifies a political structure, which he calls the "interstate system" (Goldfrank 2000; Shannon 1996). The interstate system represents a historically unique structure, within which sovereign states are connected to one another but no country is strong enough to conquer the other political centers.

Studies of societal metabolism can provide a biophysical view complementing these two dimensions. Following their approach, social and natural systems interact and influence each other. Thus, economic and political processes are dependent on and influenced by processes in natural systems (Fischer-Kowalski & Weisz 1999). In investigating socioeconomic change and in particular environmental problems arising from social processes, it is important not to ignore the role of society–nature interactions, such as patterns of material and energy use.

Cores, Peripheries, Semiperipheries, and Their Biophysical Patterns

According to world-system theory, the global division of labor leads to a distinction of countries into three categories of economic zones: cores, peripheries, and semiperipheries. Cores represent countries engaged in high-tech, capital-intensive, and high-profit production. In these countries, per capita consumption is high and cannot be satisfied only with local resources

(Goldfrank 2000; Shannon 1996). Peripheries, however, are characterized by labor-intensive production using low-tech technologies. The main part of domestic production is located in the primary sectors, and most of the produced goods are exported to the cores. In return, peripheries import manufactured products from the cores. Peripheries are exposed to intensive competition and are generally forced to accept low prices and low profits (Ibid.).

Between these two extremes, world-system theory identifies a third category: the semiperiphery. According to Wallerstein, semiperipheral countries represent a necessary structural element (Wallerstein 1974). On the one hand, semiperipheries are characterized by production that is typical of core countries, but other features are more peripheral-like. Trade flows are maintained simultaneously in two directions, that is, to peripheries as well as to core countries (Goldfrank 2000). According to Wallerstein, the role of these countries is primarily to prevent a political polarization of the world-system. The three economic zones can also be characterized according to their trade networks as formulated by Terlouw (1992:34):

> The core dominates trade in all sectors and has relations with every other block of states. The periphery is connected to the international trade system almost exclusively through trade with the core states. Semiperipheral states have strong links with the core, but they also have significant links among each other.

The perspective of societal metabolism raises the question whether this tripartite structure is also reflected in specific biophysical patterns, that is, how the position of a country in the global world economy affects its interactions with the natural environment. Bunker (1985) addressed the difference between extractive and productive economies in terms of their impact on nature and refers to the overexploitation of natural resources in developing countries as an attempt to gain profits from export intensification (Bunker 1985). In the empirical section below, we refer to these issues and analyze MFA data in relation to three focal issues: (1) The amount of domestically extracted materials in relation to trade flows; this will add an MFA perspective to the notion of "extractive economies" versus industrialized countries. (2) Physical trade balances will clarify which countries are net exporters and net importers of materials, respectively; this will illuminate the unequal distribution of environmental burdens owing to the uneven spatial distribution of resource extraction and consumption. (3) Third, we compare average unit prices of imports and exports to show how a country can gain different economic profits from its trade activities.

Ecological Unequal Trade

In the framework of world-system theory, unequal trade is characteristic of the exchange between cores and peripheries, generating the economic development of industrialized countries at the expense of the periphery (Goldfrank 2000; Shannon 1996; Wallerstein 1974). Thus, the relation between core and periphery is based on exploitation; surplus economic production is transferred to core countries and accumulated there, which in turn continually reproduces the international division of labor and the core-periphery structure.

Different approaches to unequal trade and its links to environmental issues have been discussed by several scholars (Bunker 1985; Giljum & Eisenmenger 2004; Hornborg 1998b; Muradian & Martinez-Alier 2001b; Singh 2003). Here we merely summarize the main arguments in this discussion.

Several economic and political reasons are formulated to explain unequal trade. According to Shannon (1996), the main reason for unequal trade is that peripheral countries specialize in the extraction and processing of raw materials and agricultural products. These sectors are characterized by low investments in infrastructure and a cheap and comparatively unskilled labor force. Bunker (1985) argues that the primary sectors yield decreasing returns to scale. An expansion of production will thus cause decreasing returns, that is, each additional produced unit will cost more than the previously produced unit. Large-scale production therefore increases the average costs and leads to losses in profits. Krugman and Obstfeld (2000) mention that "trade has substantial effects on the income distribution within each trading nation, so that in practice the benefits of trade are often distributed very unevenly." The so-called Prebisch-Singer thesis (cf. Muradian & Martinez-Alier 2001b) postulates that—in contrast to economic theory—increasing productivities do not result in decreasing prices because industrialized countries of the North do not convert their profits from increasing returns of scale into decreasing prices. However, prices of raw materials from developing countries tend to decrease, which results in a transfer of capital from the South to the North. The reason for this, according to Prebisch and Singer, is that, in industrialized countries, profits from production do not result in decreasing prices but in increasing wages, owing to a better organization of workers in trade unions.

Bunker (1985) adds another perspective by suggesting that unequal trade refers not only to the labor values contained in the commodities but also to the uneven appropriation of natural resources. Natural resources are increasingly extracted in peripheral countries, whereas transformation and consumption occur largely in core countries. The extractive economies thus lose "natural values" derived from their own biophysical environment.

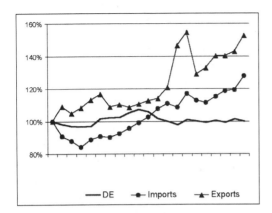

Figure 1 • EU-15 1980–2000 (Weisz et al. 2002).

In recent years, several MFA studies have been published that deal with biophysical analyses of unequal trade, for example, Muradian & Martinez-Alier (2001a) and Muradian and colleagues (2002), who analyze patterns of North-South trade in nonrenewable resources, and Giljum and Eisenmenger (2004), who discuss the distribution of environmental goods and burdens generated by North-South trade. However, much more research is still needed in this field.

Biophysical Trade Patterns

We now present some results of national material flow accounts in order to complement with empirical data the theoretical issues raised above. As mentioned, MFA is a young research area undergoing rapid development of concepts and methods. A first harmonization of MFA methods was only recently published (EUROSTAT 2001). Thus, several MFA studies exist that differ significantly in terms of the methods applied and also in terms of data quality. The number of national MFAs for developing countries is still limited. The selection of countries used in the following analysis is thus largely determined by the availability of national MFAs of comparable data quality. The countries we deal with here are Venezuela (Castellano 2001), Brazil (Machado 2001), and Chile (Giljum 2004), as representatives of developing countries, and Japan (Adriaanse et al. 1997) and the EU-15 countries (Weisz et al. 2002), as examples of industrialized countries (Figure 1). All the data presented here derive from these few studies and should thus not be used for generalizations. Still, the results reveal some interesting trends and indicate how WST and MFA can be linked in further research.

According to Terlouw (1992), Brazil, Venezuela, and Chile are generally

Table 1   Data on the socioeconomic structure of selected countries

Year 2000	Unit	Venezuela	Brazil	Chile	Japan	EU-15
Area	1,000 ha	91,205	854,740	75,663	37,780	324,269
Population	1,000 persons	24,170	170,406	15,211	127,096	376,722
Population density	persons/km2	27	20	20	336	116
GDP	Mio. USD*	79,772	788,025	81,445	5,687,635	7,502,118
GDP per capita	USD/capita	3,300	4,624	5,354	44,751	19,914

*constant 1995 prices

Sources: Area and population: FAO 2002; GDP: World Resources Institute 2004

classified as semiperipheral nations, although Brazil in some studies was classified as peripheral. Japan and the EU-15 countries are generally classified as part of the core. The countries vary significantly in geographical size, population size, and population density. Table 1 summarizes the main structural data.

From MFA data, several aggregated indicators can be derived (EUROSTAT 2001). Here we refer to the following indicators: (1) "domestic extraction" (DE), which includes all materials extracted within the territory of the chosen socioeconomic system; (2) "direct material consumption" (DMC), which is DE plus imports minus exports; and (3) "physical trade balance" (PTB), which is calculated by subtracting exports from imports.

Trade Flows Compared to Domestic Extraction

Domestic extraction in the EU-15 countries has remained rather stable over the last twenty years, whereas imports have increased about 30 percent and exports about 50 percent. The total physical amount of imports, in units of weight, is about four times as high as the exports in 2000. This clearly shows the high dependency on material imports in the EU-15 countries, as compared to a more restricted level of consumption based on domestic materials. Japan's DE is also stable over this time period, but with much higher fluctuations (Figure 2).

Material flows in the two selected developing countries show a different picture. Here, domestic extraction has grown by 50 percent in Brazil and 350 percent in Chile (Figure 3). Growth of exports and imports in Chile is slower, however, and exports have grown much slower than imports. In Brazil, exports have been growing at higher rates than DE and imports (Figure 4). These patterns indicate that the EU-15 countries and Japan are no longer intensifying

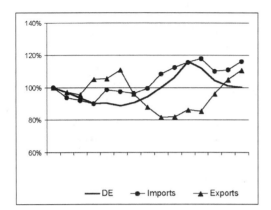

Figure 2 • Domestic extractions (DE) in Japan 1980–1994 (Adriaanse et al. 1997).

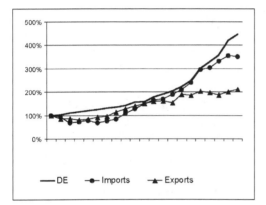

Figure 3 • Domestic extractions (DE) in Chile 1980–2000 (Giljum 2004).

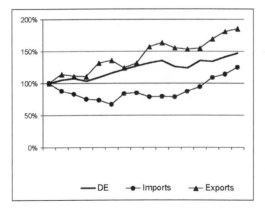

Figure 4 • Domestic extractions (DE) in Brazil 1980–1995 (Machado 2001).

the use of their own resources, but are increasingly using materials from abroad, while at the same time they are exporting greater amounts of materials. In contrast, the two developing countries seem to be further intensifying the use of their natural resources.

Domestic Extraction as an Indicator of Extractive Economies?

Developing countries are often conceived of as economies that specialize in resource extraction and have thus been referred to as "extractive economies" (Bunker 1985). Comparing MFA data on domestic extraction per capita in 1990, however, we get the following picture:

We can see in Figure 5 that in the selected five countries the amount of domestic extraction per capita in the year 1990 is of comparable quantity, that is, between twelve and seventeen tons per capita. The three developing countries should thus not be referred to as "extractive economies" in the sense that they are extracting significantly more natural resources. We can see differences, however, in the material fractions, with Brazil mainly extracting biomass, Venezuela and EU-15 extracting large amounts of fossil fuels, and Chile, Japan, and EU-15 extracting large amounts of minerals (including industrial minerals, ores, and construction minerals).

Adding imports to DE and subtracting exports, we get DMC as an indicator representing the amount of materials used in production processes and for final consumption within the domestic economy (Figure 6). For our five selected countries we get the following DMC quantities. (DMC for Japan is not available for the three material categories and thus only given as aggregate.)

Comparing DE to DMC, we get a somewhat different picture, with less material consumption in the developing countries (7 t/cap in Venezuela, 12 t/cap in Brazil) and higher DMC in Japan and the EU-15 countries (around 17 t/cap). Especially in the case of fossil fuel extraction in Venezuela, we can now see that these materials are to a large extent exported. The DMC for Chile is still rather high, at a level comparable to industrialized countries (around 16.5 t/cap). This is due to great amounts of copper extraction

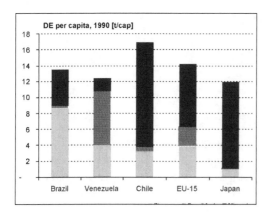

Figure 5 • Domestic extraction (DE) per capita, 1990 (Adriaanse et al. 1997; Castellano 2001; Giljum 2004; Machado 2001;Weisz et al. 2002).

and refinement in the country. Copper is a metal found only at very low concentration (around 1 percent). Mined copper thus includes huge amounts of ancillary mass that are separated during the first steps of the concentration process and mostly deposited within the domestic territory (Giljum 2004). These processes can be made visible by using the calculation of Raw Material Equivalents (RME) that account for all materials used in production or transport processes in order to provide the traded product. For a discussion on RME and their contribution to the discussion on ecological unequal trade, see Weisz (forthcoming).

As shown with these MFA data, the term "extractive economy" can be misleading, since developing countries are not extracting significantly more natural resources per capita than industrialized countries. "Extractive economies" should thus be defined as those specialized in extracting resources for exports rather than for domestic use.

Origin and Use of Materials

The DMC figures indicate a discrepancy between the regions where materials are extracted and where they are used. The indicator "Physical Trade Balance" (PTB) underlines this by identifying countries as either net importers or net exporters of materials.

Figure 7 shows a very clear picture: all three Latin American countries are net exporters of materials, whereas the EU-15 countries and Japan are net importers of materials. Based on these trade flows, it can be assumed that materials are flowing from these countries in the South to industrialized countries in the North, where they are consumed or accumulated in their physical stocks.

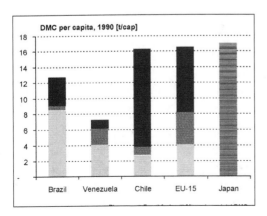

Figure 6 • Domestic Material Consumption (DMC) per capita, 1990 (Adriaanse et al. 1997; Castellano 2001; Giljum 2004; Machado 2001; Weisz et al. 2002).

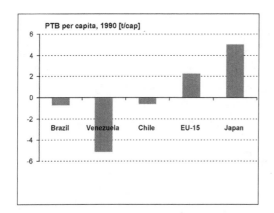

Figure 7 • Physical Trade Balance (PTB) per capita, 1990 (Adriaanse et al. 1997; Castellano 2001; Giljum 2004; Machado 2001; Weisz et al. 2002).

Unequal Trade in Biophysical Terms

By combining the biophysical data with economic data we get further support for the assumption of an unequal trade between North and South.

Figure 8 presents average unit prices of each imported and exported ton. The results show that the three Latin American countries export large amounts of materials with low economic value, reflected in low unit prices. In return, these countries are importing small quantities with high economic value, that is, with higher unit prices. The figures for the EU-15 countries and Japan are exactly the opposite. There are two possible explanations for this situation: either industrialized countries are paid higher prices for the same products, or industrialized countries export a larger share of finished products, which contain comparatively little material but high economic value (for a discussion of the latter argument see Fischer-Kowalski & Amann 2001). In either case, developing countries face a situation in which they have to export very great quantities of resources in order to gain economic profits from trade comparable to those of industrialized countries.

Summary and Conclusions

In this chapter, we have tried to link the biophysical approach of societal metabolism with world-system theory (WST) and its understanding of global socioeconomic processes, especially the phenomenon of unequal trade. The concept of social metabolism focuses on society–nature interactions by accounting for all materials exchanged between a given society and either its natural environment or other socioeconomic systems. Material flow accounts (MFA) are used as a framework in which highly aggregated indicators of environmental pressure can be derived. In order to facilitate comparability

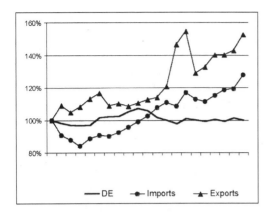

Figure 8 • Average unit prices for imports and exports, 1994 (Adriaanse et al. 1997; Castellano 2001; Giljum 2004; Machado 2001; Weisz et al. 2002).

with socioeconomic processes, material flow accounts follow analogous methodological guidelines as economic accounts. For a better understanding of global economic dependencies and long-term social changes, the concept of societal metabolism could profit from a connection to WST. WST can provide an additional perspective in discussing the driving forces behind social change and for explaining specific metabolic profiles of societies in different regions of the world.

World-system theory provides detailed insights into the world-economy and the roles, positions, and interactions of nation states in the world-system. However, WST lacks a comprehensive understanding of society–nature interactions. The concept of societal metabolism can contribute what WST is lacking in this respect. One of the main assumptions of WST is that there exists a global division of labor, generating a tripartite structure with core, periphery, and semiperiphery. A proposition often made is that countries in the South are "extractive economies," that is, specialized in resource extraction. MFA data for selected industrialized and developing countries reveal that the level of per capita domestic extraction does not significantly differ among the selected countries, irrespective of level of development. However, the three selected Latin American countries (as representatives of the global South) clearly allocate large amounts of their extracted materials to exports and thus to final use elsewhere. The industrialized countries, in contrast, import large amounts of materials, resulting in a higher DMC than that of the Southern countries.

The three countries of the South thus provide materials that are used elsewhere for production and consumption and are thus net exporters of natural resources. EU-15 countries and Japan, however, are net importers that use or accumulate materials. Because environmental pressures resulting from resource extraction are higher than in other economic sectors (Mani &

Wheeler 1998), it is important to observe that the countries that suffer most from the environmental burdens of natural resource extraction do not gain the benefits, either in terms of economic profits (owing to limited possibilities of adding value) or in terms of final domestic resource consumption (Bunker 1985). Countries in the South following a resource-intensive and export-oriented development model not only lose natural resources owing to net exports but also gain little economic profit, as illustrated by the average unit prices of imports and exports. The comprehensive picture provided by MFA can thus be used as support for the concept of ecological unequal trade that is implied by the world-system perspective.

Notes

1. This paper is partly a result of the project "GEWIN—Social Knowledge and Global Sustainability," funded by the research program *Kulturlandschaftsforschung* of the Austrian Ministry for Education, Research, and Arts. For productive discussions and critical comments during the process of writing we would like to thank particularly Heinz Schandl and Helga Weisz, as well as the whole project team of GEWIN for their contributions. We were also especially fortunate in being able to discuss this paper with Stephen Bunker during his visit to Vienna in 2004.

2. UK: (Schandl, Heinz, & Schulz 2002); Brazil: (Machado 2001); Chile: (Giljum 2004); China: (Chen & Qiao 2001); Czech Republic: (Scasny, Kovanda, & Hak 2003); Denmark: (Pedersen 2002); Finland: (Mäenpää & Juutinen 2001; Muukkonen 2000); Germany: (German Federal Statistical Office–Statistisches Bundesamt 1995; German Federal Statistical Office–Statistisches Bundesamt 2000); Hungary: (Hammer & Hubacek 2003); Italy: (Barbiero et al. 2003; De Marco, Lagioia, & Pizzoli 2000; Femia 2000); Laos: (Schandl et al. 2005); Philippines: (Rapera 2004); Poland: (Mündl et al. 1999); Sweden: (Isacsson et al. 2000); Thailand: (Weisz, Krausmann, & Sangkaman 2005); UK: (DETR/ONS/WI 2001; Schandl and Schulz 2002); Venezuela: (Castellano 2001); Germany, Japan, Netherlands, USA: (Adriaanse et al. 1997); Austria, Germany, Japan, Netherlands, USA: (Matthews et al. 2000); EU: (Bringezu et al. 2004; ETC-WMF 2003; EUROSTAT 2002; Weisz et al. 2005).

CHAPTER 21

Entropy Generation and Displacement: The Nineteenth-Century Multilateral Network of World Trade

ANDRE GUNDER FRANK

Editorial note: Andre Gunder Frank died in Luxembourg in April 2005 after a long and inspiring career. At the time of his passing he was working on a manuscript tentatively titled ReOrient the 19th Century, *a sequel to his 1998 book* ReORIENT: Global Economy in the Asian Age. ReORIENT *sought to reorganize the history of the eighteenth century, deeply flawed by western hubris, especially with regard to the nature and the role of societies of the east. Frank also sought to identify and correct the litany of erroneous conclusions that social theorists derived from that unfortunately biased historical narrative. In* ReOrient the 19th Century, *Frank hoped to apply additional historical and social theory correctives, especially with regard to the dynamics that led to the differentiation of East and West, North and South. The paper Frank prepared for this conference was based on that longer manuscript.*

Frank was often ill during his final years, and much of what he presented here was tentative in nature. I made no attempt to complete his work. I simply edited this paper for length and clarity. Among the notable innovations here is Frank's adoption of the concept of entropy to world system history. Frank decided that this was a fruitful direction, though he had not yet made the global historical applications of sociopolitical entropy completely his own. I would like to thank the editors of this volume for the chance to update Frank's essay, as I attempt to bring ReOrient the 19th Century *to publication.*

Robert A. Denemark

This is a part of my book in the making, *ReORIENT the 19th Century*, which is a sequel to my previous one that stopped in 1800. In the first *ReORIENT*, I argued that deeply flawed Eurocentric historiography gave rise to deeply flawed Eurocentric social theory, and one of the results was a lack of understanding of the many ways the whole system influences its various parts. Subsequent analyses of the South and the East have suffered ever since. The "Rise of the

West" was never the advance of one region over another from the level playing field of traditional society. The East had been significantly advanced as part of a unified global system, and the reasons for its decline (both the system and the East) and the subsequent rise of the West are particularly important issues that have yet to be sufficiently addressed. Part of the reason for the decline of the East and the rise of the West involves environmental aspects.

The theoretical and analytical tools to be used in this analysis are these:

1. The *global* political economy;
2. The study of possible *simultaneous connections* and the derivation of historical events around the world at the same time from a single global structure and dynamic;
3. The accumulation of ever more triangles of divisions of labor and trade into an increasingly complex *multiangular/multilateral system*, in which one angle of each triangle was located during this period in Britain, thus permitting it to derive benefits and most of its development from this privileged position (and not from any unique or internal attributes or advances);
4. *Physical/ecological and social entropy*, generated by economic growth and displaced from center to periphery. This displacement of entropy permits greater order and democracy than would otherwise be possible in industrial core regions and imposes greater disorder, including accelerated ecological damage, war, civil strife and political conflict, onto those who are systematically obliged to absorb that entropy.

ReOrient the Nineteenth Century

I join Kenneth Pomeranz when he argues that we need to rethink the nineteenth century, which he observes has been abandoned by a whole generation of scholars. John F. Kennedy told us that "the great enemy of truth is very often not the lie—deliberate, contrived, and dishonest—but the myth—persistent, persuasive and unrealistic" (Frank 1998:vii). If that is true, then it has certainly been persistent in the literature represented by—to meld the titles of two books—*The Nature and Causes of the Wealth and Poverty of Nations* (Landes 1999; Smith 1937 [1776]). For the received and still persistent mythological "explanations" of the most important changes of the nineteenth century, "the Great Divergence" (Pomeranz 2000) of East and West that emerged out of the structure, function, and transformation of the world economy, are altogether wide of the mark. It was this *global economy* that really gave rise to a "single worldwide system which also provided the transfer, along round about routes

. . . [of wealth and resources] to . . . particularly, the United Kingdom . . . by the much less adequately understood system of multilateral settlements of all classes of international accounts" (Hilgerdt 1942:6, 9).

My two main analytic guidelines are multilaterality and entropy. In short-cut summary, we may regard location in the multilateral system as the prime determinant of how much benefit or disbenefit a person, group, sector, region, or country can derive from its social-structural and geographical position in the world system or global economy. Elsewhere I have referred to this as the importance of *Location, Location, Location* (Frank 2001). Entropy may be regarded as the cost of participation in the system and its economic production and growth. Displacement of entropy then is the transfer or export of this entropic cost from here to there, and in the world from the rich North that generates or causes the generation of much of it to the poor South, which is obliged to absorb this displaced entropy at its own cost. The two processes of deriving benefits and absorbing costs are in turn related by the same multilaterality, through which not only the benefits are spread and derived but also the costs are channeled and absorbed.

Entropy Generation and Dissipation

Dissipative structures . . . refer(s) to the ability of complex systems to transfer their entropic costs to other parts [of the system]. . . . [We] lose sight of the fact that every system in the social order must be paid for by someone, somewhere, sometime. This essential reality is hidden from our view because human beings are very skillful at exporting the costs of their own behavior to others via dissipative structures . . . [through which] dissipation of entropy occurs when one system has the will and the ability to force others to absorb the costs of its own growth and prosperity . . . [in part] through impersonal market mechanisms so the victims on the periphery [colonial or otherwise] are not aware of what is being done to them. (Robert P. Clark, *The Global Imperative* 1997:5, 10)

The systems in which dissipation occurs have been studied especially by Prigogine & Stengers (1984) and colleagues, who have analyzed dissipative structures of open dis-equilibrium systems. Straussfogel (1998) applies this theorization to the world system, as Adams (1982) does to the British Empire. The common factor is that broken-down (expended) energy and social disorder are displaced from a center to peripheral regions and sectors. More important still in a nonlinear/nonequilibrium system is that critical points of dis-equilibrium can lead to bifurcations in the paths that may be taken, such that small changes can lead to large differences in the future. That is because taking and proceeding along one path in a nonlinear system can be an irreversible act, foreclosing the option of ever going down some alternative road. The major question for us is whether "the Great Divergence" in the nineteenth century was such a point and situation, and if so, when, why, and how?

As per the epigraph above, much of the social order and the structural complexity of the wealthy can be maintained or even be further elaborated if they can transfer the disorder that they generate to others who are obliged to absorb it, and who thereby become less orderly than they were before. This process of dissipation occurs along lines that are both more and less easily visible. The more visible ones are unidirectional. A glaring but illustrative example is the export of nuclear waste subproducts from the nuclear power stations of Europe and Japan, which have relatively much power, to Africa, with little power (in more than one sense of the word), which is paid a pittance (for the North but not for the South) to absorb this entropy.

Another, perhaps less obvious but more frequent example is how the consequences and costs of global warming generated by the burning of coal and oil by the North (much of it now imported from the South) are in turn (re-)exported to the South. There they cause flooding, soon perhaps also to submerge low-lying areas into the rising sea, and massive destruction of virgin rainforests to maintain industries and consumption in the North. These examples become even more glaring, of course, if part of the higher income in the North is the result of prior or present transfers of income from the South.

However, displacement of entropy from North to South also occurs along multilateral paths and networks. These may be less obvious or even invisible, but they are even more used and important. The transfer of entropy from one area to another can go via one or more third parties. As Folke Hilgerdt (1943:400) put it, "the development of the system of multilateral trade . . . was similar to the unfolding of a fan: more and more countries became involved, and their insertion took place in a given order, each country being farther way from the United Kingdom on the transfer routes to that country from its debtors." I would add that countries need not have been inserted one by one into Britain's charmed circle. They also entered as participants of already previously existing bi- or multilateral systems that themselves were incorporated into the worldwide web.

A sophisticated discussion of entropy and its global importance as a fundamental part of economic growth and industrialization is to be found in Alf Hornborg's *The Power of the Machine* (2001a). He stresses that machines, and industry in general, are not only technical but also social phenomena. First to build and then to run a machine requires socially provided inputs of raw material, land, fuel, and labor energy that represent greater amounts of order than the machine's output. Yet the machine can be kept running only if its products can be sold at a price that is higher than that of the inputs it uses. According to the Second Law of Thermodynamics, the machine's productive process must generate entropy, disorder, which must somehow and somewhere be disposed of. It is in the means of this disposal that machine production and products differ from organic biomass; the latter uses ultimately limitless solar energy that it converts into heat, which is dissipated into the universe. Industrialization introduced mechanical production on a growing scale that is based on fossil fuels, first coal and then oil and gas. Not only are these limited and nonrenewable, they also generate entropy that must remain with us in the form of pollution and environmental degradation. However, the locus of that entropy need not, indeed cannot, remain the same as that of the machine itself. Much of the input into the industrial process comes from nonindustrial regions, and much of the entropy is exported back to them, along with some useful industrial products. The mechanism that performs these transfers of negative entropy (exergy) from nonindustrial to industrial sites, and re-exports the entropy/disorder generated back to them or to others, is the world market, which operates on the basis of differentials in factor prices between locations. For the process to operate, the price differentials must favor the (owners of) the machine at the expense of those who, through unequal exchange, supply the wherewithal for the machine to be built and operated. And this world market mechanism is often supplemented by the exercise of political-military power.

Since the sum of the inputs into the machine, that is, to industrial production, contains more order (less entropy) than its outputs, industrial growth and "development" generally are not self-contained but are the result of the inward transfer of exergy/order and the outward transfer of entropy/disorder—both physical and social. That is, "the nonindustrial sectors experience a net increase in entropy as natural resources and traditional social structures are dismembered. The ecological and social impoverishment of the periphery are two sides of the same coin, for both nature and human labor are underpaid sources of high-quality energy" (Hornborg 2001a:11). Industry owes its existence to the availability of nonindustry, and an attempt to distribute industry and its benefits equally among all would be "as contradictory as trying to keep a beef cow alive while restoring its molecules to all the tufts of grass from which it has sprung" (Ibid.:125). Hornborg also rightly notes that since this ecological and economic structure and process are the essence of the industrial process, it is vain to claim or even to hope to ameliorate its costs by industrializing the entire Third World or by replacing dirty industrial technology with, for example, clean green but more expensive informatics. Indeed, raising the income of the Rest to that of the West would require three extra planets (Ibid.:31). Thus, capital accumulation, technological development, and economic growth in some parts of the world system are "organically linked to underdevelopment and environmental deterioration in others" (Ibid.:33). Therefore, Hornborg argues, GNP in one place is really a measure of its terms of trade with another and "reflects a country's position in socially negotiated global exchange relations" (Ibid.:32).

So that is where three major analytical categories and procedures connect in the present work: (1) the global economy and market; (2) its multiangular and multilateral structure and organization, whereby benefits and the lack thereof are unevenly distributed around the globe; and (3) the entropy costs that are generated by those most favorably placed in the "center" and displaced out to the "periphery," which is obliged to bear the costs of absorbing that entropy.

A particularly important entropic contribution to "the Great Divergence" has been analyzed by Davis (2001) under the subtitle *El Niño Famines and the Making of the Third World*. He discusses uneven climatic changes and the way agricultural societies that were advantaged by them used these events to exploit—and in effect displace some of their own entropy to—the disadvantaged. More precisely, some advanced and others suffered from the single structure and process of *global* development.

Those who were disadvantaged included much of Latin America up through Mexico, North, South and East Africa, and large parts of India, China, and probably Russia. The same *El Niño* cycles simultaneously favored more northerly regions, especially the United States' wheat-producing Great Plains, with additional rainfall. This bestowed on them both greater absolute as well as relative advantages in the global economy, and political bargaining power in the world. Davis writes that American grain production "is typically in meteorological antiphase with *El Niño* droughts and crop failures in India, north China and (most likely) the Russian *chernozem* belt. This potential to relieve the world's hunger during periods of synchronous global drought was also a partial solution to the problem of overproduction in the Plains states" (Davis 2001:261).

Thus, the simultaneous deterioration of agriculture and increase of poverty in what was becoming the Third World, combined with an agricultural boom in the United States, radically altered political-economic relations between North and South. The North did not simply advance because of a generous climate but took advantage of the South. In Africa, a missionary observed that "Europeans track famine like a sky full of vultures" (Ibid.:139). Davis quotes another late nineteenth-century observer who reported that "people saw a connection between the disaster of drought, famine, and disease on the one hand, and the advance of European political power on the other" (Ibid.:140). In "Colonial Asia: Starvation [w]as a Strategy" (Ibid.:193). In India, famine was deliberately aggravated by British colonial policy: the British overlord Curzon was "architect of brilliantly organized famine" (Ibid.:164), which was then used to extract greater concessions. In the Philippines, "the Americans . . . exceeded even the cruelest Spanish precedents in manipulating disease and hunger as weapons against an insurgent but weakened population" (Ibid.:198). In Brazil, four successive droughts between 1888 and 1902 devastated subsistence and sugar production in the old Northeast, whereas all metropolitan and Brazilian economic and state interests were concentrated on the new coffee boom in São Paulo in the South.

In other words, the North displaced its growth and adjustment costs to the South. Many states were fiscally weakened by increased military expenditures, in India through the infamous "Home Charges" that financed the British-led but Indian-manned colonial army, and in China for defense against further Western incursions. For these and other reasons, previous state intervention to stock granaries for secure food supplies and control their prices, as well as large and small-scale hydraulic management through maintenance of irrigation canals, had to be abandoned for fiscal and political reasons at the very times that *El Niño* made them more essential than ever.

In China, the First Opium War was fought at the same time as three successive floods, and the Second Opium War followed the long Taiping Rebellion that in turn followed harvest disasters. From the 1860s onward, China embarked on the "Self-Strengthening Program" of especially military expenditures, which successfully competed with the increased expenditures on agriculture that would have been necessary in order to confront the coming natural disasters from the exceptionally severe *El Niño* phases during the last third of the century.

Today, the most glaring and yet least noted instance of entropy displacement is surely the military-industrial complex against which President Eisenhower warned in his "Farewell Speech." It is probably the world's most polluting industry. It is also the example *par excellence* of entropy displacement. Military production by industrial powers uses local and imported raw materials—and often brain-drain personnel—at huge economic resource opportunity and environmental costs to produce "goods" (more properly "bads") of no social utility whatsoever. Many of these are then exported back to the suppliers of the original fuels and raw materials, who pay for them with foreign exchange derived from their export of commodities or goods of low value added, which they thereby deny to their own populations. Thus, starving Africans and Asians export foodstuffs and other raw materials to the rich so that they can import arms that they would not need if they did not face so much scarcity-based conflict. Entropy is thereby displaced from the rich to the poor.

There is a displacement of sociopolitical entropy from the richer, when they sell their military hardware and training, to the poorer abroad, who import these arms and use them to kill one another in an ever more chaotic "Third World," while the North is thereby helped to better afford "democratic order" at home. Even so, the arms producers keep enough of them for their own use to enforce and even further extend this exploitative and entropic world (dis)order, which yields benefits for themselves at enormous cost to everybody else. This is called "preserving human rights, freedom, democracy, and civilization," and most recently also "combatting terrorism." In the nineteenth century, this Western displacement of ecological and social entropy to the rest of the world was called the "civilizing mission" or the "white man's burden." Hornborg details some of the mechanisms at work, but he does not try to show us how they worked globally in the nineteenth century. This paper is part of a larger attempt to begin this heretofore neglected task, in the absence of which it has been quite impossible to offer any sensible and sensitive accounting for "the Great Divergence."

From Triangles to Multiangular Multilaterality

Already three decades ago, I wrote under the title *Multilateral Merchandise Trade Imbalances and Uneven Economic Development* (1976 [1970]:407–408):

> Contrary to orthodox international trade and national development
> theory, the uneven development of world capitalism was not accompanied
> by balanced trade (or growth) but rested in fact on a fundamental
> imbalance of international trade between the developing metropolis and
> the underdeveloping, colonialized, countries. Except for the years of
> worst depression in the metropolis, the latter had a constant but growing
> trade deficit and the underdeveloped countries a trade surplus during the
> classical imperialist period of world capitalist development at the end of
> the nineteenth and the beginning of the twentieth centuries. The almost
> exclusive theoretical and empirical interest in the balance of payments,
> and obsession with the mechanisms that make it balance, has cast a "veil
> of money" over the underlying merchandise *imbalance of trade* whose
> role, which we believe is fundamental in the process of uneven capitalist
> development and underdevelopment, has remained all but un-perceived

. . . To summarize . . . the secular excess of the underdeveloped countries' exports over imports has throughout this period made a fundamental contribution to the accumulation of capital, technological progress and economic development of the now developed countries; and the generation of this exports surplus from the now underdeveloped countries has there developed the mode of production which underdeveloped Asia, Africa and Latin America.

The study of these imbalances of trade and settlements on a world scale has been considered by very few, including Hilgerdt (1942, 1945), S. B. Saul (1960), and (through mentions in textbooks) Condliffe (1950) and Kenwood and Lougheed (1971). There is also my 1976 study of Hilgerdt's data in *The Network of World Trade*. Alas, that work has only scattered estimates for 1913 and earlier, but his sequel *Industrialization and Foreign Trade* (1945) has a few more, on which I shall draw below. However, taking advantage of the more recent literature on *Ecological Economics* (Martinez-Alier 1987) and related work, this kind of study of real merchandize flows can perhaps now also serve as a basis to analyze their absolute and relative contents of energy (Adams 1982) as well as the generation and displacement of entropy.

The multilateral or multiangular structure of the global economy permits those at privileged, angular locations to exact tribute or rent from the system as a whole and in particular from those in underprivileged positions—the role of the latter is to produce and transfer wealth and income to the privileged ones. In the nineteenth century, Great Britain came to occupy this position of privilege; and *that* is what made it "Great"—much more so than any qualities or productive or other capacities of its own. Since then, the United States has replaced Britain in this position of greatest privilege, and *that* rather than its productive capacity accounts for most of its wealth and income.

To better visualize this multilateral system, imagine a global game of musical chairs in which *n* players sit in a circle around the globe. Relations among the players are also established criss-cross. Some chairs are visibly better or worse, but their quality is in only small part due to the "essence" of their construction. Instead, the goodness or badness of the chairs is measured substantially by their location in the global circle, which generates much of the observed and/or real quality of the chairs. Now imagine, moreover, that this game of musical chairs is played, as are most real-world games, on a *not* "level playing field." When the music plays, the players scuttle about. They also move along paths that emerge out of previously established bi- but also multilateral strategic or simply tactical relations of alliance and conflict. The alliances conflict among but also within themselves. Or the other way around, the whole game is a Hobbesian war of all against all in which, even if each player is only out for him- or herself, the formation and membership of bi- or multilateral alliances can be of advantage to members relative to those who play only on their own. So now everything is set up for the cyclical and temporary cessation of the music. The shuffle results in somebody being likely not only to get a better or a worse chair but to get none at all, while the rest of the players end up going around again. (Also important, but for now disregarded here, is the potentially unequal "domestic" game of musical chairs, and how the international and "domestic" inequalities are in turn interrelated.)

All this long-winded stuff about musical chairs is included here to illustrate a short-winded point that should be obvious but is still very rarely observed: World economic development is a global game in which the players scuttle around and some manage to change positions when the cyclical music stops. Moreover, the *place* that each player has in the game is probably the most determinant factor for the players' wealth and income and for their opportunities in the next round. Any player's location also determines his/her ability to displace entropy, not just to a neighbor in the circle, but to one or many possible chairs around or across the circle. And they in turn are more often than not obliged to absorb this entropy to their own detriment. On this anything but level playing field, the specific pattern created and the place a country holds in the global system is precisely a matter of *Location, Location, Location.*

A simple graphic rendition (see Figure 1) of the system was adapted by Condliffe (1950:285) from the more detailed 1928 version in *The Network of World Trade.* However, the emphasis in all this is on the flow of payments and the derivation of benefits. What we need to do now is to complement this analysis with the flow of real goods from which people benefit or not *and* the counterflow of entropic costs along and through the channels of the same system.

Beginning with the Tropics (Underdeveloped Regions) and reading clockwise, we see that this region sends more to the United States, to Regions of Recent Settlement (Dominions), and to Continental Europe, than it receives. The United States has an export surplus with the Recently Settled regions, Europe, and Britain, though part of that surplus is canceled by its import surplus from the tropics. Regions of Recent Settlement play an intermediary role in the circuit. They receive excess merchandise from underdeveloped regions and the United States and send an excess to Europe and Britain. Europe receives an excess of imports from the Tropics, the United States and Regions of Recent Settlement, and in turn sends more to Britain than it receives. Finally, Britain receives more from each of the preceding regions, but sends more—albeit very little more—to the underdeveloped countries than it receives from them. This last relation ostensibly "completes" or "closes" the circle of this system of trade imbalances.

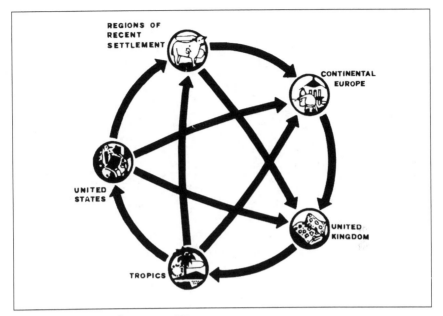

Figure 1 • The circuit of payments 1928.

A more complicated and accurate version for the period around 1910, which focuses on the special place of Britain in the system, is rendered by S. B. Saul (1960:58) and extended by me to include China (see Figure 2).

Saul omitted China for some unknown reason, so I added it. An accompanying table on the United Kingdom Balance of Payments for 1910 indicates total debits of £145 million sterling and corresponding credits of £118 million. Most revealing in the table is that the United Kingdom debits with Continental Europe, United States, Canada, and (white) South Africa account for £72 million, or more than half the debits, but that these are matched by credits of £73 billion with India and China alone, of which £60 billion from India itself, on which Britain was able to draw to cover its debits with its white settler regions.

Regarding the development, structure, and operation of this multi-lateral system, Hilgerdt (1943:394) summarized his findings as follows:

The outline of this system became clear when it was found that almost all countries could be arranged in the order of the direction of their balances of trade, so that each country had an import balance from practically all countries that preceded it in the list and an export balance to, practically all

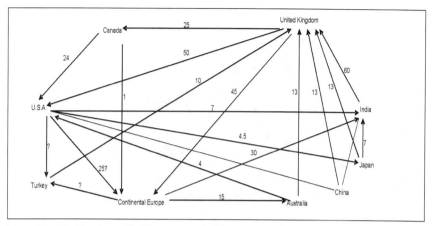

Figure 2 • World pattern of settlements 1910 [Editor's note: adapted from Figure 2 in S. B. Saul's *Studies in British Overseas Trade 1870–1914* (1960:58). Frank added China and its settlement payments to the United Kingdom but not the direction or amount of payments from/ to India or the U.S.A.].

countries that succeeded it. At beginning of this list, we find the tropical debtor countries with export balances in almost all directions, and at the end of it the European creditor countries with import balances from almost all countries, the United Kingdom being the most typical case. But between these two extremes the countries arrange themselves.

Full globalization of production, trade, capital flows, migration, and communication was thus in place already in the first decade of the twentieth century. The structure and the operation of this global system were destroyed, however, during much of the twentieth century, with the First World War, the Great Depression, and then the Second World War. It was not fully reconstructed until the 1990s and the beginning of the twenty-first century. Now, the United States is trying to occupy the place of privilege. Its foremost instrument is its monopoly on printing the world currency, which is the dollar, and this is supported in turn by the Pentagon; these are the two pillars on which the United States now rests (Frank 2005).

Historically and analytically we can recognize this process early on, with the Baltic trade between developing Western and underdeveloping Eastern Europe in the seventeenth century and then the well-known *triangular* trade across the Atlantic Ocean in the eighteenth century. In reality there were multiple triangles that connected Britain, their American colonies, France and Spain and their colonies, the Caribbean, and Africa, as illustrated in Frank (1978) and elsewhere. What they all had in common was that they ultimately had an angle in Britain and then in North America, and that they rested fundamentally on the slave trade and the silver trade that helped finance much of the rest. The obvious—if often still insistently denied—unequal and polarizing consequences of the triangular and slave trade, slavery, plantation agriculture, mining, forestry, cod fisheries, and so on were highlighted among others by Marx in his volume III of *Capital* and by Eric Williams (later Prime Minster of Trinidad and Tobago) in his *Capitalism and Slavery* (1944). But Kenneth Pomeranz (2000) and to a lesser extent Frank (1998) analyzed the concomitant "ecological exchange" through which West Europeans were able to consume much more at less ecological cost at home by displacing them to Eastern Europe and to Africa and the Americas, at the cost of their indigenous populations, soil, and other resources.

Beginning in the late eighteenth and flourishing in the nineteenth century, the Atlantic triangles were joined by the Opium Triangle between China, India, and Britain. The literature on this arrangement is best represented by Carlo Trocki in *Opium, Empire and Global Political Economy* (1999). However, the emphasis is as usual on how opium production in India yielded Indian and British expatriate remissions to Britain that were generated by Chinese imports of opium in exchange for mostly silver re-exports of what China had imported from Mexico and the United States. The ravages of opium consumption have received considerable attention as a social aberration, but not as a displacement of entropic costs from Britain.

In Asia, opium production required the conversion of land and labor first in Bihar and then in western India, Southeast Asia, and later in Szechwan. It required the dedication of terrestrial transport, shipping, finance, and so forth to the commercialization of the drug. It had serious medical and social consequences for consumers and their families in China and Southeast Asia. It debilitated the finances and thereby the infrastructural and social spending of the Chinese state through the drain of silver. It was the state's attempt to stop this drain that led to the Opium Wars and their consequences. All these events appear in a somewhat different perspective if they are viewed as the entropic counterpart of British industrial development.

Throughout the nineteenth century, more and more triangles joined the ever more multiangular, multilateral, and complex network of world trade and its division of labor and spoils. Britain remained the apex at which all these triangles joined and was eventually joined by the United States. The stages of development progressed through the addition of more and more triangles to what became a complex system of multiangular and multilateral trade and payment *im*balances. The analysis of the entropic exchange between regions in the developing North and the underdeveloping South can throw additional light and perspective on the system as a whole and the divergent paths of its various parts.

References

Abel, T. 1998. Complex adaptive systems, evolutionism, and ecology within anthropology: Interdisciplinary research for understanding cultural and ecological dynamics, *Georgia Journal of Ecological Anthropology* 2:6–29.

———2000. Ecosystems, sociocultural systems, and ecological-economics for understanding development: The case of ecotourism on the Island of Bonaire, N.A. Ph. D. dissertation, University of Florida.

———2003. Understanding complex human ecosystems: The case of ecotourism on Bonaire, *Conservation Ecology* 7(3):10.

Abel, T., and J. R. Stepp. 2003. A new ecosystems ecology for anthropology, *Conservation Ecology* 7(3):12.

Abrams, E. M., A. Freter, D. J. Rue, and J. D. Wingard. 1996. The role of deforestation in the collapse of late classic Copan Maya state. In *Tropical deforestation*. L. E. Sponsel, T. N. Headland, and R. C. Bailey, eds. New York: Columbia University Press, pp. 55–75.

Abu-Lughod, J. 1989. *Before European hegemony: The world system A.D. 1250–1350*. New York: Oxford University Press.

Adams, R. N. 1982. *Paradoxical harvest: Energy and explanation in British history, 1870–1914*. Cambridge: Cambridge University Press.

Adriaanse, A., S. Bringezu, A. Hammond, Y. Moriguchi, E. Rodenburg, D. Rogich, and H. Schütz. 1997. *Resource flows: The material basis of industrial economies*. Washington, DC: World Resources Institute.

Aikhenvald, A. Y. 1999. Areal diffusion and language contact in the Icana-Vaupés basin, north-west Amazonia. In *The Amazonian languages*. R. M. W. Dixon and A. Y. Aikhenvald, eds. Cambridge: Cambridge University Press, pp. 385–416.

Aikhenvald, A. Y., and R. M. W. Dixon. 1998. Evidentials and areal typology: A case study from Amazonia. *Language Sciences* 20:241-57.

Alés, C., and M. Pouyllau. 1992. La conquéte de l'inutile: Les géographies imaginaires de l'Eldorado, *L'Homme* 32:271–308.

Alexander, M., ed. 1976. *Discovering the New World, based on the works of Theodore de Bry*. New York: Harper and Row.

Algaze, G. 1989. The Uruk expansion. Cross-cultural exchange in early Mesopotamian civilization, *Current Anthropology* 30(5):571–608.

———2000. Initial social complexity in Southwest Asia: The Mesopotamian advantage. Unpublished paper: Department of Anthropology, UCSD.

Algaze, G., T. D'Altroy, M. Fragipane, H. Nissen, H. Pittman, S. Pollock, M. Rothman, G. Schwartz, G. Stein, and H. Wright. 1998. School of American Research Advanced Seminar: Mesopotamia in the Era of State Formation. www.science.widener.edu/ssci/mesopotamia.

Allen, P. M. 1997. *Cities and regions as self-organizing systems.* Amsterdam: Gordon and Breach Science Publishers.

Allen, R. C. 2001. The great divergence in European wages and prices from the Middle Ages to the First World War, *Explorations in Economic History* 38:411–447.

Allen, W. L., and J. H. Tizón. 1973. Land use patterns among the Campa of the Alto Pachitea, Peru. In *Variation in anthropology.* D. W. Lathrap and J. Douglas, eds. Urbana, IL: Archeological Survey, pp. 137–153.

Alvard, M. S., J. G. Robinson, K. H. Redford, and H. Kaplan. 1996. The sustainability of subsistence hunting in the neotropics, *Conservation Biology* 11:977–982.

Ambrosiani, B. 1984. Settlement expansion-settlement contraction: A question of war, plague ecology or climate. In *Climatic changes on a yearly to millennial basis.* N.-A. Mörner and W. Karlén, eds. Dordrecht: Reidel.

Amsterdam Declaration. 2001. www.sciconf.igbp.kva.se/Amsterdam_Declaration.html.

Anderies, J. 2000. On modeling human behavior and institutions in simple ecological economic systems, *Ecological Economics* 35(3):393–412

Andersen, S. T. 1995. History of vegetation and agriculture at Hassing House Mose, Thy, northwest Denmark, *Journal of Danish Archeology* 1992–1993:39–57.

———1998. Pollen analytical investigations of barrows from the Funnel Beaker and Single Grave Cultures in the Vroue area, West Jutland, Denmark, *Journal of Danish Archeology* 1994–1995:107–133.

Andersen, S. T., and B. E. Berglund. 1994. Maps for terrestrial non-tree pollen (NAP) percentages in north and central Europe 1800 and 1400 BP, *Paläoklimaforschung* 12:119–134.

Anderson, D. G. 1994. *The Savannah River chiefdoms: Political change in the late prehistoric Southeast.* Tuscaloosa, AL: University of Alabama Press.

Angel, J. L. 1972. Human skeletons from grave circles at Mycenae. In *Ho taphikos kyklos B ton Mykenon.* Athens: G. E. Mylonas.

Anon. 2001. *Öyvind Fahlström. Another space for painting.* Museu d'Art Contemporani de Barcelona, Barcelona.

Anthony, D. W. 1995. Horse, wagon & chariot: Indo-European languages and archeology, *Antiquity* 69:554–565.

———1998. The opening of the Eurasian steppe at 2000 B.C.E. In *The Bronze Age and early Iron Age peoples of eastern Central Asia.* V. H. Mair, ed. Washington, DC and Philadelphia: The Institute for the Study of Man in collaboration with The University of Pennsylvania Museum Publications, pp. 94–11.

Archer, E. R. M. 2003. Beyond the "climate versus grazing" impasse: Using remote sensing to investigate the effects of grazing system choice on vegetation cover in Eastern Karoo, *Journal of Arid Environments* 57(3):381–408.

Århem, K. 1976. Fishing and hunting among the Makuna. Annual Report, Ethnographical Museum, Gothenburg, pp. 27–44.

———1981. Makuna social organization: A study in descent, alliance and the formation of corporate groups in the north-western Amazon. Uppsala Studies in Cultural Anthropology 4, Stockholm, Uppsala University.

Asner, G. P., S. Archer, R. F. Hughes, R. J. Ansley, and C. A. Wessman. 2003. Net changes in regional woody vegetation cover and carbon storage in Texas drylands, 1937–1999, *Global Change Biology* 9(3):316–335.

Ayres, R. U. 1994. Industrial metabolism: Theory and policy. In *Industrial metabolism: Restructuring for sustainable development.* U. Ayres and Udo E. Simonis, eds. Tokyo: United Nations Robert University Press, pp. 3–20.

Bahn, P. G. 2001. Easter Island: Its rise and fall. In *Forest and civilisations.* Y. Yasuda, ed. New Delhi: Lustre Press, pp. 63–68.

Bahn, P. G., and J. Flenley. 1992. *Easter Island, Earth Island: A message from the past for the future of our planet.* New York: Thames and Hudson.

Bailey, F. G., ed. 1971. *Gifts and poison: The politics of reputation.* Oxford: Basil Blackwell.

Bain, K. B. 1993. *The new friendly islanders: The Tonga of King Taufa'ahau Tupou IV.* London: Hodder & Stoughton.

Baines, J., and N. Yoffee. 1998. Order, legitimacy, and wealth in ancient Egypt and Mesopotamia. In *Archaic states.* G. M. Feinman and J. Marcus, eds. Santa Fe, NM: School of American Research Press.

Baksh, M., and A. Johnson. 1990. Insurance policies among the Machiguenga: An ethnographic analysis of risk management in a non-western society. In *Risk and uncertainty in tribal and peasant economies.* E. Cashdan, ed. Boulder, CO: Westview, pp. 193–227.

Balée, W. 1992. People of the fallow: A historical ecology of foraging in lowland South America. In *Conservation of neotropical forests: Working from traditional resource use.* K. H. Redford and C. Padoch, eds. New York: Columbia University Press, pp. 35–57.

———1994. *Footprints in the forest: Ka'apor ethnobotany—The historical ecology of plant utilization by an Amazonian people.* New York: Columbia University Press.

———1998 (ed.). *Advances in historical ecology.* New York: Columbia University Press.

Ball, P. 2004. *Critical mass.* London: Heinemann.

Ballard, C. 1986. Drought and economic distress: South Africa in the 1800s, *Journal of Interdisciplinary History* 17, 2:359–378.

Barbiero, G., S. Camponeschi, A. Femia, G. Greca, A. Tudini, and M. Vannozzi. 2003. *1980–1998 Material-input-based indicators time series and 1997 material balances of the Italian economy.* Rome: ISTAT.

Barfield, T. J. 1989. *The perilous frontier: Nomadic empires and China.* Oxford, UK: Blackwell Publishing.

Barjamovic, G. 2005. A historical geography of ancient Anatolia in the Assyrian Colony Period. Ph.D. dissertation, Copenhagen, Denmark: University of Copenhagen.

Barrett, L. 2000. Money matters: Doing business in Vanuatu, *Island Spirit* (12):11.

Barrow, C. J. 1985. The development of the várzeas (floodlands) of Brazilian Amazonia. In *Change in the Amazon basin.* J. Hemming, ed. Vol. 1. Manchester, UK: Manchester University Press, pp. 108–128.

Barth, F. 1969. *Ethnic groups and boundaries: The social organization of cultural difference.* Boston: Little, Brown.

Basso, E. B. 1973. *The Kalapalo Indians of central Brazil.* New York: Holt, Rinehart and Winston.

Bates, D. G., and S. H. Lees, eds. 1996. *Case studies in human ecology.* New York: Plenum Press.

Bateson, G. 1972a. From Versailles to cybernetics. In *Steps to an ecology of mind.* Frogmore, UK: Paladin, pp. 445–453.

———1972b. *Steps to an ecology of mind.* New York: Ballantine.

Batistella, M., S. Robeson, and E. F. Moran. 2003. Settlement design, forest fragmentation, and landscape change in Rondonia, Amazonia, *Photogrammetric Engineering and Remote Sensing* 69(7):805–812.

Beaglehole, James, ed. 1955. *The journals of Captain James Cook on his voyages of discovery.* Cambridge: Cambridge University Press.

Beaujard, P. 2005. The Indian Ocean in Eurasian and African world-systems before the sixteenth century, *Journal of World History* 16:4(Dec.):411–465.

Beckerman, S. 1977. The use of palms by Barí Indians of the Maracaibo Basin, *Principes* 21:143–154.

Becquelin, P., and D. Michelet. 1994. Demografía en la zona Puuc: El recurso del método, *Latin American Antiquity* 5:289–311.

Behling, H. 2002. Impact of the Holocene sea-level changes in coastal, eastern and central Amazonia, *Amazoniana* 17:41–52.

Behre, K. E., and D. Kucan. 1994. Die Geschichte der Kulturlandschaft und des Ackerbaus in der Siedlungskammer Flögeln, Niedersachsen, seit der Jungsteinzeit, *Probleme der Küstenforschung im südlichen Nordseegebiet* 21:1–228.

Bell, B. 1971. The dark ages in ancient history I: The first dark age in Egypt, *American Journal of Archeology* 75:1–26.

———1975. Climate and the history of Egypt: The Middle Kingdom, *American Journal of Archeology* 79:223–69.

Bell, M., and M. J. C. Walker. 1992. *Late quaternary environmental change: Physical and human perspectives.* Essex, UK: Longman Scientific and Technical.

Benenson, I., and P. M. Torrens. 2004. *Geosimulation. Automata-based modelling of urban phenomena.* Hoboken, NJ: John Wiley.

Bennett, E. L., and J. G. Robinson. 2000. Hunting of wildlife in tropical forests: Implications for biodiversity and forest peoples. Environmental Department Papers 76, Biodiversity Series-Impact Studies. Washington, DC: The World Bank.

Berglund, B. E. 1969. Vegetation and human influence in South Scandinavia during the prehistoric time, *Oikos Supplement* 12:9–28.

———1985. Early agriculture in Scandinavia: Research problems related to pollen-analytical studies, *Norwegian Archeological Review* 18:77–105.

———1986/2003 (ed.). *Handbook of Holocene palaeoecology and palaeohydrology.* Hoboken, NJ: John Wiley & Sons.

———1991 (ed.). The cultural landscape during 6000 years in southern Sweden, *Ecological Bulletins* 41, 495 pp.

———2000. The Ystad Project: A case study for multidisciplinary research on long-term human impact, *PAGES Newsletter* 8, 3:6–7.

———2003. Human impact and climate changes: Synchronous events and a causal link? *Quaternary International* 105:7–12.

Berglund, B. E., H. J. B. Birks, M. Ralska-Jasiewiczowa, and H. E. Wright, eds. 1996. *Palaeoecological events during the last 15,000 years: Regional syntheses of palaeoecological studies of lakes and mires in Europe.* Hoboken, NJ: John Wiley & Sons.

Berglund, B. E., and K. Börjesson, eds. 2002. *Markens minnen: Landskap och odlingshistoria på Småländska höglandet under 6000 år.* Stockholm: Riksantikvarieämbetet.

Berkes, F. 1999. *Sacred ecology: Traditional ecological knowledge and management systems.* New York: Anchor Books.

Berkes, F., J. Colding, and C. Folke, eds. 2003. *Navigating social-ecological systems: Building resilience for complexity and change.* Cambridge: Cambridge University Press.

Berkes, F., and C. Folke. 2002. Back to the future: Ecosystem dynamics and local knowledge. In *Panarchy: Understanding transformation in human and natural systems.* L. H. Gunderson and C. S. Holling, eds. Washington, DC: Island Press.

Bertram, I. G., and R. E. Watters. 1985. The MIRAB economy in South Pacific microstates, *Pacific Viewpoint* 26(3):497–519.

———1986. The MIRAB process: Earlier analysis in context, *Pacific Viewpoint* 27(1):47–59.

Bilsky, L. J., ed. 1980. *Historical ecology: Essays on environment and social change.* Port Washington, NY: Kennikat Press.

Biraben, J.-N. 1975. *Les Hommes et la peste en France et dans les pays européens et méditerranéens.* Paris: Mouton.

Birks, H. J. B. 1986. Late-quaternary biotic changes on terrestrial and lacustrine environments, with particular reference to northwest Europe. In *Handbook of Holocene palaeoecology and palaeohydrology.* 1986/2003. B. E. Berglund, ed. Hoboken, NJ: John Wiley & Sons.

Bjornstad, O. N., R. A. Ims, and X. Lambin. 1999. Spatial population dynamics: Analyzing patterns and processes of population synchrony, *Trends in Ecology and Evolution* 14:427–432.

Blaikie, P. M. 1994. *At risk: Natural hazards, people's vulnerability, and disasters.* London: Routledge.

Blaikie, P. M., and H. C. Brookfield. 1987. *Land degradation and society.* London: Methuen.

Blanco, R., and R. Chakraborty. 1975. Genetic distance analysis of twenty-two South American Indian populations, *Human Heredity* 25:177–193.

Blanton, R., S. Kowalewski, G. Feiman, and L. Finsten. 2003. *Ancient Mesoamerica.* Cambridge: Cambridge University Press.

Blum, W. E. H., and L. M. S. Magalhães. 1987. Restrições edáficas de solos na bacia sedimentar amazônica à utilização agrária. In *Homem e natureza na Amazônia.* G. Kohlhepp and A. Schrader, eds. *Tübinger Geographische Studien 95.* Geographischen Instituts der Universität Tübingen, pp. 83–92.

Boomert, A. 1987. Gifts of the Amazons: "Green stone" pendants and beads as items of ceremonial exchange in Amazonia and the Caribbean, *Antropologica* 67:33–54.

Boroffka, N. 1998. Bronze- und früheisenzeitlichen Geweihtrensenknebel aus Rumänien und ihre Beziehungen, Eurasia Antiqua, *Zeitschrift für Archäologie Eurasiens* 4:81–135.

Boroffka, N., and Sava, E. 1998. Zu den steinernen "Zeptern/Stössel-Zeptern," "Miniaturesäulen" und "Phalli" der bronzezeitlichen Eurasiens, *Archäologische Mitteilungen aus Iran und Turan* 30:17–113.

Boserup, E. 1965. *The conditions of agricultural growth: The economics of agrarian change under population pressure.* London: G. Allen & Unwin.

———1966. *Population and technological change: A study of long-term trends.* Chicago: University of Chicago Press.

Bosworth, A. 1995. World cities and world economic cycles. In *Civilizations and world systems: Studying world-historical change.* S. K. Sanderson, ed. Walnut Creek, CA: AltaMira Press, pp. 206–227.

Bouamrane, M. 1993. Conclusions and recommendations of the 'Islands 2000' conference, *Insula* (1):4–6.

Boulding, K. 1973. Foreword. In *The images of the future.* Polak, F., ed. Amsterdam: Elsevier.

Bourdieu, P. 1977. *Outline of a theory of practice.* Cambridge: Cambridge University Press.

Box, G. E. P., and G. M. Jenkins. 1976. *Time series analysis: Forecasting and control.* Oakland, CA: Holden Day.

Boyle, K., C. Renfrew, and M. Levine, eds. 2002. *Ancient interactions: East and west in Eurasia.* Cambridge, UK: McDonald Institute Monographs.

Bringezu, S., H. Schutz, S. Steger, and J. Baudisch. 2004. International comparison of resource use and its relation to economic growth: The development of total material requirement, direct material inputs and hidden flows and the structure of TMR, *Ecological Economics* 51(1–2):97–124.

Brochado, J. J. J. P. 1984. An ecological model of the spread of pottery and agriculture into eastern South America. Ph.D. thesis. University of Illinois at Urbana-Champaign.

Broecker, W. S. 1991. The great ocean conveyor belt, *Oceanography* 4:79.

Brondizio, E. S. In press. *Small farmers in the global market: Caboclo agroforestry, commodity chains, and land use in the Amazon estuary.* New York: Botanical Garden Press.

Brondizio, E. S., E. F. Moran, P. Mausel, and Y. Wu. 1994. Land-use change in the Amazon Estuary: Patterns of Caboclo settlement and landscape management, *Human Ecology* 2(3):249–278.

———1996. Land cover in the Amazon Estuary: Linking of the thematic mapper with botanical and historical data, *Photogrammetric Engineering and Remote Sensing,* 62(8):921–929.

Brosius, J. P. 2001. The politics of ethnographic presence: Sites and topologies in the study of transnational movements. In *New directions in anthropology and environment: Intersections.* C. L. Crumley, ed. Walnut Creek, CA: AltaMira Press, pp. 150–176.

Browder, J. O. 1989. *Fragile lands of Latin America.* Boulder, CO: Westview Press.

Browman, D. L. 1980. Tiwanaku expansion and altiplano economic patterns, *Estudios Arqueológicos* 5:107–120.

Brown, R. P. C. 1998. Do migrants' remittances decline over time? Evidence from Tongans and Western Samoans in Australia, *The Contemporary Pacific* 10(1):107–151.

Budyko, M. I. 1980. *Global ecology.* Moscow: Progress Publishers.

Bunker, S. G. 1985. *Underdeveloping the Amazon: Extraction, unequal exchange, and the failure of the modern state.* Chicago: Chicago University Press

Bunyatyan, K. P. 2003. Correlations between agriculture and pastoralism in the northern Pontic steppe area during the Bronze Age. In *Prehistoric steppe adaptations and the horse.* M. Levine, C. Renfrew, and K. Boyle, eds. Cambridge, UK: McDonald Institute Monographs, pp. 269–287

Burch, E. S., Jr. 2005. *Alliance and conflict: A world system of the Iñupiaq Eskimos.* Lincoln, NB: University of Nebraska Press.

Burger, R. L. 1992. *Chavín and the origins of Andean civilization.* London: Thames and Hudson.

Burgess, R. L., and L. Jacobson. 1984. Archeological sediments from a shell midden near Wortel Dam, Walvis Bay, Southern Africa, *Palaeoecology of Africa* 16:429–435.

Burmeister, S. ed. 2004. *Rad und Wagen. Der Ursprung einer Innovation. Wagen im vorderen Orient und Europa.* Mainz: Verlag Phillip von Zabern.

Burns, T. J., D. L. Byron, and E. L. Kick. 1997. Position in the world-system and national emissions of greenhouse gases, *Journal of World-Systems Research* 3(3):432–466.

Burton, M., C. C. Moore, J. W. M. Whiting, and A. K. Romney. 1996. Regions based on social structure, *Current Anthropology* 37(1):87–123.

Butt, A. J. 1977. Land use and social organization of tropical forest peoples of the Guianas. In *Human ecology in the tropics.* J. P. Garlick and R. W. J. Keay, eds. London: Taylor and Francis Ltd, pp. 1–17.

Butzer, K. W. 1976. *The early hydraulic civilization in Egypt: A study in cultural ecology.* Chicago: University of Chicago Press.

———1995. Environmental change in the Near East and human impact on the land. In *Civilizations of the ancient Near East,* Vol. 1. J. M. Sasson, ed. New York: Simon and Schuster.

———1997. Sociopolitical discontinuity in the Near East c. 2200 B.C.E.: Scenarios from Palestine and Egypt. In *Third millennium B.C.E. climate change and old world collapse,* H. N. Dalfes, G. Kulka, and H. Wiess, eds. Berlin: Springer-Verlag. pp. 245–296.

———2005. Environmental History in the Mediterranean World: Cross-Disciplinary Investigation of Cause-and-Effect for Degradation and Soil Erosion, *Journal of Archaeological Science* 32:1773-1800.

Campbell, L. 1997. *American Indian languages: The historical linguistics of native America.* Oxford: Oxford University Press.

Cancian, F. 1965. *Economics and prestige in a Maya community: The religious cargo system in Zincantan.* Stanford, CA: Stanford University Press.

———1976. Social stratification, *Annual Review of Anthropology* 9578:227–248.

Capra, F. 1996. *The web of life.* New York: Anchor/Doubleday.

Carneiro, R. L. 1970. A theory of the origin of the state, *Science* 169:733–738.

Carvalho, J. C. M. 1952. Notas de viagem ao Rio Negro. *Publicaçoes Avulsas 9.* Museu Nacional, Rio de Janeiro.

Castellano, H. 2001. *Material flow analysis in Venezuela,* unpublished.

Catton, W. R., Jr. 1980. *Overshoot: The ecological basis for revolutionary change.* Urbana, IL: University of Illinois Press.

Cavalli-Sforza, L. L., P. Menozzi, and A. Piazza. 1994. *The history and geography of human genes.* Princeton, NJ: Princeton University Press.

Chapman, J. 2002. Domesticating the exotic: The context of Cucuteni-Tripolye exchange with the steppe and forest-steppe Communities. In *Ancient interactions: East and west in Eurasia.* K. Boyle, C. Renfrew, and M. Levine, eds. McDonald Monographs, Cambridge, UK: Cambridge University Press.

Chase-Dunn, C. ed. In press. *The rise and fall of Bronze Age civilizations.* Ms. In preparation for publication.

Chase-Dunn, C., and T. Boswell. 2002. Transnational social movements and democratic socialist parties in the semi-periphery. Presented at the meetings of the California Sociological Association, Riverside, CA. October 19. http://irows.ucr. edu/papers/csa02/csa02.htm.

Chase-Dunn, C., and T. D. Hall. 1991. *Core/Periphery relations in pre-capitalist worlds.* Boulder, CO: Westview Press.

———1995. Cross-world-system comparisons. In *Civilizations and world systems: Studying world-historical change.* S. K. Sanderson, ed. Walnut Creek, CA: AltaMira Press, pp. 109–135.

————1997. Rise and demise: *Comparing world-systems*. Boulder, CO: Westview Press.

————1998 Ecological degradation and the evolution of world systems, *Journal of World Systems Research* 3:403–431.

————2000. Comparing world-systems to explain social evolution. In *World system history: The social science of long-term change*. R. Denemark, J. Friedman, B. K. Gills, and G. Modelski, eds. London: Routledge, pp. 86–111.

————2001. City and empire growth/decline sequences in ancient Mesopotamian and Egyptian world-systems. Presented at the annual meetings of the International Studies Association, Chicago, February 24.

————2002. Paradigms bridged: Institutional materialism and world systemic evolution. In *Structure, culture, and history: Recent issues in social theory*. S. C. Chew and J. D. Knotterus, eds. Lanham, MD: Rowman and Littlefield, pp. 197–216.

Chase-Dunn, C., ed. In press. *The rise and fall of Bronze Age civilizations*. Ms. In preparation for publication.

Chase-Dunn, C., Y. Kawano, and B. Brewer. 2000. Trajectories of globalization since 1800: Cycles of world-system integration, *American Sociological Review* 65:77–95 (February).

Chase-Dunn, C., and K. M. Mann. 1998. *The Wintu and their neighbors: A very small world-system in northern California*. Tucson, AZ: The University of Arizona Press.

Chase-Dunn, C., and E. S. Manning. 2002. City systems and world-systems: Four millennia of city growth and decline, *Cross-Cultural Research* 36(4):379–398.

Chase-Dunn, C., S. Manning, and T. D. Hall. 2000. Rise and fall: East-west synchrony and Indic exceptionalism examined, *Social Science History* 24(4):727–754.

Chen, X., and L. Qiao. 2001. A preliminary material input analysis of China, *Population and Environment* 23(1):117–126.

Cheney, J. 1989. The neo-stoicism of radical environmentalism, *Environmental Ethics* 11:293–325.

Chernykh, E. N. 1992. *Ancient metallurgy in the USSR: New studies in archeology*. Cambridge: Cambridge University Press.

————2002. Ancient mining and metallurgical production on the border between Europe and Asia: The Kargaly center, *Archeology, Ethnology and Anthropology of Eurasia* 3(11):88–106.

Chernykh, E. N., E. E. Antipina, and E. J. Lebedeva. 1998. Produktionsformen der Urgesellschaft in den Steppen Osteuropas (Ackerbau, Viehzucht, Erzgegwinnung und Verhüttung). In *Das Karpatenbecken und die Osteuropäsichen Steppe*. B. Hänsel and J. Machnik, eds. München: Verlag Marie Leidorf, pp. 233–254.

Chernykh, E. N., L. I. Avilova, and L. B. Orlovskaya. 2002. Metallurgy of the Circumpontic Area: From unity to disintegration, *Der Anschnitt. Zeitschrift für Kunst und Kultur im Bergbau*, Beifheft 15:83–100. Anatolian Metal II.

Chernykh, E. N., and Kuzminykh, S. V. 1989. *Ancient metallurgy in the northern Eurasia (Seyma-Turbino Phenomon)*. Moscow: Academy of Sciences of the USSR, Institute of Archeology.

Chew, S. C. 2001. *World ecological degradation: Accumulation, urbanization, and deforestation 3000 B.C.–A. D. 2000*. Walnut Creek, CA: AltaMira Press.

———2002a. Globalization, ecological crisis, and dark ages, *Global Society* 16(4):333–356.

———2002b. Ecology in command. In *Structure, culture, and theory*. S. C. Chew and J. D. Knotterus, eds. Lanham, MD: Rowman and Littlefield, pp. 217–229.

Chomitz, K. M., and D. A. Gray. 1996. Roads, land use, and deforestation: A spatial model applied to Belize, *The World Bank Economic Review* 10:487–512.

Christensen, C. 1995. The Littorina transgressions in Denmark. In *Man and sea in the Mesolithic: Coastal settlement above and below present sea level*. A. Fischer, ed. Oxbow Monograph, Oxford, 53:15–22.

Christensen, P. 1993. *The decline of Iranshahr*. Copenhagen: Museum Tusculanum Press, University of Copenhagen.

Clark, K., and C. Uhl. 1987. Farming, fishing, and fire in the history of the upper Rio Negro region of Venezuela, *Human Ecology* 15:1–26.

Clark, R. P. 1997. *The global imperative: An interpretive history of the spread of humankind*. Boulder, CO: Westview Press.

Clark, W. C., et al. 2003. Assessing vulnerability to global environmental risks. Workshop on Vulnerability to Global Environmental Change: Challenges for Research, Assessment and Decision Making. Airlie House, Warrenton, VA: Belfer Center for Science and International Affairs Discussion Paper 2000–12, Environmental and Natural Resources Program, Kennedy School of Government, Harvard University.

Clastres, P. 1987. *Society against the state: Essays in political anthropology*. New York: Zone Books.

Climo, J., and M. Cattell, eds. 2002. *Social memory and history: Anthropological perspectives*. Walnut Creek, CA: AltaMira Press.

Cochrane, M. A. 2001. Synergistic interactions between habitat fragmentation and fire in evergreen tropical forests, *Conservation Biology* 15(6):1515–1521.

Cochrane, M. A., A. Alencar, M. D. Schulze, C. M. Souza Jr., D. C. Nepstad, P. Lefebvre, and E. Davidson. 1999. Positive feedbacks in the fire dynamic of closed canopy tropical forests, *Science* 284:1832–1835.

Cochrane, M. A., and W. F. Laurance. 2002. Fire as a large-scale edge effect in Amazonian forests, *Journal of Tropical Ecology* 18:311–325.

Cohen, J., and I. Stewart 1994. *The collapse of chaos*. London: Penguin Books.

Cole, J. E., R. B. Dunbar, T. R. McClanahan, and N. A. Muthiga. 2000. Tropical pacific forcing of decadal SST variability in the western Indian Ocean over the past two centuries, *Science* 287:617–619.

Colson, A. B. 1983–1984. The spatial component in the political structure of Carib speakers of the Guiana Highlands: Kapon and Pemon, *Antropológica* 59–62:73–124.

Condliffe, J. B. 1950. *The commerce of nations.* New York: Norton.

Conklin, B. A. 2001. *Consuming grief: Compassionate cannibalism in an Amazonian society.* Austin, TX: University of Texas Press.

Connerton, P. 1989. *How societies remember.* New York: Cambridge University Press.

Costanza, R., and M. Ruth. 1998. Using dynamic modelling to scope environmental problems and build consensus, *Environmental Management* 22:183–195.

Couclelis, H. 2002. Why I no longer work with agents: A challenge for ABMs of human–environment interactions. In *Agent-based models of land-use and land-cover change,* D. C. Parker, T. Berger, and S. M. Manson, eds. Report and Review of an International Workshop, October 4–7, 2001, LUCC Report Series no. 6. LUCC Focus 1 Office, Indiana University, pp. 3–6.

Coulthard, T. J., J. Lewin, and M. G. Macklin. 2005. Modelling differential catchment response to environmental change, *Geomorphology* 69:222–241.

Coulthard, T. J., M. G. Macklin, and M. J. Kirkby. 2002. Simulating upland river catchment and alluvial fan evolution. *Earth Surface Processes and Landforms* 27:269–288.

Crews-Meyer, K. A. 2001. Assessing landscape change and population-environment interactions via panel analysis, *Geocarto International* 16(4):69–79.

Crocombe, R. 2001. *The South Pacific.* Suva: Institute of Pacific Studies, University of the South Pacific.

Cronon, W. 1992. A place for stories: Nature, history and narrative, *The Journal of American History* 78:1347–1376.

Crosby, A. W. 1986. *Ecological imperialism: The biological expansion of Europe, 900–1900.* Cambridge: Cambridge University Press.

————2003. *America's forgotten pandemic: The influenza of 1918.* New edition. Cambridge: Cambridge University Press.

Crumley, C. L. 1979. Three locational models: An epistemological assessment for anthropology and archeology. In *Advances in archeological method and theory.* Michael B. Schiffer, ed. New York: Columbia University Press, pp. 141–173.

————1987a. Celtic settlement before the conquest: The dialectics of landscape and power. In *Regional dynamics: Burgundian landscapes in historical perspective.* San Diego: Academic Press.

————1987b. A dialectical critique of hierarchy. In *Power relations and state formation.* T. C. Patterson and C. Ward Gailey, eds. Washington, DC: American Anthropological Association, pp. 155–168.

————1993. Analyzing historic ecotonal shifts, *Ecological Applications* 3(3):377–384.

————1994a. ed. *Historical ecology: Cultural knowledge and changing landscapes.* Santa Fe, NM: School of American Research Press.

————1994b. The ecology of conquest: Contrasting agropastoral and agricultural societies' adaptation to climatic change. In *Historical ecology: Cultural knowledge and changing landscapes.* C. L. Crumley, ed. Santa Fe, NM: School of American Research Press., pp. 183–201.

————1995a. Heterarchy and the analysis of complex societies. In *Heterarchy and the analysis of complex societies*. R. M. Ehrenreich, C. L. Crumley, and J. E. Levy, eds. Archeological Papers of the American Anthropological Association no. 6. Washington, DC: American Anthropological Association, pp. 1–5.

————1995b. Building an historical ecology of Gaulish polities. In *Celtic chiefdom, Celtic state*. B. Gibson and B. Arnold, eds. Cambridge: Cambridge University Press, pp. 26–33.

————1998. Foreword. *Advances in historical ecology*. W. Balée, ed. New York: Columbia University Press, pp. ix–xiv.

————2000. From garden to globe: Linking time and space with meaning and memory. In *The way the wind blows: Climate, history, and human action*. R. J. McIntosh, J. A. Tainter, and S. K. McIntosh, eds. New York: Columbia University Press, pp. 193–208.

————2001a. Communication, holism, and the evolution of sociopolitical complexity. In *Leaders to rulers: The development of political centralization*. J. Haas, ed. New York: Plenum, pp. 19–33.

————2001b, ed. *New directions in anthropology and environment: Intersections*. Walnut Creek, CA: AltaMira Press.

————2001c. Archeology in the new world order: What we can offer the planet. In *An odyssey of space: Proceedings of the 2001 Chacmool conference*. Calgary: University of Calgary Press.

————2003a. Alternative forms of societal order. In *Heterarchy, political economy, and the ancient Maya: The Three Rivers region of the east central Yucatan Peninsula*. V. L. Scarborough, F. Valdez Jr., and N. Dunning, eds. Tucson: The University of Arizona Press.

————2003b. Historical ecology: A scheme for disaster preparedness and the re-interpretation of heritage resources. In *Association for preservation technology bulletin*. Albany, NY: Mount Ida Press.

————2003c. Historical ecology: Analyzing landscapes at multiple temporal and spatial scales. Paper presented at the Conference on Urban Landscape Dynamics and Resource Use, Uppsala, Sweden, August 28–31, 2003.

Crumley, C. L., and W. H. Marquardt, eds. 1987. Regional dynamics in Burgundy. In *Regional dynamics: Burgundian landscapes in historical perspective*. C. L. Crumley and W. H. Marquardt, eds. San Diego: Academic Press, pp. 609–623.

Cruxent, J. M., and M. Kamen-Kaye. 1950. Reconocimiento del área del Alto Orinoco, ríos Sipapo y Autana, en el Territorio Federal Amazonas, Venezuela, *Memoria de la Sociedad de Ciencias Naturales La Salle* 10(26):11–23.

Culbert, T. P. 1988. The collapse of classic Maya civilization. In *The collapse of ancient states and civilizations*. N. Yoffee and G.L. Cowgill, eds. Tucson, AZ: University of Arizona Press, pp. 69–101.

Daily, G., T. Söderqvist, S. Aniyar, K. Arrow, P. Dasgupta, P. R. Ehrlich, C. Folke, A. Hansson, B. O. Jansson, N. Kautsky, S. Levin, J. Lubchenco, K. G. Mäler, D. Simpson, D. Starrett, D. Tilman, and B. Walker. 2000. The value of nature and nature of value, *Science* 289:395–396.

Dale, V. H., R. V. O'Neill, F. Southworth, and M. Pedlowski. 1994. Modeling effects of land management in the Brazilian Amazonian settlement of Rondonia, *Conservation Biology* 8:196–206.

Daniels, P. L., and S. Moore. 2001. Approaches for quantifying the metabolism of physical economies, part I: Methodological overview, *Journal of Industrial Ecology* 5(4):69–93.

Danielsson, B., and M.-T. Danielsson. 1986. *Poisoned reign: French nuclear colonialism in the Pacific.* New York: Penguin.

David, W. 1997. Altbronzezeitliche Beinobjekte des Karpatenbeckens mit Spiralwirbel– oder Wellenbandornamnet und ihre Parallellen auf der Peloponnes und in Anatolien in frühmykenischer Zeit. In *The Thracian world at the crossroads of civilizations.* P. Roman, ed. Bucharest: Institutul Roma de Thracologie, pp. 247–305.

———2001. Zu den Beziehungen zwischen Donau-Karpatenraum, osteuropäischen Steppengebieten und ägäisch-anatolischen Raum zur Zeit der mykenischen Schachtgräber unter Berücksichtigung neuerer Funde aus Südbayern. Anados. *Studies of Ancient World* 1:51–80.

Davis, M. 2001. *Late Victorian holocausts: El Niño famines and the making of the Third World.* New York: Verso.

Day, J. V. 2001. *Indo-European origins: The anthropological evidence.* Washington, DC: The Institute for the Study of Man.

Dean, J. S., et al. 1999. Understanding Anasazi culture change through agent-based modeling. In *Dynamics in human and primate societies.* T. Kohler and G. Gumerman, eds. Oxford: Oxford University Press, pp. 179–205.

Dearing, J. A. 2006. Human-environment interactions: Learning from the past. In *Integrated history and future of people on Earth.* R. Costanza, L. Graumlich, and W. Steffen, eds. Dahlem Workshop Report 96. Cambridge, MA: The MIT Press.

Dearing, J. A., R. W. Battarbee, R. Dikau, I. Larocque, and F. Oldfield. 2006a. Human–environment interactions: Towards synthesis and simulation, *Regional Environmental Change* 6:1–16.

———2006b. Human–environment interactions: Learning from the past, *Regional Environmental Change* 6:115–123.

Dearing, J. A., R. T. Jones, S. Ji, X. Yang, J. F. Boyle, G. Foster, D. S. Crook, and M. Elvin. In prep. In Centennial human–environment interactions in sub-tropical south-west China: A case-study from the Erhai Lake catchment Yunnan Province.

Dearing, J. A., N. Richmond, A. J. Plater, J. Wolf, D. Prandle, and T. J. Coulthard. 2006c. Models for coastal simulation based on cellular automata: The need and potential, *Philosophical Transactions of the Royal Society of London,* Series A. 364:1051–1071.

de Bruyn, S. M., and J. Opschoor. 1997. Developments in the throughput-income relationship: Theoretical and empirical observations, *Ecological Economics* 20(3):255–268.

de Carvajal, G. 1934. Discovery of the Orellana River. In *The discovery of the Amazon according to the accounts of friar Gaspar de Carvajal and other documents*. H. C. Heaton, ed. New York: American Geographical Society, pp. 167–235.

deFries, R., C. Field, I. Fung, G. Collatz, and L. Bounoua. 1999. Combining satellite data and biogeochemical models to estimate global effects of human-induced land cover change on carbon emissions and primary productivity, *Global Biogeochemical Cycles* 13(3):803–815.

deFries, R. S., C. B. Field, I. Fung, C. O. Justice, S. Los, P. A. Matson, E. Matthews, H. A. Mooney, C. S. Potter, K. Prentice, P. J. Sellers, J. R. G. Townshend, C. J. Tucker, S. L. Ustin, and P. M.Vitousek. 1995. Mapping the land surface for global atmosphere-biosphere models: Toward continuous distributions of vegetation's functional properties, *Journal of Geophysical Res. Atmos.* 100 (D10):20867–20882.

deFries, R., R. A. Houghton, M. C. Hansen, C. B. Field, D. Skole, and J. Townshend. 2002. Carbon emissions from tropical deforestation and regrowth based on satellite observations for the 1980s and 1990s, *Proceedings of the National Academy of Sciences (USA)*, 99(22): 14256–14261.

de Landa, M. 1997. *A thousand years of nonlinear history*. New York: Zone Books/ Swerve Editions.

de Marco, O., G. Lagioia, and M. Pizzoli. 2000. Materials flow analysis of the Italian economy, *Journal of Industrial Ecology* 4(2):55–70.

de Menocal, P. 2001. Cultural responses to climate change during the Late Holocene, *Science* 292:667–673.

Denemark, R. A. 2000. Cumulation and direction in world system history. In *World system history: The social science of long-term change*. R. A. Denemark, J. Friedman, B. K. Gills, and G. Modelski, eds. London: Routledge, pp. 299–312.

Denevan, W. M. 1992. Stone vs. metal axes: The ambiguity of shifting cultivation in prehistoric Amazonia, *Journal of the Steward Anthropological Society* 20:153–165.

———2001. *Cultivated landscapes of native Amazonia and the Andes*. Oxford: Oxford University Press.

———2004. Semi-intensive pre-European cultivation and the origins of anthropogenic Dark Earths in Amazonia. In *Amazonian Dark Earths: Explorations in space and time*. B. Glaser and W. I. Woods, eds. Berlin: Springer-Verlag, pp. 135–143.

Denevan, W. M., and A. Zucchi. 1978. Ridged-field excavations in the central Orinoco Llanos, Venezuela. In *Advances in Andean archeology*. D. L. Browman, ed. Paris: Mouton Publishers, pp. 235–245.

Depew, D. J., and B. H. Weber. 1995. *Darwinism evolving: Systems dynamics and the genealogy of natural selection*. Cambridge, MA: The MIT Press.

Dergachev, V. 2000. The migration theory of Marija Gimbutas, *Journal of Indo-European Studies* 28(3–4):257–319.

Descola, P. 1981. From scattered to nucleated settlement: A process of socioeconomic change among the Achuar. In *Cultural transformations and ethnicity in modern Ecuador*. N. Whitten, ed. Urbana, IL: University of Illinois Press, pp. 614–646.

————1988. La selva culta: simbolismo y praxis en la ecologia de los Achuar. Quito: Ediciones Abya-Yala.

Descola, P., 1989. *La selva culta: simbolismo y praxis en la ecología de los Achuar.* Lima.

————1994a. Homeostasis as a cultural system: The Jívaro case. In *Amazonian Indians from prehistory to the present: Anthropological perspectives.* A. C. Roosevelt, ed. Tucson, AZ: The University of Arizona Press, pp. 203–224.

————1994b. *In the society of nature: A native ecology in Amazonia.* New York: Cambridge University Press.

————1996. *The spears of twilight: Life and death in the Amazon jungle.* New York: The New Press.

DETR/ONS/WI. 2001. *Total material resource flows of the United Kingdom* (revised and updated 2002 by ONS). Department of Environment, Transport and the Regions of the UK, Office for National Statistics of the UL, Wuppertal Institute.

Devezas, T., and G. Modelski. 2003. Power, law, behaviour and world system evolution: A millennial learning process, *Technological Forecasting and Social Change* October:1–41.

de Vries, B., and J. Goudsblom, eds. 2002. Mappae Mundi: Humans and their habitats in a long-term socio-ecological perspective. In *Myths, maps, and models.* Amsterdam: Amsterdam University Press.

de Vries, B., M. Thompson, and K. Wirtz. 2002. Understanding: Fragments of a unifying perspective. In *Myths, maps, and models.* B. De Vries and J. Goudsblom, eds. Amsterdam: Amsterdam University Press.

de Vries, D. H. 2002. Monitoring dynamic human–environmental systems: A historical and political ecological critique on the role of baseline analyses. Paper presented at the 2002 Berlin Conference on the Human Dimensions of Global Environmental Change and the 2002 Annual Convention of the Environmental Policy and Global Change Section of the German Political Science Association.

————2005. Choosing your baseline carefully: Integrating historical and political ecology in the evaluation of environmental intervention projects, *Journal of Ecological Anthropology* 9:35–50.

de Vries, P., and H. Seur. 1997. *Moruroa and us.* Lyon: Centre de Documentation et de Recherche sur la Paix et les Conflits.

Diakonoff, I. 1982. The structure of Near Eastern society before the middle of the second millennium B.C., *Oikemene* 3:1–100.

Diamond, J. 1997. *Guns, germs, and steel: The fates of human societies.* New York: W.W. Norton.

————2005. *Collapse: How societies choose to fail or succeed.* London: Allen Lane/ Viking.

Díaz del Rio, P., P. López Garcia, J.-A. López Sáez, M. I. Martinez Navarette, A. L. Rodriguez Alcalde, S. Rovira-Llorens, J. M. Vicent García, and I. De Zavala Morencos 2006. Understanding the productive economy during the Bronze Age through archaeometallurgical and palaeo-environmental research at Kargaly (southern Urals, Orenburg, Russia). In *Beyond the steppe and the sown.* D. L. Peterson, L. M. Popova, and A. T. Smith, eds. Proceedings of the 2002 University of Chicago Conference on Eurasian Archaeology. Colloquia Pontica. Series on the Archeology and Ancient History of the Black Sea Area. Leiden and Boston: Brill Academic Publishers.

Digerfeldt, G., and S. Welinder. 1988. The prehistoric cultural landscape in southwest Sweden, *Acta Archeologica* 58:127–136.

di Gregorio, A., and L. J. M. Jansen. 2000. *Land cover classification system*. Rome: FAO.

Dixon, R. M. W., and A. Y. Aikhenvald, eds. 1999a. *The Amazonian languages*. Cambridge: Cambridge University Press.

———1999b. Introduction. In *The Amazonian languages*. R. M. W. Dixon and A. Y. Aikhenvald, eds. Cambridge: Cambridge University Press, pp. 1–21.

Dolukanov, P. 1994. *Environment and ethnicity in the ancient Middle East*. Avebury, UK: Worldwide Archeology Series.

Döös, B. R. 2002. Population growth and loss of arable land, *Global Environmental Change* 12(4):303–311.

Douglas, M. 1973. *Natural symbols: Explorations in cosmology*. New York: Vintage Books.

Drews, R. 1988. *The coming of the Greeks: Indo-European conquests in the Aegean and the Near East*. Princeton: Princeton University Press.

Duster, T. 1996. The prism of heritability and the sociology of knowledge. In *Naked science: Anthropological inquiry into boundaries, power, and knowledge*. L. Nader, ed. London: Routledge, pp. 119–130.

Dzieduszycka-Machnik, A., and J. Machnik 1990. Die Möglichkeiten der Erforschung der sozialen Struktur frühbronzezeitlicher Menschengruppen in Kleinpolen–am Beispiel der Nekropole in Iwanowice. *Godisniak, Knjiga XXVII*, Centar za Balkanoloska Ispitivanja, Knjiga 26. Sarajevo, 185–196.

Earle, T. 2001. Institutionalization in chiefdoms: Why landscapes are built. In *From leaders to rulers*. J. Haas, ed. Dordrecht: Kluwer Academic/Plenum Publishers, pp. 105–124.

Eckmann, J.-P., and D. Ruelle. 1985. Ergodic theory of chaos and strange attractors, *Review of Modern Physics* 57:617–656.

Ecsedy, I. 1994. Camps for eternal rest: Some aspects of the burials of the earliest nomads of the steppe. In *The archeology of the steppes: Methods and strategies*. B. Genito, ed. Papers from an international symposium held in Naples, Italy, 9–12 November 1992, pp. 167–177.

Eden, M. J. 1974. Ecological aspects of development among Piaroa and Guahibo Indians of the upper Orinoco basin, *Antropológica* 39:25–56.

Egan, D., and E. A. Howell, eds. 2001. *The historical ecology handbook: A restorationist's guide to reference ecosystems*. Washington, DC: Island Press.

Ehrenreich, R. M., C. L. Crumley, and J. E. Levy, eds. 1995. *Heterarchy and the analysis of complex societies*. Archeological Papers of the American Anthropological Association no. 6. Washington, DC: American Anthropological Association.

Eisenmenger, N. 2002. Internationaler Handel und globale Umweltveränderungen.

Kann eine Verbindung der Welt-System Theorie mit dem Konzept des gesellschaftlichen Metabolismus zu einem besseren Verständnis beitragen? *Kurswechsel* 4:87–99.

Ekholm, K. 1976. Om studiet av det globala systemets dynamik, *Antropologiska Studier* 14:15–23.

———1980. On the limitations of civilization: The structure and dynamics of global systems, *Dialectical Anthropology* 5:155-166.

———2005. Structure, dynamics and the final collapse of Bronze Age civilizations in the second millennium B.C. In *Declining hegemonies: Present and past.* J. Friedman and C. Chase-Dunn, eds. Boulder, CO: Paradigm Press, pp. 51–87.

Ekholm, K., and J. Friedman. 1979. "Capital," imperialism and exploitation in ancient world systems. In *Power and propaganda: A symposium on ancient empires.* M. T. Larsen, ed. Copenhagen. Republished with postscript as chapter in A. G. Frank and B. Gills, eds. 1993. *The world system: Five hundred years or five thousand.* New York: Routledge.

———1980. Towards a global anthropology. In *History and underdevelopment.* L. Blussé, H. Wesseling, and C. Winius, eds. Leiden and Paris: Center for the Study of European Expansion, pp. 61–76.

———1982. "Capital" imperialism and exploitation in ancient world systems, *Reviews in Anthropology* 4:87–109.

Ellen, R. 1982. *Environment, subsistence, system: The ecology of small scale social formations.* Cambridge: Cambridge University Press.

Elton, C. S. 1924. Periodic fluctuations in the number of animals: Their causes and effects, *British Journal of Experimental Biology* 2:119–163.

Elvin, M., et al. 2002. The impact of clearance and irrigation on the environment in the Lake Erhai catchment from the ninth to the nineteenth century, *East Asian History* 23:1–60.

Emanuelsson, U. 1988. A model for describing the development of the cultural landscape. In *The cultural landscape: Past, present and future.* H. H. Birks, H. J. B. Birks, P. E. Kaland, and D. Moe, eds. Cambridge: Cambridge University Press, 111–121.

Emanuelsson, U., and J. Möller. 1990. Flooding in Scania: A method to overcome the deficiency of nutrients in agriculture during the nineteenth century, *Agricultural History Review* 38.

Enckell, P. H., and E.-S. Königsson. 1979. Ecological instability of a Roman Iron Age human community, *Oikos* 33:328–349.

Engedal, Ø. 2002. *The nordic scimitar: Exernal relations and the creation of elite ideology.* Okrod, UK: British Archeological Reports International Series 1050.

Erickson, C. L. 2000. The Lake Titicaca Basin: A Precolumbian built landscape. In *Imperfect balance: Landscape transformations in the Precolumbian Americas.* D. L. Lentz, ed. New York: Columbia University Press, pp. 311–356.

———2003. Historical ecology and future explorations. In *Amazonian Dark Earths: Origin, properties, management.* J. Lehmann et al., eds. Dordrecht: Kluwer Academic Publishers, pp. 455–500.

Erikson, P. 1993. Une Nébuleuse compacte: Le Macro-ensemble pano. In *La Remontée de l'Amazone: Anthropologie et histoire des sociétés amazoniennes*. P. Descola and A. C. Taylor, eds. *L'Homme* 126–128, XXXIII (2–4):45–58.

Escobar, A. 1999. After nature: Steps to an antiessentialist political ecology, *Current Anthropology* 40:1–16.

ETC-WMF. 2003. *Zero study: Resource use in European countries. An estimate of materials and waste streams in the community, including imports and exports using the instrument of material flow analysis.* S. Moll, S. Bringezu, and H. Schütz, eds. Copenhagen: European Topic Centre on Waste and Material Flows (ETC-WMF).

EUROSTAT. 1999. *The policy relevance of material flow accounts.* Working Paper No. 2/1999/B/1. Luxembourg: EUROSTAT.

———2001. *Economy-wide material flow accounts and derived indicators: A methodological guide.* Luxembourg: Eurostat, European Commission, Office for Official Publications of the European Communities, pp. 1–92.

———2002. *Material use in the European Union 1980–2000: Indicators and analysis.* H. Weisz, M. Fischer-Kowalski, C. Amann, N. Eisenmenger, K. Hubacek, and F. Krausmann, eds. Luxembourg: EUROSTAT, Office for Official Publications of the European Communities.

Evans, C., and B. J. Meggers. 1960. Archeological investigations in British Guiana, *Bureau of American Ethnology* Bul. 177. Washington, DC: Smithsonian Institution.

Evans, C., B. J. Meggers, and J. M. Cruxent. 1960. Preliminary results of archeological investigations along the Orinoco and Ventuari Rivers, Venezuela. Actas del 33° Congreso Internacional de Americanistas, San José, Costa Rica, pp. 359–369.

Ezzo, J., C. M. Johnson, and T. D. Price. 1997. Analytical perspectives on prehistoric migration: A case study from east-central Arizona, *Journal of Archeological Science* 24:447–466.

Fagan, B. 1999. *Floods, famines and emperors: El Niño and the fate of civilizations.* New York: Basic Books.

Fairbridge, R., O. Erol, M. Karaca, and Y. Yilmaz. 1997. Background to mid-Holocene climate change in Anatolia and adjacent regimes. In *Third millennium B.C. climate change and Old World collapse.* H. N. Dalfes, G. Kukla, and H. Weiss, eds. Berlin: Springer-Verlag.

Fajardo, G., and W. Torres. 1987. Ticuna. In *Introducción a la Colombia Amerindia.* Bogotá, Instituto Colombiano de Antropología, pp. 165–175.

FAO. 2002. *FAO-STAT 2001 statistical database.* Rome: FAO, CD-Rom and www.fao.org.

Fearnside, P. M. 1986. *Human carrying capacity of the Brazilian rain forest.* New York: Columbia University Press.

———1990. Estimation of human carrying capacity in rainforest areas, *Trends in Ecology & Evolution* 5:192–196.

Fearnside, P. M., and N. L. Filho. 2001. Soil and development in Amazonia. In *Lessons from Amazonia.* R.O. Bierregaard et al., eds. New Haven: Yale University Press, pp. 291–312.

Femia, A. 2000. *A material flow account for Italy, 1988.* Eurostat Working Paper No 2/2000/B/8. Luxembourg.

Fischer, G., and L. X. Sun. 2001. Model based analysis of future land-use development in China, *Agriculture, Ecosystems and Environment* 85:163–176.

Fischer-Kowalski, M. 1998. Society's metabolism: The intellectual history of material flow analysis, part I: 1860–1970, *Journal of Industrial Ecology* 2(1):61–78.

Fischer-Kowalski, M., and C. Amann. 2001. Beyond IPAT and Kuznets Curves: Globalization as a vital factor in analysing the environmental impact of socio-economic metabolism, *Population and Environment* 23(1):7–47.

Fischer-Kowalski, M., and H. Haberl. 1993. Metabolism and colonization: Modes of production and the physical exchange between societies and nature, *Innovation: The European Journal of Social Sciences* 6(4):415–442.

———1998. Sustainable development: Socio-economic metabolism and colonization of nature, *International Social Science Journal* 158(4):573–587.

Fischer-Kowalski, M., and H. Weisz. 1999. Society as hybrid between material and symbolic realms: Toward a theoretical framework of society–nature interrelation, *Advances in Human Ecology* 8:215–251.

Flannery, K. 1972. The cultural evolution of civilizations, *Annual Review of Ecology and Systematics* 3:399–426.

Flenley, J. R. 2001. Forest and civilisation on Easter Island. In *Forest and civilisation.* Y. Yasuda, ed. New Delhi: Lustre Press, pp. 55–62.

Fletcher, J. 1985. Integrative history: Parallels and interconnections in the early modern period, 1500–1800, *Journal of Turkish Studies* 9:37–58.

Foresta, R. A. 1991. *Amazon conservation in the age of development: The limits of providence.* Gainesville, FL: University of Florida Press.

Forman, R. T. T., and M. Godron. 1986. *Landscape ecology.* New York: Wiley and Sons.

Fox, J., V. Mishar, R. Rindfuss, and S. Walsh. 2002. *People and the environment: Approaches for linking household and community survey to remote sensing and GIS.* Amsterdam: Kluwer.

Frank, A. G. 1976. Multilateral Merchandise Trade Imbalances and Uneven Economic Development, *Journal of European Economic History* 2:407–408.

———1978. *World accumulation 1492–1789.* New York: Monthly Review Press.

———1979. *Dependent accumulation and underdevelopment.* New York: Monthly Review Press.

———1995. The modern world system revisited: Rereading Braudel and Wallerstein. In *Civilizations and world systems: Studying world-historical change.* S. K. Sanderson, ed. Walnut Creek, CA: AltaMira Press, pp. 163–194.

———1998. *ReORIENT: Global economy in the Asian age.* Berkeley and Los Angeles: University of California Press.

———2001. Location, location, location to dissipate and absorb entropy in the nineteenth century world economy. Paper presented at the 2001 meeting of the International Studies Association, Chicago.

———2005. Paper tiger, fiery dragon. In *Devastating society: The neoconservative assault on democracy and justice*. B. Hamm, ed. London: Pluto.

Frank, A. G., and B. K. Gills. 1992. The five thousand year world system: An interdisciplinary introduction, *Humboldt Journal of Social Relations* 18(1):1–79.

———1993. eds. The world-system: Five hundred years or five thousand? London: Routledge.

Frank, A. G., and W. R. Thompson. 2005. Afro-Eurasian Bronze Age economic contraction and expansion revisited, *Journal of World History* 16:115–172.

Fredskild, B. 1990. Agriculture in SW Greenland in the Norse period (A.D. 982–c. 1450). PACT 31:39–43.

Fresco, L., R. Leemans, B. L. Turner II, D. Skole, A. G. vanZeijl-Rozema, and V. Hoffman, eds. 1997. Land use and cover change (LUCC): Open science meeting proceedings, *LUCC Report Series No. 1*. Barcelona: Institut Cartogràfic de Catalunya.

Friedman, J. 1974. Marxism, structuralism, and vulgar materialism, *Man* (N.S.) 9:444–469.

———1976. Marxist theory and systems of total reproduction, *Critique of Anthropology* 7.

———1979. *System, structure, and contradiction: The evolution of Asiatic social formations*. Copenhagen: Nationalmuséet. Reprinted in 1998 as *System, structure and contradiction in the evolution of "Asiatic" social formations*. Walnut Creek, CA: AltaMira Press.

———2005. Plus ça change: On not learning from history. In *Hegemonic declines: Past and present*. J. Friedman and C. Chase-Dunn, eds. Boulder, CO: Paradigm Press.

Friedman, J., and C. Chase-Dunn, eds. 2005. *Declining hegemonies: Present and past*. Boulder, CO: Paradigm Press.

Friibergh Workshop. 2000. Sustainability science. Friibergh Workshop on Sustainability Science, Friibergh, Sweden.

Funtowicz, S. O., and J. R. Ravetz. 1992. The emergence of post-normal science. In *Science, politics and morality*, von Schomberg, ed. Dordrecht: Kluwer.

———1993. Science for the post-normal age, *Futures* 25:739–755.

Gallo, K. P., and T. Ower., n.d. Identification of urban heat islands using remotely sensed data: A multi-sensor approach, *Remote Sensing Core Curriculum*, Volume 4. http://research.umbc.edu/~tbenja1/gallo/gallo.html.

Gallois, D. 1981. Os Waiãpi e seu território. *Boletim do Museu Paraense Emílio Goeldi* No. 80. Belém.

Galloway, P. 1992. The unexamined habitus: Direct historical analogy and the archeology of the text. In *Representations in archeology*, J.-C. Gardin and C. S. Peebles, eds. Bloomington, IN: University of Indiana Press, pp. 178–195.

Galloway, P. R. 1986. Long-term fluctuations in climate and population in the preindustrial era, *Population and Development Review* 12:1–24.

Gasse, F. 2000. Hydrological changes in the African tropics since the Last Glacial Maximum, *Quaternary Science Reviews* 19:191–211.

Gassón, R. 2000. Quirípas and mostacillas: The evolution of shell beads as a medium of exchange in northern South America, *Ethnohistory* 47(3–4):581–609.

———2002. Orinoquia: The archeology of the Orinoco River Basin, *Journal of World Prehistory* 16(3):237–311.

———2003. Ceremonial feasting in the Colombian and Venezuelan Llanos: Some remarks on its sociopolitical and historical significance. In *Histories and historicities in Amazonia.* N. Whitehead, ed. Lincoln, NB: University of Nebraska Press, pp. 179–201.

Gastineau, C. F., W. J. Darby, and T. B. Turner, eds. 1979. *Fermented food beverages in nutrition.* New York: Academic Press.

Geels, F. 2002. Technological transitions as evolutionary technological reconfiguration processes: A multi-level perspective and a case-study, *Research Policy* 31(8–9):1257–1274

Geist, H. J., and E. F. Lambin. 2002. Proximate causes and underlying driving forces of tropical deforestation, *BioScience* 52(2):143–150.

Geoghegan, J. G., S. Cortina-Villar, P. Klepeis, P. Macario-Mendoza, Y. Ogneva-Himmelberger, R. R. Chowdhury, B. L. Turner II, and C. Vance. 2001. Modeling tropical deforestation in the southern Yucatán peninsular region: Comparing survey and satellite data, *Agriculture, Ecosystems and Environment* 85:25–46.

Gerasimenko, N. P. 1997. Environmental and climatic changes between 3 and 5 Ka BP in Southeastern Ukraine. In *Third millennium B.C. climate change and old world collapse.* H. N. Dalfes, G. Kukla, and H. Weiss, eds. Berlin: Springer-Verlag.

German Federal Statistical Office-Statistisches Bundesamt. 1995. *Integrated environmental and economic accounting: Material and energy flow accounts.* Fachserie 19, Reihe 5. Wiesbaden.

———2000. *Integrated environmental and economic accounting: Material and energy flow accounts.* Fachserie 19, Reihe 5. Wiesbaden.

Gernet, J. 1982. *A history of Chinese civilization.* Cambridge: Cambridge University Press.

Gershkovich, Y. P. 2003. Farmers and pastoralists in the Pontic lowland during the Late Bronze Age. In *Prehistoric steppe adaptations and the horse.* M. Levine, C. Renfrew, and K. Boyle, eds. Cambridge, UK: McDonald Institute Monographs, pp. 307–318.

Gheerbrandt, A. 1992. *The Amazon: Past, present, and future.* New York: Harry N. Abrams Inc.

Giljum, S. 2004. Trade, material flows and economic development in the South: The example of Chile, *Journal of Industrial Ecology* 8(1–2):241–261.

Giljum, S., and N. Eisenmenger. 2004. North-South trade and the distribution of environmental goods and burdens: A biophysical perspective, *Journal of Environment and Development* 13(1):73–100.

Gill, R. B. 2000. *The great Maya droughts: Water, life, and death.* Albuquerque, NM: University of New Mexico Press.

Gills, B. K. 1995. Capital and power in the processes of world history. In *Civilizations and world systems: Studying world-historical change.* S. K. Sanderson, ed. Walnut Creek, CA: AltaMira Press, pp. 136–162.

Gimblett, H. R., ed. 2002. *Integrating geographic information systems and agent-based modelling techniques for simulating social and ecological processes.* Santa Fe Institute Studies in the Sciences of Complexity. Oxford: Oxford University Press.

Glacken, C. 1967. *Traces on the Rhodian shore.* Berkeley and Los Angeles: University of California Press.

Glaser, B., and W. I. Woods, eds. 2004. *Amazonian Dark Earths: Explorations in space and time.* Berlin: Springer-Verlag.

Godwin, H. 1944. Age and origin of the Breckland Heaths, *Nature* 154:6–8.

Goldewijk, K. K. 2001. Estimating global land use change over the past 300 years: The HYDE database, *Global Biogeochemical Cycles* 15(2):417–434.

Goldfrank, W. L. 2000. Paradigm regained? The rules of Wallerstein's world-system method, *Journal of World-Systems Research* VI(2):150–195.

Goldman, I. 1966. *The Cubeo: Indians of the Northwest Amazon.* Urbana, IL: University of Illinois Press.

Goldstone, J. 1991. *Revolution and rebellion in the early modern world.* Berkeley and Los Angeles: University of California Press.

Gomes, D. 2001. Santarém: Symbolism and power in the tropical forest. In *Unknown Amazon: Culture in nature in ancient Brazil.* C. McEwan, C. Barreto, and E. Neves, eds. London: The British Museum Press, pp. 134–155.

Good, K. R. 1987. Limiting factors in Amazonian ecology. In *Food and evolution.* M. Harris and Eric B. Ross, eds. Philadelphia: Temple University Press, pp. 407–421.

Goodale, C. L., M. J. Apps, R. A. Birdsey, C. B. Field, L. S. Heath, R. A. Houghton, J. C. Jenkins, G. H. Kohlmaier, W. Kurz, S. R. Liu, G. J. Nabuurs, S. Nilsson, A. Z. Shvidenko. 2002. Forest carbon sinks in the northern hemisphere, *Ecological Applications* 12(3):891–899.

Göransson, H. 1986. Man and the forests of nemoral broad-leafed trees during the Stone Age, *Striae* 24:143–152.

Gorman, M. 1979. *Island ecology.* London: Chapman and Hall.

Goudsblom, J. 1992. *Fire and civilization.* London: Penguin.

Goudsblom, J., E. Jones, and S. Mennell. 1996. *Course of human history: Economic growth, social process and civilization.* London: Sharpe.

Gow, Peter. 2002. Piro, Apurinã, and Campa: Social dissimilation and assimilation as historical processes in southwestern Amazonia. In *Comparative Arawakan histories: Rethinking language family and culture area in Amazonia.* J. D. Hill and F. Santos-Granero, eds. Urbana, IL: University of Illinois Press, pp. 147–170.

Gragson, T. L. 1995. Pumé exploitation of Mauritia flexuosa (Palmae) in the Llanos de Venezuela, *Journal of Ethnobiology* 15:177–188.

Grimes, P. 2000. Recent research in world-systems. In *A world-systems reader: New perspectives on gender, urbanism, cultures, indigenous peoples, and ecology.* T. D. Hall, ed. Lanham, MD: Rowman & Littlefield, pp. 20–55.

Gross, Daniel R. 1983. Village movement in relation to resources in Amazonia. In *Adaptive Responses of Native Amazonians.* R. B. Hames and W. T. Vickers, eds. New York: Academic Press.

Grove, J. 1988. *The little ice age.* London: Methuen.

Grudd, H., K. Briffa, W. Karlén, T. S. Bartholin, P. D. Jones, and B. Kromer. 2002. A 7,400-year tree-ring chronology in northern Swedish Lapland: Natural climatic variability expressed on annual to millennial timescales, *The Holocene* (12)6:657–665.

Grünbühel, C. M., H. Haberl, H. Schandl, and V. Winiwarter. 2003. Socio-economic metabolism and colonization of natural processes in SangSaeng Village: Material and energy flows, land use, and cultural change in northeast Thailand, *Human Ecology* 31(1):53–87.

Grupe, G., et al. 1997. Mobility of Bell Beaker people revealed by strontium isotope ratios of tooth and bone: A study of southern Bavarian skeletal remains, *Applied Geochemistry* 12:517–525.

Guilizzoni, P., and F. Oldfield, eds. 1996. *Palaeoenvironmental analysis of Italian crater lake and Adriatic sediments (PALICLAS).* Memorie del'Istituto Italiano di Idrobiologia, 55.

Gunderson, L. H., and C. S. Holling, eds. 2002. *Panarchy: Understanding transformations in human and natural systems.* Washington, DC: Island Press.

Gunderson, L. H., C. S. Holling, and S. S. Light. 1995. *Barriers and bridges to the renewal of ecosystems and institutions.* New York: Columbia University Press.

Gunderson, L., C. Holling, L. Pritchard, and G. Peterson. 1997. *Resilience in ecosystems, institutions, and societies.* Stockholm: Beijer International Institute of Ecological Economics/Royal Swedish Academy of Sciences.

Gunn, J. D. 1994. Global climate and regional biocultural diversity. In *Historical ecology: Cultural knowledge and changing landscapes.* C. L. Crumley, ed. Santa Fe, NM: School of American Research, pp. 67–97.

———2000 (ed.). *The years without summer: Tracing A.D. 536 and its aftermath.* British Archeological Reports S872.

Gunn, J. D., C. L. Crumley, E. Jones, and B. Young. 2004. A landscape analysis of western Europe during the early middle ages. In *The archeology of global change.* C. L. Redman, ed. Washington, DC: Smithsonian Institution Press.

Gunn, J., and W. Folan. 2000. Three rivers: Subregional variations in Earth system impacts in the southwestern Maya lowlands (Candelaria, Usumacinta, and Champoton Watersheds). In *The way the wind blows: Climate, history, and human action.* R. McIntosh, J. Tainter, and S. Keech McIntosh, eds. New York: Columbia University Press.

Gutman, G., A. Janetos, C. Justice, E. F. Moran, J. Mustard, R. Rindfuss, D. Skole, B.L. Turner II, and M. Cochrane, eds. 2004. *Land change science: Observing, monitoring, and understanding trajectories of change on the Earth's surface.* Dordrecht: Kluwer Academic Publishers.

Hall, C. A. S. 1995. *Maximum power: The ideas and applications of H. T. Odum*. Boulder, CO: University Press of Colorado.

Hall, M. 1987. *The changing past: Farmer, kings and traders in southern Africa 200–1860*. London: James Currey.

Hames, R. B. 1980. Game depletion and hunting zone rotation among Ye'kwana and Yanomamo of Amazonas, Venezuela, *Working Papers on South American Indians* 2:31–66.

Hammer, M., and K. Hubacek. 2003. *Material flows and economic development: Material flow analysis of the Hungarian economy*. Laxenburg, Austria: IIASA Interim Report IR-02-057.

Hänsel, B., and J. Machnik, eds. 1998. Das Karpatenbecken und die Osteuropäsichen Steppe. München: Verlag Marie Leidorf.

Hansen, S. 2002. "Überausstattungen" in Gräbern und Horten der Frühbronzezeit. In *Vom Endneolithikum zur Frühbronzezeit: Muster sozialen Wandels?* J. Müller, ed. Tagung Bamberg 14–16 Juni 2001. UPA 90:151–173. Bonn.

Harner, M. 1970. Population pressure and the social evolution of agriculturalists, *Southwestern Journal of Anthropology* 26(1):67-86.

Harris, M. 1977. *Cannibals and kings: The origins of cultures*. New York: Random House.

———1979. *Cultural materialism: The struggle for a science of culture*. New York: Random House.

Harrison, P. D. 1999. *The lords of Tikal: Rulers of an ancient Maya city*. New York: Thames and Hudson.

Hassan, F. A. 1994. Population ecology and civilization in ancient Egypt. In *Historical Ecology: Cultural knowledge and changing landscapes*. C. L. Crumley, ed. Santa Fe, NM: School of American Research Press, pp. 155–181.

Hau'ofa, E. 1994. Our sea of islands, *The Contemporary Pacific* 6(1):147–161.

Haug, D., and M. Kaupenjohann. 2001. Parameters, prediction, post-normal science and the precautionary principle—a roadmap for modelling for decision-making, *Ecological Modelling* 144:45–60.

Häusler, A. 2003. Geschlechtsdifferenzierte Bestattungssitten und die Entstehung des grammatischen Geschlechts in den indogermanischen Sprachen. In *Morgenrot der Kulturen. Frühe Etappen der Menschengeschichte in Mittel-und Südeuropa* E. Jerem and P. Raczky, eds. Budapest: Archeolingua, pp. 39–53.

Haviland, W. A. 1985. Excavations in small residential groups of Tikal: Groups 4F–1 and 4F–2. *Tikal Report No. 19, University Museum Monograph 58*. Philadelphia: The University Museum.

Head, L. 2000. *Cultural landscapes and environmental change*. London: Arnold.

Heckenberger, M. 1996. War and peace in the shadow of empire: Sociopolitical change in the upper Xingú of southeastern Amazonia, A.D. 1400–2000. Ph.D. Thesis. University of Pittsburgh.

———2002. Rethinking the Arawakan diaspora: Hierarchy, regionality, and the Amazonian formative. In *Comparative Arawakan histories: Rethinking language family and culture area in Amazonia.* J. D. Hill and F. Santos-Granero, eds. Urbana, IL: University of Illinois Press, pp. 99–122.

Hedeager, L. 1978. *A quantitative analysis of Roman imports in Europe north of the limes (0–400 A.D.), and the question of Roman-Germanic exchange.* Copenhagen: National Museum of Denmark, pp. 743–774.

Helms, M. 1998. *Access to origins: Affines, ancestors and aristocrats.* Austin, TX: University of Texas Press.

Hemming, J. 1978. *The search for El Dorado.* London: Michael Joseph Ltd.

Henige, D. 1998. *Numbers from nowhere: The American Indian contact population debate.* Norman, OK: University of Oklahoma Press.

Henley, P. 1982. *The Panare: Tradition and change on the Amazon frontier.* New Haven: Yale University Press.

Herrera, L. F., I. Cavelier, C. Rodriguez, and S. Mora. 1992. The technical transformation of an agricultural system in the Colombian Amazon, *World Archeology* 24(1):98–113.

Hewitt, K. 1983. *Interpretations of calamity from the viewpoint of human ecology.* Boston: Allen & Unwin.

———1995. Excluded perspectives in the social construction of disaster, *International Journal of Mass Emergencies and Disasters* 13(3):317–339.

Heyerdahl, T., A. Skjølsvold, and P. Pavel. 1989. The "Walking" Moai of Easter Island, *The Kon-Tiki Museum Occasional Papers* (1):36–64.

Hiebert, F. T. 1999. Central Asians on the Iranian Plateau: A model for Indo-Iranian expansionism. In *The Bronze Age and early Iron Age peoples of eastern Central Asia.* V. H. Mair, ed. Washington and Philadelphia: The Institute for the Study of Man in collaboration with The University of Pennsylvania Museum Publications, pp. 148–162.

———2002. Bronze Age interaction between the Eurasian steppe and Central Asia. In *Ancient interactions East and west in Eurasia.* K. Boyle, C. Renfrew, and M. Levine, eds. Cambridge, UK: McDonald Institute Monographs, University of Cambridge, pp. 237–248.

Hilgerdt, F. 1942. *The network of world trade.* Geneva: League of Nations.

———1943. The case for multilateral trade, *American Economic Review* 33(1/2):393–407.

———1945. *Industrialization and foreign trade.* Geneva: League of Nations.

Hill, J. D. 1996a. Introduction: Ethnogenesis in the Americas, 1492–1992. In *History, power, and identity: Ethnogenesis in the Americas, 1492–1992.* J. D. Hill, ed. Iowa City: University of Iowa Press, pp. 1–19.

———1996b. Ethnogenesis in the northwest Amazon: An emerging regional picture. In *History, power, and identity: Ethnogenesis in the Americas, 1492–1992.* J. D. Hill, ed. Iowa City: University of Iowa Press, pp. 142–160.

———2002. Shamanism, colonialism, and the wild woman: Fertility cultism and historical dynamics in the upper Rio Negro region. In *Comparative Arawakan histories: Rethinking language family and culture area in Amazonia.* J. D. Hill and F. Santos-Granero, eds. Urbana, IL: University of Illinois Press, pp. 223–247.

Hill, J. D., and F. Santos-Granero, eds. 2002. *Comparative Arawakan histories: Rethinking language family and culture area in Amazonia.* Urbana, IL: University of Illinois Press.

Hill, K., and J. Padwe. 2000. Sustainability of Aché hunting in the Mbaracayu Reserve, Paraguay. In *Hunting for sustainability in the tropical forests.* J. G. Robinson and E. L. Bennett, eds. New York: Columbia University Press, pp. 79–105.

Hiraoka, M., S. Yamamoto, E. Matsumoto, S. Nakamura, I. C. Falesi, and A. R. C. Baena. 2003. Contemporary use and management of Amazonian Dark Earths. In *Amazonian Dark Earths: Origin, properties, management.* J. Lehmann et al., eds. Dordrecht: Kluwer Academic Publishers, pp. 387–406.

Hobson, J. M. 2004. *The eastern origins of western civilisation.* Cambridge: Cambridge University Press.

Hofstadter, D. 1979. *Godel, Escher, Bach: An Eternal Golden Braid.* New York: Basic Books.

Hole, F. 1994. Environmental instabilities and urban origins. In *Early states in the Near East: The organizational dynamics of complexity.* G. Stein and M. S. Rothman, eds. Madison, WI: Prehistory Press.

Hole, F. 1996. The context of caprine domestication in the Zagros region. In *The origins and spread of agriculture and pastoralism in Eurasia.* D. Harris, ed. London: UCL Press, pp. 263–281.

Holland, D. C., and N. Quinn. 1987. *Cultural models in language and thought.* Cambridge: Cambridge University Press.

Holling, C. 1986. The resilience of terrestrial ecosystems: Local surprise and global change. In *Sustainable development of the biosphere.* W. Clark and R. M. Clark, eds. Cambridge/Laxenburg: Cambridge University Press/IIASA.

———1987. Simplifying the complex: The paradigms of ecological function and structure, *European Journal of Operational Research* 30:139–146.

Holling, C., L. H. Gunderson, and G. D. Peterson. 2002. Sustainability and panarchies. In *Panarchy: Understanding transformations in human and natural systems.* L. H. Gunderson and C. S. Holling, eds. Washington, DC: Island Press, pp. 63–102.

Holmgren, K., J. A. Lee-Thorp, G. J. Cooper, K. Lundblad, T. C. Partridge, L. Scott, R. Sithaldeen, A. S. Talma, and P. D. Tyson. 2003. Persistent millennial-scale climatic variability over the past 25 thousand years in southern Africa, *Quaternary Science Reviews* 22:2311–2326.

Holmgren, K., A. Moberg, O. Svanered, and P. D. Tyson. 2001. A preliminary 3,000-year regional temperature reconstruction for South Africa, *South African Journal of Science* 97:49–51.

Hopkins, A. 1978. Economic growth and towns in classical antiquity. In *Towns in societies.* P. Abrams and E. A. Wrigley, eds. Cambridge: Cambridge University Press.

Horgan, J. 1996. *The end of science*. London: Abacus.

Hornborg, A. 1998a. Ecosystems and world-systems: Accumulation as an ecological process, *Journal of World-Systems Research* 4(2):169–177.

———1998b. Towards an ecological theory of unequal exchange: Articulating world-system theory and ecological economics, *Ecological Economics* 25:127–136.

———2001a. *The power of the machine: Global inequalities of economy, technology, and environment*. Walnut Creek, CA: AltaMira Press.

———2001b. Vital signs: An ecosemiotic perspective on the human ecology of Amazonia, *Sign Systems Studies* 29:121–152.

———2002. Comments on G. Pálsson and K. E. Hardardóttir, For whom the cell tolls: Debates about biomedicine, *Current Anthropology* 43(2):291–292.

———2005. Perspectives on Diamond's collapse: How societies choose to fail or succeed, *Current Anthropology* 46:S94–95.

———2007. Introduction: Environmental history as political ecology. In *Rethinking environmental history: World system history and global environmental change*. A. Hornborg, J. McNeill, and J. Martinez-Alier, eds. Lanham, MD: AltaMira Press.

Hornborg, A., J. McNeill, and J. Martinez-Alier, eds. 2007. *Rethinking environmental history: World system history and global environmental change*. Lanham, MD: AltaMira Press.

Houghton, R. A., J. E. Hobbie, J. M. Melillo, B. Moore, B. J. Peterson, G. R. Shaver, and G. M. Woodwell. 1983. Changes in the carbon content of terrestrial biota and soils between 1860 and 1980: A net release of CO_2 to the atmosphere, *Ecological Monographs* 53(3):235–262

Houghton, R. A., D. L. Skole, C. A. Nobre, J. L. Hackler, K. T. Lawrence, and W. H. Chomentowski. 2000. Annual fluxes or carbon from deforestation and regrowth in the Brazilian Amazon, *Nature* 403:301–304

Huffman, T. N. 1989. Ceramics, settlements and Late Iron Age migrations, *African Archeological Review* 7:155–182.

———1996. Archeological evidence for climatic change during the last 2000 years in southern Africa, *Quaternary International* 33:55–60.

———2000. Mapungubwe and the origins of the Zimbabwe culture. In *African naissance: The Limpopo Valley 1,000 years ago*. M. Leslie and T. Maggs, eds. The South African Archeological Society, Goodwin Series 8:14–29.

Huffman, T. N., and R. K. Herbert. 1994. New perspectives on Eastern Bantu, *Azania* 29:27–36.

Hughes, J. D. 1975. *Ecology in ancient civilizations*. Albuquerque: University of New Mexico Press.

———1994. *Pan's travail: Environmental problems of the ancient Greeks and Romans*. Baltimore: Johns Hopkins University Press.

———2001. *Environmental history of the world: Humankind's changing role in the community of life*. London: Routledge.

Hunter-Andersson, R. L. 1998. Human versus climatic impacts at Rapanui: A case study of people and their environments. In *Easter Island in the Pacific context*. C. M. Stevenson and F. J. Morin, eds. Los Osos, CA: The Easter Island Foundation, pp. 85–99.

Huntington, E. 1907. *The pulse of Asia, illustrating the geographic basis of history*. Boston: Houghton-Mifflin.

———1922. *Civilization and climate*. New Haven: Yale University Press.

———1924. *The character of races as influenced by physical environment, natural selection, and historical development*. New York: Scribners.

Huntley, J. Jäger, N. S. Jodha, R. E. Kasperson, A. Mabogunje, P. Matson, H. Mooney, B. Moore III, T. O'Riordan, and U. Svedin. 2001. Sustainability science, *Science* 292:641–642.

Hutjes, R. W. A., P. Kabat, S. W. Running, et al. 1998. Biospheric aspects of the hydrological cycle, *Journal of Hydrology* 212–3:1–21.

IGBP-PAGES. 2001. Focus 5 Past Ecosystem Processes and Human-Environment Interactions. www.liv.ac.uk/geography/PAGESFocus5.

Iliffe, J. 1995. *Africans, the history of a continent*. Cambridge: Cambridge University Press.

Indrabudi, H., A. de Gier, and L. O. Fresco. 1998. Deforestation and its driving forces: A case study of Riam Kanan watershed, Indonesia, *Land Degradation and Development* 9(4):311–322.

Ingerson, A. E. 1994. Tracking and testing the nature/culture dichotomy in practice. In *Historical ecology: Cultural knowledge and changing landscapes*. C. L. Crumley, ed. Albuquerque, NM: School of American Research Press, pp. 43–66.

IPCC. 2001. *Climate change 2001: The scientific basis*. Contribution of working group I to the third assessment report of the intergovernmental panel on climate change. Cambridge: Cambridge University Press.

Irion, G., W. J. Junk, and J. A. S. N. de Melo. 1997. The large central Amazonian River floodplains near Manaus: Geological, climatological, hydrological and geomorphological aspects. In *The central Amazonian floodplain*. W. J. Junk, ed. Berlin: Springer-Verlag, pp. 23–46.

Irvine, D. 1989. Succession management and resource distribution in an Amazonian rain forest. In *Resource management in Amazonia*. D. A. Posey and W. Balée, eds. New York: New York Botanical Garden, pp. 223–237.

Irwin, E. G., and J. Geoghegan. 2002. Theory, data, methods: Developing spatially explicit economic models of land use change, *Agriculture, Ecosystems, and Environment* 84:7–24.

Isacsson, A., K. Johnsson, I. Linder, V. Palm, and A. Wadeskog. 2000. *Material flow accounts: DMI and DMC for Sweden 1987–1997*. Luxembourg: Eurostat, Office for Official Publications of the European Communities.

ITSTAT. 1998. *Les Tableaux de l'économie polynésienne 1998*. Papeete: Institut Territorial de la Statistique de Polynésie française.

Iversen, J. 1941. Landnam i Danmarks Stenalder (Land occupation in Denmark's stone age), *Danmarks Geologiske Undersögelse* II, 66:1–68.

Jackson, J. E. 1994. Becoming Indians: The politics of Tukanoan ethnicity. In *Amazonian Indians from prehistory to the present: Anthropological perspectives*. A. C. Roosevelt, ed. Tucson, AZ: University of Arizona Press, pp. 383–406.

Jackson, K. 1976. The dimensions of Kamba pre-colonial history. In *Kenya before 1900: Eight regional studies*. B. A. Ogot, ed. Nairobi: East African Publishing House, 174–261.

Jacobsen, T., and R. M. Adams. 1958. Salt and silt in ancient Mesopotamian agriculture, *Science* 128:1251–1258.

Janssen, M., T. Kohler, and M. Scheffer. 2003. Sunk-cost effects and vulnerability to collapse in ancient societies, *Current Anthropology* 44(5):722–728.

Jantsch, E. 1980. *The self-organizing universe: Scientific and human implications of the emerging paradigm of evolution*. New York: Oxford University Press.

———1982. From self-reference to self-transcendance: The evolution of self-organization dynamics. In *Self-organization and dissipative structures: Applications in the physical and social sciences*. W. C. Schieve and P. M. Allen, eds. Austin: University of Texas Press.

Jensen, C. 1999. Tupí-Guaraní. In *The Amazonian languages*. R.M.W. Dixon and A.Y. Aikhenvald, eds. Cambridge: Cambridge University Press, pp. 125–163.

Joffe, A. H. 2000. Egypt and Syro-Mesopotamia in the 4th millennium: Implications of the new chronology, *Current Anthropology* 41:113–123.

Johnson, A. 1989. How the Machiguenga manage resources: Conservation or exploitation of nature? *Advances in Economic Botany* 7:213–222.

Johnson, A. W., and T. Earle. 1987. *The evolution of human societies: From foraging group to agrarian state*. Stanford, CA: Stanford University Press.

Johnson, C. D., T. A. Kohler, and J. Cowan. 2005. Modeling historical ecology: Thinking about contemporary systems, *American Anthropologist* 107:96–107.

Johnson, G. 1984. *Collision course at Kwajalein: Marshall Islanders in the shadow of the bomb*. Honolulu: Pacific Concerns Resource Centre.

Johnson, S. 2001. *Emergence: The connected lives of ants, brains, cities, and software*. New York: Scribner.

Johnson, T. C., S. L. Barry, Y. Chan, and P. Wilkinson. 2001. Decadal record of climate variability spanning the past 700 yr in the southern tropics of East Africa, *Geology* 29:83–86.

Johnston, B. R. 1994. *Who pays the price? The sociocultural context of environmental crises*. Washington, DC: Island Press.

———1997. *Life and death matters: Human rights and the environment at the end of the millennium*. Walnut Creek, CA: AltaMira Press.

———1998. *Water, culture, and power: Local struggles in global context*. Washington, DC: Island Press.

———2001. Anthropology and environmental justice: Analysts, advocates, mediators, and troublemakers. In *New directions in anthropology and environment: Intersections*. C. L. Crumley, ed. Walnut Creek, CA: AltaMira Press, pp. 132–149.

Kaland, P.E. 1986. The origin and management of Norwegian coastal heaths as reflected by pollen analysis. In *Anthropogenic indicators in pollen diagrams*. K. E. Behre, ed. Rotterdam: A. A. Balkema, 19–36.

Kalicz, N. 1998. Östliche Beziehungen während der Kupferzeit in Ungarn. In *Das Karpatenbecken und die Osteuropäsichen Steppe*. B. Hänsel and J. Machnik, eds. München: Verlag Marie Leidorf, pp. 163–177.

Kalnay, E., and M. Cai. 2003. Impact of urbanization and land use on climate change, *Nature* 423:528–531.

Kane, J. 1995. *Savages*. New York: Knopf.

Kates, R. W., W. C. Clark, R. Corell, J. M. Hall, C. C. Jaeger, I. Lowe, J. J. McCarthy, H. J. Schellenhuber, B. Bolin, N. M. Dickson, S. Faucheaux, G. C. Gallopin, A. Grübler, and B. Kauffman, S. A. 1993. *The origins of order: Self-organization and selection in evolution*. New York: Oxford University Press.

Kates, R. W., et al. 2001. Environment and development: Sustainability science, *Science* 292(5517):641–642.

Kauffman, S. A. 1995. *At home in the universe: The search for laws of self-organization and complexity*. New York/London: Oxford University Press/Viking.

Kaufman, T. 1989. Language history in South America: What we know and how to know more. In *Amazonian linguistics*. D. L. Payne, ed. Austin, TX: University of Texas Press, pp. 13–73.

———1994. The native languages of South America. In *Atlas of the world's languages*. C. Moseley and R. E. Asher, eds. London: Routledge, pp. 46–76.

Kelley, P. M., and W. N. Adger. 2000. Theory and practice in assessing vulnerability to climate change and facilitating adaptation, *Climatic Change* 47:325–352.

Kempton, W. 2001. Cognitive anthropology and the environment. In *New directions in anthropology and environment: Intersections*. C. L. Crumley, ed. Walnut Creek, CA: AltaMira Press.

Kempton, W., J. S. Boster, and J. Hartley. 1995. *Environmental values in American culture*. Cambridge, MA: The MIT Press.

Kenoyer, J. M. 1998. *Ancient cities of the Indus Valley civilization*. Karachi: Oxford University Press.

Kensinger, K. M. 1995. *How real people ought to live: The Cashinahua of eastern Peru*. Long Grove, IL: Waveland Press.

Kenwood, A. G., and A. L. Lougheed. 1971. *The growth of the international economy 1820–1980: An introductory text*. London: George Allen and Unwin.

Kern, D. C., G. D'Aquino, T. E. Rodrigues, F. J. L. Frazão, W. Sombroek, T. P. Myers, and E. G. Neves. 2003. Distribution of Amazonian Dark Earths in the Brazilian Amazon. In *Amazonian Dark Earths: Origin, properties, management*. J. Lehmann et al., eds. Dordrecht: Kluwer Academic Publishers, pp. 51–76.

Kirch, P. V. 1984. *The evolution of the Polynesian chiefdoms*. Cambridge: Cambridge University Press.

———2000. *On the road of the winds: An archeological history of the Pacific Islands before European contact*. Berkeley and Los Angeles CA: University of California Press.

Kirch, P. V. and T. L. Hunt, eds. 1997. *Historical Ecology in the Pacific Islands: Prehistoric Environmental and Landscape Change.* New Haven: Yale University Press.

Klooster, D. 2003. Forest transitions in Mexico: Institutions and forests in a globalized countryside, *Professional Geographer* 55(2):227–237.

Kohl, P. 2001. Migrations and cultural diffusion in the later prehistory of the Caucasus. In *Migration und Kulturtransfer. Der Wandel der vorder- und zentralasiatischer Kulturen im Umbruch vom 2. zum 1. vorchristlichen Jahrtausend.* Römisch-Germanische Kommission, Frankfurt a. M. Eurasien-Abteilung, Berlin. *Kolloquien zur Vor-und Frühgeschichte,* Band 6. R. Reichmann and H. Parzinger, eds. Bonn: Dr. Rudolf Habelt.

———2003. Integrated interaction at the beginning of the Bronze Age: New evidence from the northeastern Caucasus and the advent of tin bronzes in the third millennium B.C. In *Archeology in the borderlands: Investigations in Caucasia and beyond.* A. T. Smith and K. Rubinson, eds. Monographs 47. Los Angeles: The Cotsen Institute of Archeology, University of California, pp. 9–21.

Kohler, T., and G. Gumerman, eds. 2000. *Dynamics in human and primate societies: Agent-based modeling of social and spatial processes.* The Santa Fe Institute for Studies in the Sciences of Complexity. Oxford: Oxford University Press.

Kolata, G. 1999. *Flu: The story of the great influenza pandemic of 1918 and the search for the virus that caused it.* New York: Farrar, Straus and Giroux.

Kontopoulos, K. M. 2006. The logics of social structure. In *Structural analysis in the social sciences,* 6. M. Granovetter, ed. Cambridge: Cambridge University Press.

Kradin, N. N. 2002. Nomadism, evolution and world-systems: Pastoral societies in theories of historical development, *Journal of World-Systems Research* 8(3):368–388.

Krausmann, F. 2003. Land use and societal metabolism in 19th century Austrian villages. *Presentation at the 2nd Conference of the European Society of Environmental History: Dealing with Diversity, 3–7* September 2003, Prague.

Krementski, C. V. 1997. The late Holocene environmental and climate shift in Russia and surrounding lands. In *Third millennium B.C. climate change and old world collapse.* H. N. Dalfes, G. Kukla, and H. Weiss, eds. Berlin: Springer-Verlag.

Kremenetski, K. 2003. Steppe and forest steppe belt of Eurasia: Holocene environmental history. In *Prehistoric steppe adaptations and the horse.* M. Levine, C. Renfrew, and K. Boyle, eds. Cambridge, UK: McDonald Institute monographs, pp. 11–29.

Kristiansen, K. 1989. Prehistoric migrations—The case of the Single Grave Culture and Corded Ware Cultures, *Journal of Danish Archeology* 8:211–225.

———1998a. *Europe before history.* Cambridge: Cambridge University Press

———1998b. The construction of a Bronze Age landscape. Cosmology, economy and social organisation in Thy, Northwestern Jutland. In *Mensch und Umwelt in der Bronzezeit Europas.* B. Hänsel, ed. Kiel: Oetker-Voges Verlag, pp. 281–291.

———2001. Rulers and warriors: Symbolic transmission and social transformation in Bronze Age Europe. In *From leaders to rulers.* J. Haas, ed. Dordrecht: Kluwer Academic/Plenum Publishers, pp. 85–105.

————2004. Institutions and material culture: Towards an intercontextual archeology. In *Rethinking materiality: The engagement of mind and the material world.* C. Renfrew and E. DeMarais, eds. Cambridge, UK: McDonald Institute Monographs.

————2005. What language did Neolithic pots speak? Colin Renfrew's farming-language-dispersal model challenged, *Antiquity* 79(305): 679–691.

Kristiansen, K., and T. B. Larsson. 2005. *The rise of Bronze Age society: Travels, transmission and transformations.* Cambridge: Cambridge University Press.

Krugman, P. R., and M. Obstfeld. 2000. *International economics: Theory and policy.* Reading, MA: Addison-Wesley (World Student Series).

Kruk, J., and S. Milisauskas. 1999. Rozkwit i upadek społecze´nstw rolniczych neolitu. *The rise and fall of Neolithic societies.* Krakow, Poland: Instytut Archeologii i Etnologii Polskiej Akademii Nauk.

Kurella, D. 1998. The Muisca: Chiefdoms in transition. In *Chiefdoms and chieftaincy in the Americas.* E. M. Redmond, ed. Gainesville: University Press of Florida, pp. 89–216.

Kuzmina, E. E. 1998. Cultural connections of the Tarim Basin People and the pastoralists of the Asian steppes in the Bronze Age. In *The Bronze Age and early Iron Age peoples of eastern central Asia.* V. H. Mair, ed. Washington, DC and Philadelphia: The Institute for the Study of Man in collaboration with The University of Pennsylvania Museum Publications, pp. 63–92.

————2001. The first migration wave of Indo-Iranians to the south, *Journal of Indo-European Studies* 29(1):1–40.

————2002. Origins of pastoralism in the Eurasian steppes. In *Prehistoric steppe adaptation and the horse.* M. Levine, C. Renfrew, and K. Boyle, eds. Cambridge, UK: McDonald Institute Monographs pp. 203–232.

Lagerås, P. 1996. Farming and forest dynamics in an agriculturally marginal area of southern Sweden, 5000 B.C. to present: A palynological study of Lake Avegöl in the Småland uplands, *The Holocene* 6:301–314.

Lamb, H. H. 1972–1977. *Climate: Present, past, and future.* London: Methuen.

————1982. *Climate, history and the modern world.* London: Methuen.

————1984. Climate and history in northern Europe and elsewhere. In *Climatic changes on a yearly to millennial basis.* N.-A. Mörner and W. Karlén, eds. Dordrecht: Reidel Publishing Company, 225–240.

————1995. *Climate, history, and the modern world,* 2nd ed. (1st ed. 1982). London: Routledge.

Lamb, H., I. Darbyshire, and D. Verschuren. 2003. Vegetation response to rainfall variation and human impact in central Kenya during the past 1,100 years, *The Holocene* (13)2:285–292.

Lambin, E. F. 1994. *Modelling deforestation processes: A review.* Luxemburg: European Commission.

————1997. Modelling and monitoring land-cover change processes in tropical regions, *Progress in Physical Geography* 21(3):375–393.

Lambin, E. F., X. Baulies, N. Bockstael, G. Fischer, T. Krug, R. Leemans, E. F. Moran, R. R. Rindfuss, Y. Sato, D. Skole, B. L. Turner II, and C. Vogel. 1999.

Land-use and land-cover change implementation strategy. International Geosphere-biosphere Programme Secretariat, Stockholm: IGBP Report No. 48, IHDP Report No. 10.

Lambin, E. F., and D. F. Ehrlich. 1997. Land-cover changes in sub-Saharan Africa, 1982–1991: Application of a change index based on remotely sensed surface temperature and vegetation indices at a continental scale, *Remote Sensing and the Environment* 61(2):181–200.

Lambin, E. F., H. J. Geist, and E. Lepers. 2003. Dynamics of land-use and land-cover change in tropical regions, *Annual Review of Environment and Resources,* 28:205–241.

Lambin, E. F., M. D. A. Rounsevell, and H. J. Geist. 2000. Are agricultural land-use models able to predict changes in land-use intensity? *Agriculture, Ecosystems and Environment* 82:321–331.

Lambin, E. F., and Strahler, A.H. 1994. Indicators of land-cover change for change-vector analysis in multitemporal space at coarse spatial scales. *International Journal of Remote Sensing* 15(10): 2099–2119.

Lambin, E. F., B. L. Turner II, H. Geist, S. Agbola, A. Angelsen, J. W. Bruce, O. Coomes, R. Dirzo, G. Fischer, C. Folke, P. S. George, K. Homewood, J. Imbernon, R. Leemans, X. Li, E. F. Moran, M. Mortimore, P. S. Ramakrishnan, J. F. Richards, H. Skånes, H. Steffen, G. D. Stone, U. Svedin, T. Veldkamp, C. Vogel, and J. Xu. 2001. The causes of land-use and land-cover change: Moving beyond the myths, *Global Environmental Change* 11:2–13.

Landes, D. 1999. *The wealth and poverty of nations: Why some are so rich and some so poor.* New York: Norton.

Langton, C. G., ed. 1992. *Artificial life II: Proceedings of the Workshop on Artificial Life, Santa Fe, NM.* Redwood, CA: Addison-Wesley.

Lansing, S. J. 1987. Balinese water temples and the management of irrigation, *American Anthropologist* 89:326–341.

———1991. *Priests and programmers: Technologies of power in the engineered landscape of Bali.* Princeton, NJ: Princeton University Press.

———1994. *The Balinese.* New York: Harcourt Brace.

Laris, P. 2002. Burning the seasonal mosaic: Preventing burning strategies in the wooded savanna of southern Mali, *Human Ecology* 30(2):155–186.

Larsson, L. 1990.The mesolithic of southern Scandinavia, *Journal of World Prehistory* 4:257–309.

Larsson, T. B. 1999a. Symbols in a European Bronze Age cosmology. In *Communications in Bronze Age Europe.* C. Orrling, ed. Transactions of a Bronze Age symposium in Tanumstrand, Bohuslän, Sweden, September 7–5, 1995. Stockholm: Statens Historiska Museum, pp. 9–17.

———1999b. The transmission of an élite ideology: Europe and the Near East in the second millennium B.C. In *Rock art as social representations.* J. Goldhahn, ed. Oxford: British Archaeological Reports International Series 794, pp. 49–64.

Lathrap, D. W. 1970. *The Upper Amazon.* London: Thames and Hudson.

———1971. The tropical forest and the cultural context of Chavín. In *Dumbarton Oaks Conference on Chavín.* E. P. Benson, ed. Washington, DC: Dumbarton Oaks Research Library and Collection, Trustees for Harvard University, pp. 73–100.

Lawton, J. 2001. Earth system science, *Science* 292:1965.

Leach, E. R. 1954. *Political systems of highland Burma: A study of Kachin social structure.* London School of Economics Monographs on Social Anthropology 44. London: The Athlone Press.

LeBlanc, S. A. 1999. *Prehistoric warfare in the American southwest.* Salt Lake City, UT: University of Utah Press.

Lee-Thorp, J. A., K. Holmgren, S. E. Lauritzen, H. Linge, A. Moberg, T. C. Partridge, C. Stevenson, and P. Tyson. 2001. Rapid climate shifts in the southern African interior throughout the mid to late Holocene, *Geophysical Research Letters* 28:4507–4510.

Leeuw, S. van der, and B. de Vries. 2002. The Roman empire. In *Myths, maps, and models.* B. de Vries and J. Goudsblom, eds. Amsterdam: Amsterdam University Press.

Lehmann, J., D. C. Kern, B. Glaser, and W. I. Woods, eds. 2003. *Amazonian Dark Earths: Origin, properties, management.* Dordrecht: Kluwer Academic Publishers.

Lenski, G., P. Nolan, and J. Lenski. 1995. *Human societies: An introduction to macrosociology,* 7th. ed. New York: McGraw-Hill.

Leopold, A. 1949. *A Sand County almanac.* New York: Oxford University Press.

Leopoldo, P. R. 2000. *Ciclo hidrológico em bacias experimentais da Amazônia Central. Amazônia: Um ecosistema em transformação.* E. Salati, M. L. Absy, and R. L Victória, eds. Manaus: INPA, pp. 87–118.

Leshtakov, K. 1995. Trade centres from early Bronze Age III and middle Bronze Age in upper Thrace. In *Early Bronze Age settlement patterns in the Balkans (ca. 3500–2000 B.C., calibrated dates).* L. Nikolova, ed. Reports of Prehistoric Research Projects, Vol. 1, Nos. 2–4:239–287.

Leslie, M., and T. Maggs, eds. 2000. *African naissance: The Limpopo Valley 1,000 years ago,* The South African Archeological Society, Goodwin Series, 8.

Levin, S. 1998. Ecosystems and the biosphere as complex adaptive systems, *Ecosystems* 1:431–436.

Levi, C. 1948. *Christ stopped at Eboli.* Frances Frenaye, trans. London: Cassell and Co.

Levine, M., Renfrew, C., and Boyle, K., eds. 2003. *Prehistoric steppe adaptations and the horse.* Cambridge, UK: McDonald Institute Monographs.

Li, X., and A. G. Yeh. 2000. Modelling sustainable urban development by the integration of constrained cellular automata and GIS, *International Journal of Geographical Information Science* 14:131–152.

Lima-Ayres, D., and E. F. Alencar. 1994. Histórico da ocupação humana e mobilidade geográfica de assentamentos na área da Estação Ecológica Mamirauá. 9° Encontro de Estudos Populacionais, Cazambu, Brasil, *Memorias* 2:353–384. Belo Horizonte: Associação Brasileira de Estudos Populacionais.

Little, P. E. 1999. Environments and environmentalisms in anthropological research: Facing a new millennium, *Annual Review of Anthropology* 28:253–284.

Liverman, D., E. F. Moran, R. Rindfuss, and P. Stern, eds. 1998. *People and pixels: Linking remote sensing and social science.* Washington, DC: National Academy Press.

Livi-Bacci, M. 1992. *A concise history of world population.* C. Ipsen, trans. Cambridge, UK: Blackwell Publishing.

Lizot, J. 1974. El río de los Periquitos: Breve relato de un viaje entre los Yanomami del Alto Siapa, *Antropológica* 37:3–23.

———1980. La agricultura Yanomama, *Antropológica* 53:3–93.

———1984. *Les Yanomami centraux.* Paris: Ecole des Hautes Etudes en Sciences Sociales.

Lopinot, N. H., and W. I. Woods. 1993. Wood overexploitation and the collapse of Cahokia. In *Foraging and farming in the eastern woodlands.* C. M. Scarry, ed. Gainesville, FL: University Press of Florida, pp. 206–231.

Lovén, S. 1928. The Orinoco in old Indian times (economy and trade). In *Atti del XXII Congresso Internazionale degli Americanisti*, vol. II. Rome: Istituto Cristoforo Colombo, pp. 711–726.

Lubchenco, J. 1998. Entering the century of the environment: A new social contract for science, *Science* 279:491–497.

Lupo, F., I. Reginster, and E. F. Lambin. 2001. Monitoring land-cover changes in West Africa with SPOT vegetation: Impact of natural disasters in 1998–1999, *International Journal of Remote Sensing* 22:2633–2639.

MacArthur, R. H., and E. O. Wilson. 1967. *The theory of island biogeography.* Princeton, NJ: Princeton University Press.

Machado, J. A. 2001. *Material flow analysis in Brazil.* Unpublished.

Mäenpää, I., and A. Juutinen. 2001. Material flows in Finland. Resource use in a small open economy, *Journal of Industrial Ecology* 5(3):33–48.

Maffi, L. 2001. *On biocultural diversity: Linking language, knowledge, and the environment.* Washington, DC: Smithsonian Institution Press.

Maggs, T. 1984. The Iron Age south of the Zambezi. In *Southern African prehistory and palaeoenvironments.* R. G. Klein, ed. Rotterdam: Balkema, pp. 329–360.

Mair, V. H., ed. 1998. *The Bronze Age and early Iron Age peoples of eastern central Asia.* Washington, DC and Philadelphia: The Institute for the Study of Man in collaboration with The University of Pennsylvania Museum Publications.

Mallory, J. P. 1998. A European perspective on Indo-Europeans in Asia. In *The Bronze Age and early Iron Age peoples of eastern central Asia.* V. H. Mair, ed. Vol. 1. Washington, DC and Philadelphia: The Institute for the Study of Man in collaboration with The University of Pennsylvania Museum Publications, pp. 175–200.

Mallory, J. P., and V. H. Mair. 2000. *The Tarim mummies: Ancient China and the mystery of the earliest people from the West.* London: Thames & Hudson.

Malm, T. 1999. *Shell age economics: Marine gathering in the Kingdom of Tonga, Polynesia.* Lund: Lund Monographs in Social Anthropology.

Malthus, T. R. 1798. *An essay on the principle of population.* London: J. Johnson.

———1960 (orig. 1798 and 1803). *On population.* New York: Modern Library and Random House.

Mani, M., and D. Wheeler. 1998. In search of pollution havens? Dirty industries in the world-economy, 1960–1995, *Journal of Environment and Development* 7(3):215–247.

Mann, C. C. 2002. The real dirt on rainforest fertility, *Science* 297:920–923.

Mann, M. 1986. *The sources of social power.* New York: Cambridge University Press.

Mann, M. E. 2000. Lessons for a new millennium, *Science* 289:253–254.

Mannion, A. M. 1991. *Global environmental change.* Hong Kong: Longman Scientific and Technical.

Manolis, S. K., and A. A. Neroutsos. 1997. The middle Bronze Age burial of Kolona at Aegina Island, Greece: Study of the human skeletal remains. In *Das mittelbronzezeitliche Schachtgrab von Ägina.* I. Kilian-Dirlmeier, ed. Römisch-Germanisches Zentralmuseum Forschungsinstitut für Vor- und Frühgeschichte. Kataloge Vor- und Frühgeschichtliche Altertümer, Band 27/Alt Ägina Band IV, 3. Mainz: Verlag Phillip von Zabern.

Manzura, I. 2005. Steps to the steppe: Or, how the north Pontic region was colonised, *Oxford Journal of Archeology* 24(4):313–338.

Marchant, R., and B. de Vries. 2002. The Holocene: Global change and local response. In *Myths, maps, and models.* B. De Vries and J. Goudsblom, eds. Amsterdam: Amsterdam University Press.

Marcus, J. 1998. The peaks and valleys of ancient states: An extension of the dynamic model. In *Archaic states.* G. M. Feinman and J. Marcus, eds. Santa Fe, NM: School of American Research Press, pp. 59–94.

Marquardt, W. H., and C. L. Crumley. 1987. Theoretical issues in the analysis of spatial patterning. In *Regional dynamics: Burgundian landscapes in historical perspective.* C. L. Crumley and W. H. Marquardt, eds. San Diego: Academic Press, pp. 1–18.

Martinez-Alier, J. 1987. *Ecological economics: Energy, environment and society.* London: Blackwell Publishing.

Marx, K. 1894/1962. *Capital.* Vol. III. Moscow: Foreign Languages Publishing House.

Massey, D. 1999. Space-time, "science," and the relationship between physical geography and human geography, *Transactions of the Institute of British Geographers* NS 24:261–276.

Matthews, E., C. Amann, M. Fischer-Kowalski, S. Bringezu, W. Hüttler, R. Kleijn, Y. Moriguchi, C. Ottke, E. Rodenburg, D. Rogich, H. Schandl, H. Schütz, E. van der Voet, and H. Weisz. 2000. *The weight of nations: Material outflows from industrial economies.* Washington, DC: World Resources Institute.

Maude, H. E. 1981. *Slavers in paradise: The Peruvian labour trade in Polynesia, 1862–1864.* Canberra: Australian National University Press.

Mazoyer, M., and L. Roudart. 1997. *Histoire des agricultures du monde.* Paris: Éditions du Seuil.

McCall, G. 1994. Little Ice Age: Some proposals for Polynesia and Rapa Nui (Easter Island), *Journal de la Société des Océanistes* 98:99–104.

McConnell, W. J. 2002. Madagascar: Emerald Isle or Paradise Lost? *Environment,* October:10–22.

McConnell, W., and E. F. Moran, eds. 2001. Meeting in the middle: The challenge of meso-level integration. *Land Use and Cover Change,* Project Report Series No. 5. LUCC Focus 1 Office. Bloomington, IN.

McCracken, S., E. Brondizio, D. Nelson, E. F. Moran, A. Siqueira, and C. Rodriguez-Pedraza. 1999. Remote Sensing and GIS at Farm property level: Demography and deforestation in the Brazilian Amazon, *Photogrammetric Engineering and Remote Sensing* 65(11):1311–1320.

McCulloch, W. S. 1945. A heterarchy of values determined by the topology of nervous nets, *Bulletin of Mathematical Biophysics* 7:89–93.

———1988. *Embodiments of mind.* Cambridge, MA: The MIT Press.

McDaniel, C. N., and J. M. Gowdy. 2000. *Paradise for sale: A parable of nature.* Berkeley and Los Angeles: University of California Press.

McEvedy, C., and R. Jones. 1978. *Atlas of world population history.* New York: Facts on File.

McIntosh, R., J. A. Tainter, and S. Keech McIntosh, eds. 2000. *The way the wind blows: Climate, history, and human action.* New York: Columbia University Press.

McNeill, W. H. 1998. *Plagues and peoples.* Garden City, NY: Anchor Press.

Meggers, B. 1971. *Amazonia: Man and culture in a counterfeit paradise.* Somerset, NJ: Aldine.

———1982. Archeological and ethnographic evidence compatible with the model of forest fragmentation. In *Biological diversification in the tropics.* G. T. Prance, ed. New York: Columbia University Press, pp. 483–496.

———1987. The early history of man in Amazonia. in *Biogeography and quaternary history in tropical America.* T. C. Whitmore and G. T. Prance, eds. Oxford: Clarendon Press, pp. 151–174.

———1992. Prehistoric population density in the Amazon Basin. In *Disease and demography in the Americas.* J. W. Verano and D. H. Ubelaker, eds. Washington, DC: Smithsonian Institution Press, pp. 197–205.

———1993–1995. Amazonia on the eve of European contact: Ethnohistorical, ecological, and anthropological perspectives, *Revista de Arqueología Americana* 8:91–115.

———1994. Archeological evidence for the impact of mega-Niño events on Amazonia during the past two millennia, *Climatic Change* 28:321–338.

———1996. *Amazonia: Man and culture in a counterfeit paradise.* Revised Edition. Washington, DC: Smithsonian Institution Press.

———1999. La utilidad de secuencias cerámicas seriadas para inferir conducta social prehistórica, *El Caribe Arqueológico* 3:2–19.

———2001. The mystery of the Marajoara: An ecological solution, *Amazoniana* 16(3/4):421–440.

Meggers, B. J., and J. Danon. 1988. Identification and implications of a hiatus in the archeological sequence on Marajó Island, Brazil, *Journal of the Washington Academy of Sciences* 78:245–253.

Meggers, B., and C. Evans. 1957. *Archeological investigations at the mouth of the Amazon.* Washington, DC: Smithsonian Institution.

Meggers, B. J., and E. Th. Miller. 2003. Hunter-gatherers in Amazonia during the Pleistocene-Holocene transition. In *Under the canopy.* J. Mercader, ed. New Brunswick, NJ: Rutgers University Press, pp. 291–316.

Meillet, A. 1952. *Atlas des langues du monde.* Paris: CNRS.

Mena, P., J. R. Stallings, B. Jhanira Regalado, and L. Ruben Cueva. 2000. The sustainability of current hunting practices by the Huaorani. In *Hunting for sustainability in tropical forests.* J. G. Robinson and E. L. Bennett, eds. New York: Columbia University Press, pp. 57–78.

Métraux, A. 1940. *Ethnology of Easter Island.* Honolulu, HI: Bernice P. Bishop Museum Bulletin 160.

Meyer, W. 1996. *Human impact on the Earth.* New York: Cambridge University Press.

Miller, E. Th., et al. 1992. *Arqueologia nos empreendimentos hidrelétricos da Eletronorte: Resultados preliminares.* Brasília: Centrais Elétricas do Norte do Brasil S.A.

Millon, R. 1981. Teotihuacán: City, state, and civilization. In *Handbook of Middle American Indians,* Supplement 1, Archeology. Austin, TX: University of Texas Press, pp. 198–243.

Milner, G. P., and J. S. Oliver. 1999. Late prehistoric settlements and wetlands in the central Mississippi Valley. In *Settlement pattern studies in the Americas: Fifty years since Virú.* B. R. Billman and G. M. Feinman, eds. Washington, DC: Smithsonian Institution Press, pp. 79–95.

Milner-Gulland, E. J., E. L. Bennett, and the SCB 2002 Annual Meeting of the Wild Meat Group. 2003. Wild meat: The bigger picture, *Trends in Ecology & Evolution* 18:351–357.

Minsky, M., and S. Papert. 1972. *Artificial intelligence progress report* (AI Memo 252). Cambridge, MA: MIT Artificial Intelligence Laboratory.

Mithen, S. 1996. *The prehistory of the mind: The cognitive origins of art, religion and science.* London: Thames and Hudson.

Modelski, G. 1987. *Long cycles in world politics.* London: Macmillan.

———1999. Ancient world cities 4000 to 1000 B.C. : Center/hinterland in the world system, *Global Society* 13(4):383–392.

———2000. World system evolution. In *World system history: The social science of long-term change.* R. Denemark et al., eds. New York: Routledge

———2003. *World cities: -3000 to 2000*. Washington, DC: FAROS 2000.

Modelski, G., and W. R. Thompson. 1999. The evolutionary pulse of the world system: Hinterland incursions and migrations, 4000 B.C. to 1500 A.D. In *World-systems theory in practice*. P. N. Kardulias, ed. Lanham, MD: Rowman and Littlefield, pp. 241–274.

———2002. Evolutionary pulsations in the world system. In *Structure, culture, and history: Recent issues in social theory*. S. C. Chew and J. D. Knotterus, eds. Lanham, MD: Rowman and Littlefield, pp. 177–196.

Molion, L. C. B., and J. C. de Moraes. 1987. Oscilação Sul e descarga de rios em America do Sul tropical, Rev. Bras. Eng., *Caderno de Hidrologia* 5:53–63.

Molloy, K., and M. O'Connell. 1991. Palaeoecological investigations towards the reconstruction of woodland and land-use history at Lough Sheeauns, Connemara, western Ireland, *Review of Palaeobotany and Palynology* 67:75–113.

———1995. Palaeoecological investigations towards the reconstruction of environment and land-use changes during the prehistory of Céide Fields, western Ireland, *Probleme der Küstenforschung im südlichen Nordseegebiet* 23:187–225.

Montgomery, J., P. Budd, and J. Evans. 2000. Reconstructing the lifetime movements of ancient people: A Neolithic case study from southern England, *European Journal of Archeology* 3(3):370–385

Moore, B., R. D. Boone, J. E. Hobbie, R. A. Houghton, J. M. Melillo, B. J. Peterson, G. R. Shaver, C. J. Vörösmarty, and G. M. Woodwell. 1981. A simple model for analysis of the role of terrestrial ecosystems in the global carbon budget. In *Carbon cycle modeling (Scope 16)*. B. Bolin, ed. New York: John Wiley & Sons.

Mora, S. 2003. Archaeobotanical methods for the study of Amazonian Dark Earths. In *Amazonian Dark Earths: Origin, properties, management*. J. Lehmann, D. C. Kern, B. Glaser, and W. I. Woods, eds. Dordrecht: Kluwer, pp. 205–225.

Morales, A., and E. Antipina. 2003. Srubnaya faunas and beyond: A critical assessment of the archaeozoological information from the East European steppe. In *Prehistoric steppe adaptations and the horse*. M. Levine, C. Renfrew, and K. Boyle, eds. Cambridge, UK: McDonald Institute Monographs, pp. 329–351.

Moran, E. F. 1990. *The Ecosystem approach in anthropology: From concept to practice*. Ann Arbor, MI: University of Michigan Press.

———1993a. *Through Amazonian eyes: The human ecology of Amazonian populations*. Iowa City: University of Iowa Press.

———1993b. Deforestation and land use in the Brazilian Amazon, *Human Ecology* 21:1–21.

———2000. *Human adaptability: An introduction to ecological anthropology*. 2nd ed. Boulder, CO: Westview Press.

———2006. *People and nature*. Cambridge, UK: Blackwell Publishers.

Moran E. F., and E. S. Brondizio. 2001. Human ecology from space: Ecological anthropology engages the study of global environmental change. In *Ecology and the sacred: Engaging the anthropology of Roy A. Rappaport*. M. Lambek and E. Messer, eds. Ann Arbor, MI: University of Michigan Press.

Moran, E. F., E. S. Brondizio, J. Tucker, M. C. Silva-Forsberg, I. C. Falesi, and S. McCracken. 2000. Strategies for Amazonian forest regeneration: Evidence for afforestation in five regions of the Brazilian Amazon. In *Amazonia at the crossroads*. London: Institute of Latin America Studies, University of London, pp. 129–149.

Moran, E. F. 1993a. *Through Amazonian eyes: The human ecology of Amazonian populations*. Iowa City: University of Iowa Press.

Moran, E. F., and E. Ostrom, eds. 2005. *Seeing the forest and the trees*. Cambridge, MA: The MIT Press.

Moran, P. A. P. 1953. The statistical analysis of the Canada lynx cycle. II: Synchronization and meteorology, *Australian Journal of Zoology* 1:291–298.

Morgan, L. H. 1877. *Ancient society*. New York: Holt, Rinehart and Winston.

Müller, J., ed. 2002. *Vom Endneolithicum zur Frühbronzezeit: Muster sozialen Wandels?* Tagung Bamberg 14–16 Juni 2001. UPA 90. Bonn.

Mündl, A., H. Schütz, W. Stodulski, J. Sleszynski, and M. J. Welfens. 1999. *Sustainable development by dematerialization in production and consumption: Strategy for the new environmental policy in Poland*. Wuppertal: Wuppertal Institute for Climate, Energy and Environment, pp. 4–89.

Muradian, R., and J. Martinez-Alier. 2001a. South-north materials flow: History and environmental repercussions, *Innovation: The European Journal of Social Sciences* 14(2):171–187.

———2001b. Trade and the environment from a "Southern" perspective, *Ecological Economics* 36(2):281–297.

Muradian, R., M. O'Connor, and J. Martinez-Alier. 2002. Embodied pollution in trade: Estimating the environmental load displacement of industrialised countries, *Ecological Economics* 41(1):51–67.

Murphy, R. 1970. Basin ethnography and ecological theory, *Languages and Information* 8:13–33.

Muscheler, R., J. Beer, and B. Kromer. 2003. Long-term climate variations and solar effects, Proc. ISCS 2003 Symposium, *Solar variability as an input to the Earth's environment*, Tatranská Lomnica, Slovakia, 23–28 June 2003, pp. 305–316.

Muukkonen, J. 2000. *TMR, DMI and material balances, Finland 1980–1997*. Luxembourg: Eurostat, Office for Official Publications of the European Communities.

Myers, T. P. 2004. Dark Earth in the upper Amazon. In *Amazonian Dark Earths: Explorations in space and time*. B. Glaser and W. I. Woods, ed. Berlin: Springer-Verlag, pp. 67–94.

Myers, T. P., W. M. Denevan, A. WinklerPrins, and A. Porro. 2003. Historical perspectives on Amazonian Dark Earths. In *Amazonian Dark Earths: Origin, properties, management*. J. Lehmann, D. C. Kern, B. Glaser, and W. I. Woods, eds. Dordrecht: Kluwer, pp. 15–28.

Myneni, R. B., J. Dong, J., C. J. Tucker, R. K. Kaufmann, P. E. Kauppi, J. Liski, L. Zhou, V. Alexeyev, and M. K. Hughes. 2001. A large carbon sink in the woody biomass of Northern forests, *Proceedings of the National Academy of Sciences of the United States of America* 98(26):14784–14789.

Myrdal, J. 1997. En agrarhistorisk syntes. In *Agrarhistoria*. B. M. P. Larsson, M. Morell, and J. Myrdal, eds. Stockholm: LT:s Förlag, 302–322.

———2000. Society and land use in a long-term perspective, *LUNDQUA Report* 37:83-89. Department of Quaternary Geology, Lund University.

———2003. Digerdöden, pestvågor och ödeläggelse, *Sällskapet Runica et Mediaevalia, Scripta minora* 9. Stockholm.

Nader, L. 1996. *Naked science: Anthropological inquiry into boundaries, power, and knowledge.* New York: Routledge.

National Research Council (U.S.), Policy Division, Board on Sustainable Development. 1997. *Environmentally significant consumption: Research directions.* Washington, DC: National Academy Press.

———1999. National Research Council (U.S.), Policy Division, Board on Sustainable Development. *Our common journey: A transition toward sustainability.* Washington, DC: National Academy Press.

Naveh, Z., and A. S. Lieberman. 1990. *Landscape ecology: Theory and application* (student ed.). New York: Springer-Verlag.

Neitzel, J. E., ed. 1999. *Great towns and regional polities in the prehistorical southwest and southeast.* Albuquerque: University of New Mexico Press (An Amerind Foundation Publication, Dragoon, AZ).

Nelson, B. W. 1994. Natural forest disturbance and change in the Brazilian Amazon, *Remote Sensing Reviews* 10:105–125.

Nemani R. R., C. D. Keeling, H. Hashimoto, W. M. Jolly, S. C. Piper, C. J. Tucker, R.-B. Myneni, and S. W. Running. 2003. Climate-driven increases in global terrestrial net primary production from 1982 to 1999, *Science* 300:1560–1563.

Nepstad, D., A. Moreira, and A. Alencar. 1999. *Flames in the rain forest: Origins, impacts, and alternatives to Amazonian fire.* Brasilia, DF: Pilot Program to Conserve the Brazilian Rain Forest.

Nepstad, D., A. Verissimo, A. Alencar, C. Nobre, E. Lima, P. Lefebvre, P. Schlesinger, C. Potter, P. Moutinho, E. Mendoza, M. Cochrane, and V. Brooks. 1999. Large-scale impoverishment of Amazonian forests by logging and fire, *Nature* 398:505–508.

Netting, R. McC. 1981. *Balancing on an Alp: Ecological change and continuity in a Swiss mountain community.* New York: Cambridge University Press.

———1993. *Smallholders, householders: Farm families and the ecology of intensive, sustainable agriculture.* Stanford, CA: Stanford University Press.

Neumann, R. P. 2005. *Making political ecology.* London: Hodder Arnold.

Neves, E. G. 1999. Changing perspectives in Amazonian archeology. In *Archeology in Latin America.* G. Politis and B. Alberti, eds. London: Routledge, pp. 216–243.

———1999-2000. O velho e o novo na arqueologia Amazônica, *Revista USP* 44:86–111.

Neves, E. G., J. B. Petersen, R. N. Bartone, and C. A. da Silva. 2003. Historical and socio-cultural origins of Amazonian Dark Earths. In *Amazonian Dark Earths: Origin, properties, management.* J. Lehmann, D. C. Kern, B. Glaser, and W. I. Woods, eds. Dordrecht: Kluwer, pp. 29–50.

Neves, E. G., J. B. Petersen, R. N. Bartone, and M. J. Heckenberger. 2004. The timing of *terra preta* formation in the central Amazon: Archeological data from three sites. In *Amazonian Dark Earths: Explorations in space and time*. B. Glaser and W. I. Woods, eds. Berlin: Springer-Verlag, pp. 125–134.

Newell, B., C. L. Crumley, N. Hassan, E. F. Lambin, C. Pahl-Wostl, A. Underdal, and R. Wasson. 2005. A conceptual template for integrative human–environment research, *Global Environmental Change* 15:299–307.

Nibbi, A. 1975. *The sea peoples and Egypt*. Park Ridge, NJ: Royes Press.

Nicholas, G. P. 2001. Time, scale, and contrastive ecologies in human land-use studies. Paper presented at the 24th Annual Society of Ethnobiology Conference, Durango, CO, March 7–11.

Nicholson, S. E. 2000. The nature of rainfall variability over Africa on time scales of decades to millennia, *Global and Planetary Change* 26:137–158.

Nietschmann, B. 1980. The limits to protein. In *Studies in hunting and fishing in the neotropics. Working papers on South American Indians* 2:131–137. Bennington College, VT.

Nissen, H. J. 1988. *The early history of the ancient Near East, 9000–2000 B.C.* Chicago: University of Chicago Press.

Noble, G. K. 1965. Proto-Arawakan and its descendants, *International Journal of American Linguistics* 31, No. 3, Part II.

Nobre, C. A., and N. O. Renno. 1985. Droughts and floods in South America due to the 1982–1983 ENSO episode. In *Proceedings of the 16th conference on hurricanes and tropical meteorology*. Houston: American Meteorological Society, pp. 131–133.

Nora, P. 1984. *Les Lieux de mémoire*. Paris: Gallimard.

Nordenskiöld, E. 1930. *L'Archéologie du Bassin de l'Amazone*. Paris: Les Éditions G. Van Oest.

Nunn, P. D. 1993. Beyond the native lands: Human history and environmental change in the Pacific Basin. In *The margin fades: Geographical itineraries in a world of islands*. E. Waddell and P. D. Nunn, eds. Suva: Institute of Pacific Studies, University of the South Pacific, pp. 5–27.

———2003. Nature-society interactions in the Pacific Islands, *Geografiska Annaler* 85(4):219–229.

Oberem, U. 1974 [orig. publ. 1967]. Trade and trade goods in the Ecuadorian montaña. In *Native South Americans: Ethnology of the least known continent*. P. J. Lyon, ed. Boston: Little, Brown, pp. 346–357.

O'Connell, M., and K. Molloy. 2001. Farming and woodland dynamics in Ireland during the Neolithic, *Proceedings of the Royal Irish Academy* 101, 1–2:99–128.

Odgaard, B. 1994. The Holocene vegetation history of northern West Jutland, Denmark, *Opera Botanica* 123:1–171. Copenhagen: Council for Nordic Publications in Botany.

Odum, E. P. 1959. Fundamentals of ecology. Philadelphia: W. B. Sanders.

———1983. *Systems ecology*. New York: John Wiley.

Odum, H. T. 1988. Self-organization, transformity, and information, *Science* 2(42):1132–1139.

————1994. The emergy of natural capital. In *Investing in natural capital: The ecological economics approach to sustainability*. A. M. Jansson, C. Folke, R. Costanza, O. Johansson, S. Koskoff, eds. Covelo, CA: Island Press, pp. 200–214.

————1995. Self-organization and maximum empower. In *Maximum power: The ideas and applications of H. T. Odum*. C.A.S. Hall, ed. Boulder, CO: University Press of Colorado, pp. 311–330.

————1996. *Environmental accounting: Energy and decision making*. New York: John Wiley.

Odum, H. T., and J. E. Arding. 1991. Emergy analysis of shrimp mariculture in Ecuador. Working Paper: Coastal Resources Center, University of Rhode Island, Narragansett, RI.

Odum, H. T., and E. C. Odum. 2001. *A prosperous way down: Principles and policies*. Boulder: University Press of Colorado.

Odum, H. T., E. C. Odum, and M. T. Brown. 1998. *Environment and society in Florida*. Boca Raton, FL: CRC Press.

Odum, H. T., and R. C. Pinkerton. 1955. Time's speed regulator: The optimum efficiency for maximum power output in physical and biological systems, *American Scientist* 43:321–343.

Odum, W. E., E. P. Odum, and H. T. Odum. 1995. Nature's pulsing paradigm, *Estuaries* 18(4):547–555.

OEA. 1974. *Marajó: Um estudo para o seu desenvolvimento*. Washington, DC: Secretaria Geral da Organização dos Estados Americanos.

OECD. 2000. *Special session on material flow accounting. History and overview*. Paris: OECD.

Oldfield, F. 1963. Pollen-analysis and man's role in the ecological history of the southeast Lake District, *Geografiska Annaler* 45:23–49.

Oldfield, F., and R. L. Clark. 1990. Environmental history—The environmental evidence. In *The silent countdown*. P. Brimblecombe and C. Pfister, eds. New York: Springer-Verlag, pp. 137–161.

Oldfield, F., and J. A. Dearing. 2003. The role of human activities in past environmental change. In *Paleoclimate, global change and the future*. IGBP Synthesis Book Series. K. Alverson, R. Bradley, and T. Pedersen, eds. Berlin: Springer-Verlag, pp. 143–162.

Oldfield, F., et al. 2003a. A high resolution Late-Holocene palaeo-environmental record from the central Adriatic Sea, *Quaternary Science Reviews* 22:319–342.

————2003b. The late-Holocene history of Gormire Lake (NE England) and its catchment: A multiproxy reconstruction of past human impact, *The Holocene* 13:677–690.

Oldfield, F., and D. C. Statham. 1966. Stratigraphy and pollen-analysis on Cockerham and Pilling Mosses, North Lancashire, *Memoirs and Proceedings of the Manchester Literary and Philosophical Society* 107:1–16.

Oliver, J. R. 1989. The archeological, linguistic and ethnohistorical evidence for the expansion of Arawakan into north-western Venezuela and northeastern Colombia. Ph.D. thesis. University of Illinois at Urbana-Champaign.

————2001. The archeology of forest foraging and agricultural production in Amazonia. In *Unknown Amazon: Culture in nature in ancient Brazil*. C. McEwan, C. Barreto, and E. Neves, eds. London: The British Museum Press, pp. 50–85.

Oliver-Smith, A., and S. M. Hoffman. 1999. *The angry earth: Disaster in anthropological perspective*. New York: Routledge.

Ostrom, E. 1990. *Governing the commons: The evolution of institutions for collective action*. New York: Cambridge University Press.

Ostrom, E., J. Burger, C. B. Field, R. B. Norgaard, and D. Policansky. 1999. Revisiting the commons: Local lessons, global challenges, *Science* 284:278–82.

Ostrom, E., T. Dietz, N. Dolšak, P. Stern, S. Stonich, and E. U. Weber, eds. 2002. *The drama of the commons*. Washington, DC: National Academy Press.

Otroschenko, V. 2003. The economic peculiarities of the Srubnaya cultural-historical entity. In *Prehistoric steppe adaptations and the horse*. M. Levine, C. Renfrew, and K. Boyle, eds. Cambridge, UK: McDonald Institute Monographs, pp. 319–328.

PAGES Newsletter. 2000. *Ecosystem processes and past human impacts*, 8(3), December. www.pages_igbp.org/.

Paine, R. R., A. C. Freter, and D. L. Webster. 1996. A mathematical projection of population growth in the Copan Valley, Honduras, A.D. 400–800, *Latin American Antiquity* 7:51–60.

Painter, M., and W. H. Durham. 1995. *The social causes of environmental destruction in Latin America*. Ann Arbor, MI: University of Michigan Press.

Pare, C. 2000. Bronze and the Bronze Age. In *Metals make the world go round: The supply and circulation of metals in the Bronze Age*. C. Pare, ed. Oxford: Oxbow Books, pp. 1–38.

Parker, D. C., and T. Berger. 2002. Part 4: Synthesis and discussion. In *Agent-based models of land-use and land-cover change*. D. C. Parker et al., eds. Report and Review of an International Workshop, October 4–7, 2001, LUCC Report Series no. 6. LUCC Focus 1 Office, Indiana University, pp. 79–88.

Parker, D. C., T. Berger, and S. M. Manson. 2002. *Agent-based models of land-use and land-cover change*. Report and Review of an International Workshop, October 4–7, 2001, LUCC Report Series no. 6. LUCC Focus 1 Office, Indiana University.

Parker, D., T. Berger, S. Manson, and W. J. McConnell. 2002. *Agent-based models of land-use and land-cover change. LUCC Report Series No. 6*. Louvain-la-Neuve, Belgium: LUCC International Project Office.

Parker, D. C., S. M. Manson, M. A. Janssen, M. J. Hoffman, and P. Deadman. 2003. Multi-agent systems for the simulation of land use and land cover change: A Review, *Annals of the Association of American Geographers* 93: 316–340.

Parker, E., D. Posey, J. Frechione, and L. F. da Silva. 1983. Resource exploitation in Amazonia: Ethnoecological examples from four populations, *Annals of the Carnegie Museum* 52:163–203.

Parsons, J. J. 1985. Raised field farmers as pre-Columbian landscape engineers: Looking north from the San Jorge (Colombia). In *Prehistoric intensive agriculture in the tropics*. I. S. Farrington, ed. British Archaeological Reports International Series 232, pp. 149–165.

Parsons, N. 1993. *A new history of Southern Africa*. London: Macmillan.

Parzinger, H., and N. Boroffka. 2002. Zur bronzezeitlichen Zinngewinnung in Eurasiaen. Die Bergarbeitersiedlung bei Karnap, Uzbekistan. *Godisnjak Jahrbuch* XXXII:161–178. Sarajevo, Frankfurt am Main, Berlin, Heidelberg.

Pasciuti, D., and C. Chase-Dunn. 2002. Estimating the population sizes of cities. http://irows.ucr.edu/research/citemp/estcit/estcit.htm.

Pashkevich, G. 2003. Palaeo-ethnobotanical evidence of agriculture in the steppe and the forest-steppe of east Europe in the Late Neolithic and Bronze Age. In *Prehistoric steppe adaptations and the horse*. M. Levine, C. Renfrew, and K. Boyle, eds. Cambridge, UK: McDonald Institute Monographs, pp. 287–297.

Patterson, K. D. 1986. *Pandemic influenza: A study in historical epidemiology*. Totowa, NJ: Rowman & Littlefield.

Paulson, S., L. L. Gezon, and M. Watts. 2003. Locating the political in political ecology: An introduction, *Human Organization* 62(3):205–217.

Payne, S. 1990. Field report on the Dendra horses. Appendix to E. Protonotariou-Deilaki: The tumuli of Mycenae and Dendra. In Celebrations of death and divinity in the Bronze Age Argolid. R. Hägg, C. Gullög, and C. Nordquist, eds. *Skrifter utgivna av svenska institutet i Atéhen* 4:XL. Stockholm.

Pedersen, O. G. 2002. *DMI and TMR for Denmark 1981, 1990, 1997: An assessment of the material requirements of the Danish economy*. Copenhagen: Statistics Denmark.

Peet, R., and M. Watts. 1996. *Liberation ecologies: Environment, development, social movements*. New York: Routledge.

Penner, S. 1998. Schliemanns Schachtgräberrund und der europäische Nordosten. *Studien zur Herkunft der Mykenischen Streitwagenausstattung*. Saarbrücker Beitrage zur Altertumskunde, Band 60. Bonn: Dr. Rudolf Habelt Verlag.

Perlin, J. 1991. *A forest journey: The role of wood in the development of civilization*. Cambridge, MA: Harvard University Press.

Perota, C. 1992. Adaptação agrícola no baixo Xingú. In *Prehistoria Sudamericana*. B. J. Meggers, ed. Washington, DC: Taraxacum, pp. 211–218.

Petersen, H. C. 1993. An anthropological investigation of the Single Grave Culture in Denmark. In *Populations of the Nordic countries. Human population biology from the present to the Mesolithic*. E. Iregren and R. Liljekvist, eds. Lund University, Sweden, Institute of Archeology Report Series No. 46, pp. 178–188.

Petersen, J. B., E. Neves, and M. Heckenberger. 2001. Gift from the past: *Terra preta* and prehistoric Amerindian occupation in Amazonia. In *Unknown Amazon: Culture in nature in ancient Brazil*. C. McEwan, C. Barreto, and E. Neves, eds. London: The British Museum Press, pp. 86–105.

Petit, C. C., and E. F. Lambin. 2002. Long-term land-cover changes in the Belgian Ardennes (1775–1929): Model-based reconstruction vs. historical maps, *Global Change Biology* 8:616–630.

Petrick, C. 1978. The complementary function of floodlands for agricultural utilization: The várzea of the Brazilian Amazon region, *Applied Sciences and Development* 12:24–46.

Pfaff, A. 1999. What drives deforestation in the Brazilian Amazon? *Journal of Environmental and Economic Management* 37:26–43.

Pfister, C. 1999. *Wetternachhersage: 500 Jahre Klimavariationen und Naturkatastrophen (1496–1995)*. Bern, Switzerland: P. Haupt.

Pfister, C., B. Frenzel, and B. Glaser, eds. 1992. *European climate reconstructed from documentary data: Methods and results*. Stuttgart, Germany: G. Fischer.

Phillips, O. 1993. The potential for harvesting fruits in tropical rainforests: New data from Amazonian Peru, *Biodiversity and Conservation* 2:18–38.

Pianka, E. R. 1978. *Evolutionary ecology*. 2nd ed. New York: Harper & Row.

Pickett, S. T. A., and M. L. Cadenasso. 2002. The ecosystem as a multidimensional concept: Meaning, model, and metaphor, *Ecosystems* 5:1–10.

Pickett, S. T. A., and P. S. White, eds.1985. *The ecology of natural disturbance and patch dynamics*. Orlando, FL: Academic Press.

Poirine, B. 1995. *Two essays on aid and remittances*. Pacific Studies Monograph No. 19. Sydney: The University of New South Wales.

———1998. Should we hate or love MIRAB? *The Contemporary Pacific* 10(1):65–105.

Pollack, H. N. 2003. *Uncertain science . . . Uncertain world*. Cambridge: Cambridge University Press.

Pomeranz, K. 2000. *The great divergence: China, Europe, and the making of the modern world economy*. Princeton, NJ: Princeton University Press.

Poncelet, Eric C. 2001. The discourse of environmental partnerships. In *New directions in anthropology and environment: Intersections*. C. L. Crumley, ed. Walnut Creek, CA: AltaMira Press, pp. 273–291.

Ponting, C. 1991. *A green history of the world: The environment and the collapse of great civilizations*. New York: Penguin.

Porro, A. 1994. Social organization and political power in the Amazon floodplain. In *Amazonian Indians from prehistory to the present: Anthropological perspectives*. A. C. Roosevelt, ed. Tucson, AZ: University of Arizona Press, pp. 79–94.

Postgate, J. N. 1992. *Early Mesopotamia*. London: Routledge.

———2003. Learning the lesson of the future: Trade in prehistory through a historian's lens, *Bibliotheca Orientalis* LX(1)2:6–25.

Prescott, C., and E. Walderhaug. 1995. The last frontier? Processes of Indo-Europeanization in northern Europe: The Norwegian case, *The Journal of Indo-European Studies* 23(3–4):257–278.

Price, D. 1990. Our readers write, *Current Anthropology* 31:386.

Price, T. D., G. Grupe, and P. Schröter. 1998. Migration in the Bell Beaker period of central Europe, *Antiquity* 72:405–11.

Price, T. D., L. Manzanilla, and W. D. Middleton. 2000. Immigration and the ancient city of Teotihuacan in Mexico: A study using strontium isotope ratios in human bone and teeth, *Journal of Archeological Science* 27:903–913.

Prigogine, I., and I. Stengers. 1984. *Order out of chaos: Man's new dialogue with nature*. Toronto: Bantam Books.

Puturidze, M. 2003. Social and economic shifts in the south Caucasian middle Bronze Age. In *Archeology in the borderlands. Investigations in Caucasia and beyond*. A. T. Smith and K. S. Rubinson, eds. Monographs 47. Los Angeles: The Cotsen Institute of Archeology, University of California, Los Angeles, pp. 111–128.

Rahmstorf, S., and T. F. Stocker. 2004. Thermohaline circulation: Past changes and future surprises. In *Global change and the Earth system*, IGBP Series. W. Steffen et al., eds. Berlin:Springer-Verlag, pp. 240–241.

Ramankutty, N., and J. A. Foley. 1999. Estimating historical changes in global land cover: Croplands from 1700 to 1992, *Global Biogeochemical Cycles* 13(4):997–1027.

Ramrath, A., L. Sadori, and J.F.W. Negendank. 2000. Sediments from Lago di Mezzano, central Italy: A record of late glacial/Holocene climatic variations and anthropogenic impact, *The Holocene* 10:87–95.

Ranta, E., V. Kaitala, and J. Lindstrom. 1999. Spatially autocorrelated disturbances and patterns in population synchrony, *Proceedings of the Royal Society of London*, Series B 266:1851–1856.

Ranta, E., V. Kaitala, J. Lindstrom, and E. Helle. 1997. The Moran effect and synchrony in population dynamics, *OIKOS* 78:136–142.

Rapera, C. L. 2004. *Southeast Asia in transition. The case of the Philippines 1981 to 2000. Part 1*. Laguna, CA: SEARCA Publishing.

Rappaport, R. A. 1968. *Pigs for the ancestors*. New Haven: Yale University Press.

Rassamakin, Y. 1999. The eneolithic of the Black Sea steppe: Dynamics of cultural and economic development 4500–2300 B.C. In *Late prehistoric exploitation of the Eurasian steppe*. M. Levin, Y. Rassamakin, A. Kislenko, and N. Tatarinteseva. Cambridge: The McDonald Institute for Archeological Research, University of Cambridge.

Raulwing, P., and H. Meyer. 2004. Der Kikkuli-Text. Hippologische und methodenkritische Überlegungen zum Training von Streitwagenpferden im alten Orient. In *Rad und Wagen. Der Ursprung einer Innovation. Wagen im vorderen Orient und Europa*. S. Burmeister, ed. Mainz: Verlag Phillip von Zabern, pp. 491–506.

Raven, P. H. 2002. Science, sustainability, and the human prospect, *Science* 297:954–958.

Reale, O., and J. Shukla. 2000. Modeling the effects of vegetation on Mediterranean climate during the Roman Classical Period Part II: Model simulation, *Global and Planetary Change* 25:185–214.

Redman, C. L. 1999. *Human impact on ancient environments*. Tucson, AZ: The University of Arizona Press.

Reibsame, W. E., and W. J. Parton. 1994. Integrated modeling of land use and cover change, *BioScience* 44:350–357.

Reichel-Dolmatoff, G. 1996. *The forest within: The world-view of the Tukano Amazonian Indians*. Devon, UK: Themis Books.

Renard-Casevitz, F.-M. 1993. Guerriers du sel, sauniers de la paix. In *La Remontée de l'Amazone: Anthropologie et histoire des sociétés amazoniennes*. P. Descola and A. C. Taylor, eds. *L'Homme* 126–128, XXXIII (2–4):25–43.

————2002. Social forms and regressive history: From the Campa cluster to the Mojos and from the Mojos to the landscaping terrace-builders of the Bolivian savanna. In *Comparative Arawakan histories: Rethinking language family and culture area in Amazonia*. J. D. Hill and F. Santos-Granero, eds. Urbana, IL: University of Illinois Press, pp. 123–146.

Renard-Casevitz, F.-M., T. Saignes, and A. C. Taylor-Descola. 1986. *L'Inca, L'Espagnol et les Sauvages: Rapports entre les sociétés Amazoniennes et Andines du Xve au XVIIe siècle*. Paris: Editions Recherche sur les Civilisations. *Synthése* no. 21.

Renfrew, C. 1987. *Archeology and language: The puzzle of Indo-European origins*. London: Pimlico.

————2000 (ed.). *America past, America present: Genes and languages in the Americas and beyond*. Cambridge: Cambridge University Press.

Renfrew, C., and J. Cherry, ed. 1985. *Peer polity interaction and socio-political change*. Cambridge: Cambridge University Press.

Reynolds, J. F., and M. Stafford Smith, eds. 2002. *Global desertification: Do humans cause deserts?* Berlin: Dahlem University Press.

Rezepkin, A. D. 2000. Das frühbronzezeitliche Gräberfeld von Klady und die Majkop-Kultur in Nordwestkaukasien. *Archäologie in Eurasien* Band 10. Rahden, Germany:Verlag Marie Leidorf (VML).

Ribeiro, P. M. 1999. Os horticultores de Roraima. In *Pré-história da Terra Brasilis*. M. C. Tenório, ed. Rio de Janeiro: Editora UFRJ, pp. 339–344.

Ritchie, J., and J. Ritchie. 1979. *Growing up in Polynesia*. Sydney: George Allen & Unwin.

Rival, L. 1996. *Hijos del sol, padres del jaguar: Los Huarani de ayer y hoy*. Quito: Abya Yala.

Robbins, P. 1998. Authority and environment: Institutional landscapes in Rajasthan, India, *Annals of the Association of American Geographers* 88:410–435.

Robert Kenner Films. 1998. Influenza 1918. Script of the American experience: 1918, the year of dying and forgetting. WGBH Educational Foundation.

Roberts, J. T., and P. E. Grimes. 2002. World-System theory and the environment: Toward a new synthesis. In *Sociological theory and the environment: Classical foundations, contemporary insights*. Riley E. Dunlap et al., eds. Bd. 8. Lanham, MD: Rowman & Littlefield Publishers, pp. 167–194.

Roberts, N. 1998. *The Holocene. An environmental history*. London: Blackwell Publishing.

Robertshaw, P., and D. Taylor. 2000. Climate change and the rise of political complexity in western Uganda, *Journal of African History* 41:1–28.

Robinson, J. G., and E. L. Bennett. 2000. Carrying capacity limits to sustainable hunting in tropical forests. In *Hunting for sustainability in tropical forests*. J. G. Robinson and E. L. Bennett, eds. New York: Columbia University Press, pp. 13–30.

Rogan, J., and J. Franklin. 2002. Mapping wildfire burn severity in southern California forests and shrublands using Enhanced Thematic Mapper imagery, *Geocarto International* 16:89–99.

Roosevelt, Anna C. 1991. *Moundbuilders of the Amazon*. San Diego, CA: Academic Press.

———1993. The rise and fall of the Amazon chiefdoms. In *La Remontée de l'Amazone: Anthropologie et histoire des sociétés amazoniennes*. P. Descola and A. C. Taylor, eds. *L'Homme* 126–128, XXXIII (2–4):255–283.

Roosevelt, Anna C., R. A. Housley, M. I. da Silveira, S. Maranca, and R. Johnson. 1991. Eighth millennium pottery from a prehistoric shell midden in the Brazilian Amazon, *Science* 254:1621–1624.

Rösch, M. 1992. Human impact as registered in the pollen record: Some results from the western Lake Constance region, Southern Germany, *Vegetation History and Archaeobotany* 1:101–109.

Rose, S., L. J. Kamin, and R. C. Lewontin 1984. *Not in our genes: Biology, ideology, and human nature*. New York: Pantheon Books.

Rothman, D. S. 1998. Environmental Kuznets curves: Real progress or passing the buck? A case for consumption-based approaches, *Ecological Economics* 25(2):177–194.

Rothman, M. S. 2003. Ripples in the stream. Transcaucasia-Anatolian interaction at the beginning of the third millennium B.C. In *Archeology in the borderlands. Investigations in Caucasia and beyond*. Monographs 47. A. T. Smith and K. S. Rubinson, eds. Los Angeles: The Cotsen Institute of Archeology, University of California, pp. 95–110.

Rotmans, J., and H. Dowlatabadi. 1998. Integrated assessment modeling. In *Human choice and climate change*. S. Rayner and E. L. Malone, eds. Seattle, WA: Battelle Press, pp. 291–377.

Rowlands, M. 1980. Kinship, alliance and exchange in the European Bronze Age. In *Settlement and society in the British Later Bronze Age*. J. Barrett and R. Bradley, eds. BAR British Series 83. Oxford: BAR.

Rubinson, K. S. 2003. Silver vessels and cylinder sealings: Precious reflections of economic exchange in the early second millennium B.C. In *Archeology in the borderlands: Investigations in Caucasia and beyond*. Monographs 47. A. T. Smith & K. S. Rubinson, eds. Los Angeles: The Cotsen Institute of Archeology, University of California, pp. 128–143.

Ruddle, K. 1974. The Yukpa cultivation system: A study of shifting cultivation in Colombia and Venezuela, *Ibero-Americana* 52. Berkeley and Los Angeles: University of California Press.

Ruhlen, M. 1987. *A guide to the world's languages*, vol. 1, *Classification*. Stanford, CA: Stanford University Press.

Runnels, C. N.1995. Environmental degradation in ancient Greece, *Scientific American* March:96–99.

Sahlins, M. 1969. Economic anthropology and anthropological economics, *Social Science Journal of Anthropology* 26(1):67–86.

———1972. *Stone Age economics*. London: Tavistock Publications.

———1994. Goodbye to tristes tropes: Ethnography in the context of modern world history. In *Assessing cultural anthropology*. R. Borofsky, ed. New York: McGraw-Hill, pp. 377–394.

Sahoglu, V. 2005. The Anatolian trade network and the Izmir region during the early Bronze Age, *Oxford Journal of Archeology* 24(4):339–361.

Saloranta, T. M. 2001. Post-normal science and the global climate issue, *Climate Change* 50:395–404.

Salthe, S. N. 2003. Infodynamics, a developmental framework for ecology/economics, *Conservation Ecology* 7(3):3.

Salzano, F. M., and S. M. Callegari-Jacques. 1988. South American Indians: A case study in evolution, *Research Monographs on Human Population Biology* 6. Oxford: Oxford University Press.

Samford, P. 2000. Power flows in many channels: Pits and West African-based spiritual traditions in colonial Virginia. Ph.D. Dissertation, Department of Anthropology. University of North Carolina, Chapel Hill, NC.

Samuelson, P. A., and W. D. Nordhaus. 1995. *Economics.* New York: McGraw-Hill.

Sandars, N. K. 1978. *The sea peoples: Warriors of the ancient Mediterranean, 1250–1150 b.c.* London: Thames and Hudson.

Sanderson, S. K. 1990. *Social evolutionism: A critical history.* London: Basil Blackwell Publishing.

Sandweiss, D. H., K. A. Maasch, and D. G. Anderson. 1999. Transitions in the mid-Holocene, *Science* 283:499–500.

Santos, A. M. de Souza. 1982. Aritapera: Uma comunidade de pequenos productores na várzea amazônica (Santarám-PA). Bol. do Museu Paraense Emílio Goeldi, *Antropologia* No. 83. Belém.

Santos-Granero, F. 2002. The Arawakan matrix: Ethos, language, and history in native South America. In *Comparative Arawakan histories: Rethinking language family and culture area in Amazonia.* J. D. Hill and F. Santos-Granero, ed. Urbana, IL: University of Illinois Press, pp. 25–50.

Saul, S. B. 1960. *Studies in British overseas trade 1870–1914.* Liverpool, UK: Liverpool University Press.

Scasny, M., J. Kovanda, and T. Hak. 2003. Material flow accounts, balances and derived indicators for the Czech Republic during the 1990s: Results and recommendations for methodological improvements, *Ecological Economics* 45(1):41–57.

Schaan, D. P. 2004. The Camutins chiefdom: Rise and development of social complexity on Marajó Island, Brazilian Amazon. Doctoral Dissertation, University of Pittsburgh.

Schandl, H., C. M. Grünbühel, S. Thongmanivong, B. Pathoumthong, and P. Inthapanya. 2005. *National and local material flow analysis for Lao PDR.* Laguna, CA: SEARCA Publishing.

Schandl, H., and N. B. Schulz. 2002. Changes in United Kingdom's natural relations in terms of society's metabolism and land use from 1850 to the present day, *Ecological Economics* 41(2):203–221.

Schandl, H., H. Weisz, and B. Petrovic. 2000. Materialflussrechnung für Österreich 1960 bis 1997, *Statistische Nachrichten* 55 (NF)(2):128–137.

Scheffer, M., S. Carpenter, J. Foley, C. Folke, and B. Walker. 2001. Catastrophic shifts in ecosystems, *Nature* 413:591–596.

Schellnhuber, H. J. 1999. "Earth system" analysis and the second Copernican revolution, *Nature* 402:19–23.

Schellnhuber, H. J., P. J. Crutzen, W.C. Clark, M. Claussen, and H. Held, eds. 2004. *Earth system analysis for sustainability.* Cambridge, MA: The MIT Press.

Schimel, D., and D. Baker. 2002. Carbon cycle: The wildfire factor, *Nature* 420 (6911):29–30.

Schimel D. S., J. I. House, K. A. Hibbard, P. Bousquet, P. Ciais, P. Peylin, B. H. Braswell, M. J. Apps, D. Baker, A. Bondeau, J. Canadell, G. Churkina, W. Cramer, A. S. Denning, C. B. Field, P. Friedlingstein, C. Goodale, M. Heimann, R. A. Houghton, J. M. Melillo, B. Moore, D. Murdiyarso, I. Noble, S. W. Pacala, I. C. Prentice, M. R. Raupach, P. J. Rayner, R. J. Scholes, W. L. Steffen, and C. Wirth. 2001. Recent patterns and mechanisms of carbon exchange by terrestrial ecosystems, *Nature* 414:169–172.

Schmidt, M. 1917. Die Aruaken: Ein Beitrag zum Problem der Kulturverbreitung. Ph.D. thesis. Universität Leipzig.

———1974. [Orig. publ. 1951] Comments on cultivated plants and agricultural methods of South American Indians. In *Native South Americans: Ethnology of the least known continent.* P. J. Lyon, ed. Boston: Little, Brown, pp. 60–68.

Schneider, J. 1977. Was there a pre-capitalist world-system? *Peasant Studies* 6(1):20–29.

Schultes, Richard E. 1977. Diversas plantas comestíveis nativas do noreste da Amazônia, *Acta Amazônica* 7:317–327.

Schwartz, S. B., and F. Salomon. 1999. New peoples and new kinds of people: Adaptation, readjustment, and ethnogenesis in South American indigenous societies (colonial era). In *The Cambridge history of the native peoples of the Americas,* Volume III, *South America, Part 2.* F. Salomon and S. B. Schwartz, eds. Cambridge: Cambridge University Press, pp. 443–501.

Scoones, I. 1999. New ecology and the social sciences: What prospects for a fruitful engagement? *Annual Review of Anthropology* 28:479–507.

Sen, A. K. 1997. *Poverty and famines: An essay on entitlement and deprivation.* Oxford: Clarendon Press.

Serrão, E. A. 1995. Possibilities for sustainable agriculture development in the Brazilian Amazon: An EMBRAPA proposal. In *Brazilian perspectives on sustainable development of the Amazon region.* M. Clüsner-Goldt and I. Sachs, eds. Man in the Biosphere Series 15, UNESCO, pp. 259–285.

Service, E. R. 1971. *Profiles in ethnology.* New York: Harper and Row.

———1975. *Origins of the state and civilization: The process of cultural evolution.* New York: W.W. Norton.

Seto, K., and R. Kaufmann. 2003. Modeling the drivers of urban land use change in the Pearl River Delta, China: Integrating remote sensing with socioeconomic data, *Land Economics* 79:106–121.

Seto, K. C., R. K. Kaufmann, and C. E. Woodcock. 2000. Landsat reveals China's farmland reserves, but are they vanishing? *Nature* 406:314–322.

Shannon, T. R. 1996. *An introduction to the world-system perspective.* Boulder, CO: Westview Press.

Shea, D. E. 1976. In defense of small population estimates for the Central Andes in 1520. In *The native population of the Americas in 1492.* W. M. Denevan, ed. Madison, WI: University of Wisconsin Press, pp. 157–180.

Shen, J., T. Jones, X. Yang, J. A. Dearing, and S. Wang. 2006. The Holocene vegetation history of Erhai Lake, Yunnan Province, southwestern China: The role of climate and human forcings, *The Holocene* 16:265–276.

Sherratt, A. 1997. *Economy and society in prehistoric Europe: Changing perspectives.* Edinburgh: Edinburgh University Press.

———1999. Echoes of the Big Bang: The historical context of language dispersal. In *Proceedings from the tenth annual UCLA Indo-European conference Los Angeles, 1998.* K. Jones-Bley et al., eds. *Journal of Indo-European Studies Monograph Series No. 32.* Washington, DC, pp. 261–282.

———2003. The Baden (Pécel) culture and Anatolia: Perspectives on a cultural transformation. In *Morgenrot der Kulturen. Frühe Etappen der Menschheitsgeschichte in Mittel-und Südosteuropa.* E. Jerem and P. Raczky, eds. Festschrift für Nándor Kalicz zum 75. Geburtstag. Budapest.

Shislina, N. I., ed. 2000. *Seasonality studies of the Bronze Age northwest Caspian steppe (English summaries).* Papers of the State Historical Museum Vol. 120. Moscow.

———2001 (ed.). The seasonal cycle of grassland use in the Caspian Sea steppe: A new approach to an old problem, *European Journal of Archeology* 4:323–46.

———2003 (ed.). Yamna culture pastoral exploitation: A local sequence. In *Prehistoric steppe adaptations and the horse.* M. Levine, C. Renfrew, and K. Boyle, eds. Cambridge: McDonald Institute Monographs, pp. 353–367.

Shislina, N. I., V. P. Golikov, and O. Orfinskaya. 2000. Bronze Age textiles of the Caspian Sea maritime steppes. In *Kurgans, ritual sites, and settlements. Eurasian Bronze and Iron Age.* J. Davis-Kimball et al., eds. Oxford: BAR International Series 890.

Shislina, N. I., and Hiebert, F. T. 1998. The steppe and the sown: Interaction between Bronze Age Eurasian nomads and agriculturalists. In *The Bronze Age and early Iron Age peoples of eastern Central Asia.* V. Mair, ed. Washington, DC and Philadelphia: The Institute for the Study of Man in collaboration with The University of Pennsylvania Museum Publications, pp. 222–238.

Sierra, R., and J. Stallings. 1998. The dynamics and social organization of tropical deforestation in northwest Ecuador, 1983–1995, *Human Ecology* 26(1):135–161.

Silverberg, R. 1996. *The golden dream: Seekers of El Dorado.* Athens, OH: Ohio University Press.

Simões, M. F., and C. G. Correa. 1987. Pesquisas arqueológicas no baixo Uatumã-Jatapu (Amazonas), *Revista de Arqueologia* 4(1):29–48.

Simões, M. F., and F. de Araujo-Costa. 1987. Pesquisas arqeológicas no baixo rio Tocantins (Pará), *Revista de Arqueologia* 4(1):11–27.

Simões, M. F., and D. F. Lopes. 1987. Pesquisas arqeológicas no baixo/médio Rio Madeira. *Revista de Arqueologia* 4(1):117–134.

Simões, M. F., and A. L. Machado. 1987. Pesquisas arqueológicas no lago de Silves (Amazonas), *Revista de Arqueologia* 4(1):49–82.

Singh, S. J. 2003. *In the sea of influence: A world-system perspective of the Nicobar Islands.* Lund: Lund University (Lund Studies in Human Ecology 6).

Singh, S. J., and C. M. Grünbühel. 2003. Environmental relations and biophysical transitions: The case of Trinket Islands, *Geografiska Annaler, Series B, Human Geography* 85 B(4):187–204.

Skole, D. L., W. H. Chomentowski, W. A. Salas, and A. D. Nobre. 1994. Physical and human dimensions of deforestation in Amazonia, *Bioscience* 44(5):314–322.

Skole, D. L., and C. Tucker. 1993. Tropical deforestation and habitat fragmentation in the Amazon: Satellite data from 1978 to 1988, *Science* 260(5116):1905–1910.

Smith, A. 1776/1937. *An inquiry into the nature and causes of the wealth of nations. 1776/1937.* New York: Random House.

Smith, A., and K. S. Rubinson, eds. 2003. *Archeology in the borderlands. Investigations in Caucasia and beyond.* Monographs 47. Los Angeles: The Cotsen Institute of Archeology, University of California.

Smith, V. A. 1981. *The Oxford history of India.* 4th edition. P. Spear, ed. Delhi: Oxford University Press.

Snow, C. P. 1959. *The Two Cultures and the scientific revolution.* New York: Cambridge University Press.

Snowball, I., P. Sandgren, and G. Pettersson. 1999. The mineral magnetic properties of an annually laminated Holocene lake-sediment sequence in northern Sweden, *The Holocene* 9:353–362.

Soares, L. de Castro. 1977. Hidrografia. In *Geografia do Brasil,* Vol. 1, Região Norte. Rio de Janeiro: Fundação Instituto Brasileiro de Geografia e Estatística, pp. 95–166.

Sombroek, W. G. 1984. Soils of the Amazon region. In *The Amazon.* H. Sioli, ed. Dordrecht: Dr. W. Junk Publishers, pp. 521–535.

Sörlin, S., and A. Öckerman. 1998. *Jorden en ö: En global miljöhistoria.* Stockholm: Natur och Kultur.

Sorokin, P. A. 1937. *Social and cultural dynamics.* Vol. III. *Fluctuations of social relationships, war, and revolution.* New York: American Book Company.

Spencer, C. S. 1998. Investigating the development of Venezuelan chiefdoms. In *Chiefdoms and chieftaincy in the Americas.* E. M. Redmond, ed. Gainesville, FL: University Press of Florida, pp. 104–137.

Spencer, H. 1860. *First principles.* London: Williams & Norgate.

Stager, J. C., B. Cumming, and L. Meeker. 1997. A high-resolution 11,400-yr diatom record from lake Victoria, East Africa, *Quaternary Research* 47:81–89.

———2003. A 10,000-year high-resolution diatom record from Pilkington Bay, Lake Victoria, East Africa, *Quaternary Research* 59:172–181.

Stager, J. C., D. Ryves, B. F. Cumming, L. D. Meeker, and J. Beer. 2005. Solar variability and the levels of Lake Victoria, East Africa, during the last millennium, *Journal of Palaeo-limnology* 33:243–251.

Stark, L. R. 1985. Indigenous languages of lowland Ecuador: History and current status. In *South American Indian languages: Retrospect and prospect*. H. E. M. Klein and L. R. Stark, eds. Austin, TX: University of Texas Press, pp. 157–193.

Stearman, A. M. 2000. A pound of flesh: Social change and modernization as factors in hunting sustainability among neotropical indigenous societies. In *Hunting for sustainability in tropical forests*. J. G. Robinson and E. L. Bennett, eds. New York: Columbia University Press, pp. 233–250.

———1990. The effects of settler incursion on fish and game resources of the Yuquí, a native American society of eastern Bolivia. *Human Organization* 49:373–385.

Steffen, W., J. Jäger, D. Carson, and C. Bradshaw, eds. 2001. *Challenges of a changing Earth*. Heidelberg: Springer-Verlag.

Steffen, W., A. Sanderson, P. D. Tyson, J. Jäger, P. A. Matson, B. Moore III, F. Oldfield, K. Richardson, H.-J. Schellnhuber, B. L. Turner II, and R. J. Wasson. 2004. *Global change and the Earth system: A planet under pressure*. IGBP Global Change Series. Berlin: Springer-Verlag.

Stein, G. J. 1999. *Rethinking world-systems: Diasporas, colonies, and interaction in Uruk Mesopotamia*. Tucson, AZ: The University of Arizona Press.

Steiner, D. 1993. Human ecology as transdisciplinary science, and science as part of human ecology. In *Human ecology: Fragments of anti-fragmentary views of the world*. D. Steiner and M. Nauser, eds. London: Routledge, pp. 47–76.

Steininger, M. K., C. J. Tucker, J. R. G. Townshend, T. J. Killeen, A. Desch, V. Bell, and P. Ersts. 2001. Tropical deforestation in the Bolivian Amazon, *Environmental Conservation* 28(2):127–134.

Steward, J. H. 1955. *Theory of culture change: The methodology of multilinear evolution*. Urbana, IL: University of Illinois Press.

Steward, J. H., and L. C. Faron. 1959. *Native peoples of South America*. New York: McGraw-Hill.

Stewart, I. 1997. *Does God play dice?* 2nd ed. London: Penguin.

Stonich, S. C. 1993. *"I am destroying the land!": The political ecology of poverty and environmental destruction in Honduras*. Boulder, CO: Westview Press.

———1998. Political ecology of tourism, *Annals of Tourism Research* 25(1):25–54.

———2000. *The other side of paradise: Tourism, conservation, and development in the Bay Islands*. New York: Cognizant Communication Corp.

———2001. Political ecology. In *The international encyclopedia of the social and behavioral sciences*. B. L. Turner, ed. Oxford: Elsevier Science.

Straussfogel, D. 1998. How many world-systems? A contribution to the continuationist/transformationist debate, *Review* 21(1):1–28.

———2000. World-systems theory in the context of systems theory: An overview. In *A world-systems reader: New perspectives on gender, urbanism, cultures, indigenous peoples, and ecology*. T. D. Hall, ed. Lanham, MD: Rowman & Littlefield, pp. 169–180.

Stuiver, M., P. J. Reimer, E. Bard, J. W. Beck, G. S. Burr, K. A. Hughen, B. Kromer, F. G. McCormac, J. van der Plicht, and M. Spurk. 1998. INTCAL 98 Radiocarbon age calibration 24,000–0 cal BP, *Radiocarbon* 40:1041–1083.

Sutton, J. 2004. Engaruka: The success & abandonment of an integrated irrigation system in an arid part of the Rift Valley, c 15th to 17th centuries. In *Islands of intensive agriculture in Eastern Africa*. M. Widgren and J.E.G. Sutton, eds. Eastern African Studies, James Currey Ltd, 114–132.

Swesey, S. L., and Heizer, R. F. 1977. Ritual management of salmonid fish resources in California, *Journal of California Anthropology* 4:6–29.

Tainter, J. 1988. *The collapse of complex societies.* Cambridge: Cambridge University Press.

———2000. Problem solving: Complexity, history, sustainability, *Population and Environment* 22(1):3–41.

Tainter, J., et al. 2003. Resource transitions and energy gain: Contexts of organization, *Conservation Ecology* 7(3):4.

Tansley, A. G. 1935. The use and abuse of vegetational concepts and terms, *Ecology* 16(3):284–307.

Taylor, A. C. 1999. The western margins of Amazonia from the early sixteenth to the early nineteenth century. In *The Cambridge history of the native peoples of the Americas,* Volume III, *South America, Part 2.* F. Salomon and S. B. Schwartz, eds. Cambridge: Cambridge University Press, pp. 188–256.

Taylor, D., P. Robertshaw, and R. P. Marchant. 2000. Environmental change and political-economic upheaval in precolonial western Uganda, *The Holocene* 10, 4:527–536.

Teggart, F. J. 1939. *Rome and China: A study of correlations in historical events.* Berkeley and Los Angeles: University of California Press.

Terlouw, C. P. 1992. *The regional geography of the world-system. External arena, periphery, semiperiphery, core.* Utrecht: Koninklijk Nederlands Aardrijkskundig Gnootschap (Netherlands Geographical Studies; 144).

Thaman, R. R. 1982. Deterioration of traditional food systems, increasing malnutrition and food dependency in the Pacific Islands, *Journal of Food and Nutrition* 39:109–121.

Thirgood, J. V. 1981. *Man and the Mediterranean forest: A history of resource depletion.* New York: Academic Press.

Thomas, C. G., and G. Connant.1999. *Citadel to city-state: The transformation of Greece 1200–700 B.C.E..* Bloomington, IN: Indiana University Press.

Thompson, M., R. Ellis, and A. Wildawsky. 1989. *Cultural theory.* Boulder, CO: Westview Press.

Thompson, W. R. 2000a. Climate, water, and center-hinterland conflict in the ancient world system. Paper delivered at the annual meeting of the International Studies Association, Los Angeles, CA, March.

———2000b. K-waves, leadership cycles, and global war: A nonhyphenated approach to world systems analysis. In *A world-systems reader: New perspectives on gender, urbanism, cultures, indigenous peoples, and ecology.* T. D. Hall, ed. Lanham, MD: Rowman & Littlefield, pp. 83–104.

————2001a. Trade, collapse, and diffusion. Paper delivered at the annual meeting of the International Studies Association, Chicago, IL, February.

————2001b. The globalization of ancient near eastern trade. Paper delivered at the annual meeting of the American Schools of Oriental Research, Boulder, CO, November.

————2002. Testing a cyclical instability theory in the ancient Near East, *Comparative Civilizations Review* 46:34–78.

————2003. Climate, water, and political-economic crises in the southwest Asian Bronze Age. Paper delivered at The World System History and Global Environmental Change Conference, Lund, Sweden, September.

————2006. Early globalization, trade crises and reorientations in the ancient Near East. In *Connectivity in antiquity: Globalization as long-term historical process*. O. S. LaBianca and S. Scham, eds. New York: Continuum.

Tian, H., J. M. Mellilo, D. W. Kicklighter, A. D. McGuire, J. V. K. Helfrich III, B. Moore III, and C. Vrsmarty. 1998. Effect of inter-annual climate variability on carbon storage in Amazonian ecosystems, *Nature* 396:664–667.

Tierney, K. 1999. Toward a critical sociology of risk, *Sociological Forum* 14(2):215–242.

Tilly, C. 1993. *European revolutions: 1492–1992*. Oxford, UK: Blackwell Publishing.

Torero, A. 2002. *Idiomas de los Andes: Lingüística e historia*. Lima: Instituto Francés de Estudios Andinos.

Torrens, P. M, and D. O'Sullivan. 2001. Cellular automata and urban simulation: Where do we go from here? *Environment and Planning B: Planning and Design* 28:163–168.

Toullelan, P.-Y., and B. Gilles. 1992. *Le Mariage Franco-Tahitien: Histoire de Tahiti du XVIIIe siècle à nos jours*. Papeete: Éditions Polymages-Scoop.

Townsend, P. 2000. *Environmental anthropology: From pigs to policies*. Prospect Heights, IL: Waveland Press.

Tran van Doan, J. B. 1985. Harmony and consensus: Confucius and Habermas on politics. In *Proceedings of internation symposium on Confucius and the modern world*. Taipei: Taiwan University.

Trawick, P. 2002. *The struggle for water in Peru: Comedy and tragedy in the Andean commons*. Stanford, CA: Stanford University Press.

Triana, G. 1987. Introducción. In *La Colombia Amerindia*, pp. 97–107. Bogotá: Instituto Colombiano de Antropología.

Trifonov, V. 2004. Die Majkop-Kultur und die erste Wagen in der südrussischen Steppe. In *Rad und Wagen. Der Ursprung einer Innovation. Wagen im vorderen Orient und Europa*. S. Burmeister, ed. Mainz: Verlag Phillip von Zabern, pp. 167–177.

Trigger, B. G. 1993. *Early civilizations: Ancient Egypt in context*. Cairo: The American University in Cairo Press.

Trocki, C. 1999. *Opium, empire and global political economy: A study of the Asian opium trade, 1750–1950*. London: Routledge.

Tucker, C. M. 1999. Private vs. communal forests: Forest conditions and tenure in a Honduran community, *Human Ecology* 27(2):201–230.

Tucker, G. E., and R. Slingerland. 1997. Drainage basin responses to climate change, *Water Resources Research* 33:2031–2047.

Turchin, P. 2003a. Evolution in population dynamics, *Nature* 424:17(July):257–258.

———2003b. *Historical dynamics: Why states rise and fall.* Princeton: Princeton University Press.

———2005. Dynamical feedbacks between population growth and sociopolitical instability in agrarian states, *Structure and Dynamics* 1(1): Article 3. http://repositories.cdlib.org/imbs/socdyn/sdeas/.

Turchin, P., and T. D. Hall. 2003. Spatial synchrony among and within world-systems: Insights from theoretical ecology, *Journal of World-Systems Research* 9(1):37–64.

Turchin, P., and S. A. Nefedov. 2007. *Secular cycles.* Book manuscript in preparation. http://jwsr.ucr.edu/archive/vol9/number1/pdf/jwsr-v9n1-turchinhall.pdf.

Turner, B. L., II. 2002. Toward integrated land-change science: Advances in 1.5 decades of sustained international research on land-use and land-cover change. In *Challenges of a changing Earth.* W. Steffen, J. Jäger, D. Carson, and C. Bradshaw, eds. Heidelberg: Springer-Verlag, pp. 21–26.

Turner, B. L., II, W. C. Clark, R. W. Kates, J. F. Richards, J. T. Mathews, and W. B. Meyer, eds. 1990. *The Earth as transformed by human action.* New York: Cambridge University Press.

Turner, B. L., II, S. C. Villar, D. Foster, J. Geoghegan, E. Keys, P. Klepeis, D. Lawrence, P. M. Mendoza, S. Manson, Y. Ogneva-Himmelberger, A. B. Plotkin, D. P. Salicrup, R. R. Chowdhury, B. Savitsky, L. Schneider, B. Schmook, and C. Vance. 2001. Deforestation in the Southern Yucatán peninsular region: An integrative approach, *Forest Ecology and Management* 154:353–370.

Turner, B. L., II, J. Geoghegan, and D. R. Foster, eds. 2004. *Integrated land-change science and tropical deforestation in the southern Yucatán: Final frontiers.* Oxford Geographical and Environmental Studies. Oxford: Clarendon Press of Oxford.

Tyson, P. D., G. R. J. Cooper, and T. S. McCarthy. 2002. Millennial to multi-decadal variability in the climate of southern Africa, *International Journal of Climatology* 22:1105–1117.

Tyson, P. D., J. Lee-Thorp, K. Holmgren, and J. F. Thackeray. 2002. Changing gradients of climate change in southern Africa during the past millennium: Implications for population movements, *Climatic Change* 52:129–135.

UNEP. 2002. *Global Environmental Outlook-3.* London: Earthscan.

Uriarte, L. 1985. Los nativos y su territorio: el caso de los Jivaro Achuara en la Amazonia peruana, *Amazonía Peruana* 11:39–64.

Van de Vijver, G., S. N. Salthe, and M. Delpos, eds. 1998. *Evolutionary systems: Biological and epistemological perspectives on selection and self-organization.* Dordrecht: Kluwer.

van Geel, B., J. Buurman, and H. T. Waterbolk. 1996. Archeological and palaeoecological indications of an abrupt climate change in The Netherlands, and evidence for climatological teleconnections around 2650 BP, *Journal of Quaternary Science* 11:451–460.

van Geel, B., O. M. Raspopov, H. Renssen, J. vander Plicht, V. A. Dergachec, and H. A. J. Meijer. 1999. The role of solar forcing upon climate change, *Quaternary Science Reviews* 18:331–338.

Vance, C., and J. Geoghegan. 2002. Temporal and spatial modeling of tropical deforestation: A survival analysis linking satellite and household survey data, *Agricultural Economics* 27:317–332.

Vandkilde, H. In press. Warriors and warrior institutions in Copper Age Europe. In *Warfare in archeological and social anthropological perspective.* T. Otto, H. Thrane, and H. Vandkilde, eds. Aarhus, Denmark: Aarhus University Press.

Vayda, A. P., and B. B. Walters. 1999. Against political ecology, *Human Ecology* 27(1):167–179.

Veldkamp, A., and L. O. Fresco. 1997. Reconstructing land use drivers and their spatial scale dependence for Costa Rica, *Agricultural Systems* 55:19–43.

Veldkamp, A., and E. F. Lambin. 2001. Predicting land-use change, *Agriculture, Ecosystems and Environment* 85:1–6.

Vercoutter, J. 1967. Archaic Egypt. In *The Near East: The early civilizations.* J. Bottero, E. Cassin, J. Vercoutter, eds. R. F. Tannenbaum, trans. New York: Delacorte Press.

Veríssimo A., P. Barreto, R. Tarifa, and C. Uhl. 1995. Extraction of a high-value natural source from Amazon: The case of mahogany, *Forest Ecology and Management* 72:39–60.

Verschuren, D., K. R. Laird, and B. F. Cumming. 2000. Rainfall and drought in equatorial East Africa during the past 1,100 years, *Nature* 403:410–414.

Vicent Garcia, J. M., A. Rodriquez, J. Lopez, J. de Zavala, P. Lopez, and M. Martinez. 1999. Una propuesta metodologica para el estudio de la metalurgia prehistorica: El caso de Gorny en la region de Kargaly (Orenburg, Rusia), *Trabajos de Prehistoria* 56(2):85–113.

———2000. Catastrofes eologicas en la estepa? Arqueologia del paisaje en el complejo minro-metalurgico de Kargaly (region Orenburg,Rusia), *Trabajos de Prehistoria* 57(1):29–74.

Vickers, W. T. 1983. The territorial dimensions of Siona-Secoya and Encabello adaptation. In *Adaptive responses of native Amazonians.* R. B. Hames and W. T. Vickers, eds. New York: Academic Press, pp. 451–478.

———1984. The faunal components of lowland South American hunting kills, *Interciencia* 9:366–376.

———1989. *Los Sionas y Secoyas: Su adaptación al ambiente amazónico.* Quito: Ediciones Abya-Yala.

———1991. Hunting yields and game composition over two years in an Amazon Indian territory. In *Neotropical wildlife use and conservation.* J. Robinson and K. Redford, eds. Chicago: University of Chicago Press, pp. 53–81.

Videjko, M. 1995. Grosssiedlungen der Tripol'e-Kultur in der Ukraine. Eurasia Antiqua, *Zeitschrift für Archäologie Eurasiens* Band 1:45–48.

Vitousek, P. M., J. A. Mooney, J. Lubchenco, and J. M. Melillo. 1997. Human domination of Earth's ecosystems, *Science* 277:494–499.

Vogel, J. C. 2000. Radiocarbon dating of the iron Age sequence in the Limpopo valley. In *African naissance: The Limpopo Valley 1,000 years ago*. M. Leslie and T. Maggs, eds. The South African Archeological Society, Goodwin Series, 8, 51–57.

Wagley, C. 1977. *Welcome of tears: The Tapirapé Indians of central Brazil.* New York: Oxford University Press.

Wagner, E., and L. Arvelo. 1986. Monou-teri: Un nuevo complejo arqueológico en el alto Orinoco, Venezuela, *Acta Científica Venezolana* 37:689–696.

Walbank, F. W. 1993. *The hellenistic world.* Cambridge, MA: Harvard University Press.

Walker, B., W. Steffen, J. Canadell, and J. Ingram, eds. 1999. *The terrestrial biosphere and global change: Implications for natural and managed ecosystems.* Cambridge: Cambridge University Press.

Walker, P. A. 2005. Political ecology: Where is the ecology? *Progress in Human Geography* 29(1):73–82.

Wallace, A. F. C. 1970. *Culture and personality,* 2nd ed. New York: Random House.

Wallerstein, I. 1974. The rise and future demise of the world capitalist system: Concepts for comparative analysis, *Comparative Studies in Society and History* 16:387–415.

———1974–1980. *The modern world-system.* 3 vol. New York: Academic Press.

———1995. Hold the tiller firm: On method and the unit of analysis. In *Civilizations and world systems: Studying world-historical change.* S. K. Sanderson, ed. Walnut Creek, CA: AltaMira Press, pp. 239–247.

———2004. *World-systems analysis: An introduction.* Durham, NC: Duke University Press.

Walsh, A. C., and A. D. Trlin. 1973. Niuean migration: Niuean socio-economic background, characteristics of migrants, and settlement in Auckland, *Journal of the Polynesian Society* 81(1):47–85.

Walsh, S. J., and K. A. Crews-Meyer, eds. 2002. *Linking people, place, and policy: A GIScience approach.* Dordrecht: Kluwer Academic Publishers.

Wang, Y., et al. 2005. The Holocene Asian monsoon: Links to solar changes and North Atlantic climate, *Science* 308:854–857.

Ward, R. H., H. Gershowitz, M. Layrisse, and J. V. Neel. 1975. The genetic structure of a tribal population, the Yanomama Indians, *American Journal of Human Genetics* 27:1–30.

WCED (World Commission on Environment and Development). 1987. *Our common future.* Oxford: Oxford University Press.

Web of Science, Social Science + Humanities + Biophysical Sciences Databases. Accessed 13 March 2006. www.library.ucsb.edu.

Webster, D. 2002. *The fall of the Maya.* New York: Thames and Hudson.

Webster, J. B. 1980. Drought, migration and chronology in the Lake Malawi littoral, *Transafrican Journal of History* 9:70–90.

Weischet, W., and C. N. Caviedes. 1993. *The persisting ecological constraints of tropical agriculture.* London: Longman Scientific & Technical/ New York: John Wiley & Sons.

Weiss, H. 1997. Late third millennium abrupt change and social collapse in West Asia and Egypt. In *Third millennium* B.C. *climate change and old world collapse.* H. N. Dalfes, G. Kukla, and H. Weiss, eds. *NATO ASI Series I* 49:711–723.

———2000. Beyond the younger Dryas: Collapse as adaptation to abrupt climate change in ancient West Asia and the eastern Mediterranean. In *Environmental disaster and the archeology of human response.* G. Bawden and R. M. Reycraft, eds. Albuquerque, NM: Maxwell Museum of Anthropology, University of New Mexico.

Weiss, H., and R. S. Bradley. 2001. What drives societal collapse? *Science* 291(26):609–610.

Weiss, P. A. 1969. The living system: Determinism stratified. In *Beyond reductionism: The Alpbach symposium.* A. Koestler and J. R. Smythies, eds. New York: Hutchinson.

Weisz, H. Forthcoming. Combining social metabolism and input-output analysis to account for ecologically unequal trade. In *Environmental history: World system history and global environmental change.* A. Hornborg, J. Martinez-Alier, and J. McNeill, eds. Lanham, MD: AltaMira Press.

Weisz, H., C. Amann, N. Eisenmenger, K.-H. Erb, M. Fischer-Kowalski, and F. Krausmann. 2002. *Economy-wide material flow accounts and indicators of resource use for the EU.* Eurostat Tender 2001/S 125-084782/EN. Final Report. Vienna: IFF Social Ecology.

Weisz, H., C. Amann, N. Eisenmenger, F. Krausmann, and K. Hubacek. 2004. *Economy-wide material flow accounts and indicators of resource use for the EU: 1970-2001.* Final report Eurostat, contract no. Estat/B1/Contract Nr. 200241200002. Vienna: IFF Social Ecology.

Weisz, H., F. Krausmann, N. Eisenmenger, C. Amann, and K. Hubacek. 2005. *Development of material use in the European Union 1970–2001. Material composition, cross-country comparison, and material flow indicators.* Luxembourg: Eurostat, Office for Official Publications of the European Communities.

Weisz, H., F. Krausmann, and S. Sangkaman. 2005. *Resource use in a transition economy. Material- and energy-flow analysis for Thailand 1970/1980–2000.* Laguna, CA: SEARCA Publishing.

Welinder, S. 1975. Prehistoric agriculture in eastern Middle Sweden, *Acta Archeologica Lundensia,* Series in 8⁰ Minore 4.

———1983. The ecology of long-term change, *Acta Archeologica Lundensia,* Series in 8⁰ Minore 4.

White, L. A. 1959. *The evolution of culture: The development of civilization to the fall of Rome.* New York: McGraw-Hill

White, R., and G. Engelen. 1997. Cellular automata as the basis of integrated dynamic regional modelling, *Environment and Planning B: Planning and Design* 24:235–246.

Whitehead, N. L. 1993. Ethnic transformation and historical discontinuity in native Amazonia and Guayana, 1500–1900. In *La Remontée de l'Amazone: Anthropologie et histoire des sociétés amazoniennes*. P. Descola and A. C. Taylor, eds. *L'Homme* 126–128, XXXIII (2–4), s.285–305.

———1994. The ancient amerindian polities of the Amazon, the Orinoco, and the Atlantic coast: A preliminary analysis of their passage from antiquity to extinction. In *Amazonian Indians from prehistory to the present: Anthropological perspectives*. A. C. Roosevelt, ed. Tucson, AZ: The University of Arizona Press, pp. 33–53.

———1999. Native peoples confront colonial regimes in northeastern South America (c. 1500–1900). In *The Cambridge history of the native peoples of the Americas*, Vol. III, Part 2. New York: Cambridge University Press, pp. 382–442.

Wicken, J. S. 1987. *Evolution, thermodynamics, and information: Extending the Darwinian program*. New York: Oxford University Press.

Wiens, J. A. 1976. Population responses to patchy environments, *Annual Review of Ecological Systematics* 7:81–120.

Wilkinson, D. 1987. Central civilization, *Comparative civilizations review* 17:31–59.

———1995. Civilizations are world systems! In *Civilizations and world systems: Studying world-historical change*. S. K. Sanderson, ed. Walnut Creek: AltaMira Press, pp. 248–260.

Williams, E. 1944. *Capitalism and slavery*. Chapel Hill, NC: University of North Carolina Press.

Wilson, D. J. 1999. *Indigenous South Americans of the past and present: An ecological perspective*. Boulder, CO: Westview Press.

Wilson, E. O. 1998. *Consilience*. London: Little, Brown.

———2002. *The future of life*. New York: Random House.

WinklerPrins, A.M.G.A. 1999. Between the floods: Soils and agriculture on the lower Amazon floodplain, Brazil. Ph.D. Dissertation, University of Wisconsin, Madison.

Winterhalder, B. P. 1984. Reconsidering the ecosystem concept, *Reviews in Anthropology* 12:301–13.

———1994. Concepts in historical ecology: The view from evolutionary ecology. In *Historical ecology: Cultural knowledge and changing landscapes*. C. L. Crumley, ed. Santa Fe, NM: School of American Research, pp. 17–41.

Wirtz, K. 2005. Integrated modeling of human-climate interactions in the Holocene. ESF HOLIVAR Workshop. Mai 2005, Annaboda (SE).

Wirtz, K., and C. Lemmen. 2003. A global dynamic model for the Neolithic transition, *Climate Change* 59:333–367.

Wolf, E. 1972. Ownership and political ecology, *Anthropological Quarterly* 45(3):201–205.

Wolfram, S. 2002. *A new kind of science*. Champaign, IL: Wolfram Media.

Wood, C., and R. Porro, eds. 2002. *Deforestation and land use in the Amazon*. Gainesville, FL: University of Florida Press.

Woodcock, C. E., S. A. Macomber, M. Pax-Lenney, and W. B. Cohen. 2001. Monitoring large areas for forest change using Landsat: Generalization across space, time and Landsat sensors, *Remote Sensing of Environment* 78(1–2):194–203.

Woodwell, G. M., J. E. Hobbie, R. A. Houghton, J. M. Melillo, B. Moore, B. J. Peterson, and G. R. Shaver. 1983. Global deforestation: Contribution to atmospheric carbon-dioxide, *Science* 222 (4628):1081–1086

World Resources Institute (WRI). 2004. Earthtrends. The environmental information portal. http://earthtrends.wri.org.

Wright, R. 2000. *Non-zero: The logic of human destiny.* New York: Pantheon.

Wrigley, E. A., R. S. Davis, J. E. Oeppen, and R. S. Schofield. 1997. *English population history from family reconstruction: 1580–1837.* Cambridge: Cambridge University Press.

Wu, F., and D. Martin. 2002. Urban expansion simulation of Southeast England using population surface modelling and cellular automata, *Environment and Planning A* 34(10):1855–1876.

WWF, UNEP, Global Footprint Network. 2004. *Living planet report 2004.* Gland, Switzerland: WWF.

Yasuda, Y. 2001. Environmental change and the rise and fall of the Yangtze River Civilization, *Monsoon* 3:122–125. International Research Center for Japanese Studies, Kyoto, Japan.

Yasuda, Y., and N. Catto. 2004. Environmental variability and human adaptation since the last glacial period, *Quaternary Journal* (Special Issue):123–125.

Yoffee, N. 1995. Political economy in early Mesopotamian states, *Annual Review of Anthropology* 24:281–311.

Yoffee, N., and G. Cowgill, eds. 1988. *The collapse of ancient states and civilizations.* Tucson: The University of Arizona Press.

Yost, J. A. 1981. Twenty years of contact: The mechanisms of change in Wao ("Auca") culture. In *Cultural transformations and ethnicity in modern Ecuador.* N. E. Whitten, Jr. ed. Urbana, IL: University of Illinois Press, pp. 677–704.

Yost, J. A., and P. M. Kelley. 1983. Shotguns, blowguns, and spears: The analysis of technological efficiency. In *Adaptive responses of native Amazonians.* R. B. Hames and W. T. Vickers, eds. New York: Academic Press, pp. 189–224.

Yu, S. 2003. The Littorina transgression in southeastern Sweden and its relation to mid-Holocene climate variability, *LUNDQUA Thesis 51.* Dept. of Quaternary Geology, Lund University.

Zdanovich, G. B., and D. G. Zdanovich. 2002. The "Country of Towns" of Southern Trans-Urals and some aspects of steppe assimilation in the Bronze Age. In *Ancient interactions east and west in Eurasia.* K. Boyle, C. Renfrew, and M. Levine, eds. Cambridge, UK: McDonald Institute Monographs, University of Cambridge.

Zent, Stanford. 1998. Independent yet interdependent "Isode": The historical ecology of traditional Piaroa settlement pattern. In *Advances in Historical Ecology,* W. Balée, ed. New York: Columbia University Press.

Zent, Stanford. 1992. Historical and ethnographic ecology of the Upper Cuao River Wõthihã: Clues for an interpretation of native Guianese social organization. Ph.D. Dissertation, Columbia University.

Zent, S. 2002. Independent yet interdependent "Isode": The historical ecology of traditional Piaroa settlement pattern. In *Advances in historical ecology*. W. Balée, ed. New York: Columbia University Press, pp. 251–285.

Zhou, L. M., C. J. Tucker, R. K. Kaufmann, D. Slayback, N. V. Shabanov, and R. B. Myneni. 2001. Variations in northern vegetation activity inferred from satellite data of vegetation index during 1981 to 1999, *Journal of Geophysical Research-Atmospheres* 106 (D17):20069–20083.

Zimmerer, K. S, and T. J. Bassett, eds. 2003. Political ecology: An integrative approach to geography and environment—development studies. New York: Guilford.

Zolitschka, B., K. E. Behre, and J. Schneider. 2003. Human and climate impact on the environment as derived from colluvial, fluvial and lacustrine archives—examples from the Bronze Age to the Migration period, Germany, *Quaternary Science Reviews* 22:81–100.

Zolitschka, B., and J. F. W. Negendank. 1997. Climate change at the end of the third millennium B.C.—Evidence from varved lacustrine sediments. In *Third millennium B.C. climate change and old world collapse*. H. N. Dalfes, G. Kukla, and H. Weiss, eds. *NATO ASI Series* Vol I, 49: 679–690.

Zucchi, A. 1991. El Negro-Casiquiare-Alto Orinoco como ruta conectiva entre el Amazonas y el norte de Suramerica. In *Proceedings of the twelfth congress of the International Association for Caribbean Archeology*. L. S. Robinson, ed. Martinique, pp. 1–33.

———2002. A new model of the northern Arawakan expansion. In *Comparative Arawakan histories: Rethinking language family and culture area in Amazonia*. J. D. Hill and F. Santos-Granero, eds. Urbana, IL: University of Illinois Press, pp. 199–222.

Index